IRISH HERITAGE STUDIES – vol.1
The annual research journal of the Office of Public Works

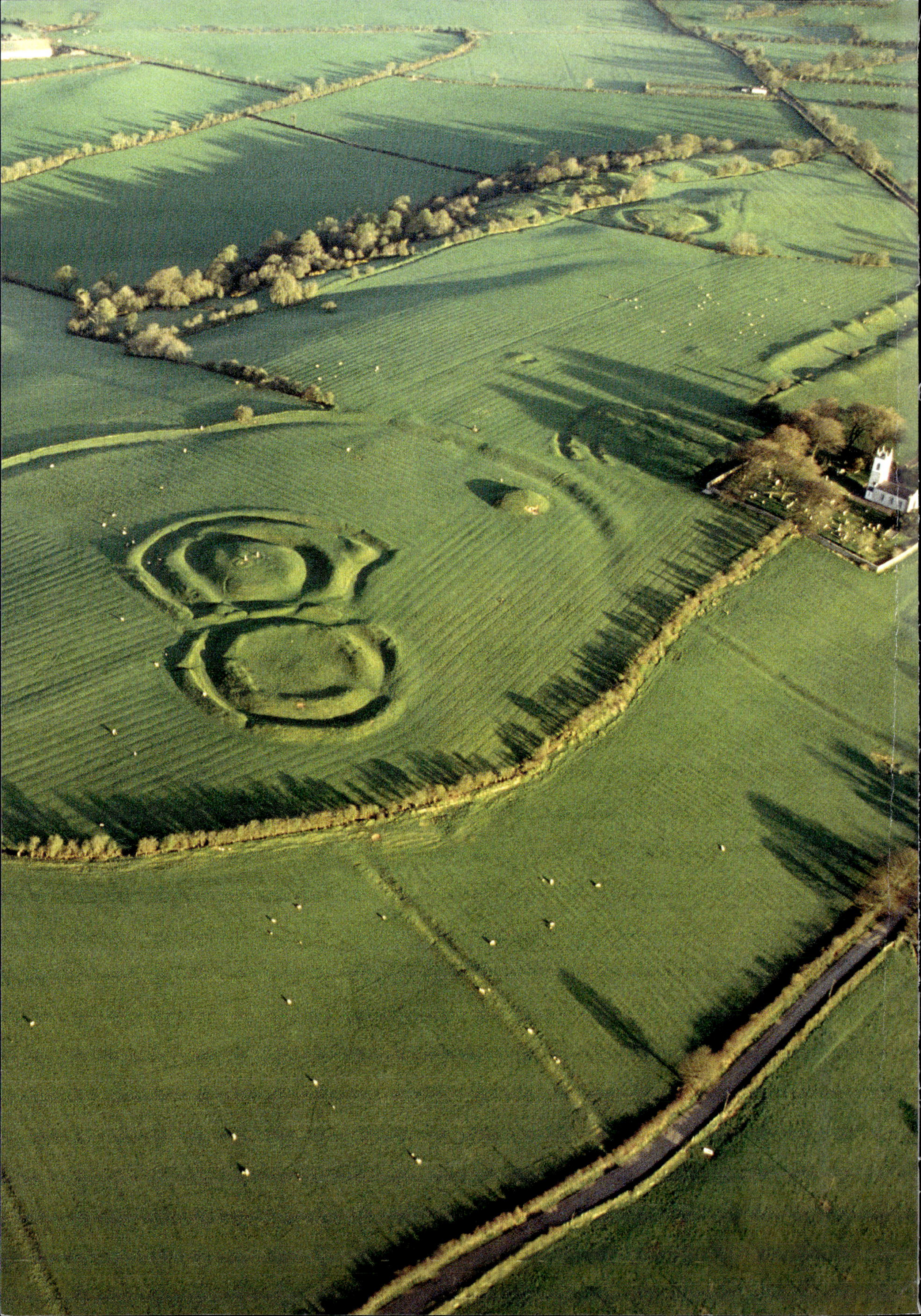

# Irish Heritage Studies

The Annual Research Journal of the Office of Public Works

1

2025

OPW
Oifig na
nOibreacha Poiblí
Office of Public Works

IRISH HERITAGE STUDIES – vol.1
The annual research journal of the Office of Public Works

Edited by Caroline Pegum
(ihsjournal@opw.ie)

OPW editorial group – Mary Heffernan, Hugh Bonar,
Dr Myles Campbell (–2023), Jacquie Moore

Co-published by the Office of Public Works and Gandon Editions



ISBN 978-1-910140-54-3

ISSN 3088-6619

Produced for the OPW by Gandon Editions Kinsale
*design* – John O'Regan (© Gandon, 2025)
*production* – Nicola Dearey, Anne Cronin (Gandon)
*printing* – W&G Baird, Belfast
*distribution* – Gandon Distribution and its overseas agents

GANDON EDITIONS
Oysterhaven, Kinsale, co. Cork, Ireland
+353 (0)21 477 0830 / <gandoneditions@gmail.com>
www.gandoneditions.com / instagram: @gandoneditions

OFFICE OF PUBLIC WORKS
Jonathan Swift Street, Trim, co. Meath, C15 NX36
+353 (0)46 942 2000 / <info@opw.ie> / www.gov.ie/opw
instagram: @opwireland

GOVERNMENT PUBLICATIONS OFFICE
Mountshannon Road, Dublin 8, D08 XA06
+353 (0)46 9423100 / <publications@opw.ie>
www.gov.ie/en/service/00fdf-government-publications/



cover – Cormac's Chapel, Rock of Cashel, co. Tipperary
(photo: Thomas P. Nelligan)
frontispiece – Aerial photograph of Tara, co. Meath
(Photographic Archive, National Monuments Service, Government of Ireland)

Irish Heritage Studies
The Annual Research Journal of the Office of Public Works

1

2025

# Introduction

CAROLINE PEGUM

THE *IRISH HERITAGE STUDIES* JOURNAL SHOWCASES ORIGINAL CRITICAL RESEARCH ROOTED IN the substantial portfolio of material culture in the care of or managed by the Office of Public Works: built heritage; historic, artistic, literary and scientific collections; the national and international histories associated with these places and objects; and its own long organisational history. Papers will contribute to a deeper understanding of this important collection of national heritage and investigate new perspectives on aspects of its history. The journal is designed for a broad public, specialist and professional readership.

Established in 1831 (and with antecedents dating back to 1670), the Office of Public Works is a central government office currently with three principal areas of responsibility: managing much of the Irish State's property portfolio; managing Ireland's flood risk; and maintaining and presenting 780 heritage sites including national monuments, historic landscapes, buildings and their collections.

We invite submissions on the following historical themes, ranging from the early medieval period to the close of the twentieth century:

- The design history of properties, demesnes and parks in the care of or managed by the OPW.
- The furniture, archives, libraries, historical botanical collection, fine and decorative art collections in the care of the OPW – including the State Art Collection – and items of material culture held elsewhere with connections to these properties and collections.
- The social, political, biographical and global histories connected with these properties and collections.
- Previously marginalised historical narratives connected to these properties and collections, such as the voices of women and members of the global majority, queer lives and disability history.
- The organisational history of public works bodies in Ireland since the seventeenth century such as the Surveyor General's activities for the Crown in Ireland and the Barrack Board, prior to the formalisation of the OPW. The full spectrum of OPW's diverse history since 1831 including civil engineering, famine relief, loan administration, architectural builds and conservation, archaeological conservation, curatorship and interpretation of monuments and historical sites. This remit encompasses activities at properties owned or managed by the OPW, as well as OPW work undertaken at other State-owned properties (e.g. Leinster House, the Four Courts).

We welcome scholarly papers from a range of perspectives, including (but not limited to) art, architectural, social, scientific and book history, cultures of collecting and display, museum and conservation studies, contested history and provenance research. We are also interested in interdisciplinary approaches and innovative methodologies. Discrete single-object case studies should seek to place the chosen subject within its broader cultural and historical context. Please note that post-2000 and current programmes and projects are not within the scope of *Irish Heritage Studies*.

We welcome submissions from academics, post-graduate students, allied professionals, independent researchers and OPW personnel, and actively encourage the work of early career scholars. Submissions should draw on original and unpublished research. Manuscripts will be anonymously peer-reviewed before definitive acceptance for publication. The journal is published in hard copy, with later release for e-book sales and, finally, free electronic version online.

Abstracts – and enquiries – are welcome at any time at ihsjournal@opw.ie. Please see https://www.gov.ie/en/campaigns/irish-heritage-studies/ for further details.

April 2025

ACKNOWLEDGEMENTS

The editor and OPW editorial group wish to thank the following peer-review readers of this volume for their generous expert feedback to the authors: DR CAROLINE CORNISH, Royal Botanic Gardens, Kew and Royal Holloway, University of London; DR VANDRA COSTELLO; EMERITUS PROFESSOR ALAN FORD, University of Nottingham; RACHEL HAND, Museum of Archaeology & Anthropology, University of Cambridge; SANDRA HEISE, National Museum of Ireland; PROF. AUDREY HORNING, Queen's University Belfast and The College of William and Mary, Williamsburg, Virginia; DR BRIAN HUGHES, Mary Immaculate College, Limerick; DR RUTH KENNY; DR MIRIAM MOFFITT, St Patrick's College, Maynooth; DR RACHEL MOSS, Trinity College Dublin; DR GRIFFIN MURRAY, University College Cork; PROF. TADHG O'KEEFFE, University College Dublin; CATHAL DOWD SMITH, Newbridge House and Malahide Castle; DR ANDREW TIERNEY, Trinity College Dublin; DR COLIN VEACH, University of Hull; DR NEIL E. WATT; and a further reviewer who wishes to remain anonymous.

*Irish Heritage Studies* is supported by the OPW's Art Management Group: JOHN CONLON (Chairman), ROSEMARY COLLIER, CONOR SREENAN, GER HARVEY, MARY HEFFERNAN, JACQUIE MOORE, JENNY DEERY, PAUL COSTELLO, MARIAN O'BRIEN.

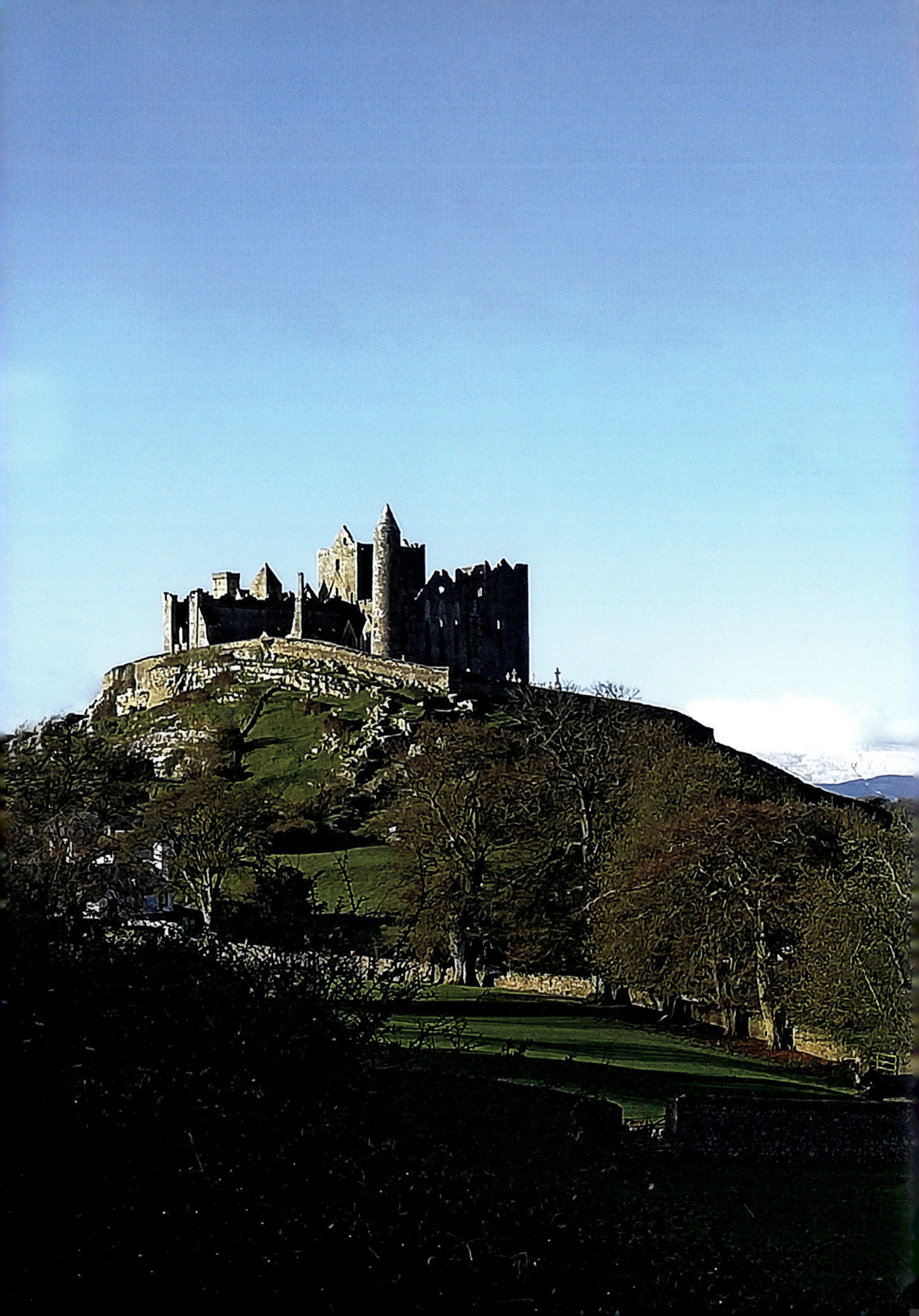

# Theology and politics in Cormac's Chapel: renewal, reform and reimagination in the twelfth century

THOMAS P. NELLIGAN

'A CHURCH WHICH WAS ERECTED BY CORMAC, GRANDSON OF CARTHACH, KING OF Caiseal, was consecrated by a synod of the clergy, assembled in one place.'[1] So mentions the 'Annals of the Four Masters' about the construction and consecration of Cormac's Chapel in 1134 at the Rock of Cashel. Commissioned by Cormac Mac Carthaig, the King of Munster, it was much more than a chapel; it was a *royal* chapel and, in essence, a theological expression of Cormac's political power and ambition. The Rock of Cashel had been the seat of power for his ancestors, the Eóganachta, since the early fifth century when, according to tradition, Conall Corc established his kingship there [fig. 1]. However, in the later tenth century the Eóganachta were ousted by the Dál Cais, who originated in co. Clare, ending centuries of Eóganacht rule in Munster. Brian Bóruma was crowned as the King of Munster at the Rock of Cashel in the year 978, but it was his great-grandson, Muirchertach Ua Briain, who would transform the Rock forever by gifting it to the Church in 1101.[2] The Rock of Cashel then appeared lost to the Eóganachta.

The twelfth century was a period of huge church reform in Ireland, and Muirchertach was at the forefront of this, convening a reforming synod at the Rock of Cashel in 1101.[3] Reform was not the only motivation for Muirchertach in handing over the Rock of Cashel to the Church. It was also a measure against the Eóganachta, a symbolic erasing of them from their ancestral seat of power.[4] It was around this time that the round tower, still extant on the summit of the Rock, was constructed. However, the death of Muirchertach Ua Briain in 1119 saw a weakening of Dál Cais power in Munster.[5] This, coupled with a resurgent Eóganachta under the leadership of Tadhg Mac Carthaig, saw the dynamic of power shift once again, and the Rock of Cashel found itself back in the hands of the Eóganachta, albeit now part of the Church. However, Munster had now been split into two smaller kingdoms, Thomond and Desmond, by Toirrdelbach Ua Conchobhair, King of Connacht, following the Treaty of Glanmire in 1118.[6] Therefore, although the Rock of Cashel was back under the influence of the Eóganachta, they had regained only part of their former kingdom. When Tadhg Mac

fig. 1 | The Rock of Cashel, co. Tipperary
(photos by the author, unless otherwise stated)

Carthaig was forced to resign his kingship due to illness in 1123, his ambitious brother, Cormac, took the reins.[7] Cormac quickly set about regaining Munster, and was a leading figure in revolt against Toirrdelbach Ua Conchobhair.[8] However, disaster seemingly struck for Cormac when, in 1127, Ua Conchobhair launched an invasion of Munster, forcing Cormac to retire to monastic life in Lismore.[9] This was to prove short-lived, and when the Uí Briain sought an unlikely alliance with Cormac, he returned from political exile and finally regained the Munster kingship – the first Eóganacht leader to do so in over one hundred and fifty years.[10] It was in this context that Cormac set about building his royal chapel at the Rock of Cashel, a powerful statement that the Eóganachta had returned to the political stage.

Constructed between 1127 and 1134, Cormac's Chapel is the only fully intact Romanesque chapel in Ireland; it is also one of the earliest, and represents an important step in the development of the Hiberno-Romanesque style [fig. 2].[11] This glorious return to the Rock of Cashel proved to be short-lived, as Cormac was assassinated only four years after the consecration of the chapel, in 1138, at the hands of the Uí Briain.[12] Munster was again divided into two kingdoms, and the Eóganachta never regained the Munster kingship.

Thirty years later a new political and military force would arrive on Irish shores in the form of the English.[13] Their arrival, and later that of their king, Henry II, would have a profound and lasting effect on Ireland. It is argued here that this would also have a profound effect on Cormac's Chapel, with the addition of fresco paintings, and that the chapel was a theatre of propaganda first for the Eóganachta, and later for Henry II.

## The ever-present past in Cormac's Chapel

IT IS TEMPTING TO VIEW MUIRCHERTACH'S GREAT GIFT TO THE CHURCH IN 1101 AS A SEISMIC shift at the Rock of Cashel when power abruptly switched from secular to ecclesiastical, but this is far from the case. It had been a powerful seat of kingship, second only to Tara, since at least the eighth century, although possibly occupied since the early fifth century.[14] In 1992 and 1993 Brian Hodkinson excavated three areas in and around Cormac's Chapel which showed that the chapel was built on the site of an earlier timber church constructed in the ninth century, and possibly extended or rebuilt in the eleventh century.[15] That several of the kings of Munster were also clerics should not come as a total surprise. This structure was entirely gone by 1101 when another church was constructed near the choir area of the present thirteenth-century cathedral.

Patrick Gleeson has convincingly argued that the location of an earlier church on the same spot as Cormac's Chapel is no coincidence, and may be intimately connected to inauguration ceremonies of the Eóganachta. The earlier timber church was possibly a royal chapel.[16] The ninth-century date is speculative, and the range of dates for its construction lie anywhere between the sixth and eleventh centuries. Gleeson, however, has argued that a ninth-century date is likely. Two hand-bells and a fragment from the base of a high cross, found in or near Cormac's Chapel, have all been dated

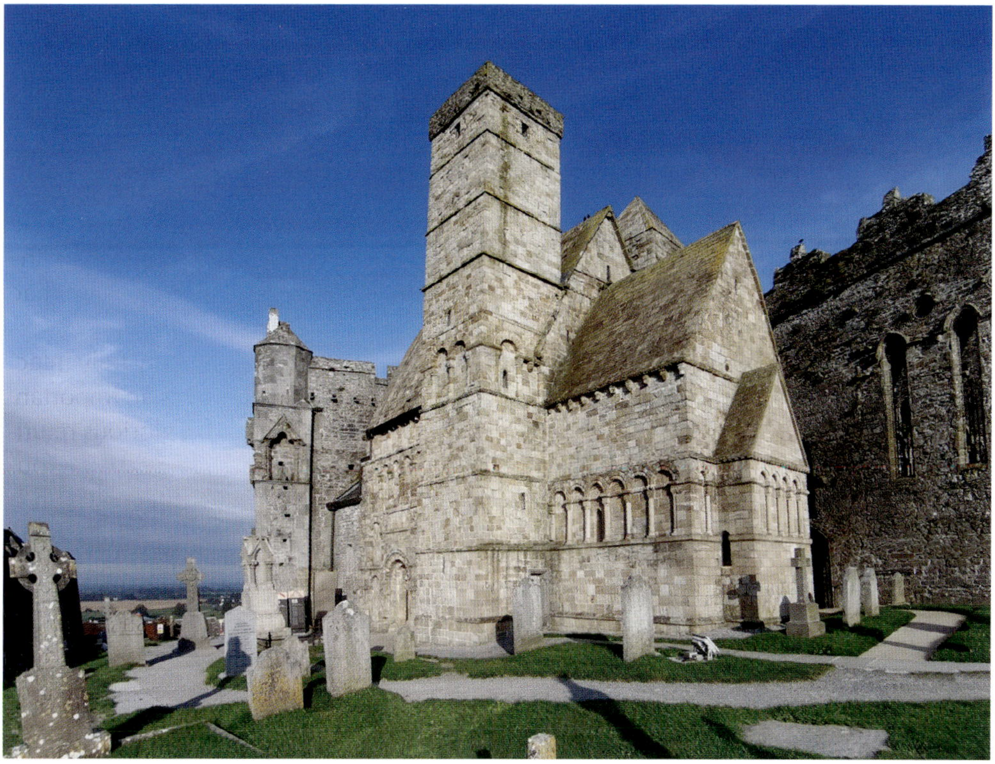

to the late eighth or early ninth century and provide evidence of a flurry of activity, likely associated with this earlier timber structure.[17] However, the most intriguing clue comes from an early ninth-century text called 'The Exile of Conall Corc'.[18] This tells the story of Conall Corc, long held to be the first king to establish a seat of kingship at the Rock of Cashel. The passage in question reads, 'I beheld a yew bush on a stone, and perceived a small oratory in front of it and a flagstone before it.'[19] This passage is relayed in the form of the vision experienced by a swineherd. The vision is then interpreted by a druid as foretelling where the residence of the King of Munster will be, and the king would be the first person to light a fire under the yew tree. That person would be Conall Corc of the Eóganachta. Gleeson argues that in this passage we get a brief glimpse of the Rock of Cashel in the early ninth century, showing a yew tree, with a small chapel and a flagstone.[20] Gleeson concluded that we are being described the timber church not long after its construction, and the 'Exile of Conall Corc' is a propaganda text projecting Eóganacht authority back to the fifth century.[21]

The archaeological evidence points to a rebuilding of this timber church, or, at the very least, a remodelling of the church, in the eleventh century, and this stood until its destruction early in the twelfth century.[22] This rebuilding or remodelling, according to Gleeson, points to the possibility that the Eóganachta were still present and active around Cashel until this late point, and may have still had access to the Rock of Cashel

fig. 2 | Cormac's Chapel, view from the south-east

without being in control of the Munster kingship.[23] It may have only been during the reign of Muirchertach Ua Briain that the Eóganachta were fully removed from the Cashel area. Muirchertach is mentioned as having maintained a house at Cashel in 1090.[24] Gleeson noted that at this time there was an evolving practice where submission was gained not only through the exchange of hostages, but through the entering of another's house. Without giving up the Dál Cais home of Kincora in co. Clare, Muirchertach managed to oust the Eóganachta from the Rock of Cashel through this symbolic act. His gift to the Church then takes on symbolic overtones in that he denied the Eóganachta their ancestral home and furthered their effacement.[25] The destruction, in the early twelfth century, of the timber chapel possibly occurred when a cathedral was built alongside the round tower.[26] Cormac Mac Carthaig may never have seen the timber chapel that had been used by his predecessors, but he was undoubtedly aware of its existence, as his later building of a new royal chapel on the same site indicates.

The building of a cathedral in *c.*1101 is of note as it would have been common practice to construct a new church on the site of an earlier one.[27] However, Muirchertach Ua Briain elected to build on entirely new ground, breaking with tradition. This can be no accident. The timber chapel must have been near-inseparable from the Eóganachta, and by removing the building and constructing something completely new on new ground, Muirchertach was furthering his symbolic erasure of the Eóganachta from the Rock of Cashel. Given that Hodkinson found a layer of ash and charcoal within the ninth-century chapel dating to the early twelfth century, it indicates that it was deliberately removed.[28] Gleeson surmised that the old chapel was ritualistically burned down upon the consecration of the *c.*1101 cathedral, a symbolic act that destroyed a long-held symbol of the old order, making way for the new and further alienating the Eóganachta from their ancestral seat of power.[29]

The act of constructing Cormac's Chapel a couple of decades later was political, restoring the Eóganachta to the Rock of Cashel and reclaiming their ancestral home and place of kingship. That it was an act of propaganda can be seen in the other activities of Cormac Mac Carthaig throughout this period. The 'Caithréim Chellacháin Chaisil' written during Cormac's reign, glorifies his ancestor Celleacháin (d.954), but is as much about glorifying Cormac as it is about honouring the former king.[30] Ó Carragáin argued that Cormac's Chapel was originally dedicated to Cormac's ancestor, the revered tenth-century bishop-king Cormac Mac Cuilennáin.[31] Churches were commonly named after the saint to which they were dedicated, so Cormac's Chapel is unusual in that it appears to be named after its founder. Ó Carragáin argued that 'Cormac' may refer to the saint and not the founder, and it is in fact, Cormac *Mac Cuilennáin's* Chapel.[32] By the twelfth century, Mac Cuilennáin was considered a saint, and several relics were associated with him, most notably the now-lost Psalter of Cashel. A twelfth-century poem 'Cormac's Metrical Testament', which was likely commissioned by Cormac Mac Carthaig, implies that the Psalter of Cashel was housed at Cashel. Ó Carragáin argued that the most likely location for this was Cormac's Chapel, making the possibility that it was dedicated to Cormac Mac Cuilennáin more likely.[33]

---

fig. 3 | View towards the chancel; note the off-centre alignment

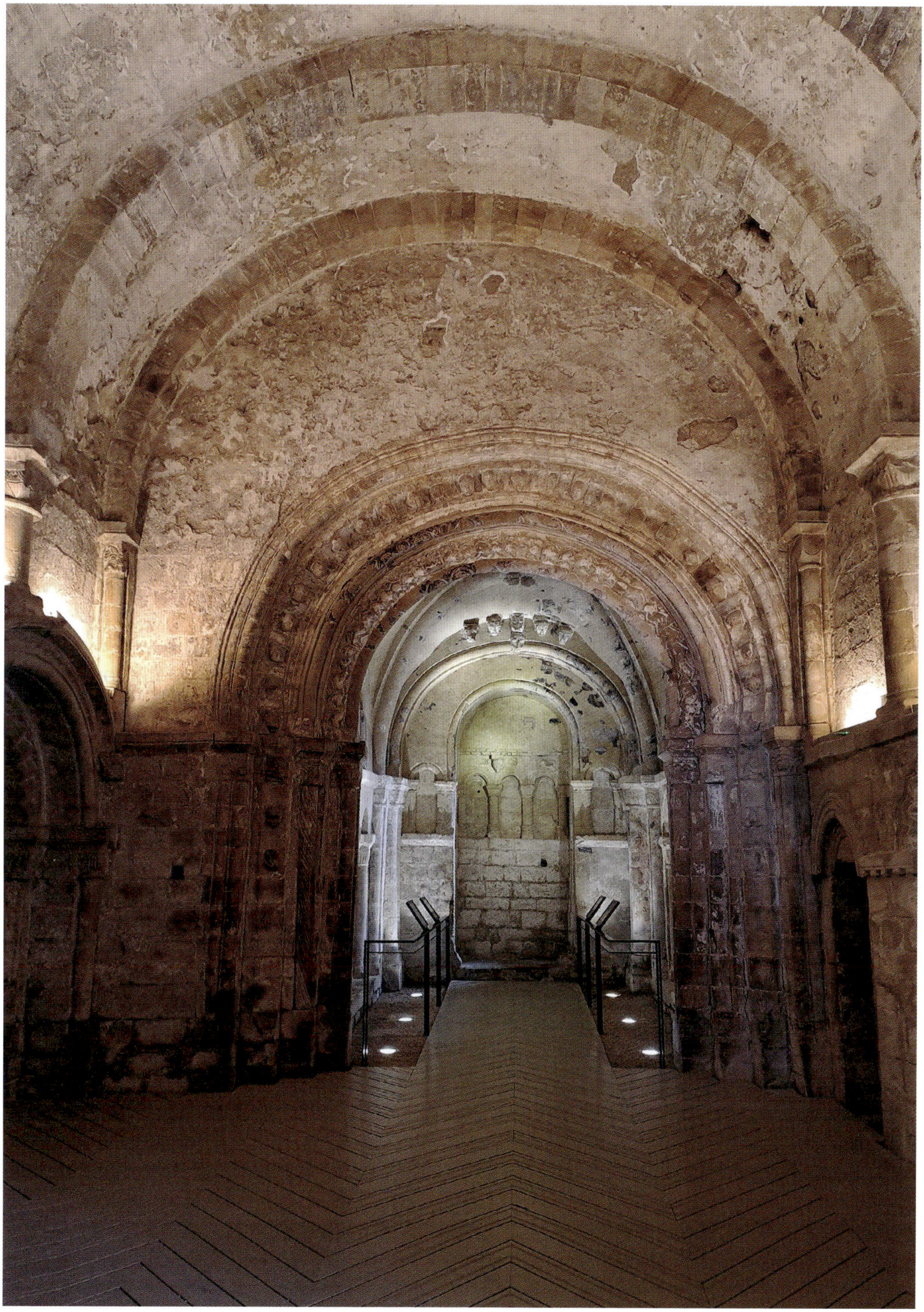

The choice of saint, if Ó Carragáin's argument is correct, was part of the process of reclaiming the Rock of Cashel for the Eóganachta. Prior to 1101, the Patrician associations of the Rock of Cashel may not have been as prominent as they were to become. Muirchertach Ua Briain, by granting the site to the Church and making the connection to St Patrick more overt, was again distancing the Rock from the Eóganachta and erasing their past.[34] Cormac, with his dedication to his ancestor, was attempting to restore their old connections.[35] Roger Stalley has described Cormac's Chapel as a 'celebration' of the Eóganachta's newfound success, while Ó Carragáin has noted that 'no other building expresses so eloquently the overlapping interests of church and "state" in medieval Ireland'.[36]

These overlapping interests may be reflected in the function of Cormac's Chapel which could have served both ecclesiastical and secular purposes. It may have been envisaged by Cormac Mac Carthaig as playing a role in the inauguration ceremonies of the Eóganachta. Gleeson drew attention to a passage from an Eóganacht genealogy which mentions that during the inauguration of a new king, he 'should be brought to the Stone of Cotraide in Cormac's great church and there proclaimed king'.[37] Cormac's Chapel, therefore, was not only a reclamation of Eóganacht power, place and tradition, it was possibly a physical encasement of the stone which represented their kingship. That the inauguration stone and the earlier ninth-century Eóganacht church were in close proximity to each other was possibly described in the 'Exile of Conall Corc', as has been discussed. The west end of this church terminated close to where the chancel arch is located in Cormac's Chapel, and the stone may have been close to this west wall. The most likely place for this stone is in the space next to the chancel arch, or within the north tower itself.[38]

Ó Carragáin has also suggested the north tower to be a place of special significance which could have housed relics, including the aforementioned Psalter of Cashel.[39] Both ideas also help to interpret the placement of the chancel arch, which is noticeably off-centre, creating extra space in front of the door to the north tower [fig. 3]. If this tower was used to house the inauguration stone of the kings of Munster or relics (or both), extra space may have been needed [fig. 4]. It also ensured that there was ample room here to prevent any activity in this area from intruding into the space in front of the chancel. It would have been considered unacceptable in the twelfth century for any encroachment on the chancel area that was not solely focused on the high altar. Yet, as Ó Carragáin has pointed out, there is seemingly no reason why the south side could not have been made wider in order to create symmetry.[40] Stalley's notion that the builders made an error in building on the wrong side of the guideline is too simplistic, and it is hard to imagine such a huge mistake would not be noticed until it was too late in the construction to amend the error.[41] Ó Carragáin suggested it was designed to draw the eye to the important north tower.[42] The very layout of the building appears to encapsulate and facilitate kingship, from the choice of location to the allocation of space.

---

fig. 4 | The elaborate entrance into the north tower

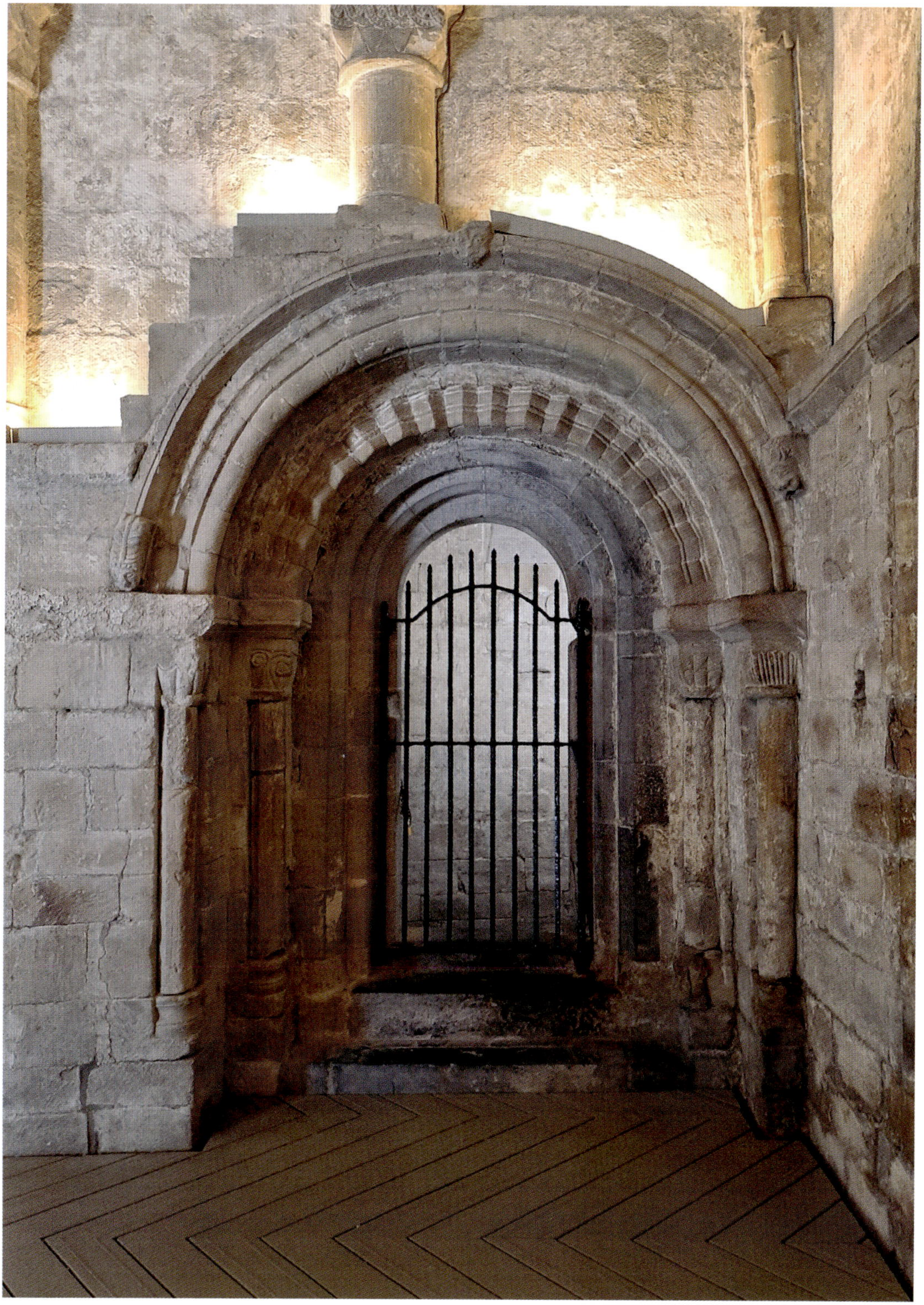

## The frescoes of Cormac's Chapel

One of the most remarkable aspects of Cormac's Chapel is the surviving series of fresco paintings, largely contained in the chancel [fig. 5]. It is one of only two extant examples of *fresco buono* in Ireland, the first being the subject of this paper, and the second being a small fragment at Lismore, co. Waterford.[43] *Fresco buono* is the application of paint to wet plaster, although details were often added using *secco*, or paint applied to dry plaster.

The existence of the paintings within the chapel has been noted since the mid-nineteenth century when they were first mentioned by George Petrie (1790–1866).[44] When the Rock of Cashel was taken into State care and the first conservation works were carried out on the chapel, it was noted that, 'careful examination has shown that figure subjects were painted on the ceiling and walls of the chancel as well as diaper work in the panels of the arcade.'[45] Traces of paint have also been noted within the north tower, the nave and the small space above the chancel. It is likely that frescoes were originally executed throughout the chapel, but most have been lost, either deliberately destroyed or damaged after centuries of poor conditions. The present argument will be confined to the figurative paintings that survive in the chancel.

In 1975, Mary McGrath published the results of pigment analysis of the frescoes, which identified seven colours: blue azurite, red vermillion, green Verdigris, St John's white, yellow ochre, brown iron oxide and carbon black. It is interesting to note that no use of ultramarine from lapis lazuli was found during this analysis, and only appears to have been discovered during later conservation work.[46]

Within the chancel, fragments of paint can be found on the chancel arch, the vaulted ceiling and the three walls [fig. 6]. The vaulted ceiling is divided into four equal triangular sections, and it is here that we find some of the best-preserved sections of fresco. In the western quadrant, above the chancel arch, several figures can be seen standing before two unevenly sized archways, surrounded with details of towered buildings [fig. 7]. On the left-hand side, in the larger of the two arches, are the remains of three figures. Only part of the red robe of the figure on the far left remains, while the central figure wears a crown and faces to the right. This figure holds an oval-shaped object. The figure on the right of this grouping looks back to the other two, is bearded with a raised hand, and also holds an object. In the smaller of the two arches, a clean-shaven figure can be seen turning to the right and presumably looking at the figure on the far right. The clean-shaven figure holds a sceptre with a fleur-de-lis on top. Unfortunately, like the figure on the far left, the figure on the far right has been largely lost, but it is clear that it is facing to the left.

In the late nineteenth century, antiquarian Michael Buckley noted that the figures could represent Christ the Redeemer, St Patrick and St Brigid. However, he offered no analysis or justification for this identification.[47] In a letter dated 30 October 1957 from Percy Le Clerc, Inspector of National Monuments, to Italian art historian Dr Michelangelo Muraro, Le Clerc identified the scene as Christ enthroned with the New

fig. 5 | The ceiling of the chancel

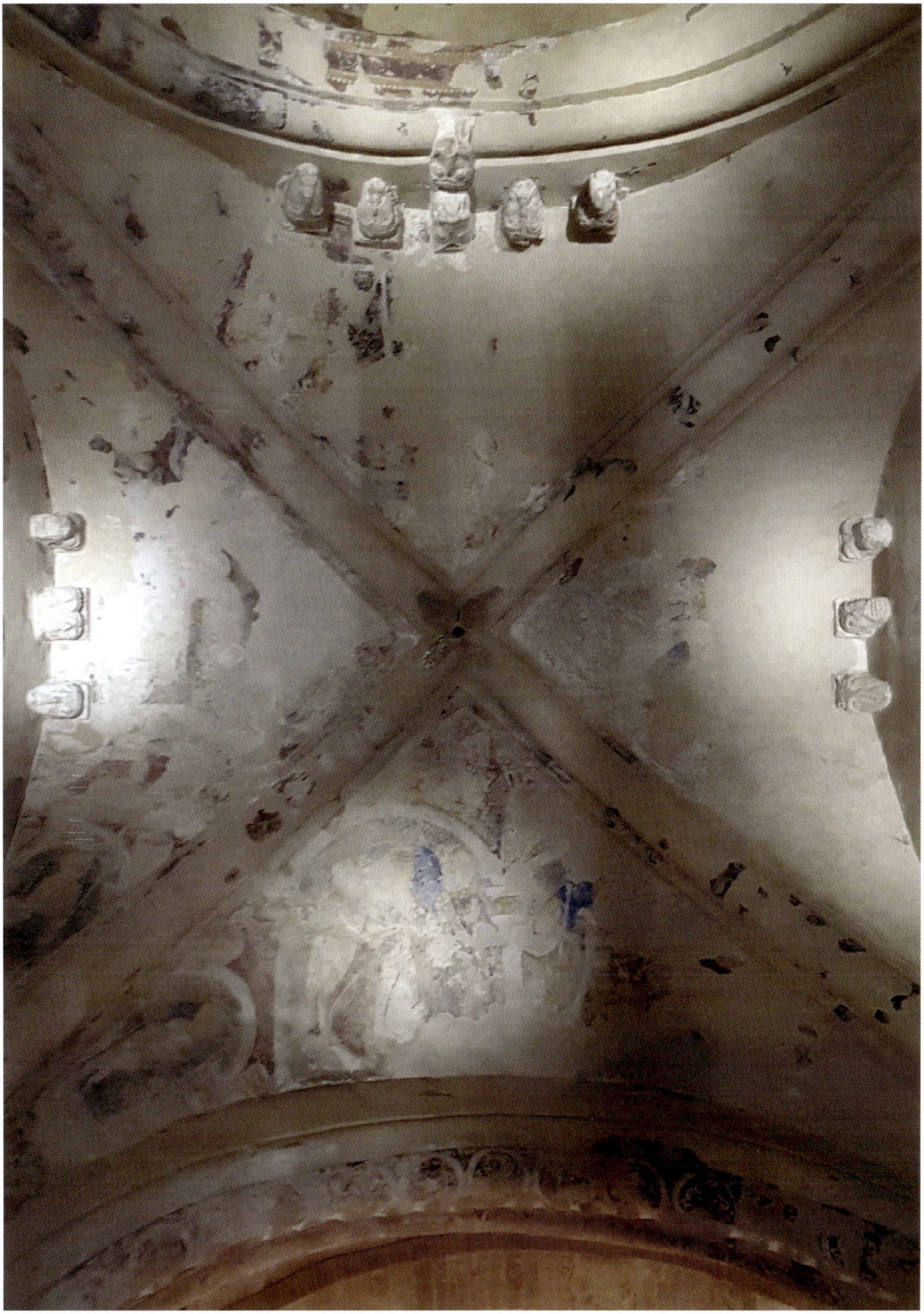

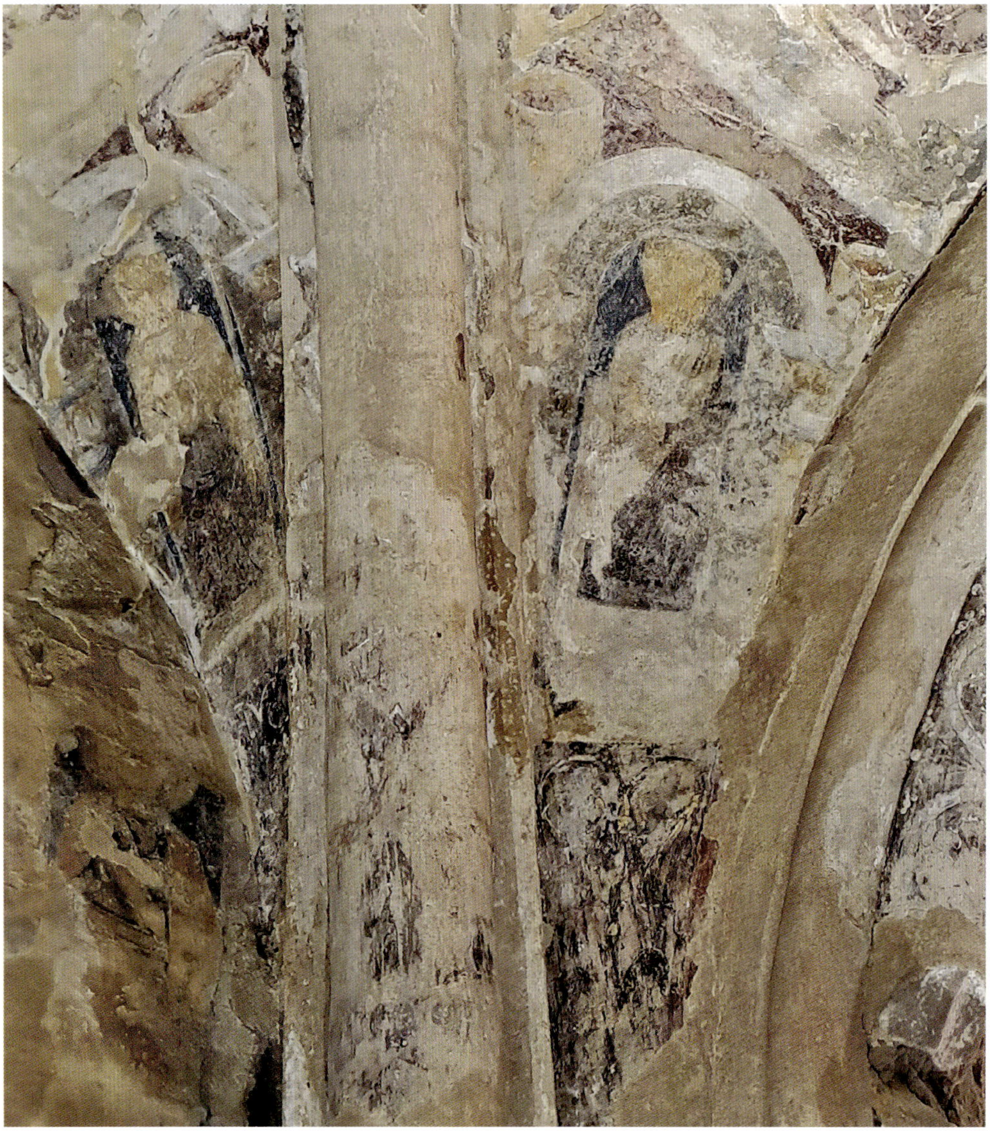

Jerusalem.[48] In 1988, Gerard Crotty attempted a more in-depth analysis of the frescoes and suggested that the scene depicted Solomon and the Queen of Sheba.[49] Crotty's identification of this scene revolved around the middle figure of the group of three on the left-hand side of the quadrant, which Crotty presumed to be female. The oval-shaped object held by this figure, Crotty argued, was a spice jar, as mentioned in 1 Kings 10:2 and 2 Chronicles 9:9, that was gifted to Solomon; the Queen of Sheba is often depicted offering a jar of spice.[50] Crotty argued that Solomon, who built the Jerusalem Temple, would have been an appropriate subject matter for a church builder like Cormac Mac

fig. 6 | Unidentified haloed figures on the south-west corner of the chancel

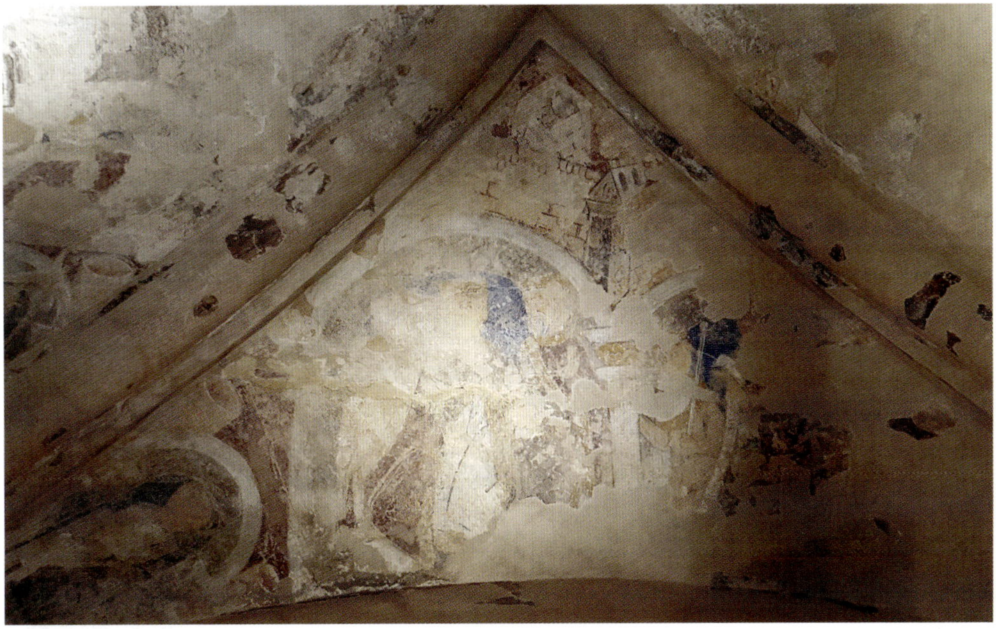

Carthaig. He further postulates that the figures on the right form part of a separate scene, namely the Judgement of Solomon (1 Kings 3:16–27). Absent, however, are the women and the child from this scene, which makes this hypothesis unlikely.[51]

More recently, Roger Stalley has argued that the scene comes from the New Testament and is part of a larger narrative sequence stretching across the chancel ceiling.[52] He contended that this scene depicts the magi before King Herod, taken from the infancy narrative of Christ. The damaged figure on the far right holds a scroll bearing the letters 'INTER' with a possible 'T' and 'R' on either side, with ample room for further lettering. He postulated that the scroll bears part of a quote from Matthew 2:8 which reads: *Et mittens illios in Bethlehem dixit, ite, et interrogate diligenter de puero; et cum inveneritis, renuntiate mihi, ut et ego veniens adorem eum* ('And sending them into Bethlehem, said: Go and diligently inquire after the child, and when you have found him, being me word again, that I also may come and adore him.').[53] 'INTER' possibly comes from *et interrogate*. If this were the case, then the damaged figure is likely to be Herod, while the figures in the larger painted arch would be the three magi. The fifth figure, then, appears to be someone presenting the magi to Herod. Supporting this interpretation is the fact that Herod and the magi is the only New Testament scene which involves several kings, and several crowns can be seen here. It is also the only scene where kings and the letters 'INTER' can be found in the corresponding text. 'INTER' can also be found in the Judgement of Solomon, as suggested by Crotty, but as noted, key elements of the scene are missing. The three magi were also a popular scene in twelfth-century art, and examples can be found at Norwich Cathedral; St Botolph's Church, Hardham, in Sussex; St Nicholas's Church, Barfreston, in Kent; St Gabriel's Chapel in

fig. 7 | The 'Magi before Herod'

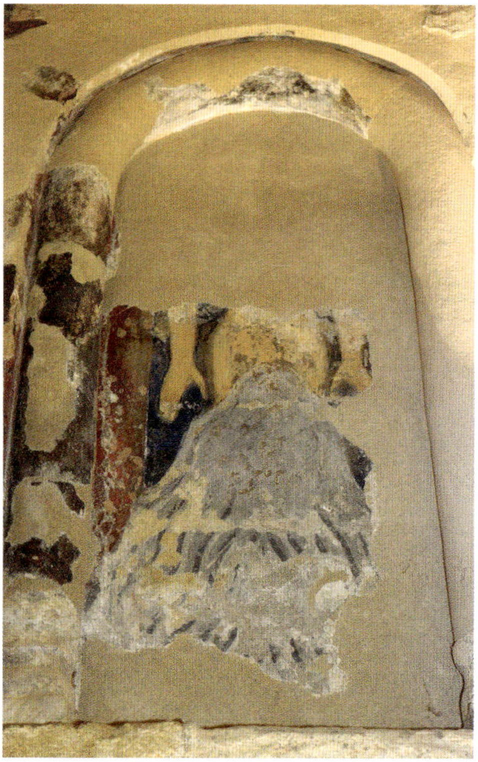

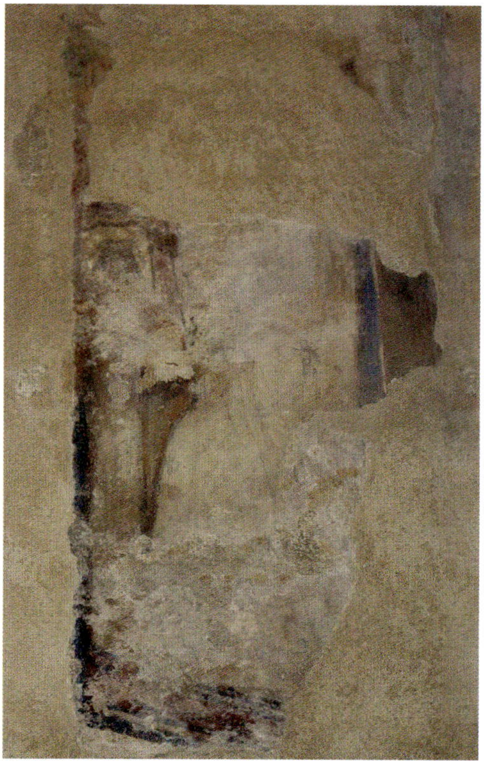

Canterbury Cathedral; and St Martin's Church, Westmeston, also in Sussex.[54] Stalley has noted that the style found in Cormac's Chapel is consistent with English art from the mid-twelfth century.[55] Stalley finds a parallel with the English-made, mid-twelfth-century Copenhagen Psalter (*c.*1170) which depicted the magi in a similar style and holding similar gifts.[56] The same conclusion was reached independently by art historian David Park.[57] Also noted were similarities with the paintings in St Gabriel's Chapel in Canterbury, dated to *c.*1155–60.[58] The identification of the magi, therefore, appears to be credible. If this scene is part of a larger narrative, what are in the other three quadrants?

Potentially easiest to identify is the south quadrant, where an inscription reading 'PASTORES' can be seen, along with a halo, and part of an animal horn.[59] Based on this, Stalley has suggested that it either shows the adoration of or the annunciation to the shepherds.[60] The north quadrant is the hardest to identify, although part of a crown can be seen which suggests another magi scene, possibly their journey towards Bethlehem. The east quadrant has potentially been identified due to the conservation efforts in the chapel, where a jewelled hem of a robe around a figure, and part of a haloed head can be seen. This is possibly part of a depiction of the adoration of the

fig. 8 | The 'Baptism of Jesus' on the south wall
(photo: Ellie McMinn)

fig. 9 | Possible Transfiguration scene on the south wall
(photo: Ellie McMinn)

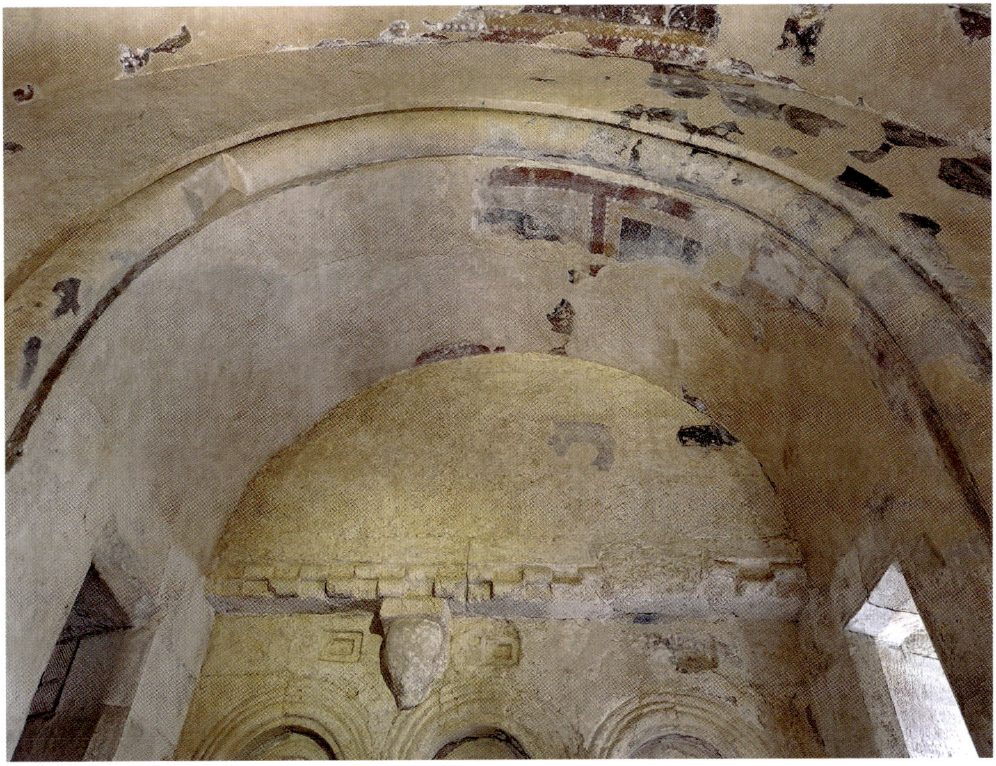

magi, and the figure uncovered – wearing a robe which appears to be blue and red in colour – is likely to be Mary.[61] The blue pigment is ultramarine, coming from the expensive stone lapis lazuli, which was only sourced in north-east Afghanistan at this time. It was commonly reserved for Mary's garments alone, not only due to its expense, but because of its symbolic overtones of purity, humility and holiness, thus making the identification in this case probable.[62] Besides Jesus, Mary was the most common subject in medieval church wall-art and was often painted close to the main altar.[63] Therefore, this location in the chancel would be an appropriate place for a depiction of Mary. There is ample room on the left-hand side of the scene for the three magi. An example of the adoration of the magi in a twelfth-century English context can be found at St Thomas's Church, East Shefford, in Berkshire, and, in Ireland, carved in stone at St Declan's, Ardmore, co. Waterford.

The identification of the Baptism of Jesus within the arch on the south wall is a sound conclusion: while we cannot see the top of the figure, the bottom half is clearly standing in water, which would correspond with the scene as depicted in the New Testament [fig. 8]. The archway to the right of the central window on the south wall also contained a scene, but it is unidentified. While it may never be known with certainty, it is proposed here that the transfiguration of Jesus would be an appropriate scene for this archway. The baptism and transfiguration of Jesus are closely connected scenes

fig. 10 | Location of possible 'Christ in Majesty' scene

on a literary level; in both God announces that Jesus is his son, and in him he is well-pleased.[64] They mirror each other, as the baptism represents the beginning of Jesus' earthly ministry, while the transfiguration represents a middle point. The baptism, as depicted in Cormac's Chapel, shows Jesus with water flowing around him and from him, while the New Testament depictions of the transfiguration describe light surrounding Christ.[65] The shape formed by Jesus' hand in the baptism can also be seen in the other archway, suggesting a similar composition, although this is speculative [fig. 9].

In Romanesque art it was common to depict Jesus as a king-like ruler of the world. A common scene was the *Majestas Domini* ('Christ in Majesty'), and it could possibly have adorned the walls of the chapel. An ideal space for this would be in the semicircular plane above the three smaller arches in the altar recess [fig. 10]. Supporting this idea is the presence of possible angels on the surrounding arch, which commonly accompanied a *Majestas Domini*.[66] Everything in the fresco paintings identified suggests kingship as its overarching theme.[67]

It has also been noted by art conservator Mark Perry that two schemes of paintings can be found in Cormac's Chapel. The first consists of a basic scheme in the form of pseudo-masonry designs, which were subsequently replaced with the figurative scheme visible today.[68] In terms of the quality of the paintings, conservators noted that,

> 'The extensive use of costly pigments and the extremely high artistic quality of the paintings, which have strong similarities to some of the finest contemporary frescoes in England and France, indicated that no expense was spared in the production of these beautiful murals.'[69]

Stalley added that, 'we are dealing with the work of major European artists.'[70]

## The historical context of the frescoes

A QUESTION THAT ARISES FROM THE ABOVE ANALYSIS IS WHETHER THERE WAS A BREAK BETWEEN the two schemes of paintings. The recent conservation work concluded that the first, masonry-style paintings date to around the consecration of the chapel in 1134. The second, and more elaborate scheme, was painted approximately thirty years later.[71] It also appears that the later artists removed some of the protruding areas of stone, such as chevron points on the chancel arch, to aid in the application of plaster.[72] Roger Stalley and David Park have both suggested a date of *c.*1170 for this later scheme.[73]

Against a *c.*1170 date, Dagmar Ó Riain-Raedel argued there is no reason for there to be a decades-wide gap between the two schemes of paintings.[74] She posited that the frescoes would have formed an important part of the original royal iconography within the chapel for Cormac Mac Carthaig.[75] Ó Riain-Raedel further argued that the *c.*1170 date proposed results from a restrictive search for models in late twelfth-century English manuscripts, and a wider search for sources is necessary. However, this argument, while intriguing, was written long before the recent conservation work, which seemingly confirmed a *c.*1170 date. Who, then, could have commissioned a scheme of paintings at this time?

Ireland around the year 1170 is difficult to define, and the century had seen much change politically, socially and ecclesiastically. Cashel had already been the site of a synod in that century, during which the site was gifted to the Church and Munster had been split, unified and split again in an ever-shifting dynamic which saw power flip-flop between the Uí Briain and Mac Carthaig family. The dawning of the twelfth century saw Munster as the most powerful kingdom in Ireland,with Muirchertach Ua Briain laying claim to the high kingship. The Mac Carthaig family were experiencing a resurgence at this time, with its peak being the construction of Cormac's Chapel and Munster's brief reunification. Both the Uí Briain and the Mac Carthaig family established themselves as great benefactors and reformers of the Church, and fostered important foreign links and alliances to bolster their power.[76] However, this prosperity was not to hold, and by 1169 the situation was far less secure. The Mac Carthaig family were once again ousted from the Rock of Cashel and pushed ever further south, and the Uí Briain, while still powerful, were not the national power they once were a mere half-century before.[77] At this time we see the Uí Briain being led by Domnall Mór Ua Briain, while Diarmait Mac Carthaig led the Eóganachta. Both are possible patrons of wall paintings in Cormac's Chapel.

Diarmait Mac Carthaig would appear as the obvious person to commission frescoes in Cormac's Chapel. He was the son of Cormac Mac Carthaig and, therefore, had vested interest in his ancestral seat of power. However, Diarmait struggled to achieve what his father had, and never held the Munster kingship. Rather, the old political divides of Thomond and Desmond once again dominated this period in Munster. Diarmait's career is one of struggle against not only the Uí Briain, but also Ruaidrí Ua Conchobhair, who claimed the high kingship.[78] While it would appear natural for Diarmait to contribute to his father's legacy with the addition of a new scheme of paintings in Cormac's Chapel, there is no evidence for his activity at Cashel in this period. Although Cashel was in the kingdom of Desmond, it was still largely under the control of Domnall Mór Ua Briain. Like Diarmait, Domnall's time as the King of Thomond was defined by struggles against Ruaidrí Ua Conchobhair, and later the English.[79] Yet, Domnall clearly had ambitions to emulate his reforming predecessor Muirchertach Ua Briain, clearly seen in his extensive building programme. He is credited with establishing nine monastic foundations, including Holycross and Kilcooly, both in co. Tipperary, and Monasteranenagh in co. Limerick. He is also credited with the construction of three cathedrals: one at Killaloe, St Mary's Cathedral in Limerick city, and at the Rock of Cashel in 1169.[80] The building of a cathedral at the Rock of Cashel is significant as it synchronises with the proposed date for the fresco paintings under discussion. Domnall, then, has to be considered as a possible patron. As a prolific church builder, works of art would have undoubtedly played an important role in these structures. However, new artwork surely would have been confined to the new structure rather than also repainting an older structure associated with his rivals. Domnall was likely emulating Muirchertach Ua Briain in building on the Rock of Cashel, and was transforming it for his own ends. However, new artworks in a building associated with Mac Carthaig power would have distracted from a grand new cathedral. There is, however, considerable doubt as to whether Domnall constructed a cathedral at the Rock of Cashel in 1169 as there is a lack of archaeological and documentary evidence.[81]

Everything, however, would be thrown into chaos with the beginning of the English conquest in 1169. The complexities of this incursion are manifold and beyond the scope of the present work, but some relevant points require attention. While the first invaders who arrived in Ireland in May 1169 were allied with Diarmaid Mac Murchada, it would be over two years before Henry II would set foot on Irish soil.[82] English incursions were quick and successful, and by 1171 they were firmly established in Ireland. Henry feared that Strongbow and other lords would carve out their own independent kingdoms, and acted swiftly.[83] It was also an opportune moment for Henry to leave for Ireland as he was under immense pressure from Rome following the murder of Archbishop Thomas Becket. Cardinals had travelled to France to demand an explanation from Henry, and he sought to distance himself from them.[84] Yet, it would be unwise to view Henry's arrival as solely reactive to unfolding events or as a way of evading difficulties elsewhere.[85]

Henry arrived in October 1171, near Waterford city, with four hundred ships and a force nearly five-thousand strong. It is in Gerald's 'Expugnatio' that we get more detailed information of Henry's movements in Ireland which have some bearing on Cashel. These events appear in Irish sources, although in less detail. Soon after arriving in Ireland, he was met by Diarmait Mac Carthaig, the King of Desmond and son of Cormac Mac Carthaig, who submitted to Henry 'doing homage and swearing fealty to him as his lord and giving hostages for the regular payment of a yearly tribute'.[86] Ralph of Diss also reported that the Irish bishops met with Henry upon his arrival in Ireland and swore loyalty to him.[87] Henry then travelled to Lismore, where he picked out a site for a castle, and then moved on to Cashel. Gerald reported that it was near Cashel, on the banks of the River Suir, that Henry received the submission of Domnall Mór Ua Briain, who was already allied with Norman forces in Ireland.[88]

While technically under interdict from the Church, Henry, strictly speaking, was not allowed to enter a church. However, considering the Irish bishops' acceptance and recognition of Henry, and his blatant disregard and desire to distance himself from his troubles with the Church, it follows that Henry would have few qualms with visiting the Rock of Cashel.[89] The significance of the Rock would not have been lost on Henry, as his selection of that site as the location for a council of the Church indicates. He had already obtained the backing of the Bishop of Lismore and, similarly, the Archbishop of Cashel, Domnall Ua hUallacháin. Irish bishops, it seems, had no issue in dealing with a man allegedly involved in the killing of an archbishop.[90]

The council of Cashel, convened by Henry, met in his absence, but with his representatives, in 1172. While not mentioned in any Irish sources, much detail is given by Gerald of Wales, who wrote that the council decided upon seven decrees covering issues of marriage, baptism, tithes, ecclesiastical immunities, murder fines and burial rites.[91] It is entirely possible that Cormac's Chapel played its part as a venue for this synod.[92] Following the council of Cashel, Henry's authority in Ireland was further recognised by Pope Alexander III in September 1172. Three letters were sent by Alexander III to Henry, the Irish bishops and the Irish kings. The Pope reminded the bishops and the kings of the oaths they took, and warned them to adhere to them. The Irish kings were threatened with ecclesiastical censure should they break their oaths, and this was to be enforced by the Irish bishops.[93] In essence, the council of Cashel formally recognised Henry's lordship of Ireland. Once again, the Rock of Cashel was at the centre of church reform, and again it was intertwined with political ambition.

A conquest of Ireland, however, had been proposed some fifteen years earlier. At a meeting of a royal council in Winchester in 1155, Henry proposed the annexation of Ireland and for it to be held by his brother William. Henry's mother, the Empress Matilda, opposed the idea, and it stalled.[94] It is possible that Henry went as far as assembling an invasion army at this stage, but it was put to different use in France.[95] Henry then dispatched emissaries to Rome, likely including John of Salisbury, who later wrote that Pope Adrian IV granted Ireland to Henry after their entreaties.[96] This refers to the controversial 'Laudabiliter' document, later quoted in full by Gerald of Wales, although no original version survives. There has been much debate as to how binding this document was, and some have questioned its existence at all.[97] Either way, Henry II appears not to have acted on such a document.

However, 'Laudabiliter' was the result of almost a century of involvement in Irish church affairs from Canterbury. Writing to Pope Alexander II in 1072, the Archbishop of Canterbury, Lanfranc, argued that Canterbury had historic primacy over the Church in York, Britain and Ireland.[98] While this does not appear to have had a legitimate basis, he received backing a year later when the new pope, Gregory VII, wrote to Lanfranc asking him to ban 'wicked' practices in Ireland. In 1074, this claim manifested into practice when the bishop-elect of Dublin, Gilla Pátraic, arrived in Canterbury seeking consecration. This may have been, from Dublin's perspective, less about recognising Canterbury's primacy than it was about rejecting Armagh's. Nevertheless, this emboldened Lanfranc and Canterbury, particularly when this move was supported by Toirdelbach Ua Briain.[99] Lanfranc's successor, Anselm, consecrated the first Bishop of Waterford in 1096, extending Canterbury's influence. Both bishops of Dublin and Waterford also swore oaths of obedience, and recognised Canterbury's primacy.

The Synod of Cashel in 1101, however, represented a shift in Irish relations with Canterbury, which took no part in this gathering.[100] The Rock of Cashel was handed over to the Church in a possible recognition of Armagh's primacy in Ireland due to their stronger associations with St Patrick, and the newly established bishopric of Limerick was consecrated in Armagh, not Canterbury.[101] Muirchertach Ua Briain and the Irish reform movement appear to be been consciously pulling away from Canterbury. This is set against the backdrop of worsening political relations between Muirchertach and Henry I.[102] The Synod of Ráith Bressail in 1111, again spearheaded by Muirchertach Ua Briain, widened the breach by creating a diocesan hierarchy in Ireland, with no mention or recognition of Canterbury.[103] The later Synod of Kells in 1152 saw this diocesan structure formally recognised by the papacy, effectively removing Canterbury from interference in the Irish Church.[104] Three years later, the council of Winchester would occur, where Henry II would first propose a conquest of Ireland. Flanagan viewed this, and the subsequent 'Laudabiliter', as an attempt by Canterbury to reinsert itself into Irish affairs by appealing to Henry II on the grounds of church reform.[105]

Why would Irish bishops, then, readily submit to Henry II after spending the better part of the twelfth century withdrawing from Canterbury's influence? Increasing political instability in the mid-twelfth century and, in particular, the rivalry between Diarmuit Mac Murchada and Ruaidrí Ua Conchobhair over the high kingship hampered continued religious reform. Henry II was likely seen as a stabilising force by the Irish bishops, one which could get church reform back on track.[106]

## Henry II and propaganda

OF THE VARIOUS CANDIDATES, HENRY II IMMEDIATELY EMERGES AS THE MOST LIKELY PATRON for the fresco paintings in Cormac's Chapel. They fit into the context of Henry II and the council of Cashel, and into Henry's larger programme of propaganda and justification of his Irish lordship. He was also a figure that had the financial and political tools at his disposal to provide complex literary and artistic justifications for his conquest.[107]

Irish sources, while mentioning the events of 1169 onwards, give little detailed information or commentary; they state what happened and move rapidly on. Therefore, we must turn to English primary sources, the most detailed of which is by Gerald of Wales, who provided a highly detailed, if biased, account of the English conquest which serves as a justification for Henry's actions.[108] The 'Topographia' and 'Expugnatio' provide the bulk of the detail regarding Henry II in Ireland. The former is dedicated to Henry and skews heavily in his favour, often at the expense of the Irish, who are portrayed as barbarous and in need of the English presence.[109] Gerald, writing at Henry's suggestion, justified Henry's rule in a variety of different ways, appealing to both mythology and more recent history. He wrote that early inhabitants of Ireland were Basque settlers who were granted an almost uninhabited island by the mythical king of Britain, Gurguintius. He argued that since the capital of the Basque country – Bayonne – fell under Henry's duchy of Aquitaine, the Irish (which Gerald maintained were Basque immigrants), were subjects of Henry II. Gerald also appealed to Arthurian legend, and mentioned that the Irish had paid tribute to King Arthur, thereby giving Henry a legitimate claim.[110] Further justifications from Gerald came from the more recent past. He referenced the controversial 'Laudabiliter' which gave Henry II papal backing, and also the oaths that Irish kings had given Henry upon his arrival into Ireland.[111] Gerald's writing is suffused with imagery from classic and biblical literature. He refers to Henry as the Alexander of the West, and compares him to Caesar and Jupiter, while drawing imagery from Virgil. He layered this with biblical themes and made reference to the Old Testament kings David and Solomon.[112]

If Henry, or at least his representatives, were responsible for the frescoes in Cormac's Chapel, why do we not find other and similar pieces of artistic propaganda in Ireland? After wintering in Dublin, Gerald reports that Henry was forced to return to England to finally face the papal legates concerning his involvement in the murder of Thomas Becket for which he received a pardon.[113] Gerald mentions that Henry had intended to return to Ireland to further his conquest and build a series of castles, but it was not to be, and Henry never gained full control in Ireland. It is impossible to know what further justifications of Henry's conquest may have been planned. While he would endow the abbey of St Thomas in Dublin's Liberties in reparation for the murder of Thomas Becket, his departure from Ireland marked the end of his involvement in Irish church reform.[114] However, his time in Ireland was marked with a clear appropriation of Irish kingship customs, such as spending Christmas in Dublin in a specially built hall, which is noted by Roger of Howden and Gerald of Wales as being a custom of Irish kings.[115] Nicholas Vincent has recently argued that even the dates of Henry's arrival and departure from Ireland are symbolic. Henry tried to sail to Ireland on 14 October, but was delayed until 16 October by poor weather. The original choice of the 14th was the anniversary of the Battle of Hastings; Henry may have been attempting to present himself as a new William the Conqueror. He returned to Britain after Easter in 1172, either on 16 or 17 April. The date, Vincent argues, allowed Henry to present himself as a Christ-like conqueror.[116]

Cashel appears to have held little strategic importance to Henry II following the council of Cashel, and he left garrisons at both Cork and Limerick, and kept the two cities, along with Dublin and Waterford, under his control.[117]

## Interpretation of the frescoes

WHILE THE THEME OF KINGSHIP HAS BEEN NOTED IN THE PAINTINGS IN THE PRESENCE OF the magi, the significance of this has not been fully explored. While the magi are often interpreted as kings or wise men, the choice of biblical scenes go far beyond them in their depictions of kingship. The scenes on the chancel ceiling depict the narrative of the birth of Christ, a king. This is not the story of the magi, but rather the birth of a foretold divinely ordained king to whom other kings would bow. The Gospel scenes with the magi (only found in the Gospel of Matthew), explicitly mention that Jesus is the king of the Jews (Matthew 2:2). The texts of the infancy narratives contained in Matthew, Luke and John (Mark contains no infancy narrative) are suffused with prophecy, and the birth of Jesus is viewed as the fulfilment of scripture.[118] It is in the Gospel of Luke that we find the strongest links to kingship, where, during the Annunciation, Mary is told that Jesus will inherit the throne of David (Luke 1:31–33).[119] In other words, it is divinely ordained.

The same message is expressed in the baptism scene on the south wall. The baptism, theologically, is akin to a crowning ceremony where Jesus' divinity is recognised by God. In Matthew, Mark and Luke, the Spirit of God descends to Jesus like a dove. This is an allusion to Old Testament texts, where the gift of the Spirit empowers the receiver with the charisma and qualities of a king.[120] These allusions are designed to link Jesus with Old Testament kings such as Saul, David and Solomon. All versions of the Baptism of Jesus contained within the synoptic gospels contain the proclamation from God that he is 'well pleased' with Jesus.[121] This is rooted in Psalm 2:7 in which a similar phrase is spoken by God. Psalm 2:7 is a royal psalm that was likely used in the coronation ceremonies of Old Testament-era kings to add divine weight to their reign.[122] Whether or not such textual allusions were apparent to English artists in the twelfth century is unclear, but the general links to kingship were unlikely to be lost on them, especially when Christ as King and a ruler of all was such a common motif in Romanesque art. If the other archway once depicted the Transfiguration, then it carries the same theological message.[123]

All the evidence at Cormac's Chapel points to Christ as King being the overarching theme. It added weight to Henry's lordship of Ireland by presenting it as having divine authority, and this was expressed through the reimagination of Cormac's Chapel. It was a tool of legitimisation. The chapel was an appropriate place to express such an idea: it was already a place inseparable from kingship, as had been its location for centuries before its construction. The message was that Henry, like Jesus, was divinely ordained. It is probably no coincidence that Henry adopted the title 'Dei Gratia Rex' or 'King by God's Grace' while in Ireland.[124] Given Henry's papal backing, this message becomes more overt. It is recorded that Henry came to Cashel, and it is likely that he came to the Rock of Cashel, one of the country's most prominent seats of kingship. The addition of these paintings within the chapel shows Henry's shrewd political manipulations at play. He took the Eóganachta's sacred place of kingship and transformed it to his own political ends, placing himself above the Eóganachta and the Uí Briain as someone divinely ordained, to whom all other kings should bow. Just as the new scheme of paintings obliterated and transformed the old, so Henry II transformed Cormac's Chapel to represent his lordship. The Eóganachta's place of kingship had now become his. Whether or not Henry directly ordered specific scenes to be painted is not clear, and it is entirely possible that Henry merely ordered paintings to be added that glorified his reign, leaving the final decision to others. The scenes selected carried the theological and political messages noted. While Henry is unlikely to have ever seen the paintings completed, as his time in Cashel and Ireland was short, he left a long legacy.

A similar scheme of paintings depicting the magi can be seen in Henry's private chapel in Petit-Quevilly near Rouen, which serves to underscore the connection between Henry and Cashel.[125] While the magi were a common theme in medieval wall painting, their presence in both chapels – at Petit-Quevilly and Cormac's Chapel, the location of a council convened by Henry – serves to strengthen this connection. The royal iconography would not have been lost on the Irish clergy.

The council of Cashel in 1172 was surely the occasion for which the frescoes were added to the chapel. It was at this council that the Irish bishops, in the single largest submission, recognised Henry's authority in Ireland. That such theological messages were successfully attached to Henry is made clear in the words of Gerald of Wales: 'With a grace that has no parallel on earth, but which was divinely conferred on you from above, you, the friend and promotor of concord, restored peace in your own dominions by your power in foreign kingdoms by your counsels and authority.'[126] The recognition by the Irish bishops of Henry's lordship and authority in Ireland was confirmed in letters from the Pope in September 1172. What better way to embody this than with the addition of paintings suffused with the theme of kingship. It would serve as a powerful and constant reminder to the Irish church, and to Domnall Mór Ua Briain and Diarmait Mac Carthaig.

———

**Dr Thomas P. Nelligan** holds a doctorate from the University of Limerick, where he studied Biblical and Classical literature, focusing on methods of textual composition. His doctoral dissertation was published in 2015 by Pickwick Publications. Thomas also runs his own website, www.thestandingstone.ie, where he has written over four hundred articles about places of historical interest in Ireland. Since 2016 he has worked as a guide for the OPW, and currently works at the Rock of Cashel.

### Author's acknowledgements

I would like to thank Dr Mairéad Carew for her help in locating hard-to-find books and her invaluable advice and wisdom throughout the writing process, and Ellie McMinn for use of her photographs. I would also like to thank Elaine Moriarty, Supervisor Guide at the Rock of Cashel, for the freedom to pursue such research projects. Lastly, I would like to thank my wife, Maria Nelligan, for her constant support and for listening to all the ideas presented here as they took shape.

### Endnotes

1 Manuscript translations throughout have been sourced from CELT (Corpus of Electronic Texts) online resource <https://celt.ucc.ie/index.html> [all acc. 10 June 2024]. 'Annals of the Four Masters' (AFM), AFM.1134.13 <https://celt.ucc.ie//published/T100005B/index.html>. The consecration of Cormac's Chapel is also mentioned in 'Annals of Tigernach' (ATig), ATig.1134.2 <https://celt.ucc.ie//published/T100002A/index.html> and 'Miscellaneous Irish Annals' (Misc.Ir.A.), Misc.Ir. A.1134.1 <https://celt.ucc.ie//published/T100013/index.html>.

2 AFM.1101.5; ATig.1101.8.

3 Marie Therese Flanagan, 'High-Kings with Opposition, 1072–1166', in D. Ó Cróinín (ed.), *A New History of Ireland. Vol.1: Prehistoric and Early Ireland* (Oxford: Oxford University Press, 2008) pp.899–933: 912. See also, Seán Duffy, '"The Western World's Tower of Honour and Dignity": the career of Muirchertach Ua Briain in context', in D. Bracken and D. Ó Riain-Raedel (eds), *Ireland and Europe in the Twelfth Century: reform and renewal* (Dublin: Four Courts Press, 2006), pp.56–73. Tadhg O'Keeffe, in 'Lismore and Cashel: reflections on the beginnings of Romanesque architecture in Munster', *Journal of the Royal Society of Antiquaries of Ireland*, vol.124 (1994), pp.118–52: 118, has argued that the emergence of Romanesque at Cormac's Chapel is entirely appropriate given that the Rock of Cashel was the epicentre of church reform in the twelfth century.

4 Tadhg O'Keeffe, *Romanesque Ireland: architecture and ideology in the twelfth century* (Dublin: Four Courts Press, 2003), pp.125–26. It is recognised that the political situation in Munster and in Ireland is far more complex than that presented here, but for the sake of space this introduction will be sufficient to provide a historical context for the construction of Cormac's Chapel.

5 AFM.1119.4; 'Annals of Ulster' (AU), AU.1119.2 <https://celt.ucc.ie//published/T100001A/index.html>; ATig.1119.1; 'Annals of Inishfallen' (AI), AI.1119.2 <https://celt.ucc.ie//published/T100004/index.html>.

6 AFM.1118.6; AI.1118.8; Misc.Ir.A.1118.3; ATig.1118.3. In the last-cited manuscript, Cormac is mentioned as having been briefly the hostage of Toirrdelbach Ua Conchobhair following the Treaty of Glanmire.

7 AFM.1123.13; AU.1124.2; ATig.1124.1; AI.1123.6 and AI.1124.2.

8 Flanagan (2008), p.918. For more on the life of Cormac Mac Carthaig, see Henry Alan Jefferies, 'Desmond: the early years and the career of Cormac Mac Carthy', *Journal of the Cork Historical & Archaeological Society*, vol.88, no.247 (1983), pp.81–99; Paul MacCotter, 'The Rise of Meic Carthaig and the Political Geography of Desmumu', *Journal of the Cork Historical & Archaeological Society*, vol.111 (2006), pp.59–76. MacCotter's article also gives a deeper insight into the politics of the early twelfth century in Munster. Various annals also mention that Ua Conchobhair executed Cormac's son, who was his hostage; AFM.1124.17; AU.1124.6; ATig.1127.4; AI.1124.6. Cormac took Limerick the following year; see AI.1125.8.

9 AFM.1127.13; ATig.1127.1; AI.1127.2.

10 AFM.1127.14; ATig.1127.2; AI.1127.4.

11 Liam de Paor, 'Cormac's Chapel: the beginnings of Irish Romanesque', in E. Rynne (ed.), North

Munster Studies (Limerick: The Thomond Archaeological Society, 1967), pp.133–45. De Paor argues that Cormac's Chapel was the genesis of the Hiberno-Romanesque style.

12 ATig.1138.5; AFM.1138.5, 'Annals of Loch Cé' (LC), LC.1138.5 <https://celt.ucc.ie//published/T100010A/index.html>; Misc.Ir.A.1138. 1.

13 While some historians use the term 'Anglo-Norman' or 'Angevin' to describe the conquest, the term 'English' has been employed here as it is the preferred usage in the primary sources discussed. See John Gillingham, *The English in the Twelfth Century* (Woodbridge: The Boydell Press, 2000), pp.145–60; John Gillingham, 'Normanising the English Invaders of Ireland', in Huw Pryce and J.L. Watts (eds), *Power and Identity in the Middle Ages: essays in memory of Rees Davies* (Oxford: Oxford University Press, 2007), pp.85–97; Nicholas Vincent, 'Angevin Ireland', in Brendan Smith (ed.), *The Cambridge History of Ireland, Vol.1: 600–1550* (Cambridge: Cambridge University Press, 2018), pp.185–221: 199.

14 Patrick Gleeson, 'Kingship and Architecture in 11th- and 12th-Century Cashel', *Journal of the Society for Church Archaeology*, vol.15 (2013), pp.1–15: 2. See also Denis G. Marnane, *Cashel: History & Guide* (Dublin: Nonsuch Publishing, 2007), pp.8–20. Even after 1101, the Rock of Cashel was undoubtedly a strong symbol of the Munster kingship. Donnchadh Ó Corráin, *The Irish Church, its Reform and the English Invasion* (Dublin: Four Courts Press, 2017), p.65.

15 Brian Hodkinson, 'Excavations at Cormac's Chapel, Cashel, 1992 and 1993: a preliminary statement', *Tipperary Historical Journal* (1994), pp.167–74.

16 Ibid.; Gleeson, p.5.

17 Ibid., p.7. See also Cormac Bourke, 'Early Irish Hand-Bells', *Journal of the Royal Society of Antiquaries of Ireland*, vol.110 (1980), pp.52–66; John Sheehan, 'A Bronze Bell-Crest from the Rock of Cashel, Co. Tipperary', *Journal of the North Munster Archaeological Society*, vol.30 (1988), pp.3–13; Peter Harbison, 'A High Cross base from the Rock of Cashel and a historical reconsideration of the "Ahenny Group" of crosses', *Proceedings of the Royal Irish Academy*, vol.93C (1993), pp.1–20.

18 Vernam Hull, 'The Exile of Conall Corc', *Publications of the Modern Language Association of America*, vol.56 (1941), pp.937–50.

19 Gleeson, p.7. Translation by Hull (1941), p.949.

20 Ibid.

21 Ibid. See also Francis J. Byrne, *Irish Kings and High-Kings* (Dublin: Four Courts Press, 2001), p.186; Tomás Ó Carragáin, *Churches in Early Medieval Ireland: architecture, ritual and memory* (New Haven and London: Yale University Press, 2010), pp.39–40.

22 Hodkinson, pp.167–74.

23 Gleeson, p.9.

24 AI.1092; AFM.1092. For an overview of the career of Muirchertach Ua Briain, see Duffy (2006), pp.56–73; Ó Corráin (2017), p.65.

25 Gleeson, p.9. O'Keeffe (2003), pp.125–26. For more on the collapse of the Eóganachta see Donnchadh Ó Corráin, *Ireland Before the Normans* (Dublin: Gill & Macmillan, 1972), pp.111–17.

26 Gleeson gives a fuller account of the ins and outs of this sequencing based on the phasing of burials observed during the excavations at the chapel in the early 1990s.

27 Gleeson, p.8; O'Keeffe (2003), p.126.

28 Gleeson, p.8. Not contained in the final published report, the mention of the ash layer can be found on Brian Hodkinson's personal website in a draft copy of the final report <http://homepage.eircom.net/~dunamase/Dunamase.html> [acc. 15 June 2024].

29 Gleeson, p.8. Gleeson gives a very tantalising argument as to its destruction involving a ritual known as *tellach*, involving the kindling of a fire, that was often employed during the possession of land; Edel Bhreathnach, *Ireland in the Medieval World, AD400–1000: landscape, kingship and religion* (Dublin: Four Courts Press, 2014), p.143; Edel Bhreathnach, 'Tara and Cashel: manifestations of the centre of the cosmos in the north and the south', in Jacqueline Borsje et al. (eds), *Celtic Cosmology: perspectives from Ireland and Scotland* (Toronto: Pontifical Institute of Mediaeval Studies, 2014), pp.165–85.

30 Donnchadh Ó Corráin, 'Caithréim Chellacháin Chaisil: History or Propaganda?' *Ériu*, vol.25 (Royal Irish Academy, 1974), pp.1–69; Jefferies, p.87; O'Keeffe (1994), p.138.

31 Ó Carragáin (2010), p.289.

32 Ibid.; Tadhg O'Keeffe, 'Wheels of Words, Networks of Knowledge: Romanesque Scholarship and Cormac's Chapel', in Bracken and Ó Riain-Raedel (eds), pp.257–69: 262–63. O'Keeffe argues that the grand consecration in 1134 was Cormac's way of cementing his name to the chapel.

33 Ibid. For more on this poem see, Erich Poppe, 'Cormac's Metrical Testament: "Mithig techt tar mo thimna"', *Celtica*, vol.23 (1999), pp.300–11.

34 Patrician associations to the Rock had existed since at least the seventh century when the famous story of St Patrick piercing the foot of King Óengus first appears in the *Vita Tripartita*. Candon has argued that Muirchertach deliberately accepted the Rock's secondary status in order to receive concession from Armagh for his claims to be High King of Ireland. Anthony Candon, 'Barefaced Effrontery: secular and ecclesiastical politics in early twelfth century Ireland', *Seanchas Ardmhacha: Journal of the Armagh Diocesan Historical Society*, vol.14 (1991), pp.1–25: 11–14.

35 Gleeson, p.10; Ó Carragáin (2010), p.289.

36 Roger Stalley, 'The Construction and Decoration of Cormac's Chapel at Cashel', in Bracken and Ó Riain-Raedel (eds), pp.162–75; Tomás Ó Carragáin, 'Relics and Recluses Revisited: some thoughts on Cormac's Chapel, Cashel', in Emer Purcell et al. (eds), *Clerics, Kings and Vikings: essays on medieval Ireland in honour of Donnchadh Ó Corráin* (Dublin: Four Courts Press, 2015), pp.326–37: 326; O'Keeffe (2003), p.125. O'Keeffe highlights that Cashel exemplifies the interconnectedness of the secular and ecclesiastical; Marie Therese Flanagan, 'Henry II, the Council of Cashel and the Irish Bishops', *Peritia*, vol.10 (1996), pp.184–211: 197–98. Flanagan sees the construction of the chapel as a sign of Cormac Mac Carthaig's ambition to attain the high-kingship of Ireland.

37 Gleeson, p.11, quoting Bhreathnach in Jacqueline Borsje et al. (eds).

38 Ibid., p.11. Gleeson has identified several possibilities as to where the stone may have been located.

39 Ó Carragáin (2010), p.289; Ó Carragáin (2015), p.330; O'Keeffe (2003), p.132. Ó Carragáin also suggests that this tower may have formed part of a *reclusium* for an anchorite.

40 Ó Carragáin (2015), p.335.

41 Stalley in Bracken and Ó Riain-Raedel (eds), p.171; O'Keeffe (2003), pp.150–51. This is an idea expressed earlier by Françoise Henry, *Irish Art in the Romanesque Period, 1020–1170 AD* (New York: Cornell University Press, 1970), pp.172–73.

42 Ó Carragáin (2015), p.336; O'Keeffe (2003), pp.150–51. A boundary feature, excavated by Hodkinson, runs underneath Cormac's Chapel and is associated with the round tower, and possibly marked the limit of the grant to the church (see Hodkinson (1994)). The area east of the boundary then belonged to the Church, while everything west remained secular. Gleeson argued that the chancel arch of Cormac's Chapel was deliberately placed on top of this feature to maintain the division between ecclesiastical and laity. There was an area for the king and an area for the Church. Gleeson, p.10.

43 O'Keeffe (1994), pp.118–52. O'Keeffe surmises that it is no coincidence that both examples of fresco paintings can be found at sites established by Cormac Mac Carthaig. O'Keeffe (2003), p.144.

44 See George Petrie, *The Ecclesiastical Architecture of Ireland: anterior to the Anglo-Norman invasion* (Dublin: Hodges and Smith, 1845), p.296; also George Petrie, 'An Inquiry into the Origin and Uses of the Round Towers of Ireland: comprising remarks on the ecclesiastical architecture of Ireland anterior to the Anglo-Norman Invasion', *The Transactions of the Royal Irish Academy*, vol.20 (1845), pp.iii–521. For more about the conservation of the paintings, see Mark Perry, 'The Romanesque Frescos in Cormac's Chapel, Cashel', *Ireland of the Welcomes*, vol.44, no.2 (March–April 1995), pp.16–19. Mark Perry, 'Recent Discoveries in Cormac's Chapel, Cashel, Co. Tipperary, Eire', in Anna Hulbert, Julie Marsden and Victoria Todd (eds), *The Conservator as Art Historian* (London: United Kingdom Institute for Conservation of Historic and Artistic Works, 1992), pp.30–31.

45 Report quoted by Mary McGrath, 'The Wall Paintings in Cormac's Chapel at Cashel', *An Irish Quarterly Review*, vol.64, no.256 (1975), pp.327–32: 328.

46 Ibid., p.330. Absent from McGrath's discussion was exactly where the samples for analysis were taken. She also discussed the exact medium of the paintings, which she argued is not true fresco, but rather tempera on set plaster. This is at odds with later reports which identify the paintings as *fresco buono* (Perry (1992), pp.30–31, and (1995), pp.16–19). Given that McGrath's analysis was carried out before the recent conservation work, it is prudent to side with Perry's analysis cited

above. Details were added *a secco* to the fresco, and it may be that this is where McGrath's samples were taken.

47 Michael J.C. Buckley, 'Ancient Irish painting at the Rock of Cashel and Molana Abbey', *Journal of the Waterford and South-East of Ireland Archaeological Society*, vol.11 (1908), pp.108–09 (originally printed in 1892).

48 Roger Stalley, 'Solving a Mystery at Cashel: the Romanesque painting in Cormac's Chapel', *Irish Arts Review Yearbook*, vol.18 (2002), pp.25–29: 26, n.3.

49 Gerard Crotty, 'A Romanesque fresco in Cormac's Chapel', *Tipperary Historical Journal*, vol.15 (1988), pp.155–58.

50 Crotty, p.157. Crotty's identification was echoed by Peter Harbison, *The Golden Age of Irish Art: the medieval achievement 600–1200* (London: Thames & Hudson, 1999), p.301.

51 Crotty, p.158. Crotty also recognised that identification of this scene as the Judgement of Solomon was fraught with problems. A later twelfth-century depiction of the Judgement of Solomon, carved on a wall panel, can be found at St Declan's in Ardmore, co. Waterford, where the women and child are all depicted. O'Keeffe (2003), p.145, pp.223–24.

52 Stalley (2002), pp.25–29. That biblical scenes were often part of a larger narrative flow is long recognised. Roger Rosewell, *Medieval Wall Paintings* (Oxford: Shire Publications, 2014), p.26.

53 Douay-Rheims English Translation <https://vulgate.org/> [acc. 26 Mar 2024]. This text comes from the Latin Vulgate of the New Testament which would have been in common use in the twelfth century. The Gospel of Matthew would have originally been written in *koine* Greek and was translated by St Jerome in the fourth century into Latin.

54 Stalley (2002), p.26; E.W. Tristram, *English Medieval Wall Painting: the twelfth century* (Oxford: Oxford University Press, 1944).

55 Stalley (2002), p.26.

56 Ibid., p.28. For more on the Copenhagen Psalter, see C.M. Kauffman, *Romanesque Manuscripts, 1066–1190, Vol. 3: a survey of manuscripts illuminated in the British Isles* (London: Harvey Miller, 1975), pp.118–20.

57 Mark Perry, 'Notes on the conservation of the wall paintings in Cormac's Chapel and St. Patrick's Cathedral' (unpublished document provided to the author, 2022), pp.1–2.

58 Stalley (2002), p.29. C.R. Dodwell, *The Pictorial Arts of the West, 800–1200* (London and New Haven: Yale University Press, 1993), p.347. Deborah Kahn, 'The Structural Evidence for the dating of the St Gabriel Chapel wall painting at Christ Church Cathedral, Canterbury', *Burlington Magazine*, vol.126 (1984), pp.225–29. K. Flynn, 'Romanesque wall-paintings in the Cathedral Church of Christ Church, Canterbury', *The Archaeologia Cantiana: transactions of The Kent Archaeological Society*, vol.95 (1979), pp.185–95.

59 Texts, normally in the form of scrolls, were an integral part of medieval wall painting. Rosewell, p.53.

60 Stalley (2002), p.28.

61 Ibid.

62 Rosewell, p.64. In an Irish context, there are no other contemporary examples of the Adoration of the Magi in wall paintings, although a slightly later twelfth-century version can be found in the sculpted wall-panels at St Declan's in Ardmore, alongside the already noted version of the Judgement of Solomon. O'Keeffe (2003), pp.223–24.

63 Rosewell, p.29.

64 The Baptism of Christ can be found in Mark 1:9–11, Matthew 3:13–17, Luke 3:21–23 and John 1:29–33. The Transfiguration of Christ can be found in Mark 9:2–8, Matthew 17:1–8, and Luke 9:28–36. There is no description of the Transfiguration in the Gospel of John.

65 Romanesque depictions of the Transfiguration are scarce; one contemporary example can be found carved into a tympanum at Notre-Dame Priory of La Charité-sur-Loire in Burgundy. If my hypothesis is correct, it would make the depiction in Cormac's Chapel a rare example in Romanesque art.

66 Stalley (2002), p.25. Rosewell, p.7. Stalley has also identified a possible *Agnus Dei* (Lamb of God) on the soffit. While there are no other Romanesque Irish examples, some contemporary instances can be found in England at St Botolph's Church, Hardham, in West Sussex, and St John's Church, Duxford, in Cambridgeshire.

[67] O'Keefe (2003), p.145 argues that the theme of kingship may have been more overt than previously allowed.

[68] Perry (1995), p.17, and (2022), pp.1–2.

[69] Perry (2022), p.2.

[70] Stalley (2002), p.29.

[71] Perry (2022), p.1.

[72] Ibid.

[73] Ibid., p.2. Stalley (2002), p.29; Stalley in Bracken and Ó Riain-Raedel (eds), p.175. O'Keeffe appears to acknowledge and agree with Stalley's dating in Tadhg O'Keeffe, *Medieval Irish Buildings 1100–1600* (Dublin: Four Courts Press, 2015), p.102, n.4.

[74] Dagmar Ó Riain-Raedel, 'Cashel and Germany, The Documentary Evidence', in Bracken and Ó Riain-Raedel (eds), pp.176–217: 216–17.

[75] Ibid., p.217.

[76] Francis J. Byrne, 'The Trembling Sod: Ireland in 1169', in Art Cosgrove (ed.), *A New History of Ireland, Vol. 2: Medieval Ireland 1169–1534* (Oxford: Oxford University Press, 2nd edn, 2008), p.29. Cormac Mac Carthaig did not only found Cormac's Chapel, but is known to have founded several other churches throughout Munster, including Gill Abbey in Cork, and Lismore in Waterford. See O'Keeffe (1994), p.119; John Bradley and Heather A. King, 'Romanesque Voussoirs at St Fin Barre's Cathedral, Cork', *Journal of the Royal Society of Antiquaries of Ireland*, vol.115 (1985), pp.146–51. Aubrey Gwynn and R. Neville Hadcock, *Medieval Religious Houses: Ireland* (Harlow: Longmans, 1970), p.167.

[77] Byrne (2008), pp.30–31. The most recent and one of the most in-depth studies of this period comes from Seán Ó Hoireabhárd, *The Medieval Irish Kings and the English Invasion* (Liverpool: Liverpool University Press, 2024), pp.198–218. I am extremely grateful to Dr Ó Hoireabhárd for kindly allowing me to read an advance copy of his book.

[78] Ruaidrí had, once again, divided Munster into two kingdoms in 1152; see AFM.1152.9.

[79] ATig.1170.9, ATig.1170.17, ATig.1171.5, ATig.1173.10, ATig.1174.9, ATig.1175.15; AI.1170.3, AI.1174.3; AFM.1170.10, AFM.1171.19; LC.1176.1; Misc.Ir.A.1169.3.

[80] Edwin C. Rae, 'Architecture and Sculpture, 1169–1603', in Art Cosgrove (ed.), pp.737–77: 743; Marnane, p.26.

[81] Conleth Manning, *Rock of Cashel, Co. Tipperary* (Dublin: Dúchas / The Heritage Service, 2000), p.7.

[82] For the first wave of invaders in 1169, see ATig.1169.3, ATig.1170.8; AFM.1169.9. For the arrival of Henry II, see ATig.1171.12; AI.1171.5; AFM.1171.29.

[83] Marie Therese Flanagan, *Irish Society, Anglo-Norman Settlers, Angevin Kingship: interactions in Ireland in the late 12th century* (Oxford: Clarendon Press, 1989), pp.168–170.

[84] F.X. Martin, 'Allies and an Overlord, 1169–72', in Art Cosgrove (ed.), pp.67–97: 80–81.

[85] This is, however, noted as a factor by Gervase of Canterbury. Flanagan (1996), p.185. Vincent (2018), p.191.

[86] Gerald of Wales, 'Expugnatio Hibernica', 1.31, in *The Historical Works of Giraldus Cambrensis, containing* [...] *the Conquest of Ireland, translated by Thomas Forester*, revised and edited by Thomas Wright (London: George Bell & Sons, 1905), p.35.

[87] Radulphi de Diceto, *The Historical Works of Master Ralph De Diceto*, ed. William Stubbs, 2 vols (London: Longmans, 1876), I, pp.350–51. For a fuller discussion of the varying accounts of the Irish bishops' reaction to Henry II, see Flanagan (1996), pp.190–91.

[88] The quick submission by both Mac Carthaig and Ua Briain could be interpreted less as a recognition of Henry's lordship than a rejection of the high kingship of Ruaidrí Ua Conchobhair. Flanagan (1989), pp.226, 247; Robin Frame, *Colonial Ireland, 1169–1369* (Dublin: Four Courts Press, 1981), p.22. Ó Hoireabhárd sees this as part of a larger pattern, especially on the part of Mac Carthaig who had a history of submitting to various different overlords, usually whichever was closer or politically beneficial. Their submission may only have been intended to be temporary and for as long as Henry II was in Ireland. Ó Hoireabhárd, pp.216, 232.

[89] Flanagan also raises the question of how such an interdict could be enforced. Flanagan (1996), p.191, n.24.

[90] Flanagan (1996), pp.184–85.

[91] Gerald of Wales, 'Expugnatio Hibernica', 1.33–34, in Thomas Wright (rev. and ed.), pp.36–37. For a larger discussion of the council of Cashel, see Flanagan (1996), pp.184–211; Ó Corráin (2017), pp.104–15.

[92] Stalley in Bracken and Ó Riain-Raedel (eds), p.175, n.33.

[93] Maurice P. Sheehy (ed.), *Pontifica Hibernica: Medieval Papal Chancery documents concerning Ireland, 640–1261*, 2 vols (Dublin: M.H. Gill, 1962–65), I, nos 5, 6, 7; Flanagan (1996), pp.188–89.

[94] Flanagan (1989), pp.38–55. Ó Corráin (2017), pp.98–99. For more on the complex relationship between Ireland and Henry II, which cannot be explored in full here, see Seán Duffy, 'Henry II and England's Insular Neighbours', in Christopher Harper-Bill and Nicholas Vincent (eds), *Henry II: New Interpretations* (Woodbridge: Boydell Press, 2007), pp.129–53 (pp.132–33).

[95] Sigebert of Gembloux, *Chronica Cum Continuatibus, Monumenta Germaniae Historica, Scriptores 6*, ed. L.C. Bethmann (Hanover, 1844), p.403; Colin Veach, 'Henry II and the ideological foundations of Angevin Rule in Ireland', *Irish Historical Studies*, vol.42, no.161 (May 2018), pp.1–25: 6.

[96] Iohannis Saresberiensis, *Metalogion*, eds J.B. Hall, K.S.B. Keats-Rohan, *Corpus Christianorum, Continuatio Mediaevalis*, vol.98 (Turnhout: Brepols, 1991), p.183. Ó Corráin (2017), p.97. Frame, pp.19–20.

[97] Anne Duggan, 'The Making of a Myth: Giraldus Cambrensis, Laudabiliter, and Henry II's Lordship in Ireland', *Studies in Medieval and Renaissance History*, 3rd series, vol.4 (2007), pp.249–312; Flanagan (1989), pp.7–55; J.A. Watt, 'Laudabiliter in Medieval Diplomacy and Propaganda', *The Irish Ecclesiastical Record,* 5th series, vol.87 (June 1957), pp.420–32; Ó Corráin (2017), pp.97–102; Vincent (2018), pp.189–98; Thomas W. Smith, 'Laudabiliter Reconsidered', in Peter Crooks and Seán Duffy (eds), *Invasion 1169* (Dublin: Four Courts Press, forthcoming). I am extremely grateful to Dr Smith for allowing me to read an advance copy of his chapter.

[98] Helen Clover and Margaret Gibson (eds), *The Letters of Lanfranc, Archbishop of Canterbury* (Oxford: Oxford University Press, 1979), pp.50–51; Ó Corráin (2017), pp.59–60. Ó Corráin argues that Lanfranc's claims were based on a possible misreading of Bede; Martin Brett, 'Canterbury's Perspective on Church Reform and Ireland, 1070–1115', in Bracken and Ó Riain-Raedel (eds), pp.13–35.

[99] Flanagan (1989), pp.14–17; Clover and Gibson (eds), pp.64–67; Ó Corráin has argued that Lanfranc's desire to expand Canterbury's influence may be a reflection of secular ambitions; Ó Corráin (2017), pp.58–60.

[100] Ó Corráin (2017), p.63. Candon, pp.1–25.

[101] Ó Corráin sees this as a possible challenge to Armagh to push them towards reform. Ó Corráin (2017), p.66; Candon, pp.11–17.

[102] Muirchertach Ua Briain and Arnulf de Montgomery, the Lord of Pembroke, entered into a marriage alliance, and Arnulf was married to the daughter of Muirchertach, Lafracoth. Arnulf had sought to depose Henry I in 1102, but his plot failed and he found himself in exile in Munster, leading to a breakdown in the relationship between Muirchertach and Henry I. Martin in Cosgrove (ed.), p.52. See also, E. Curtis, 'Murchertach O'Brien, High King of Ireland, and his Norman son-in-law, Arnulf de Montgomery, circa 1100', *Journal of the Royal Society of Antiquaries of Ireland*, 6th series, vol.11, no.2 (Dec 1921), pp.116–24; J.F.A. Mason, 'Roger de Montgomery and his sons (1067–1102)', *Transactions of the Royal Historical Society*, vol.13 (1963), pp.1–28. F.X. Martin, 'The First Normans in Munster', *Cork Historical Society Journal*, vol.76 (1971), pp.48–71: 50–51.

[103] Flanagan (1989), pp.25–26; Ó Corráin (2017), p.97; AFM.1111.5; AU.1111.8; ATig.1111.6; AI.1111.3; LC.1111.6.

[104] AFM.1152.4; ATig.1152.2.

[105] Flanagan (1989), pp.38–55. Veach saw Flanagan's analysis as going too far in its revisionism; Veach (2018), p.8.

[106] Flanagan (1996), pp.206–08. See also R.R. Davies, *Domination and Conquest: the experience of Ireland, Scotland and Wales, 1100–1300* (Cambridge: Cambridge University Press, 1990), p.17. For a larger and more in-depth study of Irish church reform, see Marie Therese Flanagan, *The Transformation of the Irish Church in the twelfth and thirteenth centuries* (Woodbridge: Boydell Press, 2010).

[107] Veach (2018), p.3. Stalley had already raised the question of Henry's involvement in the commissioning of the frescoes in Cormac's Chapel; Stalley (2002), p.29.

108 While Gerald of Wales may be detailed, he is far from reliable. Vincent (2018), p.185. Frame, pp.8–9.

109 Gerald of Wales, *Topographia*, 3.10, in Thomas Wright (rev. and ed.), pp.68–70. William of Newburgh writes in a similar way about perceived Irish barbarism. William of Newburgh, *The History of English Affairs: Book 2*, eds D.G. Walsh and M.J. Kennedy (Oxford: Aris & Phillips, 1988), 2.26.2, p.111. This is also a view that carried into modern scholarship through the influential work of G.H. Orpen who characterised pre-conquest Ireland as archaic and unable to govern itself. G.H. Orpen, *Ireland Under the Normans*, 4 vols (Oxford: Clarendon Press, 1911–20); Ó Corráin (2017), p.58.

110 The idea that Ireland had once been subject to Arthurian Britain first appeared in the works of Geoffrey of Monmouth.

111 For a more in-depth study of Henry's utilisation of the church as a justification for invading Ireland, see Veach (2018), pp.1–25.

112 Gerald of Wales, 'Expugnatio', 1.24–39, in Thomas Wright (rev. and ed.), pp.32–41. Vincent (2018), pp.186–87. Nicholas Vincent, 'Henry II', in Crooks and Duffy (eds). For more on Gerald of Wales and classical allusions, see the recent paper by Michael Staunton, 'Giraldus's "Expugnatio Hibernica" Reconsidered', in Crooks and Duffy (eds). I am extremely grateful to Professor Vincent and Professor Staunton for allowing me to read an advance copy of their chapters.

113 Gerald of Wales, 'Expugnatio', 1.36–37, in Thomas Wright (rev. and ed.), pp.38–39; Flanagan (1996), p.185.

114 Flanagan (1996), p.210.

115 Roger of Howden, *Henrici Secundi Benedicti Abbatis*, ed. William Stubbs, 2 vols (London: Longman, 1867), II, pp.24–26; Gerald of Wales, 'Expugnatio', 1.32, in Thomas Wright (rev. and ed.), pp.35–36; Colin Veach, 'From Kingdom to Colony: framing the English conquest of Ireland', *English Historical Review* (2024). I am extremely grateful to Dr Veach for allowing me to read an advance copy of his work and for his constructive comments on an early draft of this paper.

116 Vincent (forthcoming). However, it should be noted that different chroniclers give different dates for Henry's arrival and departure. Vincent bases his argument on the Brut chronicle of the Welsh which gives the dates mentioned above, while Gerald of Wales gives the date as 18 October.

117 Frame, p.84.

118 For a good overview of the infancy narrative in the gospels, see Raymond E. Brown, 'Infancy Narratives in the NT Gospels', in David Noel Freedman et al. (eds), *Anchor Bible Dictionary*, 6 vols (New York: Doubleday, 1992), III, pp.410–15. There are differences in the portrayal of Jesus in the canonical gospels found in the New Testament. In Mark, Jesus is presented as God's authorised Messiah during his baptism, while in Matthew Jesus is baptised by John in order to fulfil all righteousness. See Joel Marcus, *Mark 1–8: A New Translation, with introduction and commentary* (New Haven and London: Yale University Press, 2000), pp.149–57; W.F. Albright and C.S. Mann, *Matthew* (New York: Doubleday, 1971), pp.30–33; J.A. Fitzmyer, *The Gospel According to Luke* (New York: Doubleday, 1981), pp.479–87.

119 Adela Yarbro Collins and John J. Collins, *King and Messiah as Son of God: divine, human and angelic messianic figures in Biblical and related literature* (Grand Rapids: Eerdmans, 2008), pp.143–45.

120 Ibid., p.127; see Judges 3:10 and 1 Samuel 16:13.

121 Matthew, Mark and Luke are commonly known as the synoptic gospels, meaning 'common view', as they share similar perspectives.

122 Adela Yarbro Collins, *Mark: a commentary*, in the *Hermeneia* series (Augsburg: Fortress Press, 2007), p.150.

123 That the Baptism and Transfiguration of Christ are narratively connected has long been recognised. Collins and Collins, pp.130–32: 142. In Matthew's version of the Transfiguration, Jesus is explicitly portrayed as a king.

124 Nicholas Vincent, 'The Charters of King Henry II: The Royal Inspeximus revisited', in Michael Gervers (ed.), *Dating Undated Medieval Charters* (Woodbridge: Boydell & Brewer, 2000), pp.110–12. Vincent (forthcoming) sets out further evidence of Henry II presenting himself as a messiah-like figure.

125 Stalley (2002), p.26.

126 Gerald of Wales, *Topographia*, 3.48, in Thomas Wright (rev. and ed.), pp.87.

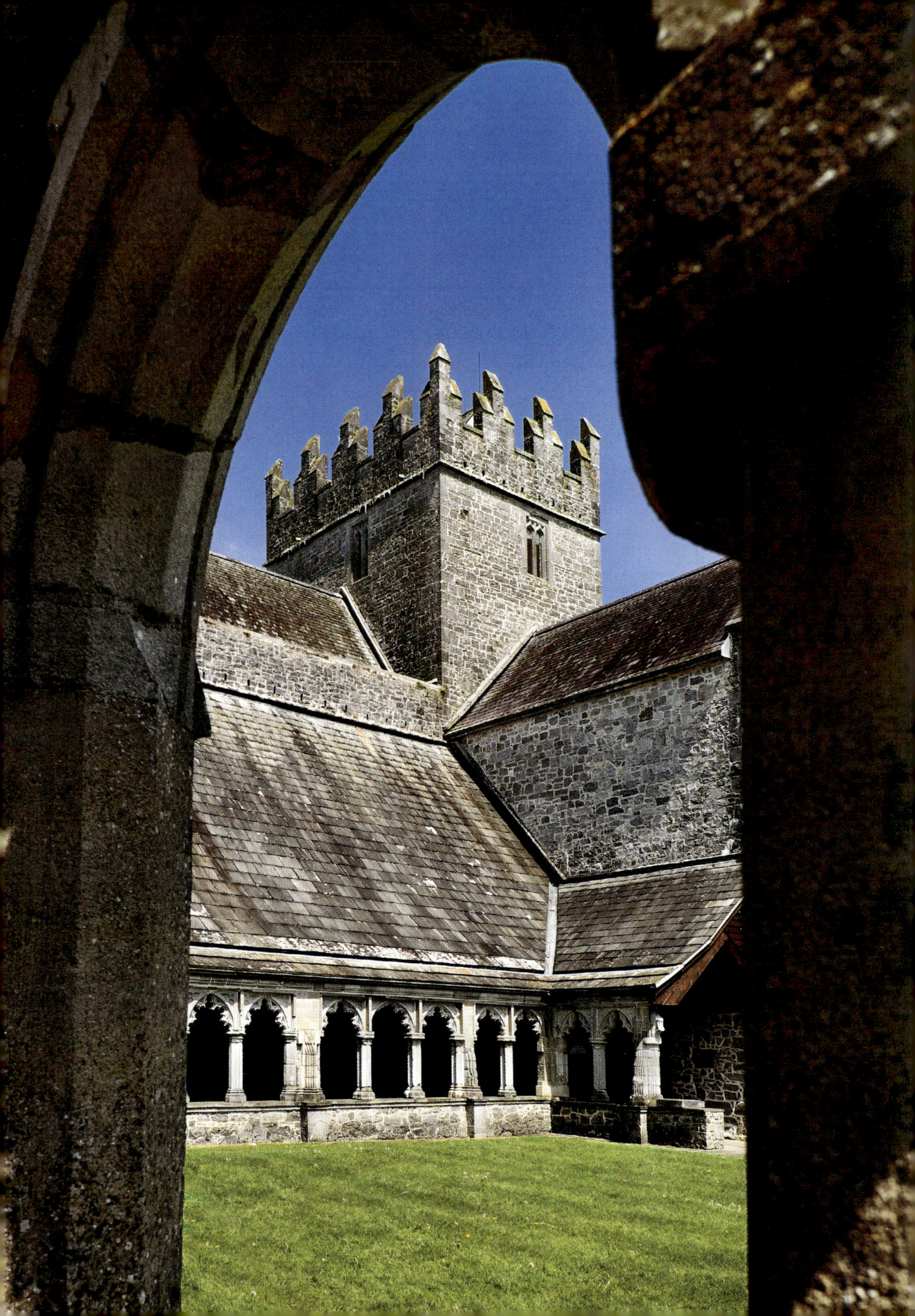

# The carved stonework of Holycross Abbey: shrines or sepulchres?

NIAMH FLOOD

THE FIFTEENTH-CENTURY RECONSTRUCTION OF THE EAST END OF HOLYCROSS ABBEY, CO. Tipperary, resulted in some instances of the highest quality decorative stonework in Ireland [figs 1, 2], from flamboyant traceried windows to tierceron ribbed vaulting and the magnificently carved sedilia in the chancel. However, the carved pier wall in the south transept [fig. 3] surpasses all the other stonework in both accomplishment and aesthetics, so much so that it might be regarded not only as microarchitecture, but also as architectural sculpture. Its emphatically premeditated positioning has ensured its survival, but its primary function is not as apparent. This paper will expand on the significance of the cross relics in the possession of the abbey that signify the carved pier wall's function as a shrine for the various cross relics. It will also explore whether a second piece of microarchitecture, formerly located in the body of the abbey, also functioned as a shrine, albeit of a hierarchical nature [fig. 4]. For clarity, these pieces will be referred to as the 'carved pier wall' and 'the second shrine'. The work of Roger Stalley is significant to this paper; it was his research that put forward the idea that the carved pier wall was a shrine. He also documented the temporary reconstruction of the second shrine during the OPW renovations in the 1970s, before it was disassembled and placed in storage. This paper will also suggest that these two pieces might have transmuted their function in tandem with the emergent prevalence of liturgical Easter rites, and served as Easter sepulchres. The existence of these two pieces of carved stonework in Holycross, one emphatically *in situ*, the other fragmented and displaced, speaks to the potential for a hierarchical form of pilgrimage and performative rituals.

## History of the abbey and the relics

ALTHOUGH THE FOCUS OF THIS PAPER IS PREDOMINANTLY CONCERNED WITH THE FUNCTION of these two pieces of microarchitecture, a brief chronicle of the abbey might inform their purpose. Given its name, the abbey of Holycross was intrinsically associated with the relics under its aegis. Concurrent with a chronology of the abbey, a brief historical synopsis of the cross relics thought to have been in the abbey might indicate the fundamental importance of the Holy Cross in both the abbey's architecture and its remarkable

fig. 1 | View into the cloister at Holycross Abbey, co. Tipperary
(photo: Alamy / Hugh Rooney, 2013)

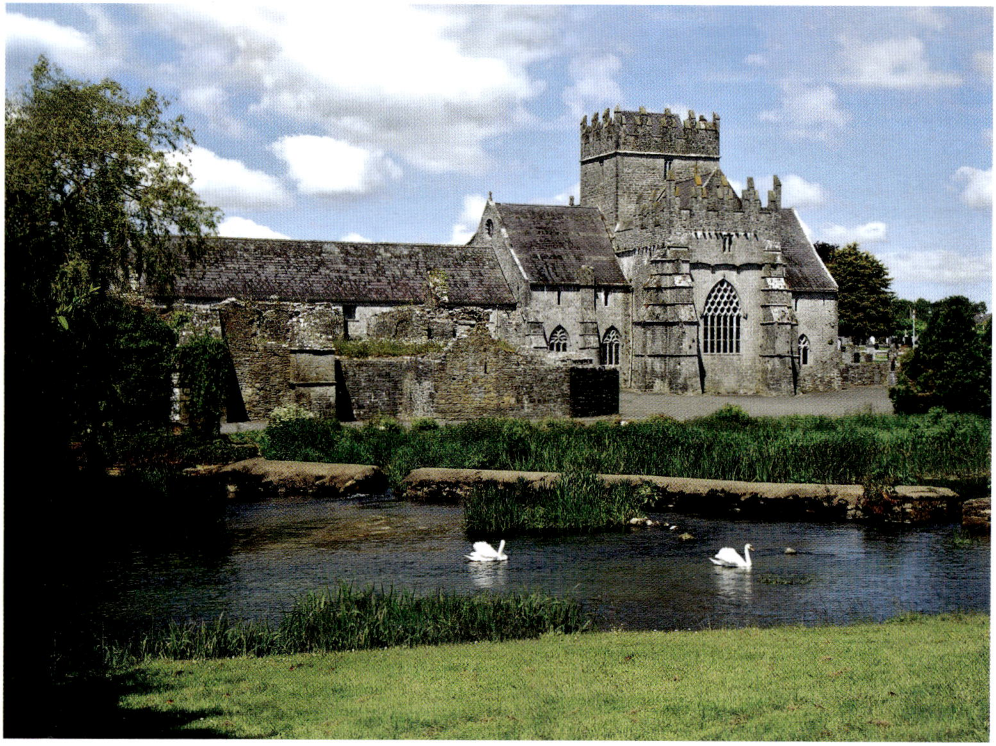

endurance, and support the argument for hierarchical shrines within the abbey.

Domhnall Mór O'Brien, the high king of Thomond, is thought to have gifted the land around Holycross to the Cistercians in *c.*1181, and also gifted a pre-existing Benedictine community with a relic of the True Cross in *c.*1169.[1] It would appear that by the thirteenth century many of the Cistercian rules had fallen into abeyance, such as allowing tenants on the abbey's farms and serfs on its lands, potentially indicating a similar relaxation of rules in terms of the relic in their possession, how it was displayed and venerated, and who was permitted into the abbey.[2] By the mid-fourteenth century, Holycross was at the centre of a feudal system that saw fairs, markets and courts all focused around the abbey, and was most likely a popular pilgrimage destination. By the time of the fifteenth-century renovations to the abbey, it seems to have been a pivotal locus for pilgrims and locals, which might have influenced the architectural decisions that saw Holycross become one of the most elaborately decorated churches in medieval Ireland, with relics having a strong influence on the refurbishments.

An almost-unbroken father-to-son line of succession from 1185 to 1405 saw the Butlers possess near-total control and power of co. Tipperary, and as patrons and protectors of Holycross; the fifteenth-century refurbishments were most likely overseen

fig. 2 | Holycross Abbey, viewed from the east
(courtesy Tipperary Tourism)

fig. 3 | South view of carved pier wall, *c.*1440, black limestone
(photos by the author (2021–24), unless otherwise stated)

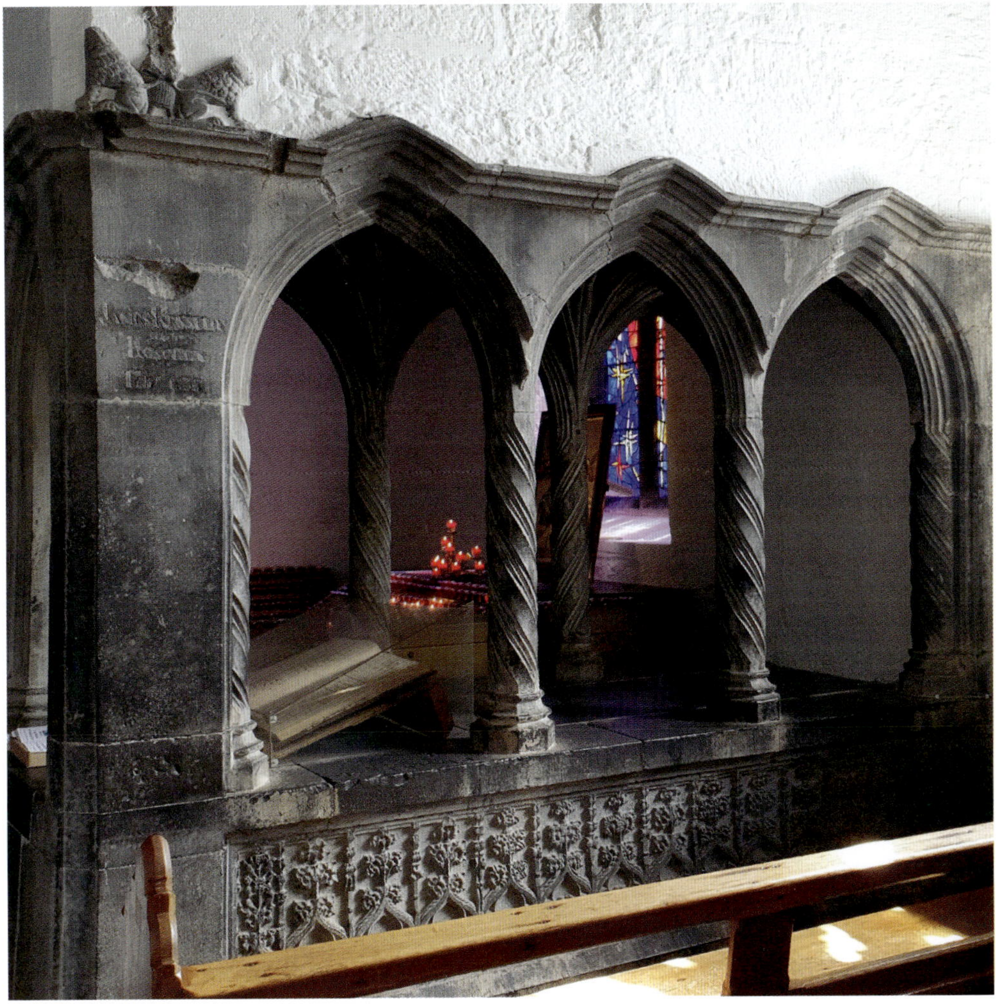

by the 'White Earl', James Butler, 4th Earl of Ormond (c.1390–1452).[3] By 1539, Holycross had become a secular provostry due to the direct intercession of the Earl of Ormond.[4] This patronage and protection of the abbey most probably ensured its survival at a time when most religious houses were either suppressed or abandoned. There is evidence from 1567 to 1601 of large crowds of pilgrims still venerating the relics there.[5] It was during this period that a monk from Holycross, Malachy Hartry, compiled a manuscript chronicling the history of the abbey which, although apocryphal in sections, is the only surviving record of events within the abbey. The Cistercians remained until 1752 when the last monk, Fr Edmund Cormick – recorded as both abbot and parish priest – left Holycross, and the abbey fell into ruin.[6]

The eighteenth and nineteenth centuries saw Holycross become a destination on travellers' itineraries, when an upsurge in the Romantic ideation of picturesque ruins integrated with a growing antiquarian focus on the architecture of medieval Ireland.[7] These records, while documenting what remained of the abbey in its ruinous state, also

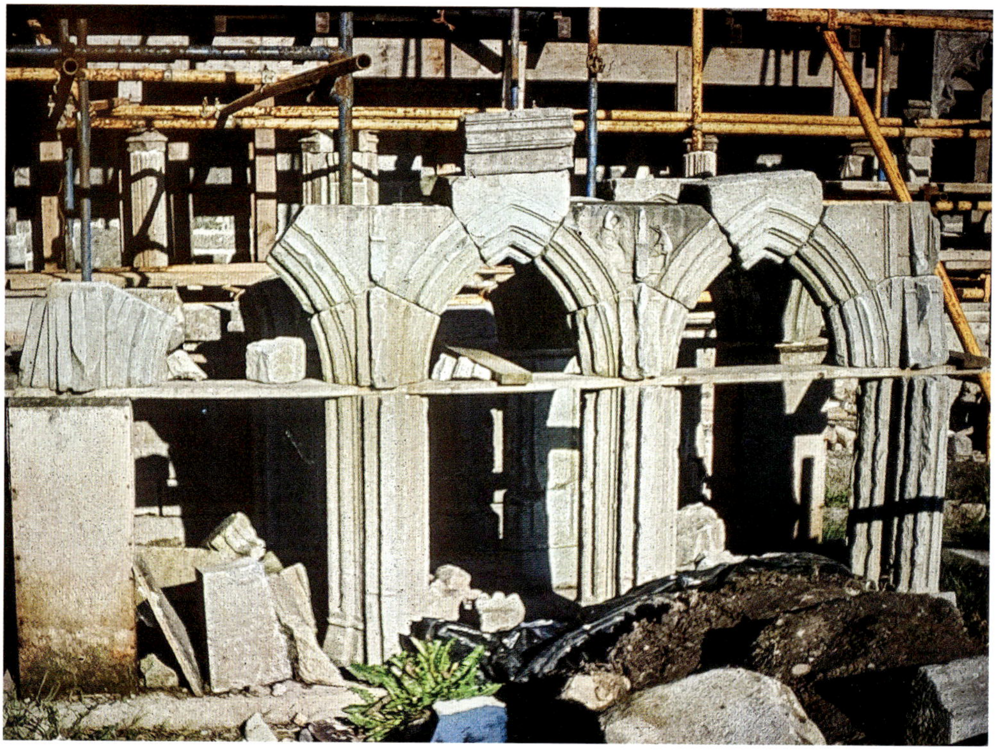

gave the first interpretations of the remaining architectural features of the abbey. These included the carved pier wall in the south transept and mentions of another shrine structure, along with nascent considerations of their functions. In 1797, John Harden struggled to categorise the carved pier wall, saying it might be 'a sepulchral shrine (or a mausoleum for I am ignorant by what name to call it)', and the anonymous 'M.E.C.', writing in 1868, called it a waking bier.[8] Writing in 1806, Richard Colt Hoare described it as of a 'very singular design, and unlike any I recollect to have seen', and also posited that it was a waking bier.[9] Another traveller, Hermann Fürst von Pückler-Muskau, writing in 1828, says the carved pier is for the repose of all the past abbots' ashes.[10] George Holmes in 1797 said he 'descended from the night stairs into the south cross and saw there the remains of a very curious shrine which had deposited in it the cross relics'.[11] Indicating the dispersal of the carved stonework, he remarked that the abbey's 'walls may be traced through all the neighbouring gardens, and half the houses in the village are composed of the spoils of this fine ruin'.[12] What remained by the twentieth century, before the 1970s OPW restoration, suggests a puzzling arrangement of carved stonework, much of it removed from its original locations with the exception of the carved pier wall in the south transept.

Fundamental to the abbey's endurance was its possession over the centuries of relics of the True Cross; indeed the abbey may have possessed a relic of the True

fig. 4 | Remnants of a second 'shrine' from Holycross, temporarily reassembled in the cloister *c.*1970 (Trinity College Dublin: Dept of History of Art & Architecture Slide Collection / Roger Stalley)

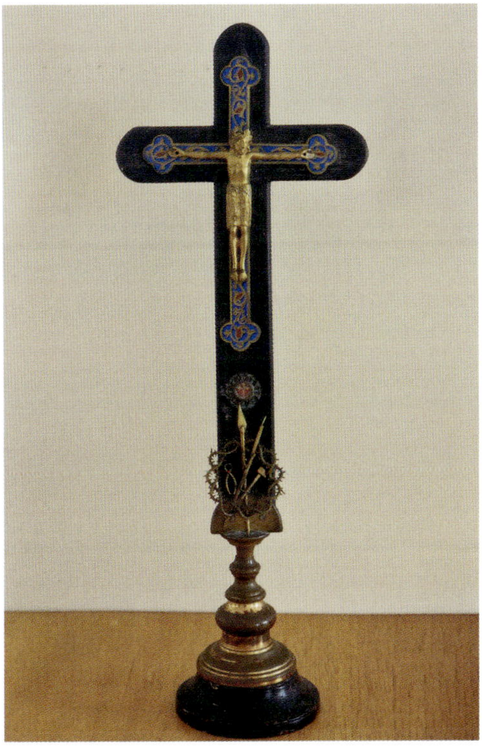

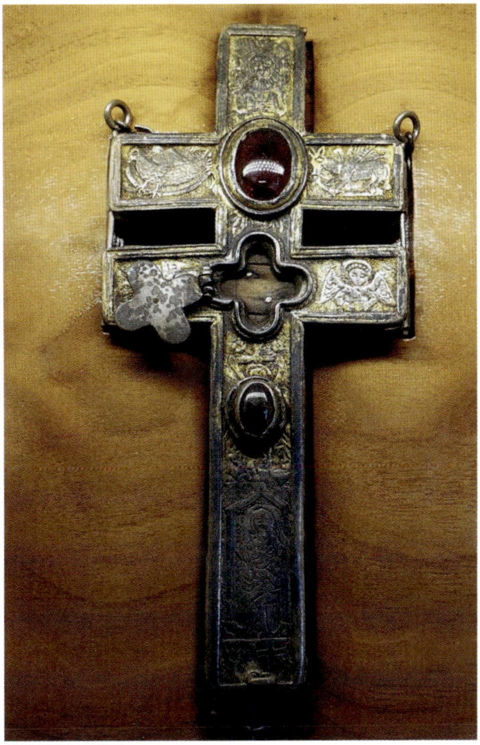

Cross from its inception, to rival the one at Cong Abbey, co. Mayo.[13] As a place of pilgrimage, Holycross was unique in Cistercian dynamics in Ireland, most likely for possession of this relic.[14] It is not known how, where, or if any relics were displayed by the Cistercians prior to the fifteenth-century refurbishments, but in keeping with the abeyance of Cistercian mores previously mentioned, and the variable condition of its finances, it might be suggested that the relics were indeed utilised to bring pilgrims, authority and money to the abbey.[15]

The Cistercian historian Colmcille Ó Conbhuidhe posits that the abbey was in possession of three relics, the earliest originating from Rome through the medium of the O'Brien family; the second either from France or Jerusalem via England; and the third from the Earls of Ormond.[16] The royal house of the O'Briens had been gifted a cross relic in *c.*1110 by Pope Pascal II in recognition of their help in integrating the Irish Church into that in Europe, and it is presumed that it was this relic that was presented to the Benedictine community that existed before the Cistercian arrival at Holycross.[17] It appears to have been in the possession of the last Cistercian at Holycross, Edmund Cormick, in the mid-1750s, before eventually being passed to the Sisters of Charity in Milltown, Dublin. It was ultimately returned to the custody of the Cistercians at Mount Melleray, co. Waterford, where it remains today, despite requests in the 1970s for its

fig. 5 | The reliquary at Mount Melleray, co. Waterford, date unknown, wood and metal
(by kind permission of Mount Melleray Abbey community)
fig. 6 | The fifteenth-century Butler Reliquary at Holycross Abbey

return to Holycross.[18] The form of this relic [fig. 5] has most likely been modified over the years; it is now presented embedded in a wooden cross that is attached to a metal base, but with evidence of an earlier suspension mechanism remaining on the rear. The mystery of how and where it was displayed in Holycross remains.

Sometime in the fourteenth century, a second relic, potentially from an English source, was given to the abbey. It has been suggested that it was a gift to the Cistercians from Isabella Marche, widow of King John, in 1223, having previously been brought to England from the Holy Land by Richard Coeur de Lion.[19] In the archives of the historian Maurice Lenihan (1811–1895) is a newspaper article authored by him in 1861 that records a relic from Holycross believed to have been inserted in the crozier of the archepiscopal See of Cashel.[20] This might potentially be the English relic thought lost. In the mid-fifteenth century, most likely during the refurbishment, and perhaps instigated by it, the abbey was presented with a third relic, the Butler Relic, within a twin-armed, Cross of Lorraine-style reliquary [fig. 6]. The *Ecclesiastical Record* of 1872 corroborates a relic with Ormond/Butler provenance, and this passed down ultimately to an Ellen Butler. She presented it to a priest, who in turn donated it to the Ursuline Convent in Cork in 1801, there to be exposed to the public for veneration purposes.[21] In 1974/75 a formal request from Archbishop Morris to the Ursulines saw it return to Holycross. The Butler Relic remains to this day in Holycross, along with a Vatican Relic which was presented to the abbey to mark the restoration project in the 1970s.[22]

From this evidence, there appeared to have been three relics of the cross in the possession of the abbey up to its abandonment in the mid-eighteenth century, lending credence to the observation that Holycross was one of Munster's most notable pilgrimage sites.[23] In early medieval Ireland, relics were often symbolic of the Church's relationship with lay society and the local elite class by way of insignia and official symbols. Relics were used as a political tool to legitimise contracts and aid in disputes; they had a secular as well as a sacred function.[24] If, as Hartry says, a relic was 'in the monastery preordained for it, in which it is preserved and venerated with piety and honour', then it might be expected that it was housed in a suitably elaborate and sacred situation.[25] This *loca sancta* would have been available for pilgrims to venerate and as a focus for oath-swearing and safekeeping.[26] The presence of more than one relic also suggests the presence of more than one shrine, creating a potential hierarchy of pilgrimage, given the sanctified location of the south-transept carved pier wall. As the abbey's allegiances and role evolved, so too must have the performative acts and congregation within the church. If the relics were intertwined with the longevity of the abbey, how they were displayed or exploited, and for what purposes, ought to be imprinted into the fabric of the building.

## The carved stonework as shrines

BY THE MID-1440S, HOLYCROSS WAS FIRMLY ESTABLISHED AS A LOCUS FOR NATIONAL PILGRIMage. Its abbots were powerful and ambitious, and the patron family, the Butlers, were amongst the most powerful families in Ireland.[27] The earlier extant building, with its simplicity of style, was in the manner of Cistercian ideals, but it also reflected a lack of funds and a naive architecture that was most likely the result of the monks assuming the role of architect. This style can still be seen in the nave of Holycross, which has remained largely untouched over the years apart from the insertion of new windows into the old fabric. However, the whole of the eastern arm was rebuilt around this time, including the transepts, the monks' choir, the chancel and a new tower. That any Cistercian church should have been refined with such elaborate and flamboyant details speaks to an unorthodox reading of monastery life at the very least.[28]

In considering the carved pier wall at Holycross as a shrine for a relic of the Holy Cross, it seems apposite to consider the relics as the stimulus for all of the multi-dated architectural interventions, but most especially the fifteenth-century refurbishment. Stalley is in no doubt that the fifteenth-century rebuilding was intended to provide a suitable setting for the Holy Cross relics.[29] These relics could already have been housed in smaller shrines, perhaps of a more ephemeral material, but it appears the refurbishments might have centred around housing these relics so that they became one with the abbey's architecture, thus consolidating their sanctity into the very fabric of the building. It appears natural and logical to reuse a structural resource, and by redefining the form of the pier wall it changed its function: a pillar of the church literally became a locus for venerating the relic of the Holy Cross. Artefacts by their nature are often reinterpreted, reused, altered and transformed – as well the carved pier wall might have been – but its position has remained unchanged since the fifteenth century, and that is exceptional. Its physical form has endured but the rituals around it almost definitely changed. Originally, it must have been created to fulfil a need that had not, or was not, being met in whatever manner the relics were utilised. The architectural implication of utilising the pier wall dividing the two chapels in the south transept raises questions of motivation and location. To create a *sanctum sanctorum* within an already holy building must have been driven by the possession of the relics, but the location in the south transept is inscrutable but evidentially intentional. The carved pier wall structurally divides and supports the side chapel's vaultings and arches. When the graves and soil were cleared back to bedrock level in the 1970s, it became clear that the carved pier wall was structurally integral as the dividing wall of the two south transept chapels. Coupled with the fact that externally the south transept was emphatically buttressed during the fifteenth-century refurbishments, but the chancel and north transept were not, it demonstrates that the pier wall was indeed subtractively carved, with later pieces such as the spiral columns most likely inserted into the hollowed-out structure. The hard black limestone was difficult to carve, but resulted in a markedly delicate finish that preserved details and lent itself to definition, but it tended to fracture, making the act of carving the pier wall even more commendable. Whatever it was designed to do, it was a function unique to Holycross at this time and must have been a complex undertaking requiring the skills of multiple craftspeople. This singling-out of the carved pier wall as the primary focus of the south transept speaks to an exclusive location.

The iconography of the cross is associated with the suffering of Christ, but also the redemption of the believer, and in medieval Ireland, stational liturgy developed around the cross all year round and not only at Easter. The feast of the Invention of the

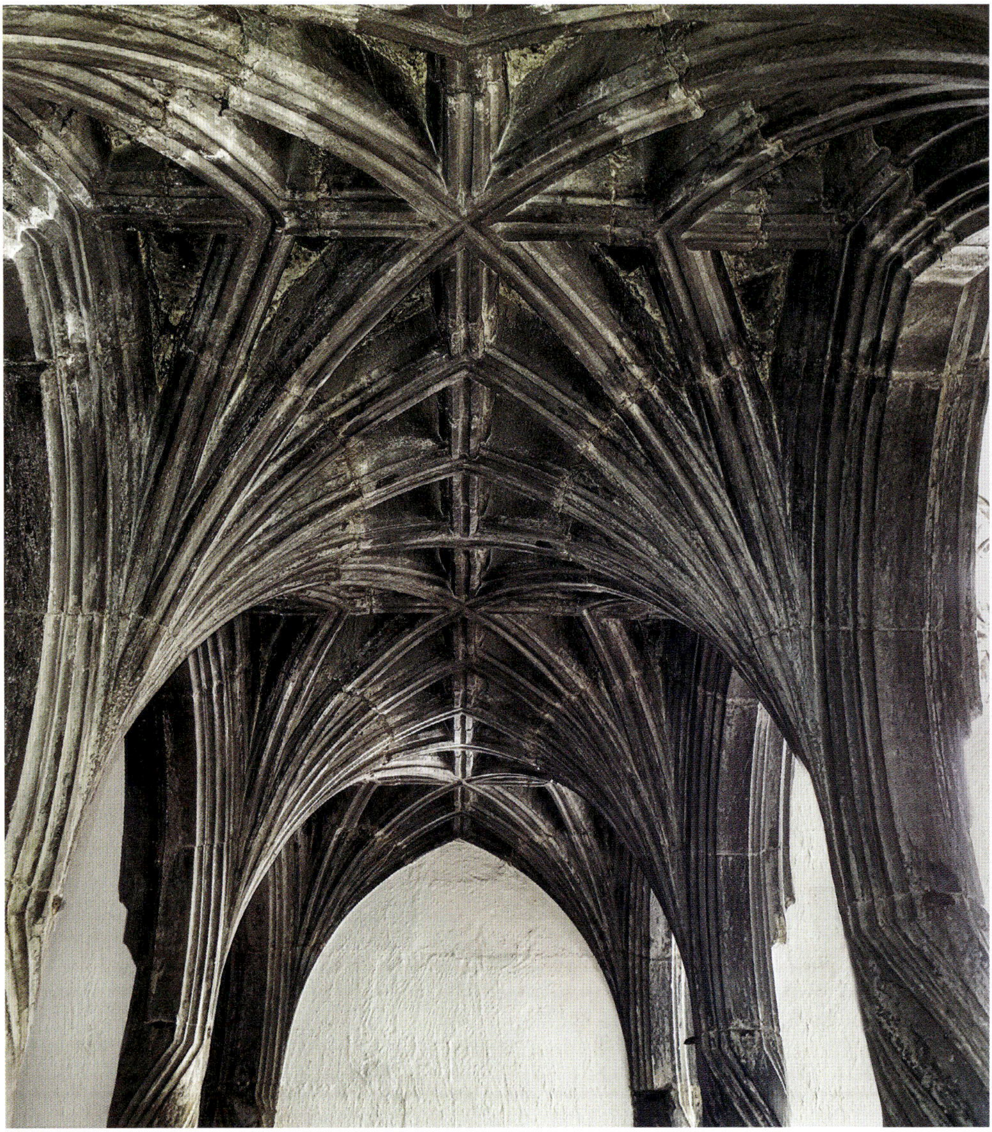

Cross is mentioned in the Ormond deeds as occurring in early May, along with the Exaltation of the Cross in September, both such significant societal markers that local courts and oath-swearing occurred around their dates.[30] These feasts had their early medieval-period roots in Jerusalem but ultimately developed in Rome, then spread throughout the West, where the performative acts differed regionally. Early Irish liturgical books make no mention of the feasts, but by the end of the ninth century they were introduced here.[31] They celebrate the True Cross, and while not site-specific ceremonies, they were performed anywhere there was a relic of the cross. The ceremonies evolved

fig. 7 | Vaulted canopy of carved pier wall, *c.*1440, black limestone, Holycross Abbey

so that every church could practice them, but it appears that a true relic was held in higher regard.[32] Given that it was a monastic community, any access to shrines behind the rood screen would have been severely curtailed to lay people, most especially women.[33] The carved pier wall's location directly beside the monks' night stairs added another dimension of restrictiveness. Writing in 2015, Tadhg O'Keefe suggests that the renovations in the mid-1400s were not merely a vanity project for the White Earl, but were intrinsically linked to – and perhaps partly funded by – pilgrim traffic.[34] There was opportunity therefore for multiple shrines given the possession of more than one relic, with access to certain shrines perhaps subject to a level of exclusivity or piety. Privileged pilgrims were even offered mass directly at some shrines in England, and this might explain the presence of a carved piscina (a drained basin using for sacramental purposes) in the carved pier wall.[35] Tomás O'Carragáin discusses how different altars were used on specific days, and the presence of this piscina might mean that the carved pier wall had a secondary function as a private place of worship, again affirming it as a location not freely accessible.[36]

In considering the physical components of the carved pier wall, its original function is not immediately apparent. Its large open-arcaded sides speak to a visual primacy in being open to view from various angles.[37] Its elaborately vaulted canopy is significant in that it is the only vaulting in the entire south transept [fig. 7]. Furthermore, it can only be seen from a kneeling position, looking upwards, potentially indicating the performative act required at the carved pier wall. Its hollowed base had a rebated slab on top, indicating its ability to be opened and closed when required with a cavity for the interment of objects. Offerings of jewellery, money and votives in the manner of wax body parts were commonly placed directly upon English shrines, affording ample latitude for the long flat surface of the rebated slab to receive similar offerings.[38] Then there are the eight (four engaged, four free-standing) exquisitely carved helical columns that give the carved pier wall such refinement [fig. 8]. Attached to these columns are remnants of iron rods that might have indicated a grille or the centralised hanging of one of the relics over the base. Extant pendant crosses all present with rings, some made of cast iron affixed to the top, from which they could either be worn as pectoral crosses or attached to a chain and hung.[39] Though no longer evident, a report in 1923 states there was a chain for suspension attached to the upper cross bar of the Butler Relic; all that remains today are small rings atop the upper cross.[40] This could imply the shrine was created specifically to house the patrons' own relic, and might indicate privileged access to the shrine for the Butlers and their guests. The two frontal piers are much worn and polished, indicating repeated touching; perhaps pilgrims' hands were placed there in order to lean in to venerate or kiss a hanging relic [fig. 9]. Writing in 1640 Hartry makes numerous mentions of pilgrims kissing the relic with 'chaste lips and holy mouth'.[41]

The base, carved directly from the pier wall, shares characteristics with English saint-shrine pedestals, and also Irish tombs, but it lacks the usual carved 'weepers' – figurative depictions of mourners, sometimes saints, on the side panel of a tomb – that would identify it as such. Instead, the base is richly carved with various foliated designs, numerous animal and bird heads, and a kneeling angel presenting the shield of

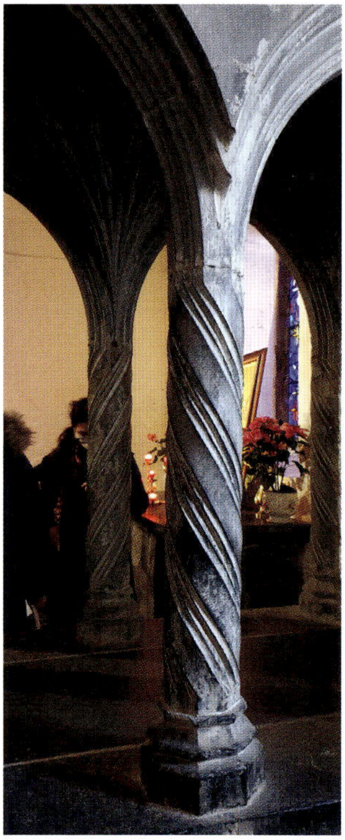

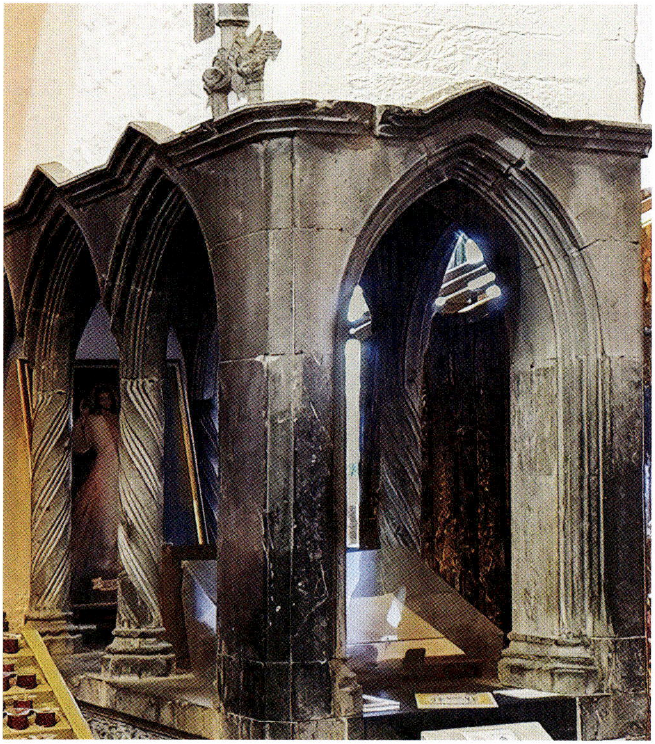

Holycross. The decoration is so profusely diverse that both sides of the base offer differing motifs [fig. 10]. The coeval sedilia in the chancel is carved with examples of heraldry that identify the families associated with the abbey, but the carved pier wall does not.[42] Holycross was described in verse in *c.*1450 as 'a sanctuary inviolable hung with gold and variegated tapestry', and although only the stone decorative iconography remains, other ephemeral ornaments such as paintwork, gilding or cloth hangings, when *in situ*, might have demonstrated function.[43]

The extant physical components of the carved pier wall, therefore, do not appear to offer any tangible evidence regarding its primary function, although the vaulted canopy can only be viewed from a kneeling position and the polished front piers would indicate innumerable hands placed upon them. Although its elements appear secular and decorative, their original meaning may have been lost over time. However, its location has remained fixed, and as such can be investigated in connection with function. The closest document pertaining to Holycross is the 1640 *Triumphalia Chronologica Monasterii Sanctae Crucis in Hibernia* by Malachy Hartry, a Cistercian monk living there. Frustratingly, Hartry never indicates where the relic is specifically kept, only saying that in 1633 pilgrims were 'led to the appointed place'.[44] Nor did he mention how many relics remained by the seventeenth century, but the implication by the use of the singular implies that there was, by then, only one. He does note that the

fig. 8 | Helical carved columns of the carved pier wall, *c.*1440, black limestone, Holycross Abbey
fig. 9 | Indication of worn and polished front piers of the carved pier wall

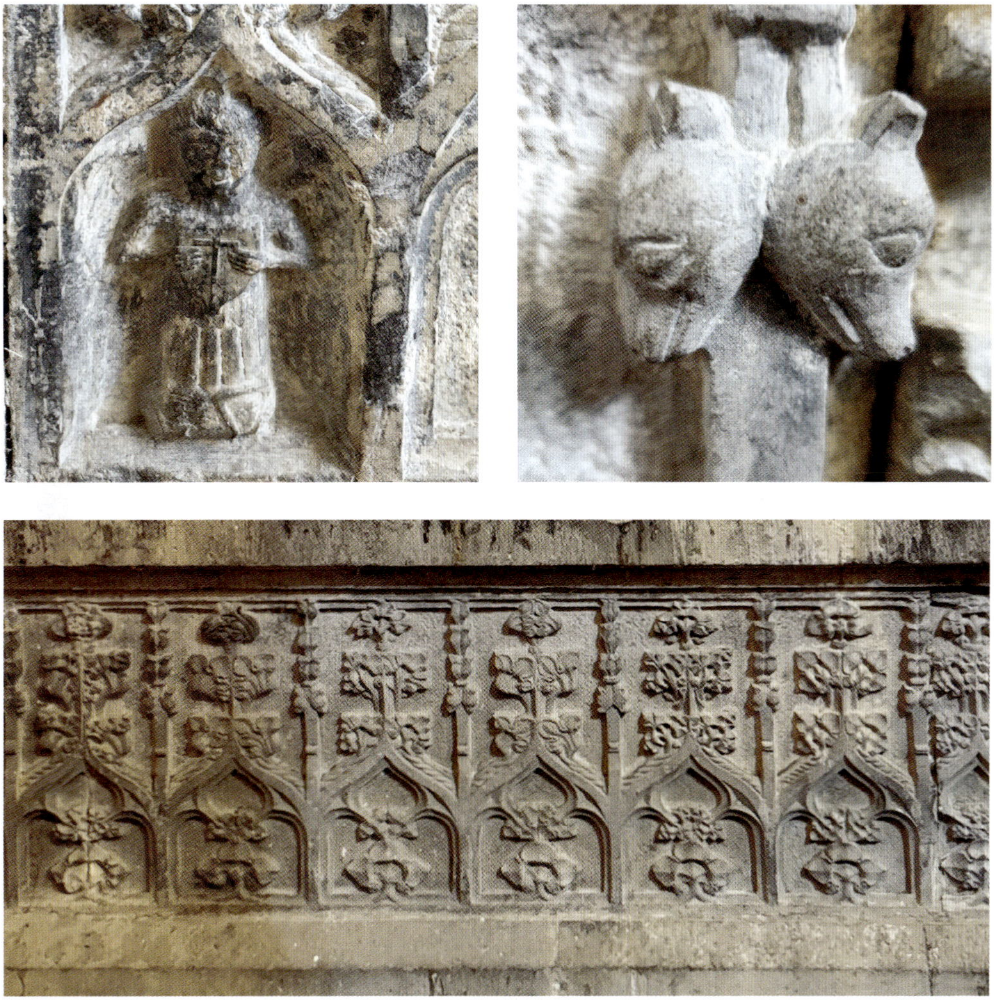

monks moved around the abbey presenting the relic to pilgrims, and one miraculous story in 1639 sees it positioned over the altar in the oratory, implying that by the seventeenth century it seemed not to have a dedicated shrine in the abbey but instead appeared to move around the building.[45] In keeping with pilgrim architectural design, access to the south transept via the south aisle may have been a factor in choosing it originally as a site for a shrine.[46] One possible reason for locating the shrine in the transept might have been to control access, as the nave had freer access to lay people.[47] This eminent – and most likely, elite – location might speak to a shrine that was reserved for patrons and their guests and evidence of another shrine at Holycross might similarly suggest a hierarchical arrangement for the veneration of the relics. The fact that one shrine is inherent to the fabric of the building only exposes the difficulty in examining the location and function of the second shrine in Holycross.

fig. 10 | Details from the carved pier wall base, indicating various animal and foliated motifs

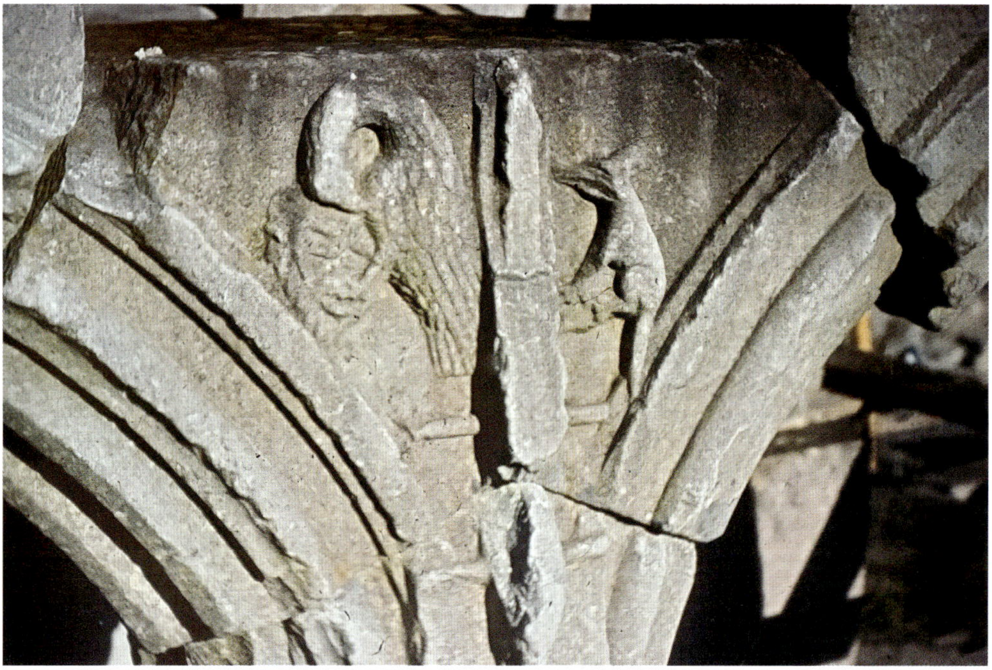

fig. 11 | Detail from second shrine from Holycross Abbey indicating pelican and fox, *c.*1440, black limestone, temporarily reassembled in the cloister *c.*1970
(Trinity College Dublin: Dept of History of Art & Architecture Slide Collection / Roger Stalley, *c.*1970)

fig. 12 | The same detail as fig. 11, photographed in 2022

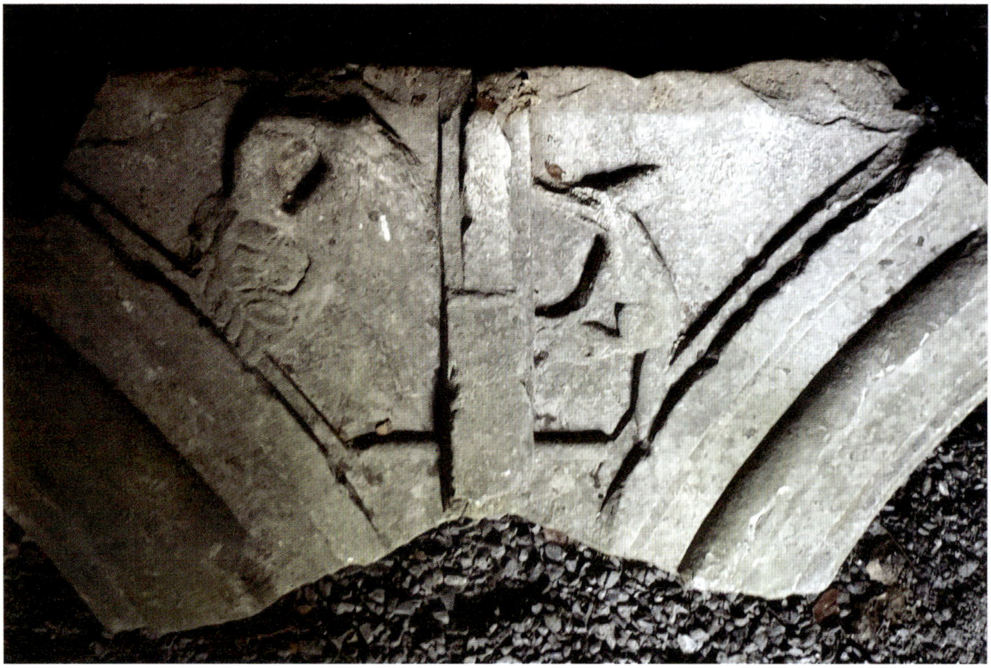

Briefly reconstructed during restoration work in the 1970s, and now deposited in fragmented form in the Stone Stores housed in what used to be the infirmary of Holycross, lie remnants of the second shrine. Stalley remarks that this shrine appears to be free-standing and possess similar characteristics to the carved pier wall: it also had a vaulted canopy, was three bays long and one bay wide, and contained carved animal sculptures including a pelican feeding her young [fig. 11]. He also surmises that the mouldings of the second shrine are so similar to those in the fifteenth-century renovations that it indicates the second shrine is contemporary with the rebuilding work.[48] In 2003, Colum Hourihane observed the level of craftmanship required for the pelican carving on this shrine, evident in the almost full-circle curve of the pelican's neck and its confident position in proportion to the spandrel's width. The opposite spandrel depicts a fox, diverse animals of vice and virtue perhaps. He suggests that another pelican depiction, now positioned in the cloister, might have been on the opposite side of this open-sided structure. The depiction of a pelican motif on both sides of the second shrine strongly suggests a eucharistic function.[49] The possibility of a multi-decorated open-arcaded shrine in turn might suggest a centralised location, enabling pilgrims to approach from a variety of angles. The second shrine was originally thought to have been situated in the north transept, another restricted and elite space.[50] Colt Hoare said in 1806 there were 'fragments of a handsome altar tomb' located in the north transept but offers no further description, so this may not have been the shrine in question.[51] However, free-standing shrines have always suffered the vagaries of time and local administration as they were capable of being moved according to changing needs.[52] Writing in 1933, Martin Callanan says that during repair work in 1914 by the Board of Works, they collected carved stones scattered throughout the abbey, partially reconstructed them, and erected them in the north transept. He described it as either a tomb or a shrine, that is formed of 'a series of arches with figures of birds and floral designs externally, while the inner aspect is finely carved'.[53] Frustratingly, the renovations and restoration of the 1970s have no formal or published records of the work carried out.[54] We do not know the original location of this second shrine, but it might possibly have been in a more public area within the abbey, such as the nave or side aisles, and been part of a stational circuit. Charles William Wall (*c.*1783–1862), vice-provost of Trinity College Dublin, who owned the abbey in *c.*1833, made several large-scale repairs to the nave and south-aisle arcades to prevent imminent collapse, resulting in all potential evidence of shrine placement being lost.[55] 'M.E.C.' said in 1868, not long after the Wall interventions, that some of his repairs 'seem rather calculated to puzzle the antiquarian'.[56]

The existence of more than one shrine proposes two potential scenarios. The first suggests stational pilgrim performance. Peter Harbison observes that Irish pilgrims visiting Rome were likely to have taken part in the tradition of the 'seven churches', a ceremonial procession begun in *c.*1553 by Philip Neri that subsequently became associated with major Irish pilgrim sites. It appears logical that without access to seven churches, localised traditions would evolve into seven altars set within one church.[57] Hartry, writing in 1640, mentions several of these altars within Holycross, noting a pilgrim 'praying seven times in a day' and visiting 'seven altars' with 'the first station being the saving wood of the holy cross'.[58] The second feasible scenario is that the shrine in the south transept was reserved for certain pilgrims only, and its location and elaborate decoration both speak to its exclusivity. This would indicate that a shrine placed in a more public section of the abbey could either be used as part of a stational procession or be available to 'ordinary' pilgrims. In 1643 Hartry tells of a woman spending twenty-four hours praying in front of the relic, perhaps suggesting a shrine positioned in the nave or aisles – locations suitable for a female pilgrim.[59] And William Camden, when talking about the cross relic in Holycross in 1586, remarked how 'incredible such a concourse of people do still throng hither out of devotion'.[60]

Perhaps similar throngs of pilgrims in the fifteenth century had motivated the White Earl to build his own shrine that was based upon his cosmopolitan travels and connections at the English court, one that was to be as exclusive as it was elaborate. David Beresford has called him 'the single most dominant figure in Irish politics in the first half of the fifteenth century'.[61] He was intimately familiar with the royal court and travelled extensively. Stalley declared that he lived his life internationally, which speaks to his cultural learning and exposure to same.[62] In the 1440s, concomitant with the Holycross renovations, the earl was at the centre of national politics (and for a time the Chief Governor of Ireland), active in Irish life and influential at the English court.[63] A lover of antiquity, archaeology, history and heraldry, his knowledge of architectural styles and cultural conditions could conceivably have influenced the scheme of work at Holycross, most particularly in the south transept.[64] O'Donovan posits that the White Earl – a 'trans-regional magnate' – was au fait with contemporary architectural trends. It might be suggested that he appropriated particulars from shrines to which he made a pilgrimage or was aware of; we know that as a particular devotee of Thomas Becket he made a pilgrimage to Canterbury in 1430.[65]

What remains in Holycross Abbey are two magnificent pieces of carved stonework, one emphatically *in situ*, the other in storage. A side-by-side comparison of the pelican spandrel of the second shrine as seen in 1970 and again in 2022 indicates the deterioration of detail (as seen in the eroding detail of the pelican's feathers) [fig. 12]. Other pieces of carved stonework in storage, including cloister remnants, are numbered, but without access to the OPW restoration documents they remain a mystery. Although the abbey is now an active and engaged parish church with contrasting priorities, as Stalley notes, 'buildings designed for relatively small monastic communities in the distant past are not necessarily ideal for modern community worship'.[66] In light of the recent advancement in plans for a flood-relief scheme and tourism centre development under the National Development Plan for Holycross village and abbey, it might be suggested that now is an opportune time to reinvestigate and preserve from environmental harm the valuable contents of the Stone Stores, and make public the records of the 1970s restoration in order to advance considerations of these shrines. It behoves the current custodians of Holycross to honour the remaining fabric of the building and the adjacent ancillary buildings. The carved pier wall appears rather disregarded and obscured in its current iteration, deterring additional academic investigation. But what remains are the worn and polished marks from innumerable pilgrim hands whose ritualistic contact with the carved pier wall has left its own indication of function, be that as a shrine or as an Easter sepulchre.

## The carved stonework as Easter sepulchres

IN CONSIDERING THE PERFORMATIVE ACTIONS AT THESE SHRINES, AND AN ALTERNATIVE FEASIBLE purpose for the south transept carved pier wall and the second shrine, the reproduction of the *sepulchrum Domini* (the Lord's tomb) as a sacred built object across medieval Europe, and its eventual metamorphosis into the Easter sepulchre along with the rituals that accompanied it, cannot be ignored. Former curate of Holycross and historian William Hayes makes mention of an undocumented and unpublished suggestion by Dagmar Ó Riain-Raedel that proposes the function of the carved pier wall as a *sepulchrum Domini*.[67] The centrality of belief in the Christian world of the resurrection of Christ is reflected in the medieval interest in representing this and the surrounding events both liturgically and architecturally, the evolution of Easter rites, and the structures from which to conduct them. Taking into account the very name of the abbey and its fundamental association with the death of Christ through its possession of relics of the cross, it appears highly credible that the rituals surrounding Easter week would merit a strong focal point within the church walls. This deep connection to the death and resurrection of Christ, along with an increasingly performative Easter liturgy, speaks to the need for a locus, or loci, within the church that would be appropriately sacrosanct, whilst satisfying the criteria involved in the dramaturgical nature of the Easter rites.

In continental Europe, most Easter rites were performed at sepulchres either outside the choir, in the nave, or in the crypt. Twelfth-century wall paintings in the north transept of the Basilica of Saint-Sernin, Toulouse, are indicative of the location of the sepulchre in this pilgrimage church.[68] The angel sitting over the extant door (as tomb) was to become a common motif of later sepulchres, along with a depiction of the three Marys. France saw incidents of the altar used as sepulchre, whereas in Italy it was usually located in the nave, and Germany saw its position in the nave or a side chapel.[69] In Germany, the pious gathered around the sepulchre were treated to 'mournful music alternated with spiritual addresses', and indeed the recommendation was to locate the sepulchre in a side chapel or side altar as a result.[70] These locations, and the processionary manner of venerating at them, indicated a growing performative nature associated with Easter rites in continental Europe.

Curtain-enclosed sepulchres were one of the more common forms in Europe. The term 'sepulchre' is variously used to describe this entire structure, or the altar, coffer or receptacle beneath its curtained exterior.[71] These enclosures could be entered or have the fabric lifted or drawn to reveal the sepulchre beneath at the appropriate part of the liturgical service. Usually drawn on Holy Saturday, the curtains would both protect the miraculous events occurring within and shroud the sepulchre with suitable gravitas while simultaneously echoing the shrouding of the body of Christ after its deposition from the cross.[72] Sepulchre frames – quadrangular in form with posts at the corners – were constructed of wood in the main, but sporadically from iron, and were placed atop the coffer-like sepulchre. Neil Brooks suggests that iron was used on these frames like an ornamental band around the sepulchre, but more likely in connection to hitching and unhitching it to the wooden coffer and prickets for the insertion of tapers.[73] The lighting of the sepulchres varied greatly from a single candle to twelve (representing the apostles), thirteen (to include a larger one representing Christ), or to many multiples. What seems apparent is that sepulchres were becoming highly adorned and visually striking. There appears to have been an obscuring of function between the 'true sepulchre' and the 'Easter sepulchre', and by 1896 the Congregation of Sacred Rites, when queried over the primacy of function as a repository of host or repository of Christ, answered, 'both one and the other'.[74]

In conjunction with the modification of sepulchre configuration came a significant change in the manner of their veneration. Sheingorn argues that the reduction in the size of the sepulchre changed its function: it became less associated with the tomb of Christ and more associated with the events that occurred around it in the days before and after the crucifixion.[75] The Easter sepulchre was 'a kind of theatrical effect designed to communicate the events of Easter more clearly and graphically to the faithful'.[76] The Sarum Rite originated in Salisbury and appears to have been used in continental Europe and Ireland. One aspect of it indicated an often elaborate and localised (depending on the configuration of the church) processionary route to be performed during Easter Week.[77] It included the burial of the host as well as a cross during the Easter rituals.[78]

By the high middle ages, Easter ceremonies comprised three main components: the first, *adoratio crucis*, involved ritualistic adoration of the cross, and the second, the *depositio*, involved the symbolic burial of liturgical objects to signify Christ's entombment (all the more significant if the church possessed an actual relic of the cross). These were then exposed and elevated to symbolise the resurrection in the final element, the *elevatio*. The Easter rites involved a procession through the church on Good Friday to the sepulchre, where, having been veiled through the procession, the cross was revealed and kissed by the priest and veiled again.[79] This was followed by the *depositio* of perhaps the host or the relic (both covered in cloth akin to the shroud of Christ) into the sepulchre. The sepulchre could contain a host, a crucifix, a relic of the cross or a carved image – sometimes all or several of these objects.[80] When the sepulchre was closed, it was sometimes sealed or tied with cords, or a symbolic stone placed on it to emulate the tomb of Christ. Candles or tapers were lit, and guards placed around it.[81] In this manner, the sepulchre was then watched through to Easter Sunday when the sacred objects, previously 'buried', were raised from the sepulchre and exposed in a highly visible place to be venerated and then paraded once more around the church. This *elevatio* happened in the early morning after matins, and for the monks only, but later it began to be performed in the presence of the laity. Given the significance of the resurrection to Christian doctrine, the Sunday ritual was the most elaborate and involved bell-ringing, adulation of the cross, perfume and incense and processionary displays around the church of the 'resurrected' relics.[82] It became more a dramaturgical event than a liturgical one that lent itself to ceremonial performative rituals involving the entire congregation.[83]

The 'Office of the Sepulchre' was a ceremony, especially popular in monasteries, that was generally performed after the sepulchre was opened on Easter Sunday, and usually by monks dressed as women representing the three Marys who, upon looking into the tomb, found that Christ had risen. This dramatisation of the Passion directly succeeding the more solemn rites was accompanied by children dressed as devils, mass congregation participation, much singing, bell-ringing and burning of incense.[84] The sepulchre's function became the *mise en scène* for this expanded ceremony.[85] The Easter rites appeared to have been surpassed by the Easter play, and these ceremonies appeared to have evolved at a very local level.[86] In Ireland, there is manuscript evidence from the fifteenth century of the Church of St John the Evangelist in Dublin (on Fishamble Street) regarding the performance of an Easter play, the *Visitatio Sepulcri*. Performed on Easter Sunday, it involved a processional performance of the three Marys seeking Christ, with attendant apostles and angels, that involved stational actions through the church up to the Easter sepulchre (thought to be in either transept of the east end). The play incorporated speeches, music, singing and lighting, with costumes and props, all bound within a strict liturgical context.[87] The church of St John the Evangelist was under the Augustinian order, but it does indicate that these elaborate plays were performed in Ireland and at monasteries. The Reformation abolished most of these liturgical rituals but they lingered in various iterations, with the Easter play surviving until the latter half of the sixteenth century when these elaborate ceremonies seem to have passed out of use.[88]

Taking into account the above description of the evolution of Easter sepulchres throughout the later medieval period, it might be suggested that the carved pier wall in the south transept of Holycross Abbey was intended to be one such Easter sepulchre when it was created during remodelling in the mid-1400s. As previously discussed, the abbey was in possession of several relics of the cross, and the association of Easter sepulchres with the cross is pivotal. In other churches, during the Easter rites only the host was ceremonially buried; to have one or more cross relics might have motivated the patron to provide a suitable sepulchre from which to celebrate the Passion. Evidence of the *Visitatio Sepulcri* being performed in Ireland also speaks to the evolution at local level of these liturgical acts, and might offer another function for the second shrine (with its eucharistic motifs) as part of the elaborate staging of the Easter play.

As to the sepulchre itself, the form of the carved pier wall, that of a highly decorated vaulted canopy with ceremonial spiral columns atop a tomb-like pedestal, certainly corresponds to previous descriptions of Easter sepulchres. Its openness on three sides would speak to the visual necessity in displaying the 'risen' objects on Easter Sunday, while the pedestal with its rebated slab fulfils the 'burial' requirement of the Easter rites and the precondition that the tomb is sealed. The slab top might also act as an altar from which to both display the 'risen' objects and also to perform any sacred rites associated with the Passion. Altars were a visual representation of the *anastasis* – Christ's tomb within the Holy Sepulchre – where liturgical rites occurred daily, so perhaps the carved and drained piscina on the north side of the structure indicates sacred rites being carried out there at Easter and other times. If the abbey did 'bury' the host along with the cross relics, then this would have necessitated storage of this specially reserved host, and would have required a separate suitable place, a *locus aptus*, which was usually a secondary altar, remote from the usual tabernacle.[89] The 'buried' and 'resurrected' relics and host would have found an appropriate location befitting their sanctity, the host perhaps contained within a hanging pyx, the cross relics displayed on the

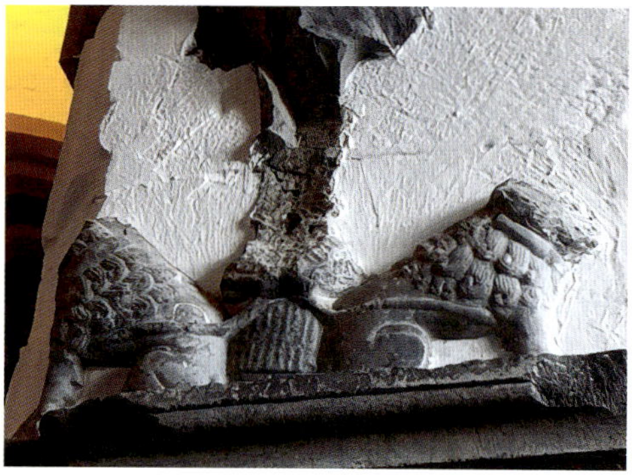
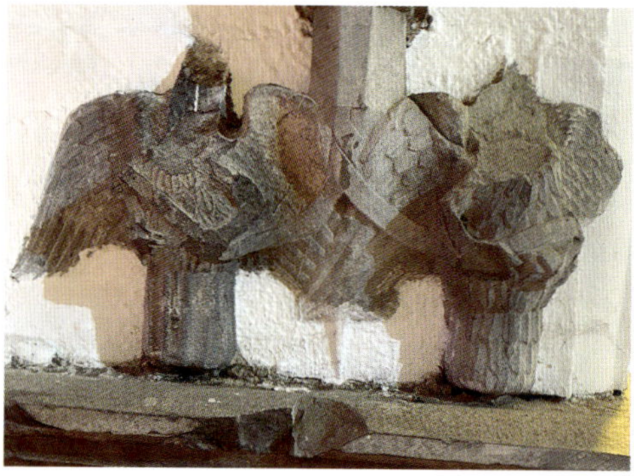

slab top beneath the intricately vaulted ceiling, expressing the glory of the three stages of the Easter rites.

On, or immediately before, Good Friday the sepulchre would be adorned with cloths and tapers. These cloths – red, gold and black were popular colours for them – were richly woven and habitually painted or embroidered with Passion scenes. Some sepulchres' curtains were hung on wires or iron rods, and so could easily and more ceremoniously be opened and closed.[90] John Bonnell in 1916, describing the shrouding of a sepulchre, wrote: 'The columns supporting the canopy were frequently, if not always, fitted with rods running horizontally, on which curtains were hung so that the altar could be made private during the *secretum*.'[91] These curtains were then left drawn until after matins on Easter Sunday when the *elevatio* ritual would take place. There is evidence remaining on the columns of the carved pier wall of small pieces of ironwork. From their positioning it appears most likely that they were connected both laterally and medially, with the inference being they were to provide both a screening function and a hanging function. The presence of richly embellished curtains adorned with scenes from the Passion, or perhaps the *Arma Christi*, might also explain why the stone structure lacks similarly carved ornamentation that could inform its purpose.

As to the decorative scheme of the carved pier wall, although it lacks the explicit Passion motifs evident in the second shrine, its highly ornate pedestal with an abundance of foliated and animal designs, intricately carved helical columns and extravagantly vaulted canopy speak to a structure that was to be a significant and prominent space within the abbey walls. Above the mouldings and at the base of the corbels on both the north and south side of the stone structure are carved figures. Both are much damaged, but enough remains that can indicate their original configuration. The south-side carving features a central figure holding two leashed lions [fig. 13]. As a point of comparison, St Stephen's Church on Coleman Street in London had unusually elaborate knights positioned above its sepulchre, perhaps an allusion to the watchers or the guardians.[92] This protector role might be attributed to the figure and the lions in Holycross. The north-side carving is two winged angels with joined hands that might have contained books or functioned as a receptacle for candles [fig. 14]. There is English

figs 13, 14 | Corbel carvings on carved pier wall of lions and human figure (on south side) and pair of angels (on north side), c.1440, black limestone, Holycross Abbey

evidence of angels above the posts of the wooden sepulchre frame, and sometimes 'angel-tapers', which were most likely carved angels with a pricket for a taper.[93]

The second shrine at Holycross indicates evidence of stational progression, most likely in a suitable location that enabled wider access for performing segments of the Easter procession along with more general acts of devotion and pilgrimage. The south transept, however, with its materially integral carved Easter sepulchre, seems entirely apposite as a *sanctum sanctorum*, a suitably distinguished locus for the end of the Easter procession in addition to being a more exclusive location for devotions.

## Conclusion

AS NOTED BY A VISITOR TO HOLYCROSS IN 1922, 'ITS HISTORY LIVES ON IN THE WHISPERING of tradition, the hearsay of passing generations'.[94] There are many apocryphal narratives associated with Holycross and its stonework, and in the case of the shrines there exists a fine balance between informed speculation and beguiling fiction. What appears explicit, however, is the significance of the relics to the history of the abbey; they ensured its success and survival, and most likely motivated its architectural design. The existence of two shrines raises the question of hierarchical privatisation of both space and worship, consolidated by the enduring immotility of the carved pier wall. It seems almost certain that the primary function of the carved pier wall and the second shrine is intrinsically linked to the cross relics either as a shrine (be it an exclusive place of veneration or not), or, in the case of an Easter sepulchre, the focus of liturgical and dramaturgical rites. What also seems evident is that this organic transmutation of function most likely echoed the evolving nature of pilgrimage and worship and the dynamic political machinations of medieval Ireland. These pieces of microarchitecture, unique to Holycross Abbey, have the ability to articulate in stone the rituals of our past that are an integral component of our national patrimony, and as such, merit safeguarding.

---

**Niamh Flood** holds a first-class BA degree in the History of Art and Architecture, and a first-class MPhil in Irish Art and Architecture, both from Trinity College Dublin. Her postgraduate field of research is in medieval Irish ecclesiastical architecture. She is the Honorary General Secretary of the Royal Society of Antiquaries of Ireland, while working part-time in the Civil Service and lecturing part-time in both TCD and UCD on medieval Irish art and architecture.

### Endnotes

1 Colmcille Ó Conbhuidhe, *The Cistercian Abbeys of Tipperary*, ed. Finbarr Donovan (Dublin: Four Courts Press, 1999), p.166.

2 Ibid., pp.174–80.

3 Danielle O'Donovan, 'Building the Butler Lordship 1405–1552' (unpublished doctoral thesis, Trinity College Dublin, 2008), pp.30, 33.

4 National Library of Ireland, Dublin, D.2255. 'Covenant between William (O'Dwyer), Abbot of Holy Cross and Philip Purcell as to the terms of the former's resignation of his office as Abbot', 10 May 1534.

5 Ó Conbhuidhe and Donovan (1999), p.233.

6 Colmcille Ó Conbhuidhe, *Studies in Irish Cistercian History*, ed. Finbarr Donovan (Dublin: Four Courts Press, 1998), pp.248–50.

7 Colum Hourihane, *Gothic Art in Ireland 1169–1550* (New Haven and London: Yale University Press, 2003), p.24.

8 John Harden, 'Tour in Ireland in 1797', *Journal of the Cork Historical and Archaeological Society*, vol.58, no.187 (1953), pp.26–32: 31; Anon., ('M.E.C.'), *A Short Account of Holy Cross Abbey* (Dublin: Edward Ponsonby, 1868), p.21.

9 Richard Colt Hoare, *Journal of a Tour in Ireland, AD 1806* (London: W. Miller, 1807), p.146.

10 Hermann Fürst von Pückler-Muskau, *Tour in England, Ireland, and France, in the Years 1828 & 1829*, 4 vols (London: Effingham Wilson, 1832), II, p.47.

11 George Holmes, *Sketches of some of the Southern Counties of Ireland, collected during a tour in the autumn, 1797, in a series of letters* (London: Longman and Rees, 1801), p.34.

12 Ibid., p.35.

13 Marie Therese Flanagan, *The Transformation of the Irish Church in the Twelfth Century* (Woodbridge: Boydell Press, 2010), p.224.

14 Roger Stalley, *The Cistercian Monasteries of Ireland* (New Haven and London: Yale University Press, 1987), p.117.

15 Ó Conbhuidhe and Donovan (1999), pp.174–80.

16 Ibid., pp.165–66.

17 Ibid.

18 Ó Conbhuidhe and Donovan (1999), p.258; William J. Hayes, *Holycross, The Awakening of the Abbey* (Roscrea: Lisheen Publications, 2011), pp.289, 294–95.

19 Geraldine Carville, *The Heritage of Holy Cross* (Belfast: Blackstaff Press, 1973), p.113.

20 Limerick City Council Archives, Maurice Lenihan private papers, 'Maurice Lenihan Scrap-book', p.48. Maurice Lenihan, 'The Abbey of the Holycross of Tipperary: notes of a short and unexpected visit', *Limerick Reporter and Tipperary Vindicator*, 7 Oct 1861 <https://www.limerick.ie/discover/explore/historical-resources/limerick-archives/archive-collections/maurice-lenihan-papers> [acc. 26 Aug 2024].

21 'Some Relics of the Holy Cross formerly preserved In Ireland', *Irish Ecclesiastical Record* (1872), pp.256–59.

22 Hayes, pp.294, 328.

23 Carville, p.116.

24 Niamh Wycherley, *The Cult of Relics in Early Medieval Ireland* (Turnhout: Brepols, 2016), p.159.

25 Malachy Hartry, *Triumphalia Chronologica Monasterii Sanctae Crucis in Hibernia: De Cisterciensium Hibernorum Viris Illustribus*, trans. Denis Murphy (Dublin: Sealy, Bryers & Walker, 1891), p.59.

26 Paula Gerson, 'Art and Pilgrimage: mapping the way', in Conrad Rudolph (ed.), *A Companion to Medieval Art: Romanesque and Gothic in Northern Europe* (Malden: Wiley-Blackwell, 2010), p.599.

27 Edmund Curtis (ed.), *Calendar of Ormond Deeds*, 6 vols, Irish Manuscripts Commission (Dublin: Stationery Office, 1932–43), III: *1413–1509* (1935), p.70.

28 Harold G. Leask, *Irish Churches and Monastic Buildings*, 3 vols (Dundalk: Dundalgan Press, 1955–60) III: *Medieval Gothic: The last phases* (1960), p.64.

29 Roger Stalley, *Ireland and Europe in the Middle Ages* (London: Pindar, 1994), p.213.

30 Curtis (ed.), *Calendar of Ormond Deeds, vol.II: 1350–1413 AD* (1934), pp.12, 98.

31 Louis van Tongeren, *Exaltation of the Cross: toward the origins of the Feast of the Cross and the meaning of the Cross in early medieval liturgy* (Leuven: Peeters, 2000), p.276.

32 Ibid., p.76.

33 Ben Nilson, 'The Medieval Experience at the Shrine', in J. Stopford (ed.), *Pilgrimage Explored* (York: York Medieval Press, 1999), pp.97–98.

34 Tadhg O'Keeffe, *Medieval Irish Buildings, 1100–1600* (Dublin: Four Courts Press, 2015), p.50.

35 Nilson (1999), p.113.

36 Tomás Ó Carragáin, *Churches in Early Medieval Ireland: architecture, ritual and memory* (New Haven and London: Yale University Press, 2010), p.211.

37 Leask, p.67.

38 Nilson (1999), pp.108–12.

39 Colum Hourihane, ''Holye Crossys': a catalogue of processional, altar, pendant and crucifix figures for late medieval Ireland', *Proceedings of the Royal Irish Academy: archaeology, culture, history, literature*, vol.100C, no.1 (2000), pp.1–85: 31.

40 Henry S. Crawford, 'A Descriptive List of Irish Shrines and Reliquaries, Part I', *Journal of the Royal Society of Antiquaries of Ireland*, 6th series, vol.13, no.1 (1923), p.90.

41 Hartry, pp.15, 131, 139.

42 O'Donovan (2008), p.71.

43 *Aiṫdioġluim Dána: a miscellany of Irish bardic poetry, historical and religious*, ed. Lambert McKenna, 2 vols (Dublin: Irish Texts Society, 1939–40) II, p.324 (88. The Holy Cross).

44 Hartry, p.143.

45 Ibid., pp.125, 131, 139, 145, 157.

46 Roger Stalley, *Early Medieval Architecture* (Oxford: Oxford University Press, 2007), p.164.

47 Nilson (1999), p.100.

48 Stalley (1987), p.117.

49 Hourihane (2003), pp.106–07.

50 Stalley (1987), p.115.

51 Colt Hoare, p.148.

52 Ben Nilson, *Cathedral Shrines of Medieval England* (Woodbridge: Boydell Press, 1998), p.67.

53 Martin Callanan, *The Abbey of Holy Cross* (Dublin: printed privately, 1933), p.20.

54 Danielle O'Donovan, 'Holycross and the Language of Irish Late Gothic', in Roger Stalley (ed.), *Limerick and South-West Ireland: Medieval Art and Architecture* (Leeds: Maney Publishing, 2011), p.133.

55 Stalley (1987), p.251.

56 Anonymous ('M.E.C.'), p.27.

57 Peter Harbison, *Pilgrimage in Ireland: the monuments and the people* (London: Barrie and Jenkins, 1991), p.236.

58 Hartry, pp.15, 143, 147.

59 Ibid., p.155.

60 William Camden, *Britannia*, 2 vols (London: Churchill, 1722), II, p.1348.

61 David Beresford, 'James Butler (*c*.1390–1452), 4th Earl of Ormond', *Dictionary of Irish Biography* <https://doi.org/10.3318/dib.001253.v1>.

62 Stalley (1987), p.113.

63 Steven G. Ellis, *Ireland in the Age of the Tudors, 1447–1603: English expansion and the end of Gaelic rule* (London: Longman, 1998), pp.52, 365.

64 Lord Dunboyne, *Butler Family History* (Kilkenny: Wellbrook Press, 3rd edn, 1972), p.10.

65 O'Donovan (2008), pp.70, 121, 126.

66 Roger Stalley (ed.), *Irish Gothic Architecture: construction, decay and reinvention* (Dublin: Wordwell, 2012), p.11.

67 Hayes, p.105.

68 Thomas W. Lyman, 'Theophanic Iconography and the Easter Liturgy', in Otto von Simson, Lucius Grisebach and Konrad Renger (eds), *Festschrift für Otto Von Simson zum 65. Geburtstag* (Frankfurt am Main: Propyläen-Verlag, 1977), pp.72–93.

69 Neil C. Brooks, *The Sepulchre of Christ in Art and Liturgy with special reference to the Liturgic Drama* (Chicago: University of Illinois, 1921), pp.53, 58.

70 Brooks, p.66.

71 Ibid., p.63.

72 Ibid., p.67.

73 Ibid., p.77.

74 Ibid., p.51.

75 Pamela Sheingorn, *The Easter Sepulchre in England* (Kalamazoo: Medieval Institute, Western Michigan University, 1987), p.17.

76 Veronica Sekules, 'Easter Sepulchre' Grove Art Online, 2003 <https://doi.org/10.1093/gao/9781884446054.article.T024749>.

77 Alfred Heales, 'Easter Sepulchres: their object, nature, and history', *Archaeologia*, vol.42 (1869), p.267.

78 Brooks, p.71.

79 Justin E.A. Kroesen, *The Sepulchrum Domini through the Ages: its form and function*, trans. Margaret Kofod (Leuven: Peeters, 2000), pp.150–51.

80 Brooks, p.67.

81 Ibid., pp.68–69.

82 John David Chambers, *Divine Worship in England in the Thirteenth and Fourteenth Centuries, contrasted with and adapted to that in the Nineteenth* (London: Basil Montagu Pickering, 1877), p.xxxix.

83 Brooks, p.8.

84 Heales, pp.277–80.

85 Kroesen, pp.151–71.

86 Brooks, p.71.

87 Máire Egan-Buffet and Alan J. Fletcher, 'The Dublin "Visitatio Sepulcri" Play', *Proceedings of the Royal Irish Academy: archaeology, culture, history, literature*, vol.90C (1990), pp.162, 163, 167, 179.

88 Kroesen, p.182.

89 Brooks, p.49.

90 Ibid., pp.79–81.

91 John K. Bonnell, 'The Easter Sepulchrum in its Relation to the Architecture of the High Altar', *PMLA*, vol.31, no.4 (1916), pp.692–93.

92 Brooks, p.83.

93 Sheingorn, pp.48, 152.

94 John B. Cullen, *The 'Santa Croce' of Ireland* (Dublin: Catholic Truth Society of Ireland, 1922), p.1.

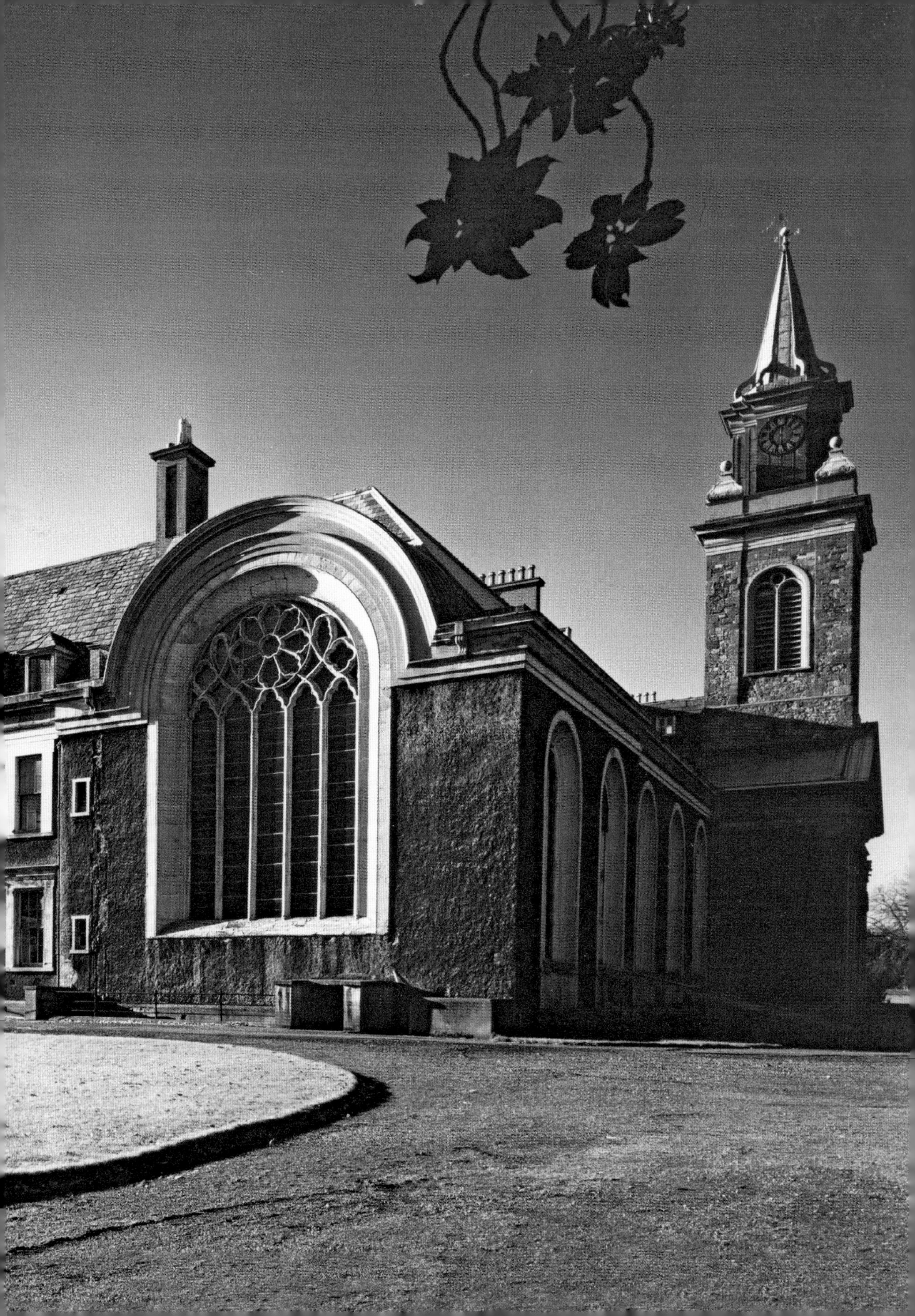

# 'Did a Dutch architect influence the design of the Royal Hospital Kilmainham?

FREDERICK O'DWYER

WHILE THE ROYAL HOSPITAL KILMAINHAM (RHK), ERECTED BY JAMES BUTLER, 1ST DUKE of Ormond (1610–1688), is regarded as being 'the first great classical building in Ireland', the sources of its plan and its quirky design details have never been clear [figs 1, 2].[1] This paper sets out to explore the apparent influences of the Amsterdam architect Hendrick (otherwise Hendrik) de Keyser (1565–1621), including the designs posthumously published in Salomon de Bray's *Architectura Moderna* (Amsterdam, 1631), and to examine the possibility that two members of his family, known to Ormond, may have been involved in its design and construction. These were his son William (otherwise Willem) de Keyser (b.1603) and William's son Hendrick III (b.1634) The erection of the hospital began in 1680, Ormond having been appointed viceroy in 1677, the fourth time he had served as lord lieutenant in a long political career beginning before Cromwell's Commonwealth, during which he was in exile in Europe with the future King Charles II. The building was erected under the superintendence of William Robinson (fl. *c.*1643–1712), who had held the office of Surveyor General since 1670.[2] It has been described as 'the grandest example' of the type of Carolean classicism established in Ireland in the late seventeenth century, though its incorporation of Gothic and Mannerist elements gave it a unique air.[3]

## Style or rhetoric: considering the Royal Hospital Kilmainham as a design statement

WHILE UNDOUBTEDLY ECLECTIC, THE HOSPITAL WAS CONSTRUCTED IN A PERIOD – THE early decades of the Restoration – which has defied agreed stylistic labelling. In 1953, Sir John Summerson invented the term 'Artisan Mannerism' to cover the style of the period 1615–75, 'the natural successor [he claimed] to Jacobean [which] has never been given a name' and one which he associated *inter alia* with the influence

fig. 1 | View from the north-east of the Royal Hospital Kilmainham, with the prominent east window of the chapel at the angle
(Irish Architectural Archive / David Davison)

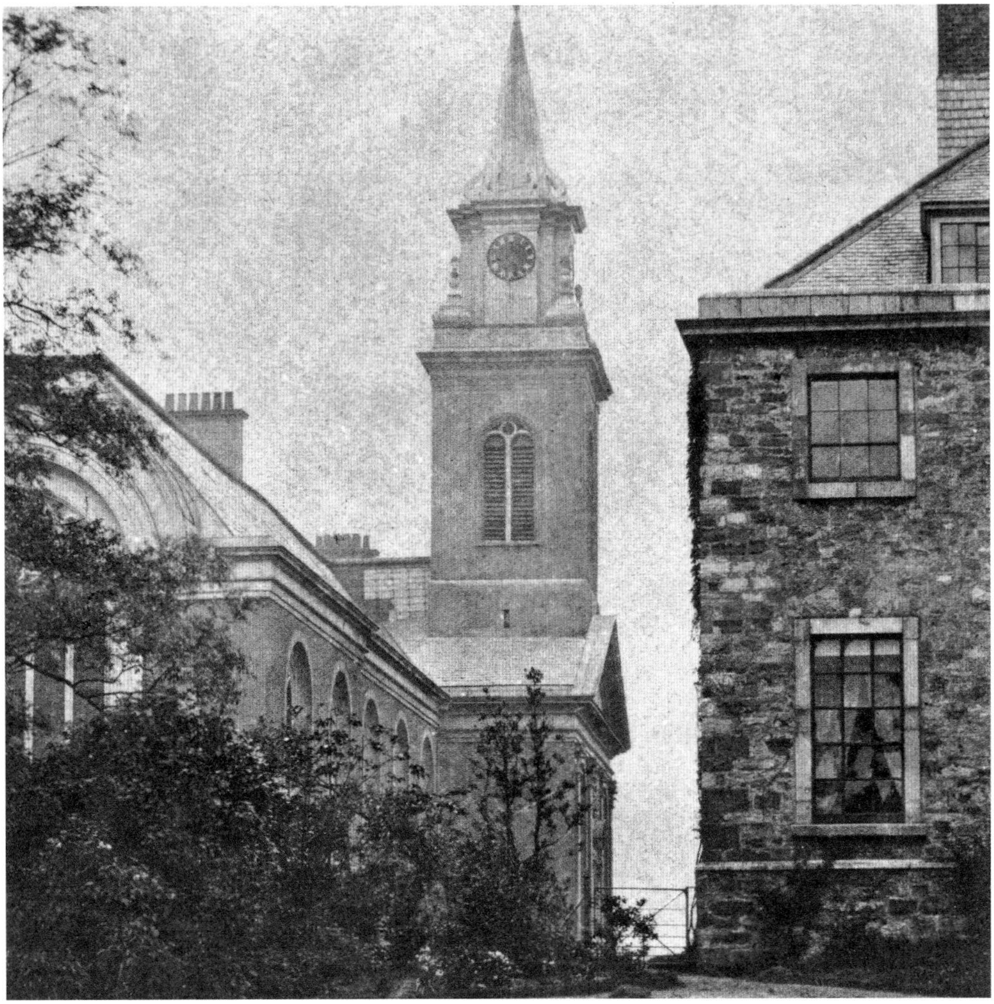

of Hendrick de Keyser.[4] Although the term has been criticised by such architectural historians as Giles Worsley and Caroline van Eck since the early part of the present century, it has remained in persistent use, but its applicability is surely to a limited cohort of buildings rather than the architecture of a whole era.[5] While the RHK was constructed in the 1680s, a decade to which Summerson assigned no particular architectural appellation, as a product of the Irish Royal Works it can hardly be labelled 'artisan'. The era of the English Baroque, now generally accepted as pertaining to the period from the late 1680s to the revival of Palladianism around 1719, did not have a distinctive Irish counterpart. There is a counter-argument, made by Professor van Eck (and others), that the concept

fig. 2 | Victorian photograph of RHK tower, showing the biforate belfry window
(Irish Architectural Archive)

fig. 3 | View from the north-east of the RHK, showing the eastern and northern ranges
(Irish Architectural Archive / David Davison)

of style as we know it did not exist in the seventeenth century; rather that the aesthetics of buildings of the early modern era should be considered as being grounded on rhetoric. She has written: 'Recent studies of Artisan Mannerism have shown that educated patrons [...] often made stylistic choices against classicism and in favour of decidedly unclassical ways of handling a design.'[6] Lucy Gent has written of the links between rhetoric and Elizabethan architecture, and as it will be seen that some aspects of the design of the RHK were grounded in that period, these links may be relevant to our study.[7] While the influence of Netherlandish Mannerist architecture was considered somewhat negatively by admirers of Palladio, Kathleen James-Chakraborty has written that the 'slowness of northern Europeans to adopt Renaissance forms should not be credited to ignorance or provincialism', albeit that 'the buildings that resulted do not fit easily into Italian-dominated accounts of architecture in early modern Europe'.[8]

The RHK, proposed as early as 1677, was built as a home for old soldiers, just like the recently constructed Hôtel des Invalides in Paris (1670–76). While it was undoubtedly an institutional model, Les Invalides was a much larger building but with one striking similar feature – the curved cornice erected over the east-end window of the chapel, described by Christine Casey as 'a startling curvilinear archivolt-like hood moulding' [fig. 3].[9] However, beneath it lies not a classical window but one subdivided by sandstone Gothic tracery, traditionally regarded as either 'a reuse of late medieval stonework from the chapel of the Knights Hospitaller, or a tenacious instance of Gothic survival'.[10] A modern observer might consider the placing of what looks like a Romanesque arch over a Gothic window to be a solecism; however, round-headed arches had largely superseded pointed ones in the language of Renaissance Ireland – part of a European trend.[11] The distinctions between Romanesque and Gothic architecture, as we understand them today, were not codified in England until the eighteenth and nineteenth centuries.[12] The chapel of the old priory on the Kilmainham site was similarly placed in the north-east corner of its complex, as can be discerned from a drawing of 1655–56 of the building in ruins by Robert Girdler for the Down Survey.[13] It is many years since the reuse theory has had currency. However, while an early

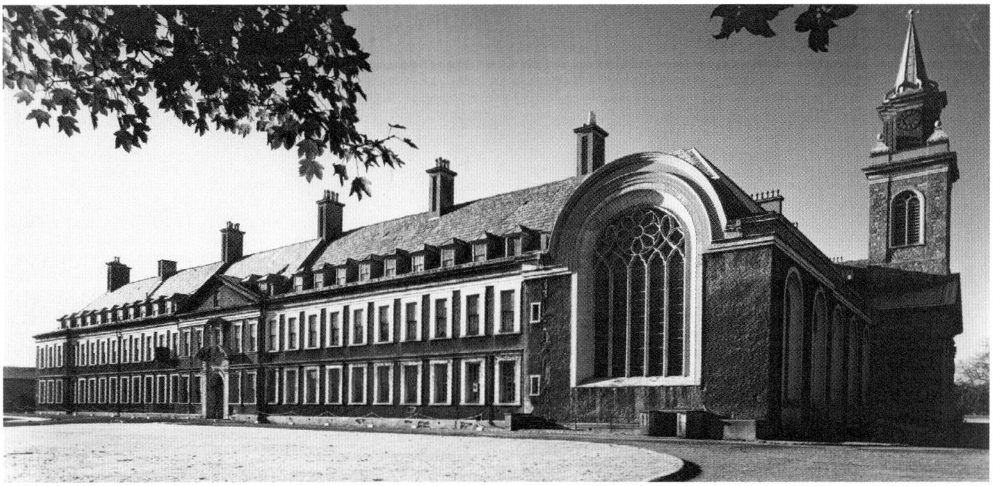

account that stones from the old chapel were used in the new one probably refers to rubble walling, the decision to construct a Gothic traceried window in what was otherwise a substantially classical building suggests a conscious attempt to link the ancient with the new.

The chapel window tracery of the RHK is not its only non-classical feature, as the use of Y-tracery (a Gothic type) in the round-headed windows of the north range and of a copper spire over its otherwise classical centrepiece attest.[14] These features and others, including the Dutch Mannerist doorcase to the courtyard, imply that the RHK is either a stylistic hybrid or an example of the application of rhetoric, depending on one's point of view. Such melanges were not unknown in seventeenth-century Britain, particularly in the university cities where, as Steven Brindle has noted, Archbishop Laud had exercised a strong influence over contemporary architecture.[15] Laud had been executed in 1645 as the reign of Charles I unravelled during Ormond's first lord lieutenancy (1643–46). However, it may be noted that Laud had been a friend of Thomas Wentworth, Earl of Strafford, who as Lord Deputy (1632–40) had shown great favour towards Ormond, securing for him the post of commander of the army in Ireland. Wentworth and Laud had been arrested at the same time, in 1640, but the former had been executed first, in 1641. In discussing the Duke of Ormond's views on religion, the late Raymond Gillespie noted both his consciousness of the Catholicism of his forbears and his partiality towards Archbishop Laud's views on Protestantism, anathema to the king's enemies.[16] If, as seems likely, the decision to erect a large Gothic window at the RHK was Ormond's, it may be seen as reflecting aspects of long-held religious beliefs.

Laudian university architecture was not, as Brindle adds, 'the court classicism of Inigo Jones, which did not really lend itself to hybridisation. Inspiration seems to have come from northern European figures like the Dutch mason Hendrick de Keyser and the painter Peter Paul Rubens.' Rubens assisted with the design of the church of St Charles Borromeo (1615–21) where he lived in Antwerp, in the Southern (Spanish) Netherlands, a monument of the Catholic counter-reformation.[17] His wider architectural influence is debatable, and, ironically, he received a late commission to paint the ceiling panels (1629–34) of Jones' Banqueting Hall in Whitehall, one of the two royal structures (the other was the Queen's House in Greenwich, 1616–35) that most exemplified Jones's disciplined Italian-inspired court style.

## From micro to macro:<br>exploring the extent of the Royal Hospital's Dutch inspiration

HENDRICK DE KEYSER HAS BEEN DESCRIBED BY JAMES STEVENS CURL AS ONE OF THE TWO most important architects working in the Netherlands in the early seventeenth century [fig. 4].[18] He was a native of Utrecht, in the largely Protestant Dutch Republic (the Northern Netherlands), where he was municipal mason and sculptor (effectively city architect) in Amsterdam. He designed a number of new Protestant churches there, including the Zuiderkerk (1606–14) and the Westerkerk (1620–31), which Curl described as 'models for Protestant churches in the Netherlands and

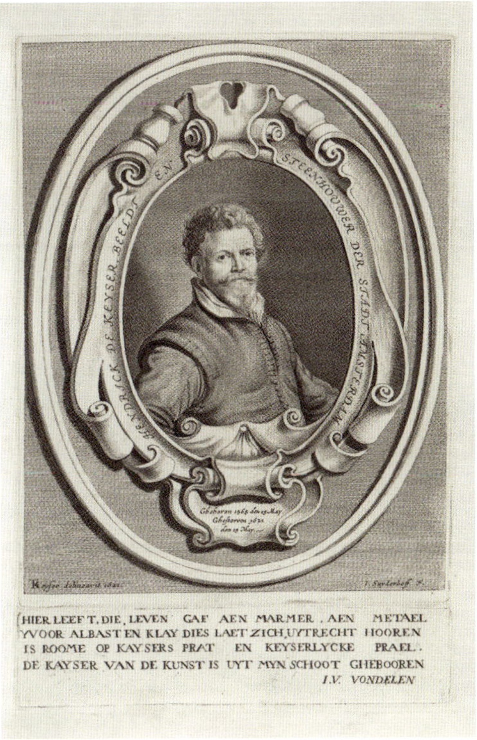


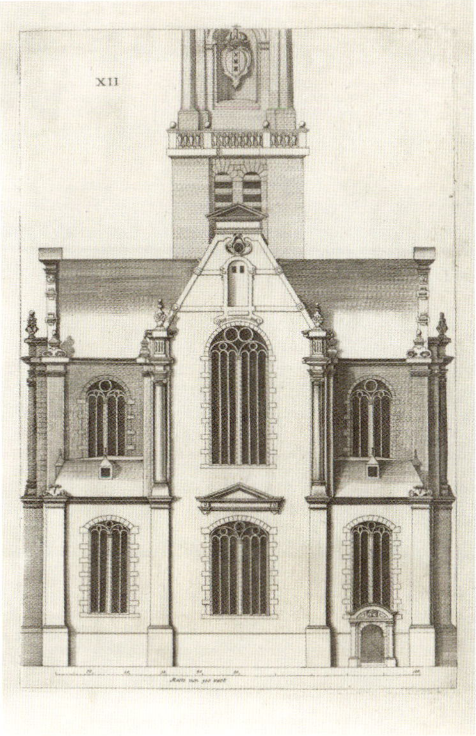


Northern Germany, partly through their publication in *Architectura Moderna* (1631) by Salomon de Bray (1597–1664)'. In fact, Netherlandish architectural influences in this era spread much further than Germany, being found as far afield as Stockholm, Seville, Gdańsk and Lviv.[19] Curl thought that de Keyser's steeples might have had some influence on Christopher Wren's designs for the (post-1666 fire) London City churches. This was certainly the case, though Wren's steeples (another of which, at St Magnus the Martyr, is based on that of St Charles Borromeo, Antwerp) were generally much smaller.

For the present writer, who has long been interested in the architecture of the RHK, the notion that it might be a Dutch-influenced building only arose during the course of a lecture he attended in London some years back on the Westerkerk. The semicircular-headed biforate (circle over two round-headed arches) louvred windows of the belfry of the hospital [fig. 2] struck him as being similar to those of the Amsterdam church, albeit that in the latter building the motif is multiplied within the tall glazed windows of the nave and transepts in a series of divisions and subdivisions [fig. 5]. De Keyser is regarded today as one of the later architects of the Dutch Mannerist School and a key figure in steering its transition into the more stately style of Dutch classicism,

fig. 4 | Hendrick de Keyser (1565–1621), engraving by Jonas Suyderhoef after a drawing of 1621 by Thomas de Keyser, Rijksmuseum, RP-P-1940–383

fig. 5 | Westerkerk, Amsterdam (1620–31) by Hendrick de Keyser, showing use of biforate divisions and subdivisions of windows. From Salomon de Bray, *Architectura Moderna* (Amsterdam: Cornelis Danckerts, 1631), plate XII, Rijksmuseum, RP-P-2016-321.

moving from exuberantly decorated gabled façades to more sober-looking buildings with horizontal rather than vertical emphases, and often (like the RHK) with hipped roofs.[20] He was particularly interested in Venice, where a number of palazzi had biforate windows, including the Palazzo Corner-Spinelli (from 1480) and the Palazzo Vendramin-Calergi (1500–09), both by Mauro Codussi; a variant of the type was used earlier in Florence.[21] The seventeenth-century acceleration of their utilisation in Protestant Northern Europe, after the publication of *Architectura Moderna* in 1631, came after their prolonged, though not widespread, use in Catholic churches in France, examples ranging from the apse of the church of St Pierre in Caen (Hector Sohier, 1518–45) to the west front of St Gervais in Paris (Salomon de Brosse, 1616–21). It has been remarked that unlike Hans Vredeman de Vries (1527–1606), a noteworthy Flemish Mannerist architect and pattern-book publisher who influenced him and indeed had a following in England, de Keyser was also interested in the classicism of Italian renaissance architects including Michaelangelo.[22] However, a glance at plate 21-B1 in de Vries' *Architectura* (Antwerp, 1577), reveals the presence of strikingly similar biforate windows to those of de Keyser's Westerkerk.

Ian Campbell has written that the use of biforate windows by Scottish masons occurred as early as the 1560s.[23] The earliest biforate windows used in a prominent building in England appear to be those in the prospect room of the eclectic Wollaton Hall in Nottinghamshire, begun by Robert Smythson for Sir Francis Willoughby in 1580. The Willoughby family accumulated a library of treatises and pattern books (Vredeman de Vries was a major influence on Wollaton).[24] Thomas Butler, 'Black Tom', the 10th Earl of Ormond (*c.*1531–1614), forbear of the Duke of Ormond, displayed a similar penchant for Flemish design in his more modest but unique Irish Elizabethan manor house at Carrick-on-Suir, begun *c.*1565 as an adjunct to Ormond Castle. He imported panelling and glass from Flanders, the internal plasterwork being also of Flemish inspiration.[25] Black Tom's architectural taste for Northern European Renaissance features has been discussed by both Jane Fenlon and Hanneke Ronnes.[26] This era was Flanders' heyday as a centre of architectural innovation and influence. It was not to last much longer. When the Northern Netherlands separated to form the autonomous Dutch Republic in 1581, Flanders remained under Habsburg rule as the Spanish Netherlands. In 1585, the Dutch blockaded the upper stretches of the River Scheldt, later taking control of its left bank, Zeelandic Flanders, and cutting off access to the sea. This led to the decline of Antwerp and the rise of Amsterdam as both an economic powerhouse and the main Netherlandish centre of architectural and artistic endeavour and influence, aptly named its Golden Age.

While biforate windows are rare in seventeenth-century English churches, they were much used in Protestant churches in Ireland after the restoration of the monarchy in 1660, and remained in common usage in Munster up until the early 1800s.[27] Like that of the RHK, the tower of a contemporary London building, Edward Jerman's Royal Exchange (1667–71, destroyed 1838), built on the site of its Elizabethan predecessor burnt in the 1666 fire, had prominent biforate windows; the upper stage had contrasting Y-tracery.[28] It was Rolf Loeber, the most prolific writer on Netherlandish influences on Irish architecture, who discovered that Samuel Molyneux, the son of William

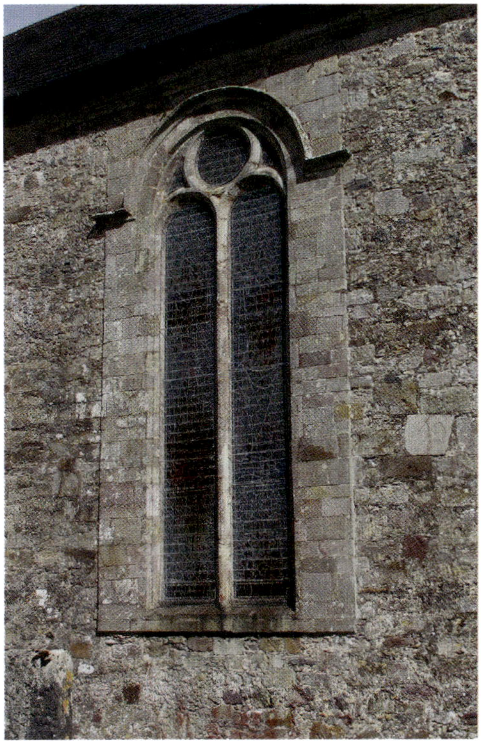

Robinson's sometime co-surveyor general William Molyneux (post-1684), owned a copy of de Keyser's book, sold with other architectural pattern-books in 1730.[29] Loeber convincingly suggested that the biforate windows used by Robinson in the rebuilding of St Carthage's Cathedral, Lismore (from 1679), had come from a reading of *Architectura Moderna*.[30] His St Mary's Church on Mary Street, Dublin (begun 1700) was similarly influenced. However, Loeber mistakenly stated that the windows at St Carthage's prefigured the 'concave mouldings' of those at the RHK, a reference to the dished reveals of its north wing.[31] The windows on the principal (south) elevation of the nave and the south transept at Lismore were framed by flat rectangles of cut stone; only the latter pair survive [fig. 6] but the ensemble is known from Jonas Blaymire's engraving of 1739.[32] Close examination indicates that these flat surrounds were intended to contrast with a rough-cast finish to the walls, since removed. The influence of *Architectura Moderna* on St Carthage's can be confirmed by an examination of a survey drawing of *c.*1810 of Robinson's gabled west elevation which had a circular window based on the Zuiderkerk; this was swept away in James Pain's rebuilding in the 1820s.[33]

Loeber has suggested that the round-arched windows at the RHK 'are similar to the ones used by Hugh May at Windsor Castle' (installed 1675–84, removed in the 1820s).[34] This work, in the buildings of the Upper Ward, would have been known to Ormond, though the Windsor windows did not have Y-tracery.[35] Surprisingly, Loeber never made a de Keyser connection with the tower windows in the RHK, nor did he ever refer to the hospital's architecture as being Dutch-inspired. While Robinson was clearly interested in the work of Hendrick de Keyser, so too, as will become clear, was the Duke of Ormond, who may well have had his own copy of the book.

In addition to the biforate windows, another feature of the RHK that may be seen as related to the plates in *Architectura Moderna* is the main doorcase in the courtyard leading from the dining hall, which has affinities with the doorcases of the Zuiderkerk [figs 7, 8]. The stonework of the upper stage has unusual carved consoles

---

fig. 6 | St Carthage's Cathedral, Lismore, co. Waterford, a biforate window in the south transept; architect William Robinson, begun 1679. The walling around its cut-stone frame would originally have had a rough-cast finish.

(photos by the author (2021–2024), unless otherwise stated)

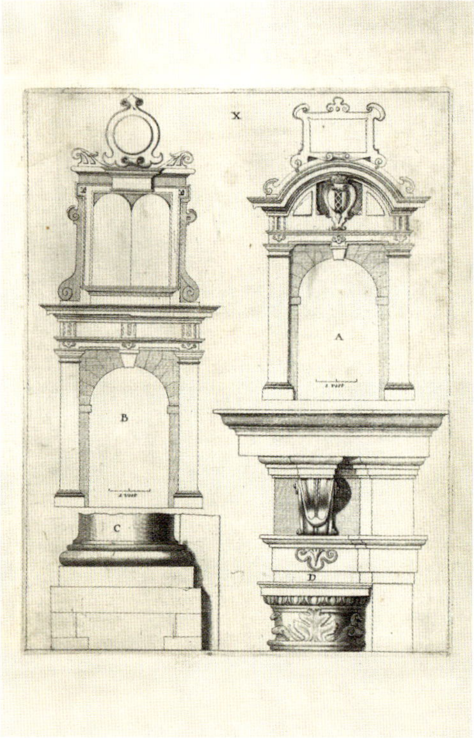


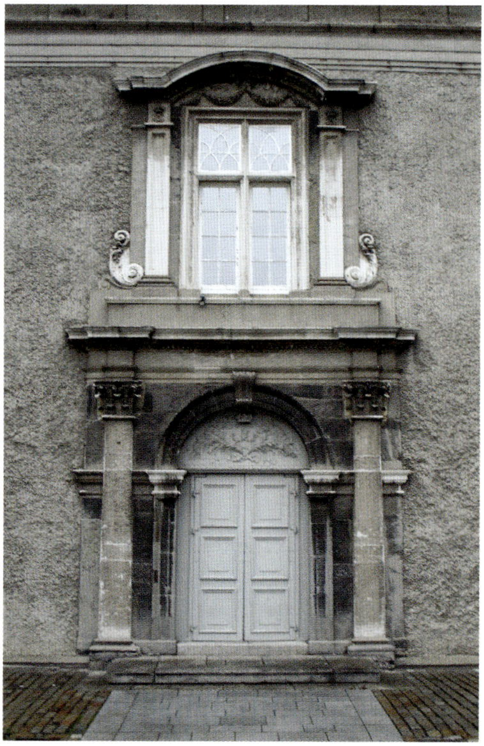

which look turned backwards; this is consistent with the quirkiness of Dutch Mannerism. While Edward McParland noted that this doorcase had been altered, this change was not to the carved stonework which remains intact.[36]

Another feature derived from the *Architectura Moderna* plates is the ensemble of brackets at the base of the spire [fig. 9]. Hendrick de Keyser used such brackets in the spires of a number of buildings, including the Zuiderkerk, and in the remodelling of several city towers, including the surviving Montelbaanstoren (1606), and they may be seen in one of the plates of the Westerkerk, though these were not included in the executed design, completed after his death by his son Pieter [fig. 10]. While the bracket motif relates more to the sixteenth-century strapwork seen in de Vries's books than contemporary architectural fashion, their visual quality adds a certain charm to the steeple profile in contrast to the solidity of the volutes used by Wren in London church spires, though one of them was constructed, about 1695, with lead-clad open brackets – St Augustine's, Watling Street.[37] Brackets were a feature of Dutch spires of this period, and while championed by de Keyser, were used by other architects there.[38] Wren's earliest

fig. 7 | Zuiderkerk, Amsterdam (1606–14), designs for doorcases by Hendrick de Keyser. The quirky scrolls on the window reveals of 'B' and the pediment of 'A', typical of Hendrick de Keyser's detailing, are arguably reflected in the quirky scrolls in the upper stage of the RHK courtyard doorcase. From de Bray, *Architectura Moderna*, op. cit., plate X, Rijksmuseum, RP-P-2016-320.

fig. 8 | RHK courtyard doorcase. The carved details included Dutch mannerist elements as in the Zuiderkerk doorcases.

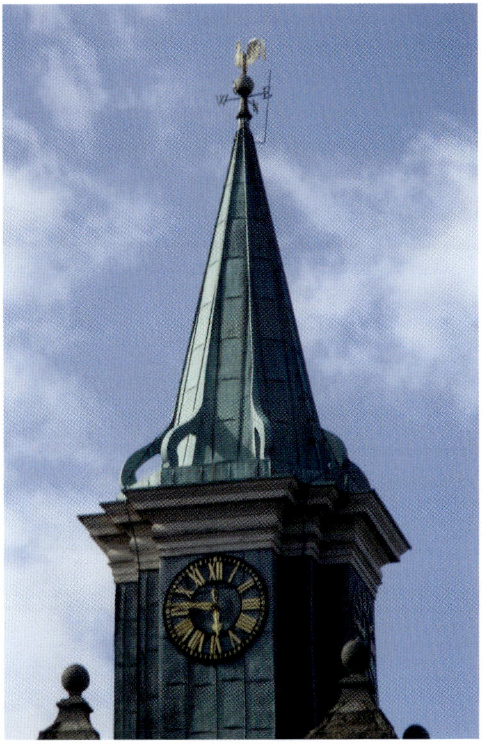

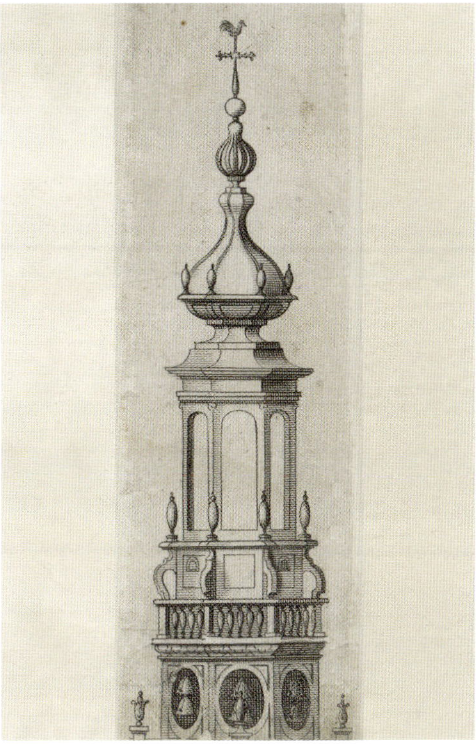

use of brackets, albeit in the form of stone consoles, was in the steeple of St Mary-le-Bow, Cheapside (1670–80).[39] Maurice Craig, who wrote lyrically about the RHK in his 1952 book on Dublin, was particularly charmed by the spire and the 'eight graceful appendages in the form of open consoles, which look rather like handles but seem to be the product simply of a happy fantasy of the designer'.[40]

When the hospital was completed in the 1680s there were no funds to erect a steeple, a temporary pyramidal roof being constructed over the tower. This matter was not finally addressed until 1701. Although Robinson had retired as surveyor general in April 1700, with Thomas Burgh replacing him in July, he continued to work at the hospital until at least 1703, continuing also as an acting governor up to 1707. On 9 June 1701, Robinson 'having presented to the Governors a draught or model of the Steeple for the Hospital as the same was first intended to be finished, the same was approved by the Governors'.[41] Construction was subsequently delegated to Burgh and the spire erected with funding from a lottery in 1703–05. The hospital seal, of early date, in the possession of the Office of Public Works, shows a different design for the ensemble, where the upper stage envisaged was not a spire but rather a classical octagonal structure with a domed top, similar to an Amsterdam church [fig. 11].[42] The hospital minutes

---

fig. 9 | RHK copper spire, showing the brackets at the base, mirroring a popular detail found in seventeenth-century spires in Dutch churches

fig. 10 | Zuiderkerk, Amsterdam (1606–14) showing use of brackets in spire.
From de Bray, *Architectura Moderna*, op. cit., plate I [detail], Rijksmuseum, RP-P-2016-312.

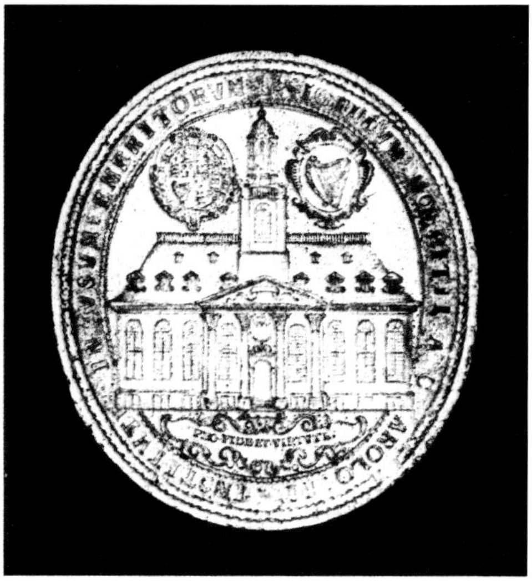

are ambiguous; but whichever the 'original design' was, either spire or octagon, it was Dutch-inspired, which suggests that the use of Netherlandish motifs had been intended in the original scheme of things, possibly with the involvement of William de Keyser.[43]

Craig began his chapter on the building by lambasting those who had claimed the design for Christopher Wren, to whom it had been incorrectly ascribed for generations. This was presumably on the assumption that it post-dated Wren's Chelsea Hospital, which was, in fact, a later construction, not begun until 1682. While Craig undoubtedly put Robinson centre stage, it was Walter Strickland who first drew the public's attention to the error, in 1923.[44] Intriguingly, Craig ended his chapter by concluding that Robinson 'had somewhere acquired a feeling for grand scale. It was certainly not in Ireland, and at the time it was perhaps hardly even in England. It is of course pure conjecture, but the basis of such conjecture is fortunately still standing.'[45]

If the Chelsea Hospital can be ruled out as an influence, what of Wren himself – could it be that elements of the RHK resemble features that Wren had used in his own oeuvre such as the church of St Mary-le-Bow, begun in 1670? Unlike the many Wren steeples deferred because of funding shortages until the 1690s and early 1700s, this one was contemporary since, as noted by Anthony Geraghty, it had been given priority in the post-fire rebuilding programme.[46] The costly spire was erected in 1678–80 to a design that was much enhanced and more de Keyser-like than the original concept. The steeple has two series of open consoles, carved from Portland stone, one set cut into the pyramidal cushions in the four corners of the tower (which resemble the solid cushions of the RHK in outline). The second set are higher up, curving like flying buttresses to link the drum to the top stage. Geraghty has pointed out the similarity of the windows of Wren's original proposal for the church's façade to those of de Keyser's Noorderkerk in Amsterdam, which he noted had been illustrated in de Bray's *Architectura Moderna*.[47] More conventional windows were used in the final scheme.

fig. 11 | Seal of the RHK, pre-1701. Imprint (in the collection of the OPW) showing the original classical proposal for the upper stage of the tower, which is similar to the octagonal domed tops of Dutch Renaissance steeples. Other differences from the executed design include the unexecuted carving in the tympanum, the subdivisions of the glazing and the form of the doorcase and the arms over it. The roof of the north range, as built, was neither balustraded nor articulated in this way though it had two rows of dormers, many inserted for the sake of symmetry rather than function. Those over the dining hall and chapel, which had high ceilings, lit only voids and were removed in later renovations. They are depicted in Francis Place's topographical drawings of 1698.
(OPW)

If the church spire shares the use of consoles/brackets with the RHK, the church also shares the use, in the building proper, of substantial dished surrounds to its openings: the principal doorcases in the case of St Mary's, the windows of the north range in the case of the hospital. These are not Dutch but French-inspired, from François Mansart's Hôtel de Conty (otherwise Conti), Wren having met the architect on a study tour in Paris in 1665.[48] Interestingly, Geraghty has noted that William de Keyser was working for Wren in 1671.[49] While the de Keyser family were already using dished surrounds in the 1660s, albeit smaller ones, a Wren influence on those at the RHK remains a possibility.

If some of the details of the RHK are Dutch or Netherlandish, what of the general plan and elevations? Little analysis has been carried out of the plan. John Olley's suggestion in 1991, that the planning relationship of the chapel to the hall is similar to that in two early seventeenth-century English hospitals seems reasonable, albeit that similar arrangements may be found in the old universities.[50] However, McParland's suggestion that the hollow-square plan is reminiscent of an unexecuted design of 1666 by John Evelyn for a naval infirmary at Chatham is not conclusive; unlike the RHK, this plan was quite different with double-banked rooms and no arcades. It will be argued here that the main influence on its plan and elevations was probably Hendrick de Keyser. His most important civic building in Amsterdam was the Bourse (1607–11) which, while not illustrated in *Architectura Moderna*, was well known from contemporary prints. Like the RHK, its principal element was a hollow rectangle with arcades at ground floor level, a piano nobile above (though with niches rather than windows facing the courtyard) and a dormer-windowed attic. While the Bourse was highly ornate, the RHK was more functional, with simple piers, without mouldings on the backs of the capitals, rather than expensive columns [figs 12, 13]. The building was used as a merchants' exchange and shops as was the London building on which it was modelled – the Flemish architect Hendrik van Paesschen's Royal Exchange, built by the entrepreneur Thomas Gresham with Flemish craftsmen and some imported materials in 1566–69.[51] This too had been a derivative – of the Antwerp Bourse of 1531 (which was a late-Gothic rather than a Renaissance design) – but it was to London that de Keyser was sent by the Amsterdam authorities in 1606 or 1607 to carry out a survey of Gresham's building. In this he was assisted by the local sculptor Nicholas Stone (*c.*1587–1647), probably originally from Devon, who returned with him to Holland and worked as his assistant, marrying his daughter Mayken (Maria) in 1613 before coming back to London to set up a practice. Among Stone's sculptural works in Amsterdam was the carving of a gateway of one of de Keyser's churches, generally accepted today as the surviving cemetery gateway of the Zuiderkerk.[52]

The widespread influence of Gresham's arcaded Royal Exchange, including on the RHK, was noted by the American scholar John Fitzhugh Millar in a dissertation in 1981.[53] Jane Fenlon has suggested that the local merchants who erected arcaded shops in Kilkenny from the 1590s may have shared the Ormond contacts with Flemish agents. She also notes that 'in time several public buildings, such as the later seventeenth-century Royal Hospital Kilmainham would have internal courtyards incorporated into their design, although not for commercial uses'.[54]

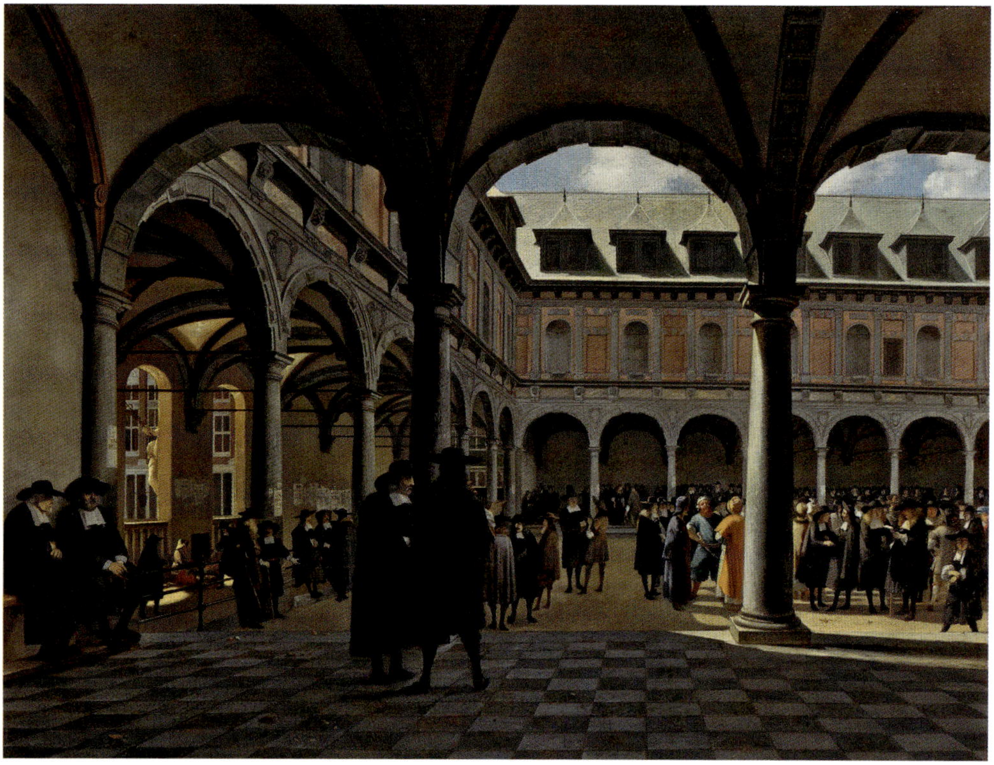

## Ormond and the Netherlands

In surmising that William Robinson may have based the RHK on a building he had seen abroad, Craig was placing him in the role of an architect of the post-Renaissance period, the central figure on the design team. Loeber noted that at around the time the hospital was being conceived, in 1677, Robinson had been sent abroad 'in the King's service', speculating that this had been to see Les Invalides but conceding 'nothing is known about the extent of his travels'.[55] However, if we examine Ormond's connections with the Stone/de Keyser family of English and Dutch architects and sculptors, and his European connections generally, a different possibility emerges – that the duke's working relationship with his surveyor general may have been more akin to a hierarchical Renaissance one. We do not know how Black Tom operated in Carrick-on-Suir, but his mansion has no known architect. The possibility that the Duke of Ormond was in the driving seat – albeit that Robinson was the designated project manager – might be considered. This is not to suggest that Robinson was unqualified for the job, but while a talented architect, he was also a placeman, simultaneously holding many remunerative posts as well as working privately for Ormond at Kilkenny and personally importing timber from Scandinavia. It can hardly be a coincidence that his timber yard was located a few hundred yards to the west of the RHK site.[56] With so many interests, it was a considerable achievement to keep the hospital on track. Ormond's experience of European architecture, including civic buildings, from his years

fig. 13 | RHK courtyard, view from the south-west corner illustrating its compositional similarities to the Amsterdam Bourse

opposite

fig. 12 | *The Old Stock Exchange of Amsterdam* by Job Berckheyde (1630–*c.*1693), *c.*1670, oil on canvas, 85.5 x 105.5 cm, Museum Boijmans Van Beuningen, Rotterdam, 1043 (OK). This was painted shortly after renovations and alterations in 1668.
(photo: Studio Tromp)

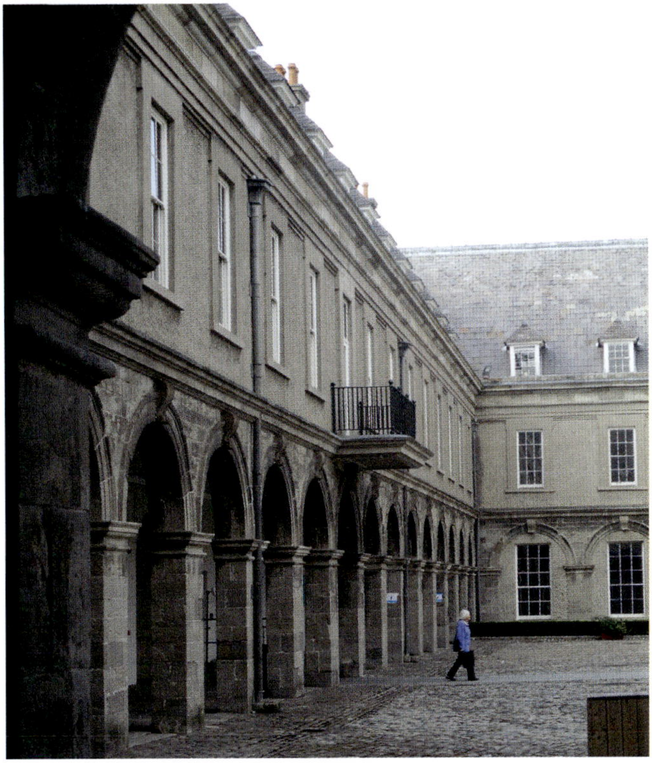

of exile would have been greater than anything Robinson might have obtained. That Ormond had his own firm architectural opinions might be gleaned from an account traced by Loeber of a dispute he had with Hugh May in 1681 over the design of piers for Kilkenny Castle.[57] May declined to change the proportions and advised Ormond's agent, the Earl of Longford, that he was consulting Christopher Wren.[58]

Architectural historians have been divided for years on the extent of the influence of Dutch architecture on the public and private works of Charles II and his courtiers, but it did exist, among the best-known examples being Hugh May's use of giant orders at Eltham Lodge in Kent (1664), based on the Sint Sebastiaansdoelen in the Hague (by Arent van 's-Gravesande, 1636), and at Cornbury Park in Oxfordshire (1666).[59] Writing in 1971, Margaret Whinney was of the opinion that 'May, like many members of [Charles's] court had visited Holland during their exile [...] from now on Dutch [architectural influence] superseded Flemish.'[60] This superseding did occur, albeit that in reality May was the only English architect who could travel freely in the Commonwealth-supporting Dutch Republic, obtaining passage from England in 1656 by posing as a servant of his friend the artist Peter Lely. He later made his way south to join Charles's court. The alternating influences of southern and northern Netherlandish architecture on Britain in the seventeenth and early eighteenth centuries has been discussed by a number of authors, including Hentie Louw.[61] In Ireland, the notion of Dutch influence in the period is not a new one; in 1726 Edward Lovett Pearce, subsequently architect of the Dublin Parliament House, was asked by Lord Burlington to inspect the ruins of the palace at Jigginstown, co. Kildare, built in the 1630s by the lord deputy Thomas Wentworth (later Earl of Strafford), to see if it might have been the work of Inigo Jones. He concluded that the facing brickwork was most likely Dutch.[62] Most of its stone dressings had been removed by this time, but a doorcase and some other features, rebuilt into a neighbouring house, were described by Pearce, probably incorrectly, as 'grey Italian marble'. Wentworth's eclectic design may have been influenced by his friend Archbishop Laud. While Loeber established that Wentworth's builder John Allen came from Holland,[63] an analysis commissioned by the Office of Public Works in 2004 concluded that, although elaborately pointed, most bricks came from a local source.[64] What neither Burlington nor Pearce succeeded in establishing was that Inigo Jones was in fact well aware of the Jigginstown project, and had criticised it, foolhardily telling one his clients, the Earl of Arundel, who passed on the remark to Wentworth, that Jones 'would be sorry if [Wentworth's] skill should be entered into the lists of his [own]'.[65] In more recent times, the term 'Dutch Billies' has gained popular usage to describe the largely disappeared curvilinear-gabled houses erected in Dublin and a few other places between the 1690s and the 1740s. The term was used by Loeber as the title of a 2014 essay, though its appearance in print reputedly goes back no further than Craig's 1952 Dublin book.[66]

While we do not know the extent of Robinson's travels, we do know that during the Commonwealth Ormond lived on the Continent for almost ten years. Ormond's exile had begun at the end of 1650 when he sailed from Galway to join his previously evacuated family at Caen in Normandy. Commander-in-chief (since 1640), he had retreated to Connacht some months earlier but failed to retain the support of the Catholic bishops, losing his alliance with their Confederates.[67] In early March 1650, he left threatened Kilkenny in the hands of his kinsman Sir Walter Butler and a small force; after a strong resistance they were obliged to surrender but obtained safe passage. From Caen, Ormond moved in late 1651 to join the court of the future Charles II in Paris, where they were to remain for three years. After periods in Cologne, the court moved to the Spanish Netherlands. Only the last two months or so of Ormond's exile was spent in the Dutch Republic, to which Charles's court was able to move in April 1660 after the Commonwealth had collapsed and the monarch was in negotiations with General George Monck to return to Britain. Monck had previously served as an officer under Ormond in Ireland; both men were cosignatories of the Declaration of Breda, dated 4 April but drafted some months earlier in the Spanish Netherlands. Ormond was joined in the court at Breda by his two sons. The elder, Thomas, Earl of Ossory (1634–1680), was exiled to the Dutch Republic in 1656 and married in Utrecht in November 1659 Emilia van Nassau, daughter of Louis of Nassau, Lord of de Lek and Beverweerd, an illegitimate son of Prince Maurice of Orange.[68] Ormond's wife and cousin Elizabeth, who owned much of their property in her own right, had done a deal with the Commonwealth to return home in 1652 with her children, provided she did not maintain correspondence with her husband (she did, clandestinely).[69] Ormond and his sons, Ossory and Richard, Earl of Arran (1639–1686), returned to England with Charles and his entourage in late May 1660.[70] From mid-May, Charles's court was based in Utrecht, Ormond being appointed Lord High Steward.[71] This post was largely ceremonial, though it nominally placed him above Charles's other senior aide Edward Hyde, Earl of Clarendon, who was made Lord Chancellor. While Ormond can, by this time, be said to have connections with Holland, we do not know if he saw the Amsterdam Bourse. He would have been familiar in any case with its progenitor the Elizabethan Royal Exchange in London (as would Robinson), in use up to the 1666 fire. An important Dutch classical building Ormond would have seen was the Mauritshuis in the Hague, by Jacob van Campen (1633–34), where a banquet was held before their departure.

Following the Restoration, Ormond was elevated in the Irish peerage to a dukedom, in March 1661, and regained the Butlers' palatinate in co. Tipperary from the monarch, which Charles I had declined to return in 1641. However, due to competing demands for royal appointments, Ormond, while a senior member of the court, did not regain the lord lieutenancy of Ireland (from lord deputy Monck) until November 1661, returning to Dublin in July 1662.[72]

### Ormond, the Stone/de Keyser family and architecture

ONE OF THE CASUALTIES OF THE ROUNDHEAD'S OCCUPATION OF KILKENNY IN 1650 WAS the destruction of the black marble tomb in St Canice's of Ormond's antecedent, the 10th Earl, carved and erected by Nicholas Stone in 1614. This had been commissioned while Black Tom had been in declining health by his heir Sir Walter Butler, who became 11th Earl.[73] Local tradition, as cited by the historian Paul Cockerham,[74] has it that a panel with which Stone faced the tomb, carved with a coat of arms and a Tudor rose, survives, built into another Butler chest tomb, but this view is not shared by Jane Fenlon.[75] We have contemporary descriptions of its magnificence, including that it was surmounted by a recumbent effigy of the earl. This was one of Stone's first works after he had returned to London from Amsterdam with his new wife Mayken de Keyser. He was to become pre-eminent as a tomb carver, with over eighty to his credit. He was also in the royal service from 1616, rising to Master Mason to the crown in 1632, and worked as a contractor for Inigo Jones as well as carrying out architectural commissions, some such as Goldsmith's Hall in London coming through Jones. Stone's style of architecture was more eclectic and, indeed, Mannerist than that of Jones's court style.

If we leap ahead, we can see from Loeber's and Colvin's biographical dictionaries, and indeed from the *Dictionary of Irish Biography*, that in the 1680s William de Keyser (b.1603), one of Hendrick's four sons, worked in Ireland, where Ormond employed him alongside Robinson and Hugh May at Kilkenny Castle.[76] William carved two fountains there, and was subsequently engaged by Dublin Corporation, in 1683, to carve the statues of Charles I and Charles II for the new Tholsel.[77] Many accounts of William end in the 1670s when he was in London, without noting an Irish career, and none have a date of death. He would have been in his late seventies when he was working on the castle, which makes it likely that he was assisted by his son Hendrick de Keyser III (b.1634).[78] He had a second son Willem, of which nothing is apparently known, not even if he survived childhood.

The question arises, can we establish a continuity of contact between the Butlers and the Stone/de Keyser family in the period between Nicholas Stone's work on the tomb in 1614 and his brother-in-law William's employment by the duke at Kilkenny Castle in the 1680s? This writer believes that we can. In 1635, when the duke was the 12th Earl of Ormond and a close ally of Thomas Wentworth, he was appointed to the privy council. Two years later, Inigo Jones ordered 3,000ft of 'black marble' from Wentworth to be shipped to London for the steps of the new portico he was adding to (Old) St Paul's Cathedral, of which a third was needed urgently. Tom Williamson, in his book *Inigo's Stones*, speculates as to whether these were from the area where Wentworth was building his mansion, at Jigginstown in co. Kildare, Galway or Kilkenny. In view of delivery problems with the balance, Nicholas Stone, who was the contractor, had to order 'about two thousand feet of the geologically similar "Belgian black" Dinant marble'.[79] This implies that it was Kilkenny marble that was being supplied, an obvious choice given Wentworth's alliance with Ormond. As the portico was a royal project, Ormond would surely have made it his business to discuss matters with the building team of whom Stone would have been known to him as the fabricator of the celebrated family tomb in St Canice's. Two of Stone's brothers-in-law were working with him in London, William de Keyser since 1621 and Hendrick II since about 1634. Both had married Englishwomen, Walpurga Parker and Elizabeth Bellamy.[80] A third brother, Pieter, was sending them stone from the Netherlands, and the fourth brother, Thomas, a Dutch Baroque artist, was also a stone trader at this time (he later sold out to Pieter). Their father, Hendrick de Keyser I, had previously been a partner of the van Neurenberg family who ran the black marble and 'Belgian bluestone' quarries.[81] While Wentworth fell from grace and was executed in 1641, Ormond is known to have visited Jigginstown in 1643 (to sign a ceasefire with the Irish Catholic Confederation). Although the house subsequently fell into disrepair, Ormond maintained an interest in it and purchased the doorcases and chimneypieces from its ruins from Wentworth's son in 1674.[82] It is unclear if this was for Kilkenny Castle or for the duchess's house at Dunmore.

It may be presumed that Ormond was transporting black marble down the Nore. The nineteenth-century antiquaries Prendergast and Graves wrote that in the duke's time conventional boats (supplying Caen stone dressings for the castle) could get up as far as Inistioge with smaller (flat-bottomed) craft being used for the upper stretch.[83] Such transportation of Kilkenny stone, via the port of Waterford, continued up to the coming of the railways. In 1664, Ormond arranged through his local architect Captain John Morton to ship Kilkenny marble for a chimneypiece for the mansion the Earl of Clarendon was building in London, with Sir Roger Pratt as his architect.[84] Morton had been employed since 1663 in renovating Kilkenny Castle and Dunmore. While Morton died in 1668, the castle renovations, in the French style, continued through the 1680s. In 1678, the Ormonds sent Kilkenny marble to England for two chimneypieces for Lady Arlington.[85]

During Ormond's two months in the Dutch Republic in April–May 1660, pending Charles's return to England, the court was lobbied by a stream of British visitors canvassing for various offices and positions under the new administration. Among these was Nicholas Stone's youngest and sole surviving son John (1620–1667), who came to

Breda seeking the post of King's Mason, held by his late father.[86] He lost out to Edward Marshall and was subsequently given the lesser post of mason to Windsor Castle. As an acquaintance of the Stone family, Ormond would have been well-disposed towards them, but the machinations as to how this played out have not been previously considered. These began when John Stone was stricken with palsy while in Breda. His foreman, Caius Gabriel Cibber, was summoned from London to bring him home, and while Stone 'never recovered sufficiently to resume the management of his affairs, and eventually died as an inmate of the Hospital of St Cross at Winchester in 1667',[87] the Windsor appointment was, nevertheless, confirmed to him in August, a few months after his collapse. Cibber, a native of Schleswig, arrived in London to join the Stone workshop 'about 1655, possibly with an introduction from the de Keyser workshop in Amsterdam'.[88] He may have continued the business after his master's incapacitation, but it was probably Stone's uncle William de Keyser that was in charge.[89] William had left London in 1640 during the political crisis, and returned to Amsterdam where he ran a successful practice, working in the new Dutch classical style. He assisted Jacob van Campen with the new town hall, and in 1647 was appointed master mason for the city. He was, however, dismissed from office in 1653 on the grounds of fraud.[90] He appears to have avoided imprisonment as van Campen continued to give him work, including as a sculptor on elaborate tombs. However, he went bankrupt in 1658 and headed back to London, probably to rejoin the Stone workshop.[91] The gate of St Olave's Church, Hart Street in the City, bedecked with sculpted skulls and clearly derived from plates in *Architectura Moderna*, was carved that year and must surely be his. Its connection to Hendrick de Keyser is mentioned in the relevant volume of *The Buildings of England* (1997).[92]

Howard Colvin notes that in July 1661 William was paid £2 for drawing 'the draughts with the uprights [plans and elevations] for the intended Building at Greenwich'.[93] This was the proposed new palace for the king and these were likely just tracings of someone else's design, probably John Webb, given that the new surveyor general Sir John Denham was a placeman with no architectural credentials.[94] Such employment seems an unusual honour for de Keyser, who had been convicted of fraud and gone bankrupt not long before. This payment was a small sum, even in the seventeenth century, but the reality was that he was already being handsomely remunerated as a sculptor on the King's Works, earning £40 for interior carvings in Whitehall Palace in February 1661 and a further £140 that year for carvings in Somerset House.[95] William clearly had a friend in court, and it is not hard to guess who that might have been.

Ormond's importance in securing commissions is implied in a letter sent to him in the spring of 1662 by Webb's son-in-law, Dr John Westley, master in chancery in the Irish administration and an amateur architect. Westley claimed that, in fairness, Webb should be rebuilding Whitehall Palace, pointedly adding that he would now be surveyor general had he not been overlooked at Breda.[96] Although the letter seems prickly, Westley was also angling (unsuccessfully) with Ormond at this time to design new buildings at Dublin Castle, saying that Webb could assist him.[97] In 1664, Westley prepared designs for a house for Sir George Lane, Ormond's secretary since the 1640s and the holder of several public offices. This can be identified as the mansion on Capel

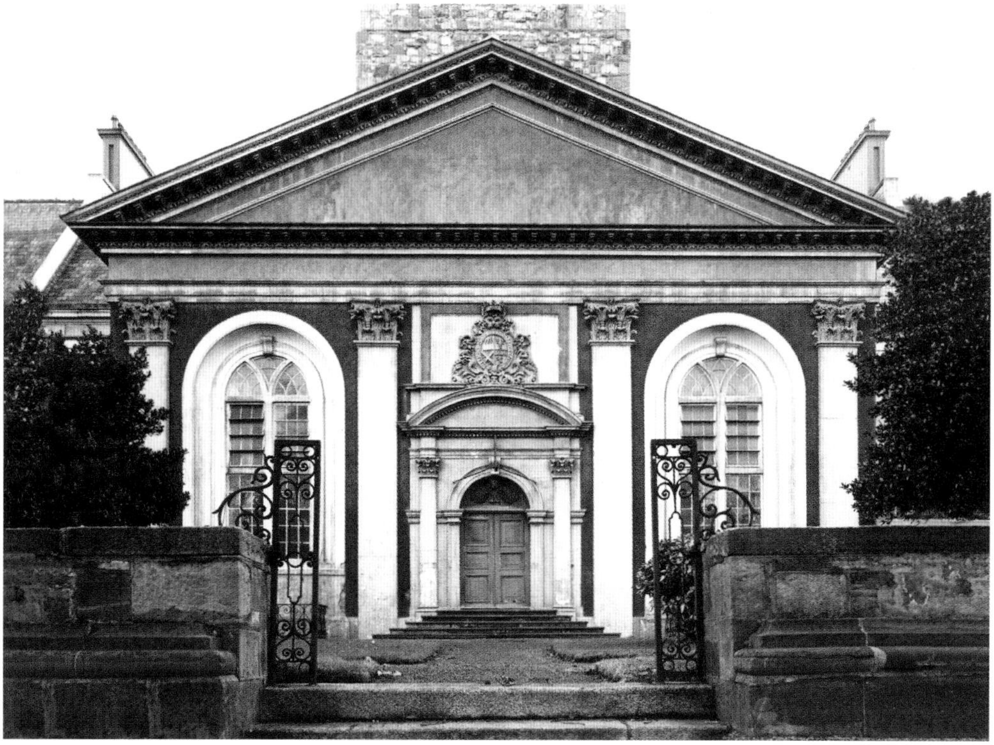

Street later occupied by the Conolly family.[98] Ormond might have built a 'palace' of his own on a seven-acre site in Oxmantown given to him in 1665 by Dublin Corporation, but by 1667 he was running out of funds.[99] By 1669 he was out of office and remained so until 1677.[100]

It seems likely that de Keyser's work at Whitehall Palace extended beyond the carvings. He may have designed the five-bay house, with full-height pilasters, that Ormond built there for his own use in 1661–62.[101] He has been suggested, by both Simon Thurley and John Bold, as the author of an unexecuted design of around this time for a seven-bay house, with a set of French or arguably Dutch-style gables, to be erected nearby, in the Privy Garden.[102]

William continued to live in London through the 1670s and was made a 'foreign member' of the Masons' Company in 1678. By 1680 he was in trouble again in Amsterdam, this time involving a dispute over payment as an assistant sculptor on the carving of an important tomb. If, as it would appear, Ormond had come to his rescue in 1660/61 in arranging commissions, he would do so again in Ireland after 1680. Loeber thought it 'likely that de Keyser set up a workshop in Dublin' after his arrival here.[103] This seems a reasonable conclusion, but it is arguable that the workshop may well have been at the RHK.

fig. 14 | RHK north front showing the giant-order pilasters and the Ormond coat of arms.
The carved Corinthian capitals are painted wood rather than stone.
(Irish Architectural Archive / David Davison)

Historically, the sculpted elements at the hospital that have received the attention of scholars have been the timber carvings in the chapel by the French Huguenot James Tabary, which were carried out between late 1683 and 1687, after the main construction works. As a craftsman working on the RHK, he is a uniquely well-documented figure both from the hospital minutes and from other sources.[104] Robin Usher has written an illuminating account of the carved tympana over the doorways of the west, south and east doorways to the courtyard, which he thought could be by Tabary.[105] Documentation does not appear to survive for the authorship of these nor for any of the stone and wood carvings on the façades, including the dining hall doorcase in the quadrangle, the sandstone tracery in the east window of the chapel, the capitals of the giant orders on the north front, and, most significantly, the Duke of Ormond's arms above the north entrance [fig. 14]. Could it be that these carvings were carried out by a team led by William de Keyser or his son? The ducal arms, pilasters and most of the dressings of these features were Portland stone, probably the first time this material, favoured by Inigo Jones, had been used on a public building in Ireland.[106]

And what of the chapel window as a hybrid piece of Gothic-survival? There is a precedent in England with a de Keyser connection – St Peter's Chapel, Bishop Auckland in co. Durham. This project was commenced by Bishop John Cosin in 1661 and involved the conversion of a twelfth-century Great Hall into a church. Cosin's works, completed about 1665, included the alteration of the clerestory 'with segmental heads and modified geometric tracery'.[107] Interestingly, the stonework beneath the heads is dished [fig. 15]. These modifications and those of the west window tracery created effects similar to that found in the chapel window of the RHK. Colvin attributes the overall design to Cosin's master mason, John Langstaffe.[108] Other writers have noted that Hendrick de Keyser, 'sculptor, of Bishop Auckland', provided the black-and-white paving; his contract, of 1663, included the possibility of importing stone from Holland.[109] An examination of Cosin's published accounts and correspondence reveals more, and implies that de Keyser was on the project from the start, apparently serving as clerk of works.[110] Cosin had been an exile, with Ormond, in Paris in the early 1650s, and remained a friend after the Restoration.

Was this Hendrick William's brother, Hendrick II, or his son, Hendrick III? Mark Girouard, in his 2021 book, says that it was William's son, a view also held by Loeber and well founded.[111] An essay in the 2008 reprint of *Architectura Moderna* indicates that Hendrick II, who had left England in 1647, lived in Amsterdam through the 1660s. He died in 1665 and was buried in the cemetery of the Noorderkerk, one of the churches designed by his father, Hendrick I.[112]

Loeber noted that the RHK was the first building in Ireland to have giant orders, a feature which, in the case of Hugh May's work in England, is considered to be Dutch-inspired.[113] Interestingly, William de Keyser had built a giant order façade at an Amsterdam house on Kloveniersburgwal (1642), designed by Philips Vingboons for Joan Poppen.[114] It seems likely that the 'piers' May was planning to erect for Ormond at Kilkenny Castle in 1681 were also giant orders, those that survive at the entrance front to the Parade.[115]

The ducal arms, elegantly and boldly worked, were clearly a statement of

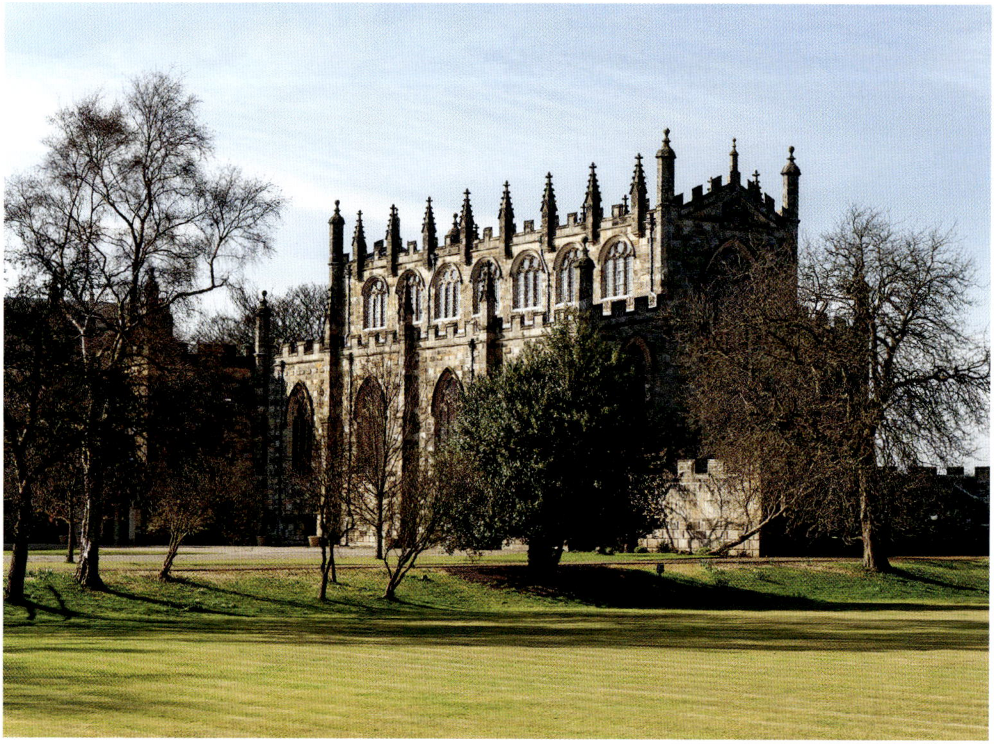

Ormond's personal confidence given that such a prominent location would normally be reserved for the royal arms. For Ormond, whose family suffered the indignity of having their Nicholas Stone tomb in St Canice's broken up by the Roundheads, having his own arms carved above a major public building by one of Stone's relatives might have offered him some solace and perhaps a quiet sense of triumph. The quality of the carving appears consistent with that of a drawing, tentatively attributed to William de Keyser, for royal arms surmounting a doorcase at St Margaret's Church, Westminster, in the collection of Sir John Soane's Museum.[116]

As well as serving a practical purpose, as a shelter for old soldiers on inclement days, the arcades (or piazzas as they were known at the time) appear to fit in with a penchant of Ormond's. His first building to have them was the Main Guard in Clonmel (1674–75), probably designed by his local architect James Archer. Robinson was to use them again in rebuilding the State Apartments at Dublin Castle after the fire of 1684. Mention has been made of the arcaded shops in Renaissance Kilkenny, believed by Fenlon to be unique in an Irish town, of which the surviving Rothe House of the 1590s is an example. It may be no coincidence that a new Dublin street constructed during Ormond's incumbency had arcaded shops, known as the Piazzas, on

fig. 15 | St Peter's Chapel, Bishop Auckland. The Gothic clerestory windows were reconstructed with segmental heads during Bishop Cosin's conversion of the building in 1661–c.1665, a project on which Hendrick de Keyser III was employed.
(Alamy / Alex Ramsay)

both sides.[117] This was Essex Street, named after the lord lieutenant who, as noted by Robin Usher, approached Dublin Corporation, in 1673, to build it to relieve traffic around the Castle.[118] Construction may not have begun in earnest until Ormond's time, after Essex had personally handed over his sword of office to him in 1677. While the properties were privately owned, an arcaded street must surely have required a master plan. There was a recognised combination of public and private interests in the construction of Essex Bridge (1677–88), on which Robinson acted as a technical advisor and about which Essex wrote to Ormond.[119] From 1682, the duke was involved in laying out [Upper] Ormond Quay, running to its west. Given such viceregal ties with the corporation, it seems probable too that Ormond secured William de Keyser's employment on the Tholsel.

To return to the question posed in the title of this paper, it is the writer's belief that the Royal Hospital was considerably influenced by the work of Hendrick de Keyser, but not just from de Bray's book *Architectura Moderna*. As to whether any of the de Keyser family worked on it is a matter of conjecture, but the fact that, as recorded by Loeber, William de Keyser was working side-by-side with Robinson at Kilkenny Castle in the 1680s (probably assisted by his son Hendrick III) suggests at least the possibility that Ormond might have made a similar arrangement at the RHK. Hitherto, William's career has never been considered as a continuum, and neither has Ormond's patronage been fully investigated. It has been put forward here that the seventy-year Butler family connection with the extended Stone/de Keyser family must have counted for something. The architectural influences on the RHK are complex, but it is arguably best viewed as a European building influenced by the broad reach of the Dutch Golden Age and its diaspora. It is also a building which, in the 1950s, Maurice Craig found both intriguing and delightful, an assessment with which the author would agree.

---

**Dr Frederick O'Dwyer** is an architectural historian, the author of three books and numerous articles on the subject. As an OPW district architect in the 1980s he looked after the Royal Hospital, where he restored the Garden House, attributed to Edward Lovett Pearce. He has written histories of various aspects of public works architecture in Ireland, including, with Vivien Igoe, an article entitled 'Early Views of the Royal Hospital, Kilmainham' (*Irish Arts Review Yearbook 1988–89*).

**Author's acknowledgements**

With thanks to the CEO and staff of the Irish Architectural Archive.

**Endnotes**

1 Arthur Gibney, 'The Classical City', in John Graby and Deirdre O'Connor (eds), *Phaidon Architecture Guide: Dublin* (London: Phaidon Press, 1993), p.24.

2 Robinson was sole Surveyor General of works and buildings from 1670–84, jointly with William Molyneux (with whom he shared the patent by choice) from 1684–87/88, and again with Molyneux

(d.1696) between 1690 and 1700. Ormond was Lord Lieutenant of Ireland from 1677 to 1685. He was replaced by Henry Hyde, 2nd Earl of Clarendon (in office 1685–87), brother-in-law of the new king, James II.

3 Edward McParland, *Public Architecture in Ireland 1680–1760* (New Haven and London: Yale University Press, 2001), p.1.

4 John Summerson, *Architecture in Britain 1530–1830* (Harmondsworth: Penguin Books, 1953), p.97.

5 Giles Worsley, 'Wren, Vanbrugh, Hawksmoor, and Archer: the search for an English Baroque', *Studies in the History of Art, vol. 66, Symposium Papers XLIII – Circa 1700: architecture in Europe and the Americas* (2005), pp.98–117. Caroline van Eck, 'Artisan Mannerism: Seventeenth-century Rhetorical Alternatives to Sir John Summerson's Formalist Approach', in Frank Salmon (ed.), *Summerson and Hitchcock: centenary essays on architectural historiography* (New Haven and London: Yale University Press, 2006), pp.85–104.

6 Ibid., p.99.

7 Lucy Gent, 'Elizabethan Architecture: A View from Rhetoric', *Architectural History*, vol.57 (2014), pp.73–108.

8 Kathleen James-Chakraborty, *Architecture since 1400* (Minneapolis and London: University of Minnesota Press, 2014), p.91.

9 Christine Casey, *The Buildings of Ireland: Dublin* (New Haven and London: Yale University Press, 2005), p.677.

10 Ibid.

11 See Konrad Ottenheym (ed.) *Romanesque Renaissance: Carolingian, Byzantine and Romanesque buildings (800–1200) as a source for new All' Antica architecture in early modern Europe (1400–1700)*, (Leiden: Brill, 2021).

12 See Thomas H. Cocke, 'Pre-nineteenth-century attitudes in England to Romanesque architecture', *Journal of the British Archaeological Association*, vol.36, no.1 (1973), pp.72–97.

13 Vivien Igoe and Frederick O'Dwyer, 'Early Views of the Royal Hospital Kilmainham', *Irish Arts Review Yearbook 1988–89* (1988), pp.78–88.

14 Nineteenth-century paintings (see n.13) appear to indicate that the RHK spire was originally clad in lead. The present copper cladding dates from the 1960s.

15 Steven Brindle, *Architecture in Britain and Ireland 1530–1830* (New Haven and London: Yale University Press, 2023), pp.109–13.

16 Raymond Gillespie, 'The Religion of the first Duke of Ormond', in Toby Barnard and Jane Fenlon (eds), *The Dukes of Ormonde, 1610–1745* (Woodbridge and New York: Boydell and Brewer, 2000), pp.101–13.

17 The Spanish Netherlands comprised the territory now occupied by Belgium and parts of northern France.

18 James Stevens Curl and Susan Wilson, *The Oxford Dictionary of Architecture* (3rd edn, Oxford: Oxford University Press, 2015), p.410. The second architect cited as being of major importance was Lieven de Key (1560–1627).

19 See Konrad Ottenheym and Krista De Jonge (eds), *The Low Countries at the Crossroads: Netherlandish architecture as an export product in early modern Europe (1480–1680)*, (Turnhout: Brepolis, 2013).

20 Wouter Kuyper, *Dutch Classicist Architecture: a survey of Dutch architecture, gardens and Anglo-Dutch architectural relations from 1625 to 1700* (Delft: Delft University Press, 1980), p.33.

21 Michele Furnari, *Formal Design in Renaissance Architecture* (New York: Rizzoli International Publications, 1995), pp.149–50. The earliest biforate windows traced by the present writer are in the buildings erected from 1459 by Pope Pius II in the Tuscan town of Pienza.

22 Hanneke Ronnes and Arnold Witte, 'The Dutch Renaissance in a Straightjacket: Recent Research on Netherlandish Art and Architecture in the Netherlands', *Explorations in Renaissance Culture*, vol.41, no.1 (March 2015), p.108.

23 Ian Campbell, 'The Scottish Renaissance Revival Revisited (Again)', in Ottenheym (ed.), (2021), see n.11. Biforate windows are curiously used in a fanciful image of 1587 by Raphael Holinshed illustrating the long-demolished St Mary's Abbey in Dublin. See his *Chronicles of England, Scotland and Ireland.*

24 Mark Girouard, *Robert Smythson and the Elizabethan Country House* (New Haven and London: Yale University Press, 1983), pp.88–90.

25 Jane Fenlon, 'The Decorative Plasterwork at Ormond Castle: A unique survival', *Architectural History*, vol.41 (1998), pp.70, 74–76. The 10th Earl imported from Sir Thomas Gresham's agent in Antwerp, Richard Clough.

26 Ibid. See also Jane Fenlon, 'Kilkenny Merchants in the Sixteenth and Early Seventeenth Century: their houses and their wealth', in Jane Fenlon and Sarah Maguire (eds), *Magnates and Merchants in Early Modern Kilkenny* (Dublin: Four Courts Press, 2023), pp.120–22; Hanneke Ronnes, 'Continental Traces at Carrick-on-Suir and contemporary Irish Castles: a preliminary study of date-and-initial stones', in Thomas Herron and Michael Potterton (eds), *Ireland in the Renaissance c.1540–1660* (Dublin: Four Courts Press, 2007), pp.255–73.

27 Among the few English churches to have biforate windows inserted in the seventeenth century was the chapel of St Mary in Arden, at Great Bowden in Leicestershire (1692–94), by Henry Dormer; it was unroofed in the 1950s. The most prominent late example in Munster was Christ Church, Fermoy, co. Cork (1805–06), by Abraham Hargrave.

28 Illustrated in several plates in Christine Stevenson's *The City and the King: architecture and politics in Restoration London* (New Haven and London: Yale University Press, 2013).

29 Rolf Loeber, *Irish Houses and Castles 1400–1740* (Dublin: Four Courts Press, 2019), p.215. This volume, drawn from Loeber's multitudinous writings on the subject from 1970 onwards, was progressed by him before his untimely death in 2017 and completed by his editors Kevin Whelan and Matthew Stout. The dates of Loeber's many discoveries are not always clear, so a reference cited in this essay may be to an insight gained by him at an unknown point in his long career.

30 Ibid., p.240.

31 Ibid.

32 Dr Nessa Roche has advised the author that, in the specifications for the seventeenth-century mansion at Blessington, co. Wicklow (probably designed by Charles Lucas; demolished), this type of surround was described as a Boswell. See Brian de Breffny, 'The Building of the Mansion at Blessington, 1672', *Irish Arts Review Yearbook 1991–92* (1991), pp.65–72. The RHK's rows of rectangular windows were also originally framed by panels of rubbed brickwork, later plastered over.

33 The survey drawings (of which there are photographs and photocopies in the Irish Architectural Archive) were made by James Dwyer, a local architect working for Richard Morrison on renovations and a new chancel.

34 Rolf Loeber, *A Biographical Dictionary of Architects in Ireland 1600–1720* (London: John Murray, 1981), p.94.

35 It is possible that the use of double-height window embrasures in the north front of the Master's lodgings of the RHK, where there were two floors behind, came from a similar idea of Hugh May's in his reconstruction of the south range of the Upper Ward at Windsor. At the latter, the spandrels between each floor were faced in stone, while in the RHK they were concealed behind the glazing, the present windows being eighteenth-century-sash replacements. This would have allowed the arrangement of tall windows on this elevation to appear uniform. McParland established that this was a late change, in or after 1682, to provide more accommodation for the Master, the original plan being to have a double-height kitchen at this location. See McParland (2001), p.63.

36 The alteration was the insertion of a cantilevered wooden balcony under the window, probably by Thomas Burgh, in the early eighteenth century; it was taken down after 1922. A nineteenth-century Lawrence photograph, taken from a high level, shows the consoles preserved behind the balcony.

37 The church proper was built by Wren in 1680–84, with the spire probably added by Nicholas Hawksmoor, whose initial drawing had volutes rather than brackets. The spire, altered in the nineteenth century, was destroyed in the Blitz and rebuilt along the original lines by Seely and Paget in 1966; see Simon Bradley and Nikolaus Pevsner, *London 1: The City of London,* The Buildings of England series (London: Penguin Books, 1997), pp.336–37.

38 Kuyper, p.53 *et passim*.

39 The author kindly acknowledges the recommendation to examine certain features of this church by one of the anonymous peer reviewers of a draft of this paper.

40 Maurice Craig, *Dublin 1660–1860: a social and architectural history* (London, Cresset Press: 1952; 2nd edn Dublin: Allen Figgis, 1969), p.61.

41 National Archives of Ireland, Dublin, Minute books of the governors of the Royal Hospital, RHK 1/1/1, f.172.

42 This is not unlike the completed upper stage of the tower of Christopher Wren's Royal Hospital Chelsea, a building that postdates the RHK, but given Wren's partiality to Netherlandish towers and spires this might not be unexpected.

43 William de Keyser had been involved with the rebuilding of the fifteenth-century Nieuwe Kerk in Amsterdam after its destruction by fire in 1645 to which it was proposed to add a new tower, to be the tallest in the city. The initial design, by Jan Adriaensz Leeghwater, for a tower of more than 103m, was followed by one by de Keyser which was to be 126m tall. He was appointed municipal stone mason in December 1647 to advance it, although the final designs, from 1648 or later, are attributable to Jacob van Campen. While the authorities had agreed to rebuild the church in the Gothic style, van Campen offered alternative Gothic and classical towers, the models for which survive. This may have been because the new Town Hall next door, begun in early 1648, was classical. Both designs, as at the RHK, have octagonal upper stages. Due to the outbreak of war with Britain in the summer of 1652, funds were withdrawn with only the piling and the first 12m of masonry completed. See Gabri van Tussenbroek, 'The Foundations of the Nieuwe Kerk Tower in Amsterdam (1645–52)', in Ine Wouters et al. (eds), *Building Knowledge, Constructing Histories, volume 2* (London: CRC Press, 2018), chapter 79.

44 W.G. Strickland, 'The Royal Hospital at Kilmainham, and its Architect,' *Journal of the Royal Society of Antiquaries of Ireland*, 6th series, vol.13, no.1 (30 June 1923), pp.101–04. Among the publications that had perpetuated the myth of Wren authorship was the *Dublin Penny Journal*, vol.2, no.89 (15 March 1834), p.1. The author of the piece was not a fan of the spire, which they described as 'being of no great height or beauty'.

45 Craig (1952), p.67.

46 Anthony Geraghty, *The Architectural Drawings of Sir Christopher Wren at All Souls College, Oxford: a complete catalogue* (London: Lund Humphries, 2007), p.87.

47 Ibid.

48 The Mansart connection to the doorcases was noted in the journal of the The Wren Society in 1942 (vol.19, p.149), but the carriage entrance of the Hôtel de Conty (built 1648–52, demolished 1768) was not identified as the actual source until the 1950s, by the writer Viktor Fürst. See Nikolaus Pevsner, *London, Volume 1: The Cities of London and Westminster* (rev. by Bridget Cherry), The Buildings of England series (Harmondsworth: Penguin Books, 1973), p.170. This influence of the Hôtel de Conty continued with Wren's pupils, as evidenced in Hawksmoor's St Mary Woolnoth (1716–27) which is heavily rusticated like the Parisian prototype.

49 Geraghty, p.88.

50 John Olley, 'Sustaining the narrative at Kilmainham', *Irish Arts Review Yearbook 1991–92* (1991), pp.65–72.

51 For an account of the Royal Exchange, see Marjorie Rubright, 'An Urban Palimpsest: Migrancy, Architecture, and the Making of an Anglo-Dutch Royal Exchange', *Dutch Crossing*, vol.33, no.1 (2009), pp.23–43.

52 Mark Girouard, *A Biographical Dictionary of English Architecture 1540–1640* (London: Paul Mellon Centre for Studies in British Art, 2021), p.284.

53 John Fitzhugh Millar, 'Hendrik van Paesschen, architect of the Northern European Renaissance' (unpublished MA dissertation, William and Mary College, Virginia, 1981). Millar includes many arcaded buildings, not just ones with central courtyards, as being possibly influenced by the Royal Exchange (or Gresham's Exchange as it was initially known). Nikolaus Pevsner in his study of building types regarded Antwerp (1531) by Domien (otherwise Dominicus) de Waghemakere as the prototype, with London and Amsterdam copying it, noting also that Jermyn's replacement for the former, begun in 1667, had the same layout. However, he also mentions, in an endnote, that the exchange at Seville (begun in 1582 after a plan by Juan de Herrera but not completed until 1646) used 'the same plan type'. See Pevsner, *A History of Building Types* (London: Thames & Hudson, 1976), pp.195–99, 318. As befits the climate, Seville has a smaller courtyard. Unlike the

two London exchanges, Antwerp and Amsterdam, all destroyed by fire, it survives. However, it had a short life, about seventy-five years, as an exchange and has housed the General Archives of the Indies since the 1780s.

54 Fenlon (2023), p.122.

55 Loeber (1981), p.89.

56 Loeber (1981), pp.88–97. At his death in 1717 he reputedly left an estate of over £50,000.

57 Ibid., p.71.

58 Historical Manuscripts Commission (HMC), *Calendar of the manuscripts of the Marquess of Ormonde*, new series, 8 vols (London: HMSO, 1902–20), VI (1911), pp.282–83. May probably also designed the water house for the castle, built around this time; see Loeber (1981), p.71.

59 Giles Worsley, *Classical Architecture in Britain: the Heroic Age* (New Haven and London: Yale University Press, 1995), pp.30–33; Paul Drury and others, 'Visualising Hugh May's Eltham Lodge', *The Antiquaries Journal*, vol.99 (Sept. 2019), pp.297–345.

60 Margaret Whinney, *Wren* (London: Thames & Hudson, 1971), p.18.

61 See H.J. Louw, 'Anglo-Netherlandish Architectural Interchange *c.*1600–*c.*1660', *Architectural History*, vol.24 (1981), pp.1–23 and pp.125–44; and H.J. Louw, 'Dutch Influence on British Architecture in the Late-Stuart Period, *c.*1660–*c.*1714', *Dutch Crossing*, vol.33, no.2 (2009), pp.83–120.

62 Maurice Craig, 'New Light on Jigginstown', *Journal of the Co. Kildare Archaeological Society*, vol.15, no.1 (1971), pp.50–56. The English bookseller and traveller John Dunton, who visited Jigginstown in 1698, also thought the brickwork was Dutch.

63 Loeber (1981), p.13. Allen is described as a bricklayer whose family had moved from England to Holland in the late seventeenth century. A bricklayer of his name was admitted to the freedom of the City of Dublin in 1630.

64 The author would like to thank Dr Sara Pavía, TCD, for this information; see Ana Dolan, 'Case Study: Jigginstown House 1635–37, Naas, County Kildare', in Gerard Lynch (ed.), *The History of Gauged Brickwork: conservation, repair and modern application* (Oxford and Burlington MA: Butterworth-Heinemann, 2007), pp.99–110. See also Susan Roundtree, *Brickmaking in Ireland: a gazetteer* (Dublin: Wordwell, 2023), p.153, which notes that while most of the bricks were made on the site, ornate examples used in some dressings could have been imported from Holland. Lynch (p.79) refers to the possible Flemish origins of yellow bricks in the plinth. The likelihood that the Jigginstown bricks were mostly local rather than Dutch was apparently first put forward by the antiquary Arthur Vicars in the 1890s; see *Journal of the Co. Kildare Archaeological Society*, vol.1 (1891–95), pp.19–24.

65 Tom Williamson, *Inigo's Stones: Inigo Jones, royal marbles and Imperial power* (Kibworth Beauchamp: Matador, 2012), p.262. Like Wentworth, the 14th Earl of Arundel had an interest in marble as a building material. He also collected marble *objects d'art*. In 1617, Arundel's friend Richard Boyle, 1st Earl of Cork, planned to export Cork red marble from his quarry on Little Island to London for Inigo Jones's Queen's House at Greenwich. This seems to have come to nought. Asked to investigate different Irish marbles for the king in 1638, Wentworth mentioned Cork red, but said it did not maintain its colour when 'set in Work' (Williamson, p.268). Given their poisonous relationship, it seems unlikely Boyle was consulted on the matter. There is a Belgian connection here in that Cork red marble (actually a lime conglomerate) was called 'red Ranse', presumably after Rance in Flanders where a similar stone is found. See Williamson, pp.268, 270, and Colin Rynne 'Colonial Entrepreneur and Urban Developer: the economic and industrial infrastructure of Boyle's Munster estates', in David Edwards and Colin Rynne (eds), *The Colonial World of Richard Boyle, First Earl of Cork* (Dublin: Four Courts Press, 2018), pp.107–08. The Little Island marble quarry was acquired by the Boyles in 1610 from the Matthew family of Cork who had operated it for decades (information from Dr Rynne, UCC, in conversation with the writer).

66 Rolf Loeber, 'Dutch Billies', in Andrew Carpenter (ed.), *Art and Architecture of Ireland*, 5 vols (Dublin, New Haven and London: RIA and Yale University Press, 2014), IV: Rolf Loeber et al. (eds), *Architecture 1600–2000*, pp.421–22.

67 Ormond's credibility as military commander had been suffering since his loss of the Battle of Rathmines in August 1649. By the spring of 1650, the Confederate forces, of which he had joint

command with his Royalist troops, had effectively lost confidence in him.

68 In some documents her name is spelt Amelia and the family name as Beverwaert. In a cynical age, this was a love match, though the duchess had her doubts; she was unhappy with the marriage settlement which obliged her to pay an annuity of £1,200. Her husband, on the other hand, obtained a dowry of £10,000 which was supposed to be distributed around the immediate family but was probably used to pay his debts. His years in exile had left him in straitened circumstances, and he reputedly saw the marriage as benefitting him politically.

69 Naomi McAreavey (ed.), *Elizabeth Butler, The Letters of the First Duchess of Ormonde*, Renaissance English Text Society, vol.40 (New York and Toronto: Iter Press, 2022).

70 Some Dutch sources give the date as early June, possibly explained by the different calendar systems then in use in European countries.

71 The rank of Lord High Steward was nominally the first of the great offices of state in England, ranking above that of Lord Chancellor. Ormond was to hold it up until his demise in 1688.

72 Ormond's Dutch links were strengthened after his son-in-law, Prince Louis, was made ambassador to the new court in London (1660–62). However, Britain's relationship with the Dutch Republic was an unstable one, and Ossory found himself as a naval officer participating in the wars between the former allies in 1665–67 and 1672–74. In the latter conflict, Charles II was allied with the French but made peace in the spring of 1674. During the following three years Ossory was among those tasked with improving relations between Britain and Prince William of Orange. This led to William's marriage to his cousin, Charles's niece Mary, in November 1677.

73 W.L. Spiers (ed.), 'The Note-Book and Account Book of Nicholas Stone', *Walpole Society*, vol.7 (1918–19), pp.3, 4, 38. Because of Walter Butler's Catholicism, King James I broke up the Ormond estates. When he contested the decision, he was imprisoned in London from 1619 until James's death in 1625. In 1629 he found a means to reunite the estates by obtaining the agreement of Charles I to the marriage of his grandson James, the future Duke of Ormond, who had been raised a Protestant, to Black Tom's granddaughter, Lady Elizabeth Preston.

74 Paul Cockerham, 'Renaissance Ideals in Irish Funerary Monuments', in Herron and Potterton (eds), pp.218–20. See also Cockerham, '"My body to be buried in my owne monument": the social and religious context of co. Kilkenny funeral monuments, 1600–1700', *Proceedings of the Royal Irish Academy*, vol.109C (2009), pp.239–365; Adam White, 'A Biographical Dictionary of London Tomb Sculptors, *c.*1560–*c.*1660', *Walpole Society*, vol.61 (1999), pp.119, 129.

75 Jane Fenlon, review of Herron and Potterton (eds), *Ireland in the Renaissance, c.1540–1660* in *Eolas: The Journal of the American Society of Irish Medieval Studies*, vol.3 (2009), pp.120–23.

76 Loeber (1981), pp.45–46; Howard Colvin, *A Biographical Dictionary of British Architects 1600–1840* (4th edn, New Haven and London: Yale University Press, 2008), p.990; Ruth Devine, 'William de Keyser (c.1603–p.1685)', *Dictionary of Irish Biography* <https://doi.org/10.3318/dib.002463.v1>. See also A.W. Weissman, 'De Schoonzoon van Hendrik de Keyser', *Oud Holland*, vol.38 (1920), pp.155–64.

77 This job caused de Keyser much difficulty and he undoubtedly lost money on the contract, completed in 1685. The Portland stone statues survive in the crypt of Christ Church. De Keyser did not provide the stone, which was obtained from a Dublin supplier Nicholas Ward.

78 Loeber (1981), p.46. Hendrick Willemsz de Keyser had previously worked in England.

79 Williamson, *Inigo's Stones*, p.273.

80 Girouard (2021), p.282.

81 Gabri van Tussenbroek, *The Architectural Network of the Van Neurenberg Family in the Low Countries (1480–1640)* (Turnhout: Brepols, 2007), p.169 *et passim*.

82 HMC, *Ormonde*, III (1904), p.357.

83 J.P. Prendergast and James Graves, 'A Journey to Kilkenny in the Year 1709. From the MS. Notes of Dr Thomas Molyneux', *Journal of the Kilkenny and South-East of Ireland Archaeological Society*, vol.3, no.2 (1861), p.279. The pre-railway transportation of Kilkenny limestone has been studied by Dr Tony Hand; see his paper; '"Doing Everything of Marble wch can be Done with it": some descriptive accounts of the Kilkenny Marble Works', *Irish Architectural and Decorative Studies*, vol.11 (2008), pp.74–99, and his dissertation 'The Kilkenny Marble Works: a family business enterprise' (unpublished doctoral thesis, Trinity College Dublin, 2011).

84 Loeber (1981), p.78.

85 HMC, *Ormonde*, IV (1906), p.170. Isabella, Lady Arlington, was the sister of Ormond's daughter-in-law Emilia. A little earlier, Ormond's predecessor as Lord Lieutenant, the Earl of Essex, shipped a number of Irish marble chimneypieces to Hertfordshire for use in Cassiobury, the new country house designed for him by Hugh May (*c*.1677–80, dem. 1922). They were noted by John Evelyn in a diary entry recording his visit on 18 April 1680; he thought them 'not much inferior to Italian'. See William Bray (ed.), *The Diary of John Evelyn*, 2 vols (Washington and London: M. Walter Dunne, 1901), II, p.142.

86 Colvin (2008), p.990.

87 Ibid.

88 Katharine Gibson, 'Caius Gabriel Cibber', *Oxford Dictionary of National Biography*, vol.11 (Oxford: Oxford University Press, 2004), p.699.

89 He may have been joined in 1659 by his son Hendrick III, who moved to England in that year; see Louw (2009), p.90.

90 William de Keyser's best-known building in Amsterdam, 211 Waterlooplein (today the Academy of Architecture), was completed in 1654. It shares some features with the RHK, including a hipped roof and rubbed brick arches over some windows. Those at the hospital were later plastered over.

91 Louw (2009), p.90.

92 Bradley and Pevsner (1997), p.254. Ottenheym (2013), pp.123–24, suggests the alternative possibility that the St Olave's gate could have come from the cemetery of the Westerkerk in Amsterdam.

93 H.M. Colvin (ed.), *The History of the King's Works*, 6 vols (London: HMSO, 1963–82), *V: 1660–1782* (1976), p.140.

94 While the online catalogue (text by Anthony Geraghty) of the All Souls College, Oxford, collection, once owned by Christopher Wren, refers to these drawings, numbered 179–83, as a 'Preliminary design by John Webb […] *c*.1661–63' and mentions de Keyser, it ascribes their authorship to 'an unidentified draughtsman' (Anthony Geraghty, *The Architectural Drawings at All Souls College, Oxford: Wren and Hawksmoor* <https://library.asc.ox.ac.uk/wren/greenwich_palace.html> [acc. 29 July 2024]). Colvin took the view in 1976 that as Webb was not formally assigned to the project until 1663, he could not have prepared the 1661 scheme. However, this disregards the pre-existing dispute between Webb (Inigo Jones's pupil and assistant) and Sir John Denham over Webb's claims that he, rather than Denham, a Dublin-born poet-turned-placeman, should have been appointed Surveyor General of the King's Works. Webb did visit the site in 1661 and de Keyser was probably asked to copy the plans while the row was raging. Colvin conceded in the last edition of his biographical dictionary that the unsigned drawings at All Souls College are probably de Keyser's tracings (Colvin, 2008, p.308). The pavilions in these resemble those of Webb's later scheme, one wing of which was constructed to shell-state and subsequently completed as a hospital rather than a palace. Simon Thurley is also of the view that Webb designed a scheme in 1661; see his essay 'A Country Seat Fit for A King: Charles II, Greenwich and Winchester', in Eveline Cruickshanks (ed.), *The Stuart Courts* (Stroud: Sutton Publishing, 2000), p.236. He illustrated a plan from the RIBA Drawings Collection [fig. 1, p.216) which appears to be a reworking of the one de Keyser traced, with *inter alia* additional wings to the rear.

95 Colvin et al. (1976), pp.255, 266.

96 John Bold, *John Webb: Architectural Theory and Practice in the Seventeenth Century* (Oxford: Clarendon Press, 1989), p.107. Westley's argument was in part founded on the fact that Webb had designed a scheme for rebuilding Whitehall for Charles I in 1647, and wished to resurrect it. Having remained in England during the Commonwealth, he was entrusted with preparing the palace for reuse in 1660. In 1664, Webb was made Denham's deputy, but he continued to lobby for the surveyorship right up to Denham's death in 1669. However, he lost out to the rising star Christopher Wren. Wren erected some new buildings at Whitehall between 1685 and 1693, but most of the complex was destroyed by fire in 1698. His plans for a replacement never got off the drawing board; see Colvin (2008), p.1158.

97 Loeber (1981), p.113. The Dublin Castle works were allowed to remain with the Irish surveyor general, John Paine, who completed them in 1667.

98 Loeber noted that Westley and William Dodson, his successor as Ormond's architect at Phoenix

Lodge, Dublin, each submitted proposals for the Lane house, which Loeber considered might have been in Dublin but did not research further, finally concluding that it was on his estate at Rathcline, co. Longford; see Loeber (1981), pp.51, 113. That the house was the one on Capel Street is verifiable from the records of Dublin Corporation, examined by the present writer in the 1990s in conjunction with an inspection of its site, then being redeveloped. A document shows that the house was owned in the 1680s by Lane's widow, Frances, Lady Lanesborough. It was subsequently sold to William Conolly, speaker of the Irish House of Commons, whose successors occupied it up to the 1760s. It was demolished around 1770 by the developer Ralph Ward, who built six terraced houses on the site. Its plan, recorded on Rocque's map and the imprint of its quoins, seen by the author *c.*1995, suggest that it resembled Schomberg House on Pall Mall, London (1698), where the partly reconstructed façade survives.

99 Loeber (1981), p.51, describes how Dodson (a former London contractor) surveyed the site in 1664 and was preparing stonework two years later, only for Ormond's 'worsening finances' to halt the project. The site was walled but not developed, being ultimately used in the early 1700s to build the Royal Barracks.

100 It is generally believed that the corporation's grant of the site in Oxmantown to Ormond was intended to draw wealthy individuals into the area. Various modern accounts of the building of Aungier Street, begun in 1661 by Ormond's agent Francis Aungier (*c.*1632–1700), later Earl of Longford, have suggested that he or one of its residents, Sir Robert Reading (*c.*1640–1689), offered a house on the street to Ormond, possibly for the same motives, after Ormond's return in 1677. This is not correct. Reading did offer him the use of a Dublin house but not on Aungier Street and not in the 1670s. Reading had built no.21 Aungier Street in the 1660s and eventually sold it to Viscount Rosse. He embarked, in the early 1680s, on the construction of a much bigger house at the corner of York Street and St Stephen's Green. This was the house he offered for Ormond's residency. Reading, who was a friend of Ormond's, was laying out York Street on an undeveloped part of the Whitefriars estate after Aungier had run out of credit. The offer was made after the Dublin Castle fire on 7 April 1684 which destroyed much of the accommodation while his son Lord Arran was acting as Lord Deputy. While Robinson was immediately tasked with designing new State Apartments, Ormond needed lodgings for his winter visit to Dublin. The relevant letter from him, dated 17 June 1684, indicates that he was considering three options for his planned return: Reading's offer; a proposal to lease two or three adjoining houses at an unspecified location; or to reside in the Master's lodgings and some annexed rooms of the RHK for a 'short time'. He felt disinclined to accept Reading's proposal because he thought the house (seen on a previous visit to Dublin) probably still unfinished and 'standing almost alone'. See HMC, *Ormonde*, VII (1912), pp.249–50. A further offer emerged, to occupy temporarily Aungier's own house on the Whitefriars site, and this was duly fitted up. The U-shaped Reading mansion, entered from York Street, was subdivided into three houses after 1802.

101 Simon Thurley, *The Whitehall Palace Plan of 1670* (London: London Topographical Society, 1998), pp.49–50. It can be seen in Leonard Knyff's bird's-eye view of Whitehall Palace, *c.*1695. Ormond probably only lived in this house for a few years, though he may have retained it as an office. He briefly occupied Clarendon House in Piccadilly after the downfall and exile of its builder, his friend the Lord Chancellor, in 1667. His final London home, acquired in 1682 from the Earl of St Albans, was Ormond House on St James's Square. Clarendon House was sold after its owner's death in 1674 to the 2nd Duke of Albemarle, son of General Monck. He resold it to speculators who dismantled it in 1683.

102 Simon Thurley, *The Lost Palace of Whitehall*, exhibition catalogue (London: RIBA, Historic Royal Palaces, 1998), pp.21–22. Two drawings survive: Thurley's plate 22 is of the main elevation (known as Z1), now in Chatsworth; the other, a detail (Z2), is in Worcester College, Oxford. See also Bold (1989), p.121. Drawing Z1 was first discussed by Margaret Whinney in an article on John Webb's drawings for Whitehall Palace published in 1946 (*Walpole Society*, vol.31 (1942–43), pp.45–107). She thought the design 'bold and free' but closer to that of 'mason architects' (which is what William de Keyser was) rather than anything that might have been produced by Inigo Jones or his immediate circle. The new block may have been intended to accommodate Henrietta Maria, Charles II's mother, but did not proceed, a wing being added instead, probably by Webb, to Somerset House

to house both her and the queen. Charles married Catherine of Braganza in May 1662.

103 Loeber (1981), p.46.

104 Daniel Beaumont, 'James Tabary (fl. 1650–87)', *Dictionary of Irish Biography* <https://doi.org/10.3318/dib.008441.v1>.

105 Robin Usher, 'The Sculptural Decoration of the Royal Hospital, Kilmainham: a Franco-Roman triumph in Restoration Ireland', *Irish Architectural and Decorative Studies*, vol.24 (2021), pp.10–35.

106 In 1673, Bernard de Gomme had proposed to face the gatehouse of his Citadel at Ringsend with Portland stone, but this project did not proceed. This gatehouse may be assumed from the specifications to be similar to his surviving Mannerist one at the Royal Citadel, Plymouth (1670), also faced with Portland stone. See J.T. Gilbert and R. Mulholland Gilbert (eds), *Calendar of Ancient Records of Dublin*, 19 vols (Dublin: Joseph Dollard, 1889–1944), V: *1671–1692* (1895), pp.566–73. Some accounts, originating in the eighteenth century, say that Hendrick de Keyser had an interest in the Portland quarry, but this is incorrect, though he attempted to procure stone from it. See Tom Williamson, 'Hendrick de Keyser, Nicholas Stone, Inigo Jones and the founding of the modern Portland Stone industry', *Proceedings of the Dorset Natural History and Archaeological Society*, vol.133 (2012), pp.33–36.

107 Historic England, Official List of Buildings: Chapel of St Peter Bishop Auckland <https://historicengland.org.uk/listing/the-list/listentry/1292120> [acc. 28 May 2024].

108 Colvin (2008), p.632.

109 Louw (2009), p.85, and others since.

110 'The Correspondence of John Cosin, D.D., Lord Bishop of Durham', *Publications of the Surtees Society*, vol.55 (1872), Part II, Appendix XIV, Agreements relating to the restorations [...] in the Castle of Durham and Auckland, pp.357, 362, 363. In 1862, a local newspaper reporting a visit by antiquaries recorded that 'Hendrick de Keyser, sculptor, [had] contracted for the carving' at the chapel, *Newcastle Daily Journal*, 19 Nov 1862.

111 Girouard (2021), p.282.

112 Koen Ottenheym, Paul Rosenberg and Niek Smit, *Architectura Moderna: moderne bouw-kunst in Amsterdam 1600–1625* (Amsterdam: Uitgeverij SUN, 2008), p.27.

113 Loeber (2019), p.198. It may be assumed that Loeber was referring to giant orders in stone; in the same book he refers (pp.229–30) to Eustace House on Dame Street, built in the early 1660s, as having 'giant pilasters' in brick. He also includes a reconstruction drawing which he made in 1974, based on a description of the house at the time of its demolition in 1782. He attributes the design to Dr John Westley. The client, Sir Maurice Eustace (*c.*1590–1665), an old friend of Ormond's and a cousin of Sir George Lane, was lord chancellor of Ireland and a lord justice.

114 Louw (2009), p.91.

115 The fact that Dr Thomas Molyneux described this gateway as unfinished in 1709 has led some authors to describe it as of that date, but Prendergast and Graves in 1861 (see n.83 above) were of the view it was a work of the 1st Duke, who died in 1688, and that the unfinished elements were the two northernmost capitals, of Caen stone. The gateway was remodelled by William Robertson in the 1820s, with the original capitals replaced and new swags added, all in Portland stone.

116 Sir John Soane's Museum, London, SM drawer 69/1/11, 'Presentation design for ceremonial entrance to St Margaret's Church, Westminster Palace'. This pre-Reformation church was assigned to the parish of the Palace of Westminster in 1614. The museum catalogue records the assessment that in view of designs for sculpture on the back (and presumably because Margaret is spelt in a continental way) that the drawing is by a Dutch architect/sculptor, possibly William de Keyser.

117 See John Montague, 'A Shopping Arcade in Eighteenth-century Dublin: John Rocque and the Essex Street "piazzas"', *Irish Architectural and Decorative Studies*, vol.10 (2007), pp.224–45; Colm Lennon and John Montague, *John Rocque's Dublin: a guide to the Georgian city* (2nd edn, Dublin: Royal Irish Academy, 2019), pp.22–23.

118 Robin Usher, *Protestant Dublin, 1660–1760: architecture and iconography* (Basingstoke: Palgrave Macmillan, 2012), p.46.

119 HMC, *Ormonde*, IV (1906), p.327. See also Gilbert and Gilbert (eds), *Calendar of Ancient Records of Dublin, vol. VI, 1692–1715/16* (1896), pp.582–98.

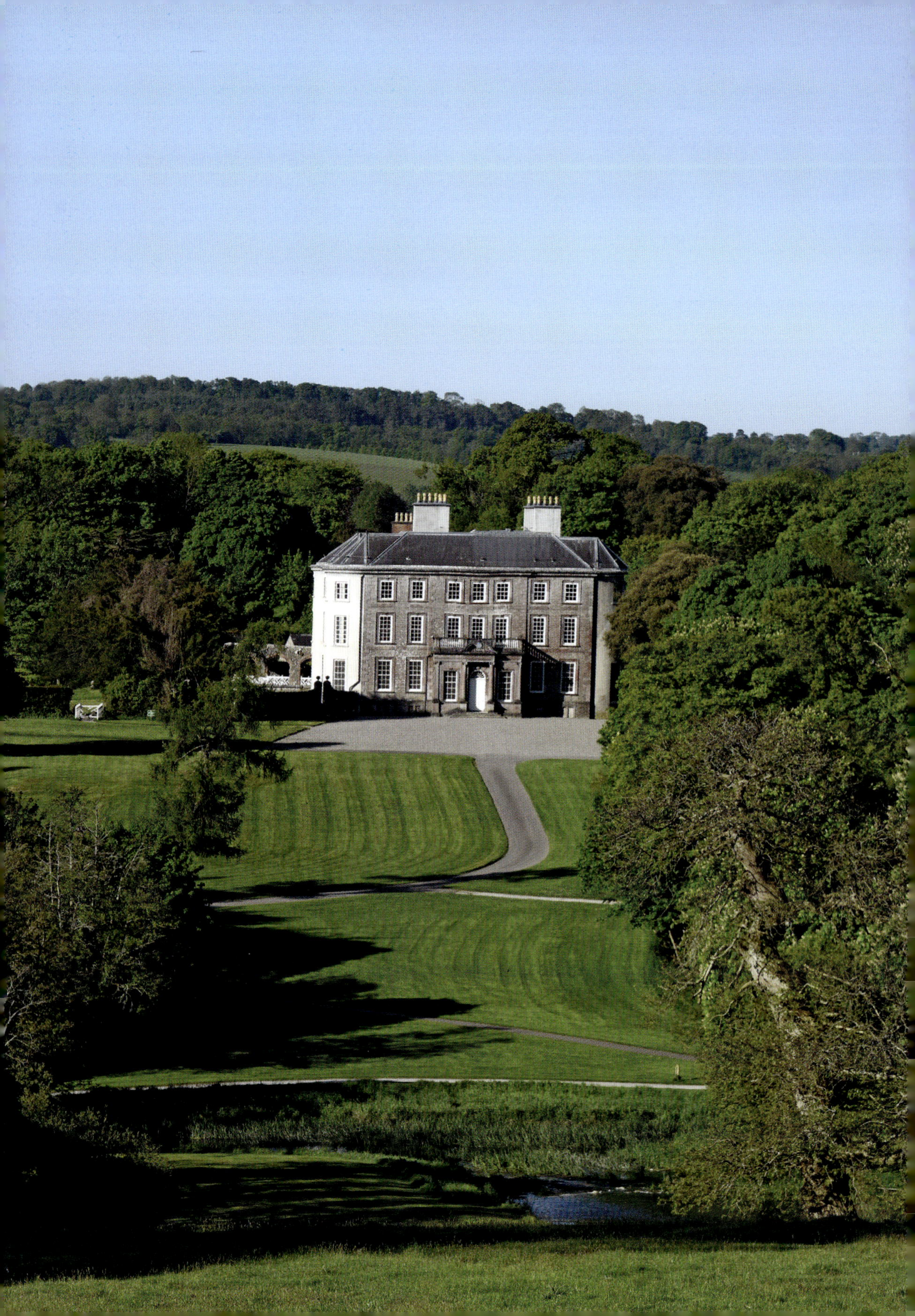

# of Doneraile Demesne,
# t 1

)EMESNE HAS BEEN IN THE STEWARDSHIP OF THE STATE SINCE 'as the longtime home of the St Leger family (Viscounts ) between 1630 and 1969 [fig. 1]. Knowledge of d from an absence of scholarship. This paper attempts situation and to place this important estate in the con- ished designed landscapes and gardens in Ireland and

the garden and demesne features at Doneraile has not explicable, perhaps, as there are no known architectural leed family correspondence on the subject. To overcome y sources, a multidisciplinary approach is taken to form f the demesne in the seventeenth and eighteenth centuries is paper will consider the demesne developments during centuries.

f the subject is limited. Vandra Costello makes reference features at Doneraile in a catalogue-like fashion, and 'ledges the quality of its eighteenth-century Brownian ınd E. Charles Nelson focus on the gifts of Irish lace to Kew Gardens, during the middle years of the nineteenth itemplates the history of the landscape at Doneraile but gn influences or architects.[2] This paper seeks to align the ›neraile with fashionable garden designs, particularly in h centuries. This is married to an understanding of the ay, their wider family and peer groups, and links to the Parallels are drawn with garden projects in Ireland,

per has relied upon fieldwork over an extended period preparation of a number of topographical, cultural and orts. Cartographic examination was focused closely upon

.ourt from the north park, showing River Awbeg and cascade,
eeline as backdrop to house

(illus © the author, unless otherwise stated)

**Seventeenth/Eighteenth Century Family Links**

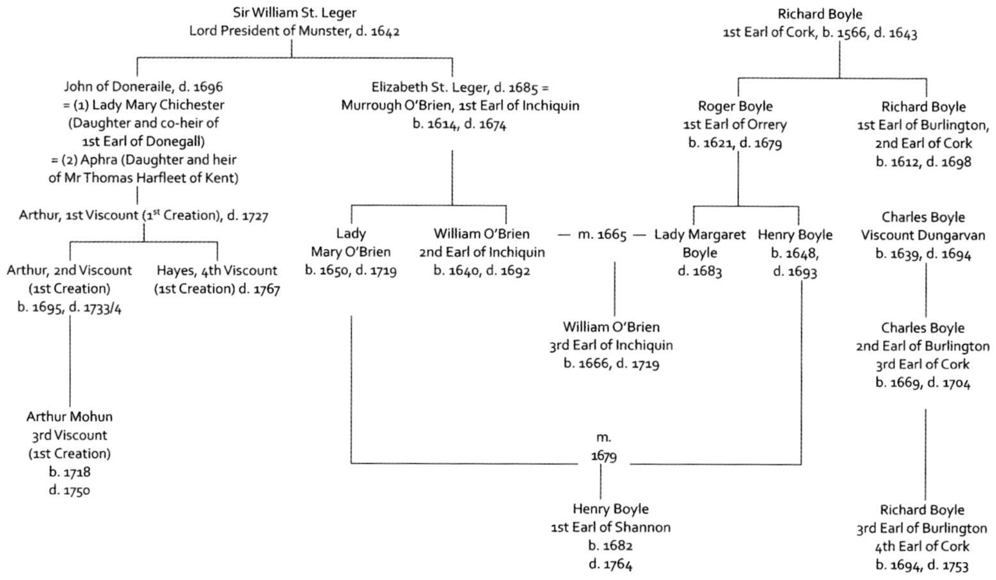


the Doneraile estate plan of 1728, and the nineteenth-century first-edition Ordnance Survey map of Doneraile demesne. Manuscript sources included the St Leger, Boyle and Orrery family papers, and the relevant Ormonde files in the Carte collection at the Bodleian Library.

The St Leger (Viscounts Doneraile), Boyle (Earls of Cork, Orrery and Burlington) and O'Brien (Earls of Inchiquin) families all had close associations with Doneraile [fig. 2]. In this, the marriages of Elizabeth St Leger to Murrough O'Brien (later 1st Earl of Inchiquin) in 1635; John St Leger to Lady Mary Chichester (daughter to 1st Earl of Donegall) in 1655; and of Lady Margaret Boyle (daughter to Roger Boyle, 1st Earl of Orrery) to William O'Brien (2nd Earl of Inchiquin) in 1665 are key. This kinship represented an important grouping of Old Irish and New Protestant families in seventeenth-century Plantation Munster. They and their successors were influential in the evolution of the demesne at Doneraile. The relevant incumbents at Doneraile and the associated circle of actors are considered here in turn. These include Sir William St Leger, Lord President of Munster, and his son John St Leger in the seventeenth century, and Hayes St Leger, 4th Viscount Doneraile (1st creation) in the eighteenth century.

---

fig. 2 | St Leger family tree (concise version) for the seventeenth and eighteenth centuries

fig. 3 | Sir William St Leger (c.1580–1642), attributed to William Dobson (1611–1646), oil on canvas. From *A Series of Historical Portraits selected from the National Portrait Exhibition of 1866*, no.734 (London: Arundel Society, 1866/67). The portrait was lent to the exhibition by William H. Blaauw.
(National Portrait Gallery, London: Heinz Archive & Library)

fig. 4 | Sir William St Leger's wife, believed to be his first wife Gertrude de Vries (m.1616), artist unknown, location unrecorded
(from Donough O'Brien, *History of the O'Briens* (London: B.T. Batsford, 1949))

## THE SEVENTEENTH CENTURY

### Sir William St Leger (d.1642)

Sir William St Leger, Lord President of Munster, took up residency at Doneraile in 1630 [figs 3, 4].[3] Richard Boyle, 1st Earl of Cork and a Lord Justice of Ireland, recorded on 24 April 1630: 'This day in my studie [...] I delivered to the L. president of Munster the ancient deed of Shynnan of donnarayle.'[4] St Leger constructed a church, a manor house adjacent to a Norman tower house built by William Synan in 1402 (the combined building known as Doneraile Castle), and, as considered here, the contiguous open garden terraces in the 1630s.[5] All was completed by 1637, as in that year Cork wrote, 'I sent John Jackson & Andrew Tucker to tak a model of the L. president's howse of donneraile to make like by ffor my son ffrances Boyle.' Murrough O'Brien (Lord Inchiquin) and Elizabeth St Leger married in 1635. In January 1638, Cork and his daughter Alice, Countess of Barrymore, were made godparents to William O'Brien (son to Murrough O'Brien and Elizabeth St Leger) at his christening in Doneraile.[6]

*Description of Carolean terrace*

A long, open, earthen-bank garden terrace orientated eastward from the site of Doneraile Castle on the north bank of the River Awbeg survives in the landscape today. The 1728 estate plan shows this terrace to have been some 1,000ft long by 250ft wide, with a central gravel pathway about 40ft wide aligned at its western end on the castle.[7] The terrace slopes gently towards the river, declining gradually from a height at its eastern

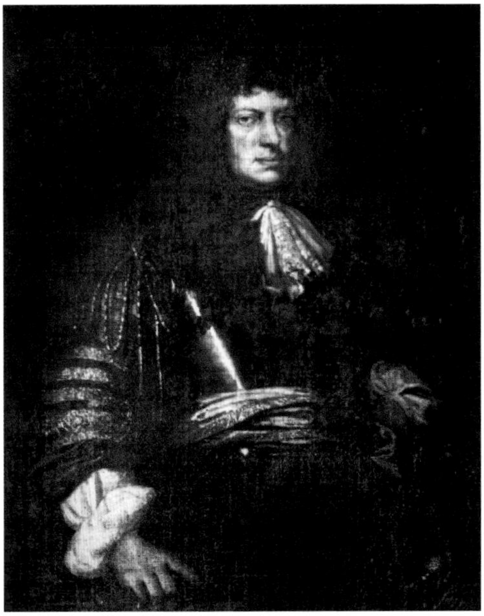

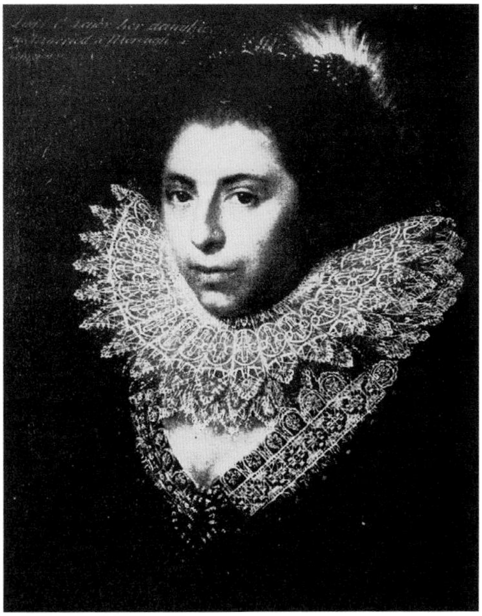

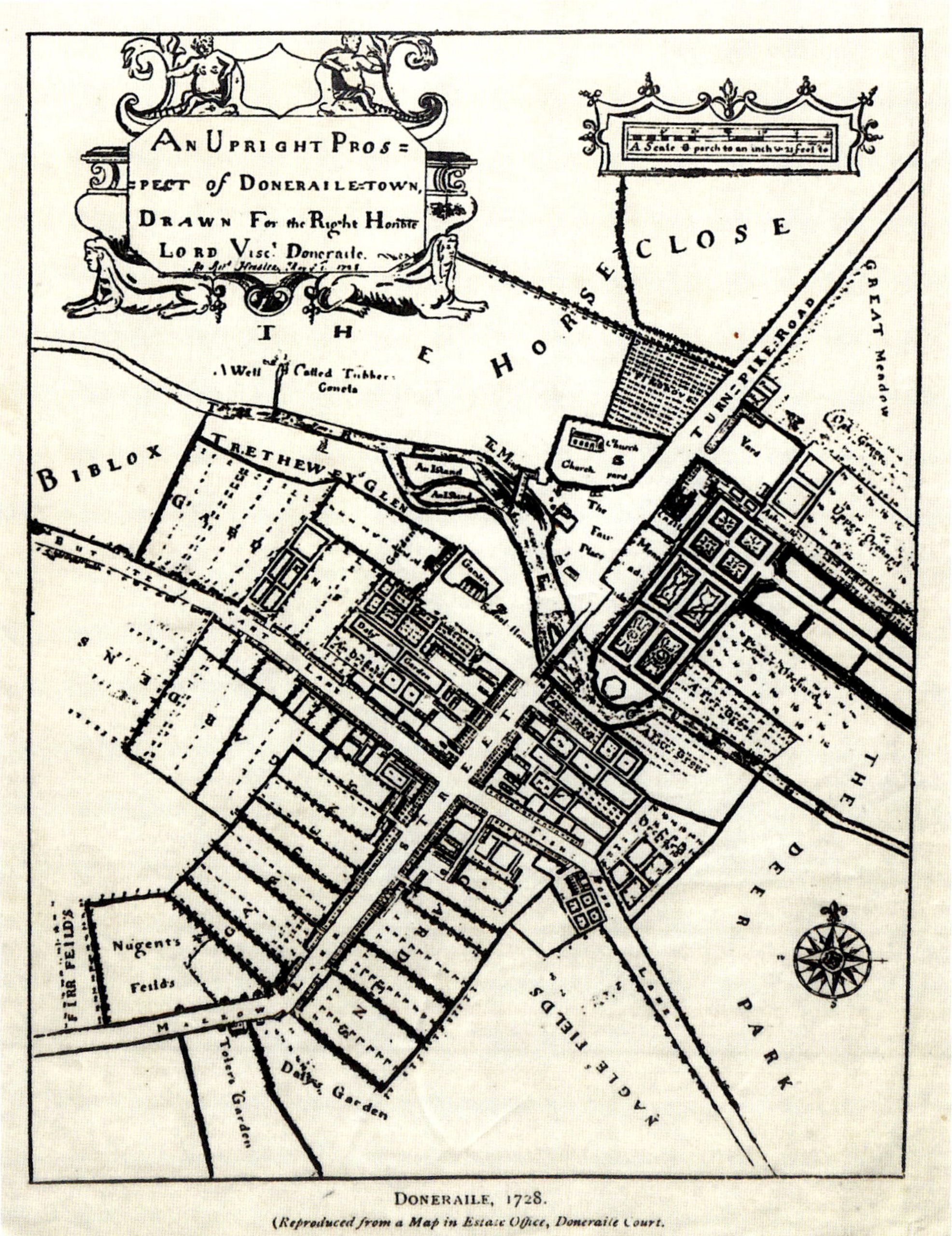


fig. 5 | 'An Upright Prospect of Doneraile town drawn for the Right Honourable Lord Viscount Doneraile', 1728. Reprinted in the *Journal of the Cork Historical & Archaeological Society*, vols 19–22 (1913–16), p.20.

opposite fig. 6 | Bridge and cascade features at Doneraile Demesne
clockwise from top left: seventeenth-century village bridge; eighteenth-century cascade and view of Carolean terrace in the north park; eighteenth-century hunting bridge; eighteenth-century avenue bridge

extremity to the castle [figs 5, 6]. The terrace is overprinted at its western extremity by later walled terrace gardens, and subsumed in its eastern part into the long northern vista of Doneraile Court. Its disposition on the ground, and placement on the 1728 estate map, point to this terrace as the first garden intervention in the demesne. There are no representations of this terrace on the first-edition Ordnance Survey six-inch-to-one-mile or subsequent maps.

*Design influences*

Notwithstanding the isolated and provincial nature of Doneraile in the mid-seventeenth century, St Leger had had direct access to courtly fashion by way of his patron, the 1st Duke of Buckingham, and the duke's gardener, John Tradescant the elder.[8] To illustrate the relationship, St Leger and Tradescant (both Buckingham confidantes and adepts at sea) were at Île de Ré off the coast of France on Buckingham's behalf in 1627.[9] Tradescant the elder, the celebrated seventeenth-century gardener and plant collector, was employed by the duke as head gardener and finder of exotics in the early 1620s. It was he who supervised the works in the duke's demesnes at Burley and New Hall.[10] Buckingham took a close interest in his properties and in park development. In a letter to James I, comparing New Hall to Burley, he wrote,

> 'I have found this morning another fine wood that must in with the rest, and two hundred acres of woodland, with broome closes [gorse enclosures] and

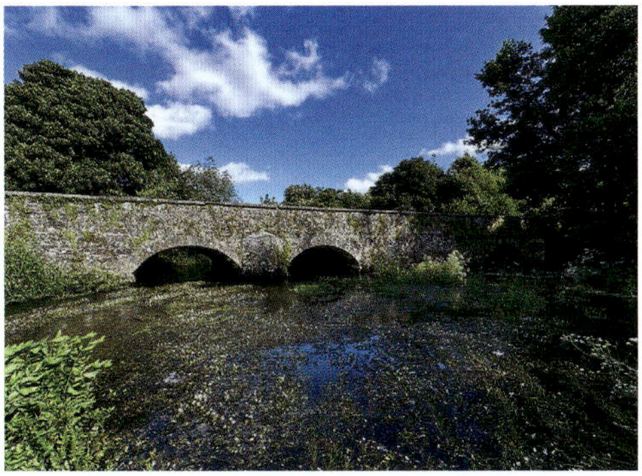

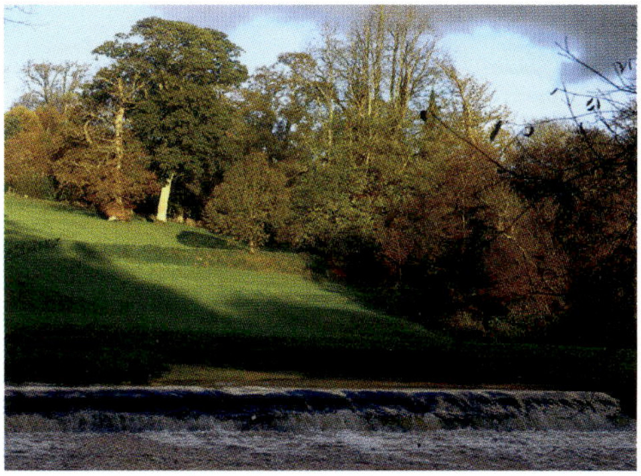

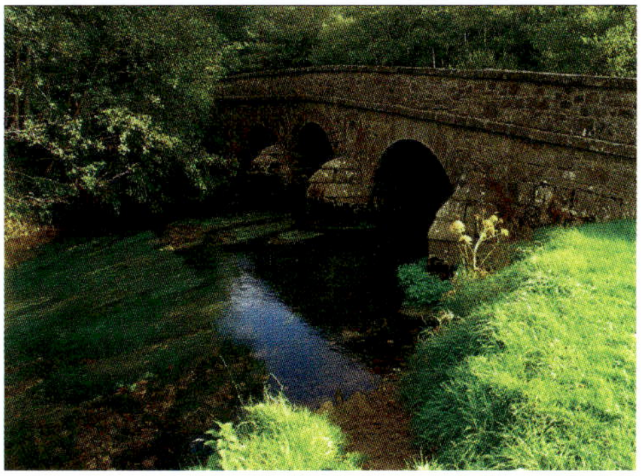

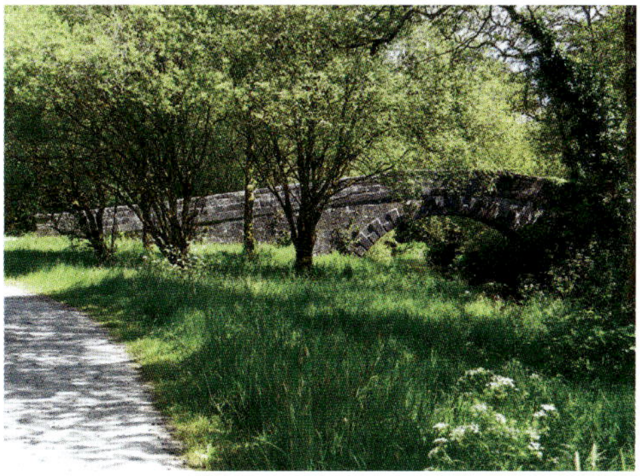

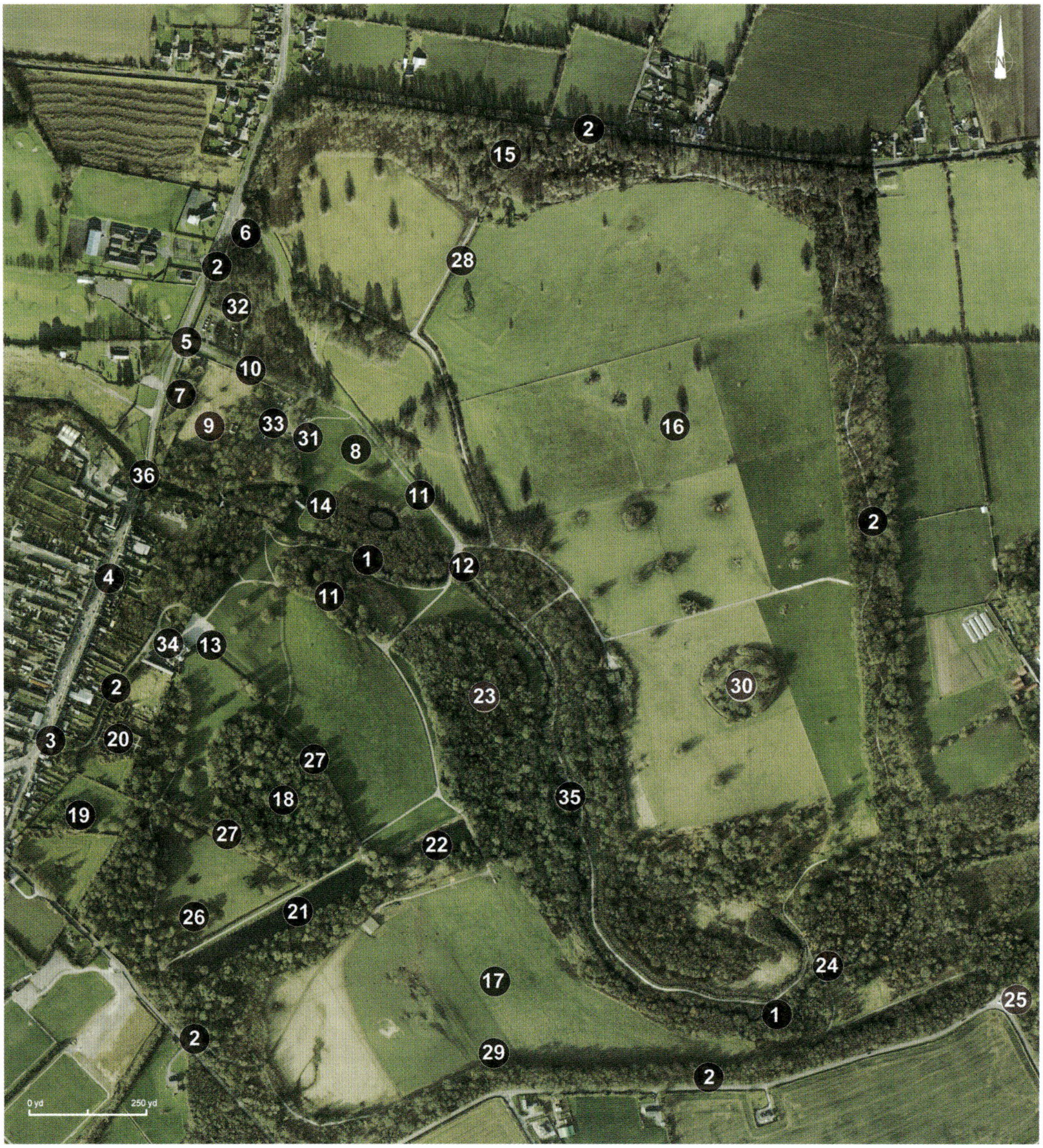


fig. 7 | Aerial view of residual demesne
(© OSI, licence CYAL50284317)

1. River Awbeg
2. Demesne wall
3. Lord's Gate entrance
4. Fishpond Lane entrance
5. Beech walk entrance
6. Triumphal arch entrance
7. Doneraile Castle (site)
8. Carolean terrace (remains)
9. Restoration garden
10. Beech walk
11. Avenue
12. Avenue bridge
13. Doneraile Court
14. Cascade
15. Colonel's plantation
16. North park
17. South park
18. Wilderness
19. Coronation walled gardens
20. American and parterre garden
21. Fish pond (upper)
22. Fish pond (lower)
23. Duck decoy (site)
24. Hunting bridge
25. Creagh Castle gate
26. Deer enclosure
27. Lime walk and ha-has
28. Great meadow ha-ha
29. Toll stone (old Fishpond Lane)
30. Ringfort
31. Car park
32. Overflow car park
33. Playground / toilets
34. Tearooms
35. Stag Island
36. Village bridge

plentiful springs running through them, so that I hope New Hall Park shall be nothing inferior to Burlie.'[11]

While there is no particular record of St Leger visiting Burley or New Hall, the garden interests of his patron and his patron's gardener are contextual. In the event, it is more likely that St Leger was influenced by the Munster Boyle and O'Brien families. The terrace at Doneraile bears favourable comparison with the coeval garden terrace construction at Castlelyons, co. Cork, for the Countess of Barrymore, and the garden terraces adjacent to the tower and manor house at Leamanagh, co. Clare for the O'Briens (the Earl of Inchiquin's family).[12]

It may also be said that the 1st Earl of Cork directly assisted St Leger in the development of the wider demesne at Doneraile. In the 1620s Cork had sufficient purse to develop a new park at Lismore Castle on the Blackwater, some thirty miles downstream of Doneraile. In 1622, poles, posts and rails to enlarge his park were acquired from Sir John Jephson of Mallow Castle, also on the Blackwater.[13] By late 1623 his park was stocked with a deer herd, a park keeper employed, and a park lodge and brick pigeon house built. Carp and tench were imported from Amsterdam to stock the fish ponds.[14] In May 1627 he proposed to 'enclose me a garden in my park' and to finish a walled orchard at Lismore. It was to his park lodge at Lismore that Cork and St Leger often repaired to confer privately. On 21 September 1627, Cork wrote in his diary, 'I gave Sir Wm St. Leger our new lorde president, two fair breeding mares and two coltes at their ffeet.' Later 'WSL and I rodd to my park, where I did bestow a brace of bucks on him.'[15] On 22 September 1630 he asked his son, Lord Dungarvan, 'to let my lo. president to have as many Rascall deer owt of my parck as he pleased to take'.[16] In 1634 Boyle also gave a gift of tench and carp to St Leger for his fish ponds.[17]

The long-lived existence of 'fish ponds' on the demesne remains close in the folklore and anecdote of the older inhabitants of Doneraile, not least as the original access route to Doneraile Court from the main street of the village continues today to be known as Fish Pond Lane [fig. 5]. The fish ponds were located within the demesne some 600 yards from the east of Doneraile Castle on a small southern tributary of the River Awbeg [figs 7 (sites 21, 22), 8] – the southern, larger pond most likely the *vivarium* (breeding pond), and the smaller, northern pond the *servatorium* (holding pond).[18] A duck decoy was also located in the so-called 'Decoy Wood' some 400 yards to the east of the castle. James B. Fox considers that 'a remarkable similarity exists between this Doneraile decoy and the one at Beaulieu near Drogheda', which lends credence to a seventeenth-century origin for this feature.[19]

### Civil wars and interregnum

THE CIVIL WAR EXTENDED TO MUNSTER IN LATE 1641. IN FEBRUARY 1642, THE WIFE OF THE Munster president, Gertrude de Vries [fig. 4], and the wife of Lord Inchiquin, Elizabeth St Leger, were sent to Bristol for safety.[20] In quick succession thereafter, William St Leger died in July 1642 and the 1st Earl of Cork died in September 1643. Doneraile Castle was sacked and burnt in 1645 by Lord Castlehaven for the Confederate

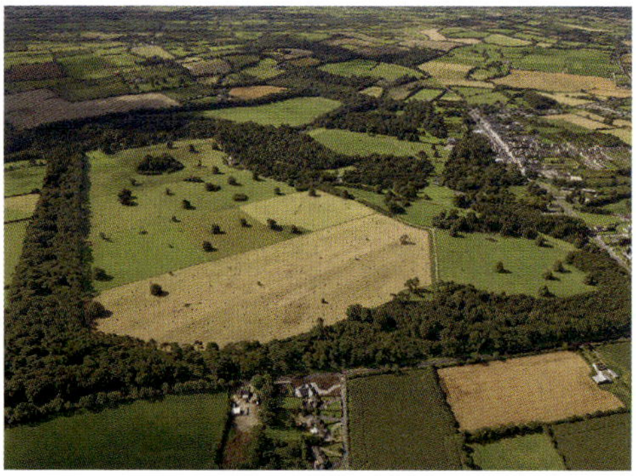
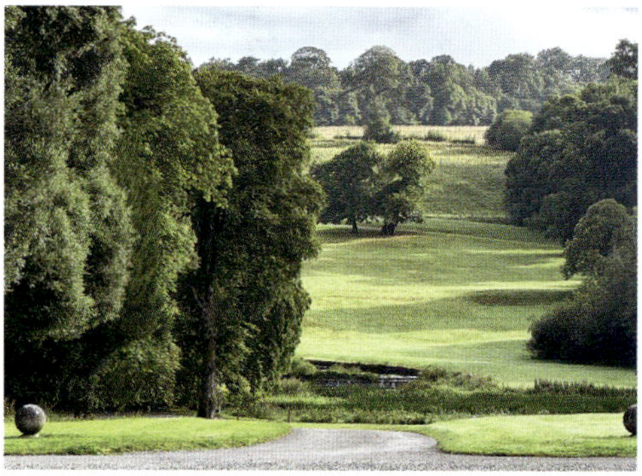
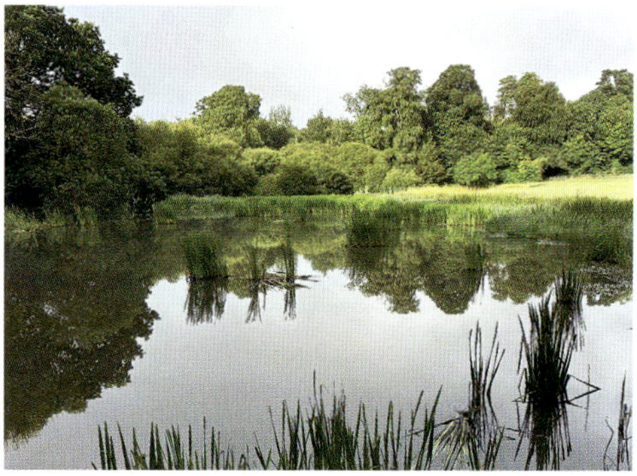
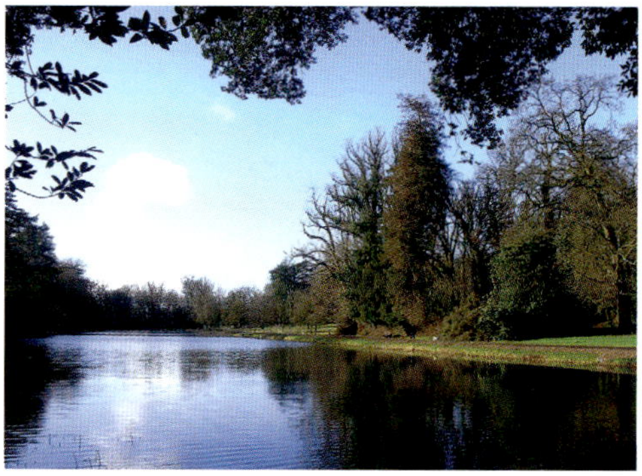

Army. William St Leger, son of the Munster president, died on the royalist side at the Battle of Newbury in 1644. Another son, John St Leger, succeeded at Doneraile.[21] It is most likely at this time that a two-storey, seven-bay house was built by the St Legers on rising ground to the south of the River Awbeg, accessed by Fish Pond Lane from Doneraile village [fig. 5]. It is also likely that John St Leger became dislocated from his lands in Doneraile in the late 1640s and 1650s. In 1655 he married Lady Mary Chichester, daughter of the 1st Earl of Donegall, who was delivered of a son (also John) the following year at Carrickfergus, co. Antrim.[22]

The 1728 estate map identifies an upper orchard and oak grove north of the terrace, and an orchard and fir grove below to the south. Whilst it is possible that these plantations were laid out at the same time as that of the Carolean terrace construction, it is more likely that they were planted during the interregnum in the 1650s in the style of Samuel Hartlib, a close member of the circle of Lady Ranelagh, daughter to the 1st Earl of Cork [fig. 9].[23]

fig. 8 | Eighteenth-century demesne features at Doneraile
clockwise from top left: aerial photograph of Doneraile demesne taken from the north-east; view of River Awbeg and north park from Doneraile Court; upper fish pond; lower fish pond

opposite fig. 9 | Conjectural evolution of seventeenth-century gardens at Doneraile Castle
(A) Carolean gardens, *c.*1630s; (B) Interregnum gardens, *c.*1650s; (C) Restoration gardens, *c.*1660s; (D) Combined seventeenth-century gardens
(© OSI, licence CYAL50284317)

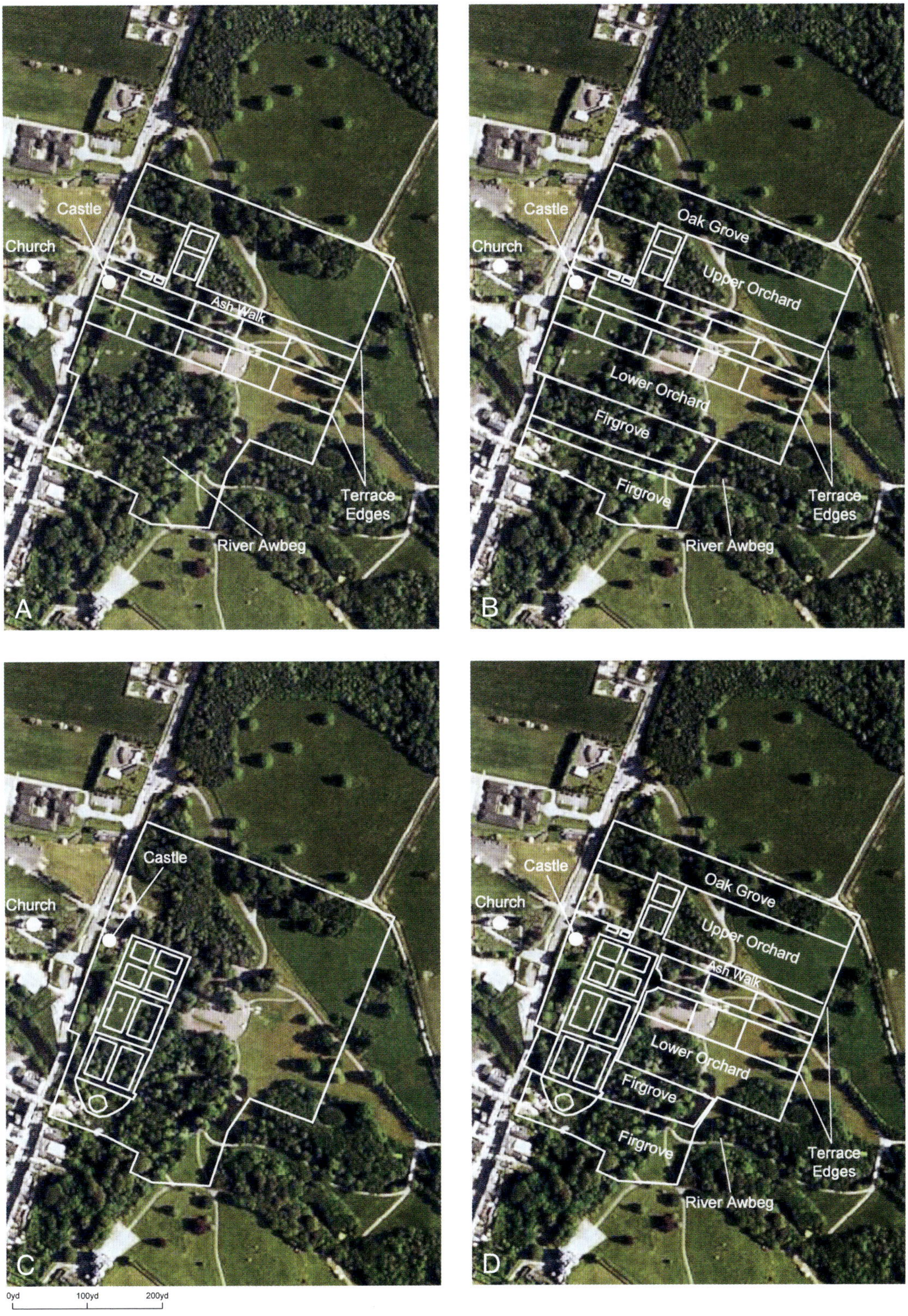
A
Castle
Church
Ash Walk
Terrace Edges
River Awbeg
B
Castle
Church
Oak Grove
Upper Orchard
Lower Orchard
Firgrove
Firgrove
Terrace Edges
River Awbeg
C
Castle
Church
D
Castle
Church
Oak Grove
Upper Orchard
Ash Walk
Lower Orchard
Firgrove
Firgrove
Terrace Edges
River Awbeg
0yd
100yd
200yd

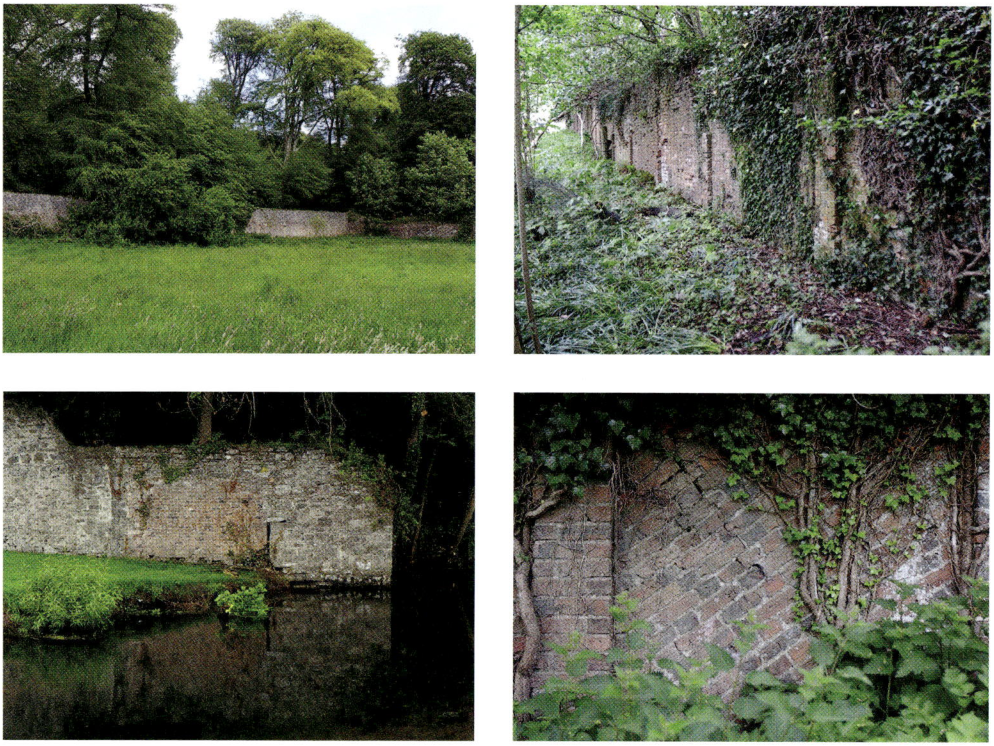

## Circle of John St Leger (d.1696)

John St Leger was the incumbent at Doneraile in the 1660s. John's sister, the 1st Countess of Inchiquin, returned to Doneraile from the court of Charles II in exile in the late 1650s. Her husband, Murrough O'Brien, 1st Earl of Inchiquin, followed in 1663. Roger Boyle, 1st Earl of Orrery, appointed Lord President of Munster and a lord justice of Ireland in September 1660, repaired to Charleville (formerly Rathgoggin), twelve miles north of Doneraile in the early 1660s.[24] Lady Margaret Boyle (daughter of Roger Boyle) and William O'Brien (son of Murrough O'Brien and future 2nd Earl of Inchiquin) married in 1665. Their first child, a son, also named William (future 3rd Earl of Inchiquin), was born in 1666.

fig. 10 | Images of extant boundary walls of the Restoration garden
clockwise from top left: view to north-east showing northern and eastern boundary wall backed by the beech walk (known as the ash walk in seventeenth/eighteenth century); brick-lined interior wall showing regular pillars; interior brick wall with bricks angled at 45° denoting the location of each plat front; outer rubble limestone skin of garden wall showing bricked-up archway access to the River Awbeg, immediately east of the village bridge

opposite fig. 11 | Underwater archaeology survey
(1) River Awbeg; (2) River bridge; (3) Restoration garden walls; (4) Indicative location of southern garden wall (seventeenth century); (5) Sections of wall upstanding in riverbed, identified during underwater survey; (6) Indicative location of southern bank of widened river
(© Mizen Archaeology, 2022; © Aidan Fidgeon Drone Solutions, 2022)

Sir Richard Cox in 1687 confirmed that the heir of St Leger, once the Lord President of Munster, kept his presidency court in Doneraile and 'had a fine house and a curious park adjoining, but the house was burnt by the Irish in 1645 and is since rebuilt'[25] ('curious' in the meaning of being fine or exceptional). Mark Bence-Jones records that the rebuilt seventeenth-century castle had a great formal garden laid out on two sides of it, while Keith Lamb and Patrick Bowe suggest that on stylistic grounds this garden may be a Restoration-era garden.[26] Taking the above into consideration, and noting that the Earl of Orrery also placed a garrison of militiamen at Doneraile in 1666 (one of only three locations in the county), it is not unreasonable to posit a mid-1660s date for the construction of this formal space.

*Description of Restoration gardens*

The 1728 estate plan depicts Doneraile Castle north of the village and to the east of Turnpike Road, overlooking the bridge crossing of the Awbeg. A large rectangular walled garden 750ft long by 250ft wide, about five acres in area, is shown to the east of the castle. The garden, extant today, was laid out in a formal fashion with elaborate parterres [fig. 5].

The garden wall enclosed three terraces, each about one acre in area, with regimented, regular square and rectangular enclosed plats. Four square plats of about one-tenth of an acre are marked on the most northern terrace [fig. 5]. Two rectangular

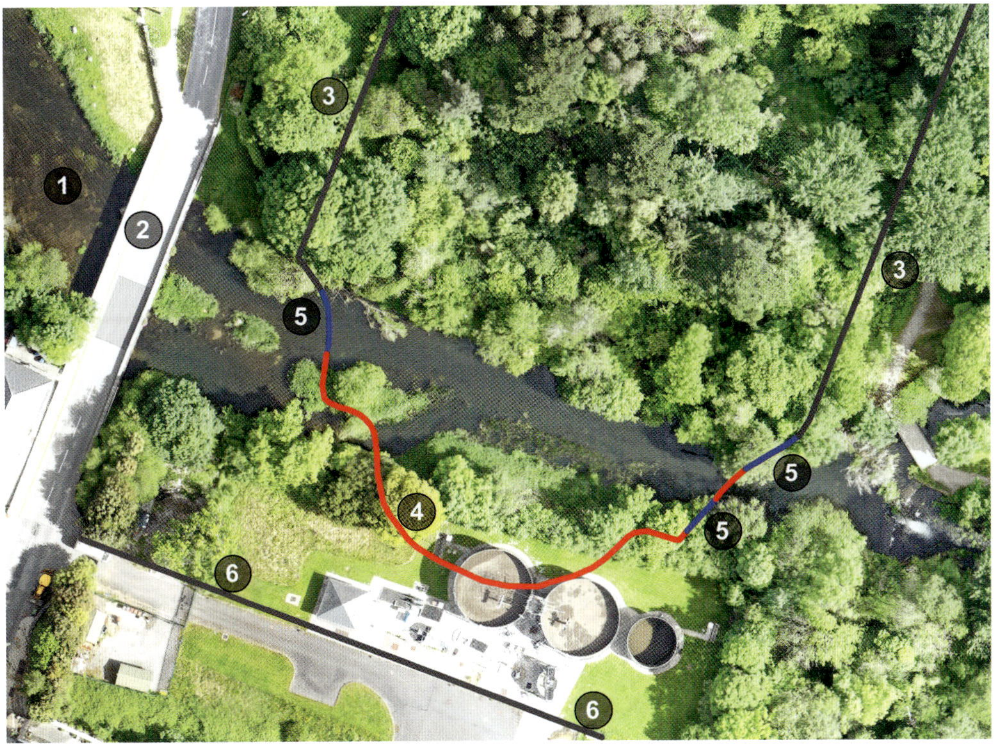

plats of about one-third of an acre are shown on both the central and southern terraces. Whilst each terrace sloped gently to the river, the southern terrace edges were delineated by an earthen bank slope about 6ft in height. The brick-lined boundary walls also reflect this transition, with bricks aligned at 45° to the south at each terrace edge [fig. 10].[27] The layout is marked by pathways around the edges of each terrace and through the centre of the garden.

The northern margin of the parterre garden joined with the ash walk, which extended eastwards parallel to the open Carolean terrace. On the most northerly terrace, a semicircular area also aligned with the castle and the earlier open terrace. Here, the open terrace was overlain in part by the walled parterre garden. At the river margin, the garden wall ended as a curved feature built out into the bed of the river. The plan shows that the river was widened considerably to accommodate the garden structure [figs 5, 11].[28]

The residual garden today is enclosed by a limestone rubble wall 8ft high, faced internally with red brick. Small piers, also of red brick, are located at regular intervals along the inner face of the walls. There is a batter (receding slope) along the base of the eastern garden wall. The latter retains a substantial height of soil in the garden. Approximately 600 yards of the perimeter wall and the three principal garden terraces remain.

An additional space once abutted the river in a bastion-like enclosure where the walls extended into the broadened river. This 'river terrace' allowed for close interplay with the river which surrounded the curved southern garden wall. Upstream of the garden and the village bridge, the river was significantly widened to divide around a series of artificial islands. The southern boundary wall does not stand today, most probably removed by flood waters or modified during the eighteenth century to provide views from the park to the bridge upstream [fig. 11].[29]

### *Design influences*

This was an unusual and perhaps unique period of opportunity and development in Restoration Munster. Following twenty years of turbulence, the Doneraile circle of John St Leger displayed an elite cohort, members of which had closely supported the king in exile and in restoration. A demonstration of loyalty to the crown would have been an important consideration to underpin and maintain provincial security and privy influence. What greater way to show solidarity than to emulate the king's newfound passion for promoting European garden influences in the realm – reflected, indeed, in his personal intervention with the assistance of the French landscape gardener André Le Nôtre at St James's Palace gardens.

The Doneraile circle was not without the sensibility for such an endeavour. John St Leger's father-in-law, the 1st Earl of Donegall, was nephew to Arthur Chichester, Lord Deputy of Ireland 1605–16. Chichester had important formal gardens in Dublin, Belfast and at Joymount, Carrickfergus.[30] John's sister and brother-in-law, the Inchiquins, had spent a lengthy period in exile with Charles II in France in the 1650s. Inchiquin had served as high steward to the household of the English Queen Mother, Henrietta

Maria, at the court of her nephew King Louis XIV of France, at the Château de Saint-Germain-en-Laye outside Paris for a number of years prior to his return to Ireland. Inchiquin, as head of the household to the queen mother, would have been familiar with the work of André Le Nôtre at Saint-Germain in the early 1660s.[31] Orrery had married Lady Margaret Howard of Audley End, daughter of the 2nd Earl of Suffolk, in 1641. Expansive formal gardens had been laid out at Audley End by Thomas Howard, 1st Earl of Suffolk, in the period 1610–14.[32] Howard built a palace to accommodate the king and queen and the travelling court at Audley End, not only in regal grandeur but also in a bid to outdo their other subjects.[33] Orrery established his presidential court at Rathgoggin (named Charleville by Orrery) some twelve miles to the north of Doneraile.[34] Taking a leaf from his in-law's book, he expended time there in the early 1660s constructing a grandiose house. Consequently, there is no doubt that this elite grouping had the wherewithal to conceive and progress the construction of a large, fashionable and unified garden development at this time.

One might be forgiven for anticipating such an elite and formal Restoration garden expression may have been progressed at Charleville, the home of Orrery, as the Restoration president. However, notwithstanding his explicit engagement with the king in the lead up to the Restoration, the nexus of court loyalty lay at Doneraile with the multi-generational administrative support of the St Legers and the Inchiquins who had spent long years with the king in France. Of equal consideration, of course, was the lie of the ground or *genus loci*. Charleville was without topographical features or flowing water; these characteristics were in abundance at Doneraile.

Regardless, all of this would have been grist to the mill for Orrery who would have had the ability to oversee these works. In correspondence with the Duke of Ormonde in December 1661 he wrote, 'I am now building a house for myself in Munster, of which I am the architect and therefore pretend something to engineership.'[35] He was also engaged with the duke in the commissioning of a seven-mile perimeter wall to enclose the royal hunting park at the Phoenix Park, Dublin. Soon afterwards, in the summer of 1667, he commissioned the earthworks for a major defensive site, named Charles Fort, at Kinsale Harbour, co. Cork. His land agent at Charleville, Sir St John Brodrick, had employed a competent team of artificers there during 1661–63, and it was he who most likely fulfilled a similar role at Doneraile. Indeed, it is known that Brodrick constructed a fortified house and large walled garden (with a red-brick grotto) for himself at Ballyannan, Midleton, about this time.[36] It should also be noted that Doneraile had expansive quantities of construction material nearby: river gravels and floodplain clays were available upstream of the garden. In the excavation of these materials to construct the plats, the river was widened, which allowed for an expansive area of pleasure boating around artificial islands. Limestone bedrock was excavated on the southern bank of the river in Trethewey's Glen [fig. 5]. Suitable brick clay was excavated from the townland of Cornahinch to the south of the village.

Equally, given his restlessness to impress the king, a garden to entice a royal visit would not be beyond Orrery's ambition (perhaps to celebrate the marriage of his daughter Lady Margaret Boyle to William O'Brien (future 2nd Earl of Inchiquin) in 1665).[37] This, in its own right, was a significant event in plantation Munster as it brought

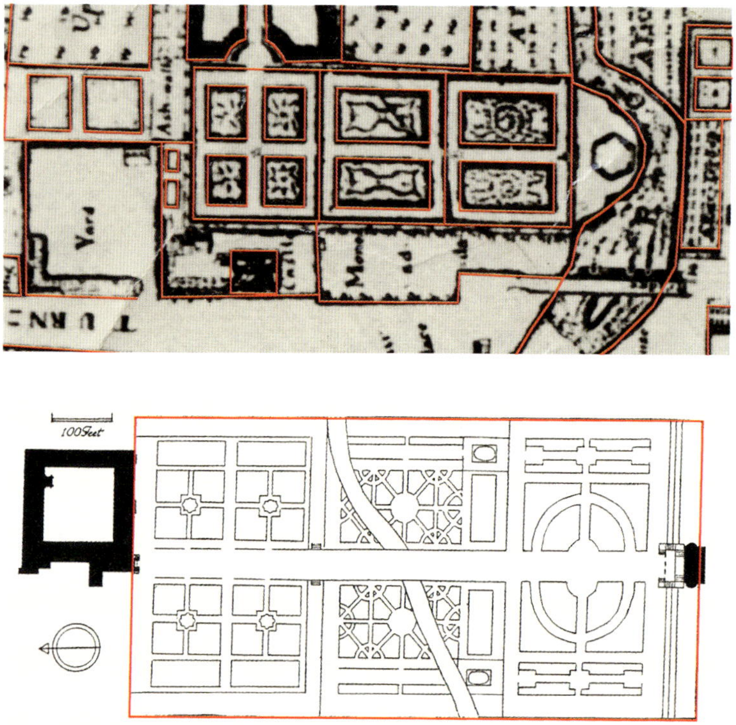


fig. 12 | Comparative plans (to scale) of Restoration gardens at Doneraile, and seventeenth-century gardens at Wilton, Wiltshire.
(from Howard Colvin, *Essays in English Architectural History* (New Haven and London: Yale University Press, 1999), p.142)

together Old Irish and planter families at the highest level in the province. Charles II had always sought a 'right understanding' between Orrery and Inchiquin, and required Orrery to conduct his presidency of Munster as 'might formerly have bin lawfully used, in the tyme during the Government of Sir William St. Leger'.[38] To that end, Orrery appointed Inchiquin as Vice-President of Munster in 1663, a role he had also fulfilled for St Leger in the early 1640s.[39] The opportunity to express the project as a vehicle of 'diplomatic bravado' (to coin a phrase from David Jacques) was patent.[40]

To contemplate a prospective royal visit to Munster at this time might not have been so fanciful. Inchiquin was central to the planning of the restoration of Charles II through Munster in the late 1640s.[41] Following the Ormonde peace in January 1648, Queen Henrietta Maria and Prince Charles acknowledged their concern for the Catholics of Ireland and their intent to send a fleet from the Hague to support Inchiquin and his army.[42] On 10 October the prince wrote to Ormond, 'mee think it most necessary to give all possible encouragement to that army under Lord Inchiquin'.[43] Over the winter of 1648–49, strenuous efforts were made to victual and dispatch a royal fleet of support from the Hague to Inchiquin in Cork.[44] Indeed, Ormond reported on Inchiquin making the army 'in a fit state to receive Prince Charles in Ireland'.[45] In 1657, Roger Boyle proposed to the king in exile that his restoration would be possible in Munster as he 'had 5000 of his protestant subjects, all tryed men, at or near Cork, ready to attend his majesty'.[46] Whilst Charles II initially agreed to this proposal, his restoration eventually progressed in London.[47] Upon the event, however, Charles II did not forget his close supporter, as he acknowledged that Orrery 'was the first of all his subjects, who invited him to his kingdom, and declared themselves ready to settle him in his undoubted rights, and therefore they did certainly deserve favour'.[48]

In laying out the Restoration garden of Doneraile, the designer eschewed all of the garden designs one might anticipate, including those of the Chichesters at Joymount; the Boyles at Lismore, Youghal, Castlelyons and Stalbridge; the Burkes at Portumna; the O'Briens at Leamanagh; the Howards at Audley End, and even the Butlers at Moor Park, Hertfordshire.[49] Instead it would appear that the garden at Wilton, Wiltshire, was the template [fig. 12].[50] The Wilton gardens were set out by Inigo Jones for the 4th Earl of Pembroke (Lord Chamberlain to the king) in 1632.[51] Aubrey used the term 'curious' to describe Wilton; Cox used the same term in reference to Doneraile.[52] It is true that the Boyles were familiar with Wilton at this time. The 1st Earl of Cork (father to Orrery) was a senior royal courtier in the 1630s, at which time he purchased the Stalbridge estate, Dorset, only twenty-seven miles to the south-west of Wilton House.[53] In August 1638 he procured the assistance of 'mounsier decon [Isaac de Caus] [...] who belongs to my L. chamberleyn [...] for drawing me a plott [...], my new intended bwylding over the great sellar of Stalbridge'.[54] Orrery would be forgiven for seeking to erect a memorial to his father and his links with Wilton. However, a greater point remains, as Aubrey records, 'King Charles the first did love Wilton above all places, and came thither every summer. It was he that did put Philip first Earle of Pembroke upon making this magnificent garden.'[55] In passing, in *c.*1629–30 the sculptor Hubert Le Sueur made a bronze cast of the so-called 'Borghese Gladiator' for Charles I. He also sculpted a duplicate for the Earl of Pembroke, which become the centrepiece of Isaac de Caus's parterre at Wilton. In 1750 Charles Smith referred to Doneraile Court, where 'in the front court on a pedestal stands the statue of a gladiator, with other lesser figures'.[56] The 'court' Smith mentions is the open gravel space which the house overlooks. The gladiator of Smith was clearly the most impressive of the statues at Doneraile, and most probably a copy of the Borghese warrior. The 1728 estate map, which shows that the Restoration garden had been kept up, identifies three sites at which statues stood on its terraces – a central location on the highest terrace, in line with Doneraile Castle, and two locations on the lower terrace close to the river. The statue possibly stood on the upper terrace of the Restoration garden between the 1660s and 1730s, and was subsequently moved to a position in front of Doneraile Court during its reconstruction in the 1730s.

Orrery would have been closely familiar with the association of Charles I with Wilton, not only through the relationship of his father with the 4th Earl of Pembroke, but also the proximity of Stalbridge to Wilton, which allowed for knowledge of the comings and goings at each property. He visited his brother, Robert Boyle (the scientist) at Stalbridge, where Robert had taken up residence in the 1640s. Orrery would no doubt have known of the enforced grubbing-up of the Wilton gardens in 1648 during the latter years of the civil wars.[57] To restore a replica of the garden, albeit on a smaller scale, would have appealed not only to Charles II, but also to his mother, Henrietta Maria, who, in her own right, counted the 1st Earl of Inchiquin and 2nd Earl of Cork (Orrery's older brother) as favourites.[58]

The Wilton and Doneraile gardens do, however, differ on one fundamental point. At Wilton, the River Nadder traverses the middle of the tripartite division of the garden. A wilderness was developed upon its banks, specifically to 'disguise the river', in the words of Wendy Bishop.[59] In contrast, the River Awbeg at Doneraile is widened to three times its natural width along the southern margin of the Restoration garden. A conspicuous extension of the southern garden wall into this expansive flowing water, allied to arched access points to the river in the garden wall, demonstrate an explicit and conscious incorporation of the river into the garden design.

## THE EIGHTEENTH CENTURY

### Hayes St Leger, 4th Viscount Doneraile (1st creation) (1702–1767)

THE 'BROWNIAN' STYLE OF THE EIGHTEENTH-CENTURY LANDSCAPE AT DONERAILE IS WELL accepted in the secondary literature. Finola O'Kane has said it best: 'Perhaps the finest example of Brownian landscape in Ireland, Doneraile's classic approach route winds through rolling parkland studded with broadleaf trees to cross a triple-arched bridge leading to the focus of the great house.' [figs 6, 7, 8, 13].[60] However, no attempt has been made to assign a particular timeframe or landscape designer to the works. Smith in 1750 notes that 'this place is indebted for the greatest part of its beauty to the fine house and extensive improvements of Hayes St. Leger, esq.'[61] Hayes St Leger (4th Viscount Doneraile 1750) was the resident St Leger at Doneraile following the death of his father Arthur St Leger, 1st Viscount Doneraile in 1727 [fig. 14].[62] It is known that he and his wife petitioned the Irish parliament in 1731 for heads of a bill to sell her estates, 'lying dispersed' and remote from their dwelling house, and to purchase, with the monies arising, lands more contiguous.[63] This suggests that the land purchase and the development of the demesne occurred sometime between the mid-1730s and the mid-1740s.[64]

It is considered here that Doneraile Court, a seven-bay, three-storey building, was constructed on the site of the seventeenth-century five-bay, two-storey building to the south of Fish Pond Lane at this time. The elevated position of the court allowed for long vistas to the north over the River Awbeg, to the east over the fish ponds, and to the south past the lime walk to Dreenagh Wood. The eighteenth-century features of building and demesne are largely intact today and demonstratable on the ground.

#### *Description of demesne*

The demesne, which lies mostly to the east of Doneraile village, was delineated by an 8ft-high masonry wall. In plan, the demesne appears as a five-sided enclosure centred on the Awbeg, which flows along a sinuous path from west to east through the park [fig. 7 (site 1)]. To the south and west are the townlands of Dromdeer and Horseclose, also partially enclosed by demesne walls. In all, the walls extended to over five miles in length. The demesne boundaries are largely unchanged today from when originally set out.

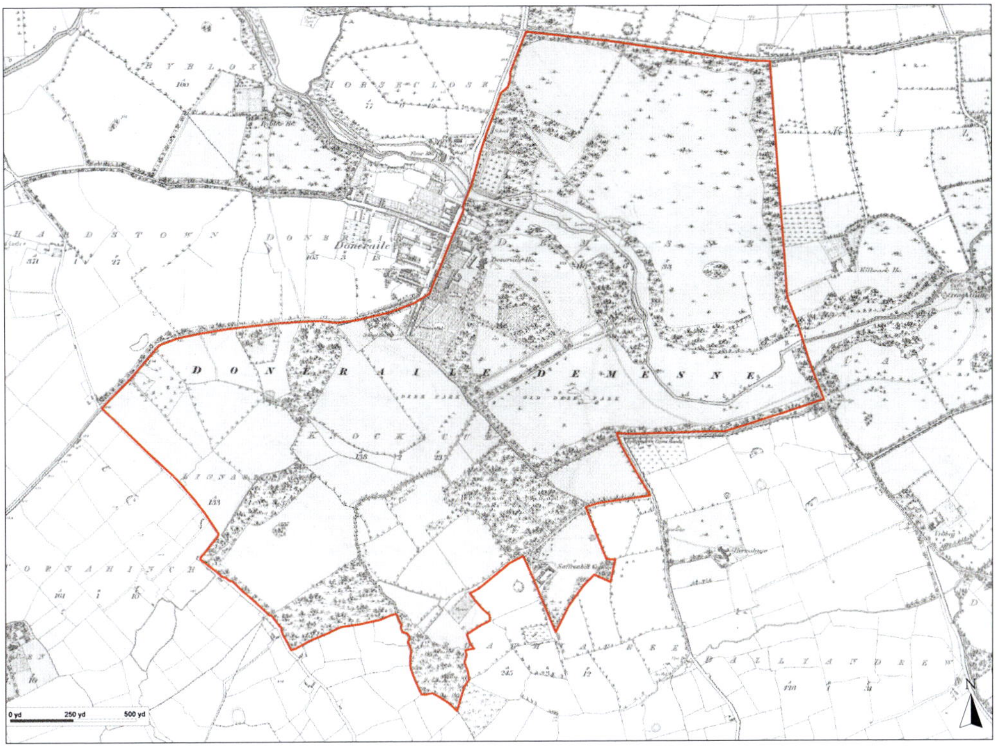


Prior to the eighteenth-century walling-in, the north park was known as the great meadow and the south park as Nagle's fields. The seventeenth-century formal gardens centred on Doneraile Castle, while elongated domestic gardens stretched out on either side of the main street to the south of the river [fig. 5]. Significant physical modification, however, was required to meet with the needs of an expansive landscape demesne. Domestic gardens to the east of the main street were shortened and screened with a double blind of beech and holm oak. Fish Pond Lane was closed, and a new road built around the new demesne wall to the south of Nagle's fields. Long and deep stone-wall ha-has were constructed to enclose a wilderness to the east of the court. The ha-has ended against an extensive sheet of formal water, shaped from the early fish ponds on a minor tributary of the Awbeg.

Carriage and foot-bridges were constructed across the river. A diversionary channel was dug on the north bank of the river, terminating in a south-facing cascade at the bottom of the valley. Grand vistas were set out from the façade of the court across the river to the northern demesne boundary, east to the formal water, and south past the lime walk on the southern ha-ha to the woods at Dreenagh. A new and lengthy approach avenue now extended from the beech-walk entrance, across the avenue bridge to the court. A deep oak boundary screen was planted round the inner perimeter of the demesne wall, and lime trees were dotted strategically on the entirety

fig. 13 | First edition Ordnance Survey map showing extent of Doneraile demesne
(© OSI, licence CYAL50284317)

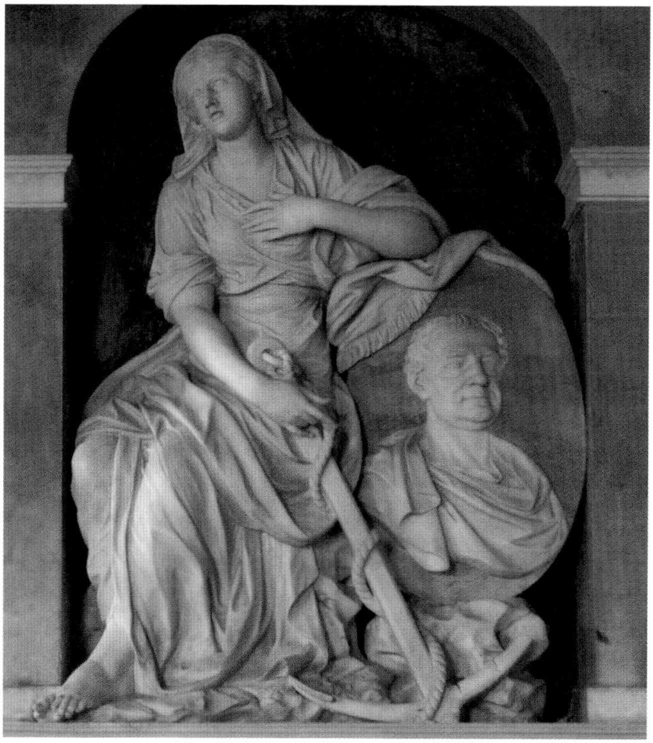

fig. 14 | Monument to Arthur St Leger (c.1657–1727), 1st Viscount Doneraile, by Henry Cheere (1703–1781), 1759, Doneraile Church. The detail shows the figure of Hope leaning on an oval portrait medallion of the deceased.

of the north park – all in all, a significant investment by the St Leger family in landscape design.

Doneraile Court had been accessible from the village by way of Fish Pond Lane since the seventeenth century. Indeed, notwithstanding the scale of the parkland, the court lies only 150 yards to the east of the village street. It was the development of the demesne landscape which resulted in a fashionable avenue and river crossing to connect the north and south parks. Finding a suitable location for the crossing was not an easy task. The north bank was occupied by the seventeenth-century gardens, a newly designed cascade and its feeder channel, and a spring line which made for wet ground in the valley bottom. On the south bank a limestone bluff extended from the river bridge in the village to the duck decoy wood. Ultimately, a site was chosen with height on the northern bank and an expanse of floodplain on the south [fig. 7 (site 12)].

The skill and artifice of the landscape designer is clear to see in this bridge. Ornamentation on the upstream side and a plain façade on the downstream point to a desire to see the bridge on its approach from the entrance gate. Also, the choice of a small bend in the river and the angling of the structure towards the southern bank allow for long vistas of the upstream face from across the southern parkland.

Yet this is not all; another positive sleight of hand is recognisable. The Awbeg is no more than twelve yards wide in any unaltered stretch of its course through the demesne. The three-arched avenue bridge is more than fifty yards long and six yards wide. A much shorter single-arched structure would clearly have sufficed. Instead, a substantial notch was excavated on the northern bank, doubling the width of the river at the bridge site. From the beech-walk entrance to the court, this crossing point necessitated an avenue of about three-quarters of a mile in the eighteenth century. As a result, a combination of vistas over the river to the house and demesne, a pleasant cascade in the valley bottom, and an elaborate bridge crossing all allowed for a stately and fashionable home drive.

Despite its elevation, the River Awbeg proper could not be seen from the façade of Doneraile Court. What can be seen today is a body of water which disappears sinuously into the undergrowth at either end of its short exposure. This south-flowing channel is crossed by a cascade midway along its length. The decision to marry a north-facing façade with a south-facing flowing body of water within its vista was successful. The centre line of the cascade aligns with that of the court, some 300 yards to the south. The channel at the cascade is twenty yards wide; however, this expands to thirty yards immediately to the south at the confluence with the river. Coincidentally or otherwise, this is similar to the width of the northern façade of the house. Additionally, by widening at a considerable rate to the south of the cascade, this positive sleight of hand provides the perspective of a receding river, much greater in compass than the Awbeg itself.

The skill of the designer may also be applauded for creating such an effect in so small a floodplain. A long feeder channel was not possible owing to the immediate upstream constraint of the seventeenth-century garden wall. The north park also rises quickly from the bank of the river, allowing only a small area of flat ground to fit an apparently expansive river bend and cascade. The pièce de résistance, however, is the construction of the cascade itself [fig. 6]. It is of rough limestone blocks arranged horizontally, with a number of smooth ridges, square in section, protruding into the flow of water. This has the effect of creating an attractive waterfall which can be heard clearly at the court and in wider parts of the demesne. This is a fine eighteenth-century construction which has a significant impact on the principal vista from the house, and an intervention not unknown to the most progressive landscape demesne developments at the time.

The 1728 estate plan identifies Fish Pond Lane as the fourth arm of a crossroads located in the centre of Doneraile village [fig. 5]. The lane was soon thereafter closed up as a public thoroughfare owing to the development of the demesne. The waterbodies, as identified on the early nineteenth-century first-edition Ordnance Survey map, and extant today, represent an eighteenth-century modification of the original fish ponds as an extensive two-part rectangular and formal expanse of water [fig. 7 (sites 21, 22)]. The long axis of the ponds, which is orientated north-east–south-west, follows the line of an old tributary of the Awbeg. The ponds lie at a slight angle to each other, the smaller and more northerly one separated by the old Fish Pond Lane causeway from the southern. The southern waterbody is 1,000ft long by 100ft wide, with an expanse of *c.*3.5 acres. The northern body is approximately 400ft long by 100ft wide, and encloses an area of 1.25 acres.[65] An overflow channel lies outside a retaining boundary wall along the southern margin of the southern waterbody. This channel, which follows the original tributary drainage line, falls from south to north along its length, and parallels the northern waterbody at a lower level. The early eighteenth-century canals at

Doneraile would be among the larger of this type of water feature in demesne gardens from this period.[66]

Charles Smith noted in 1750 that the canal (fish ponds) was 'constantly supplied by a large wheel that casts up a part of the River Awbeg' into this waterbody.[67] The suggestion from Smith is that the Awbeg was the only source of water supply; however, there are a number of features which point to the fact that this was a supplementary supply during summer months only. The formal canals are built upon the fish ponds which were fed by a southern tributary of the river. These waterbodies continue to be fed solely by this tributary to this day. Fieldwork confirms that the overflow channel fills during periods of winter flooding of this tributary, thus acknowledging the intrinsic utilisation of the stream for water supply. Observations also confirm that the spillway between the upper and lower fish ponds dries up in periods of low flow, which underpins the benefit of a supplementary source of water at these times. Neither Smith nor any other source identified the location of this 'Persian' wheel. It is posited here that the most opportune location was at Stag Island at the site of the fish pond's exit channel to the Awbeg [fig. 7 (site 35)]. Arthur Young recorded in 1776 that the water was raised 28ft.[68] It is likely that this wheel was also a 'destination' feature within the demesne during the eighteenth and early nineteenth centuries as the southern bank of the Awbeg was walled, most likely to support a bank edge pathway between the avenue bridge and Stag Island.

Smith also identified a 'wilderness' in the Doneraile gardens in 1750. This feature is identified on the early nineteenth-century first-edition Ordnance Survey maps. Oval in plan and occupying about two acres, its outline can be identified today [fig. 7 (site 18)]. Two 7ft-deep rubble limestone ha-has, one to the north and another to the south, protect this forest garden. The ha-has trend at an acute angle to each other and fall to the south-east from the garden front of the court. The southern ha-ha is approximately 300 yards in length, aligned with the Lord's Gates, and is marked by a fine avenue of lime trees. The northern ha-ha is, by contrast, about 500 yards long. It commences near the northern façade of the court and ends at the spillway between the fish ponds. To avoid interference with the principal garden-front vista, this ha-ha bends and curves away to the south, out of view of the house [fig. 7 (site 27 north)].

*Design influences*

Whilst Hayes St Leger may well have been singular in the setting out of the landscape park – much as Charles Hamilton was in the setting out of Painshill, Cobham, Surrey (from 1738) – it is worth briefly considering the social milieu of the St Leger family, especially during the 1740s.[69] The 2nd Viscount died in 1733/34, whilst the 3rd Viscount, Arthur Mohun St Leger (1718–1750), was a member of the English House of Commons between 1741 and 1750.[70] What is more, he was Lord of the Bedchamber to Frederick, Prince of Wales, between 1747 and 1750.[71] Notably, William Kent was architect to the Prince of Wales from 1732 until his death in 1748. There are a number of threads which also link Arthur's uncle, and successor to the title, Hayes St Leger, to the Burlington House circles. Edmund Spenser wrote *The Faerie Queene* whilst in residence at

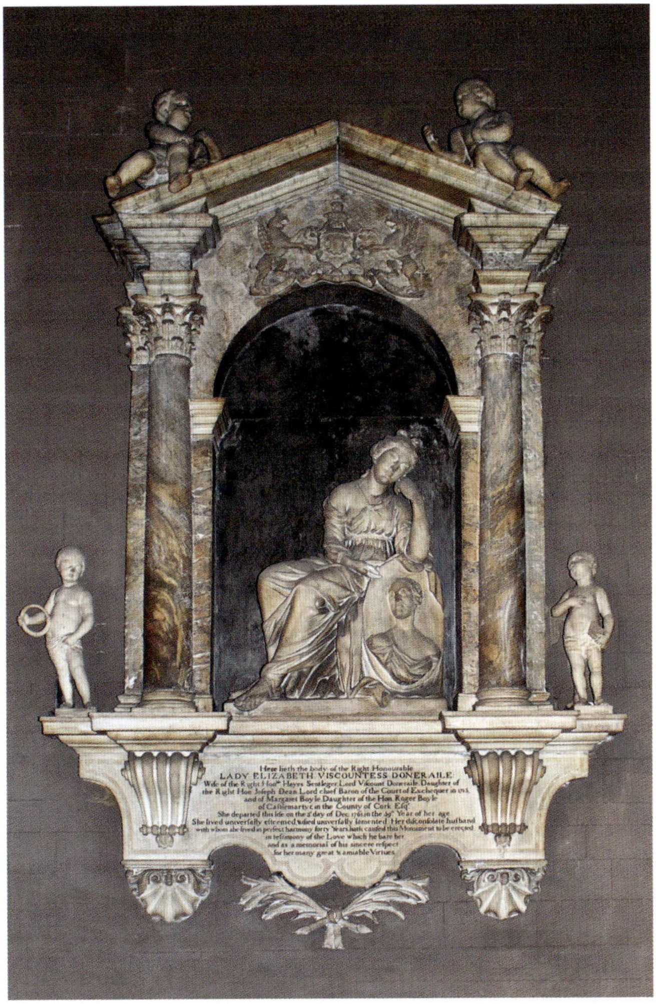


fig. 15 | Monument to Elizabeth St Leger (*c.*1702–1761), Viscountess Doneraile, by Simon Vierpyl (*c.*1725–1810), 1762, St Patrick's Cathedral, Dublin. A female figure in mourning leans on an oval portrait medallion of the deceased. (Alamy / Sergey Strelkov)

Kilcolman Castle, Doneraile, in the late sixteenth century.[72] William Mason reminds us that 'Mr Kent frequently declared he caught his taste in gardening from reading the picturesque descriptions of Spenser'.[73] The Temple of Venus at Stowe, designed by Kent, has a stylistic affinity with illustrated buildings of *The Faerie Queene*, and murals in the temple are considered to be inspired by Spenser's imagery.[74] Indeed, it is also known that he executed thirty-two drawings depicting scenes from *The Faerie Queene*, posthumously published in 1751.[75] In turn, there appears to be a common thread and a certain similarity in the manipulation of water at Chiswick, Castlemartyr and Doneraile. This suggests an alignment of these early examples of the landscape movement style promoted by Kent and others in the properties of Burlington, Shannon and St Leger at this time.[76] The link in all of the above was Richard Boyle, 3rd Earl of Burlington. Burlington (also 4th Earl of Cork) was closely related both to the Earls of Shannon and the Viscounts Doneraile. His property in Ireland lay in proximity to the Castlemartyr and Doneraile demesnes in co. Cork. It is he who, in all likelihood, promoted the 3rd Viscount Doneraile as MP for the rotten boroughs of Winchelsea and Old Sarum, and most likely introduced Kent and Doneraile to the Prince of Wales. Burlington may equally have been the person to introduce the writings of the poet Edmund Spenser to Kent. In all, it is posited here that one cannot be blind to the potential influence of the fashionable Burlington circle upon Hayes St Leger in his development of an expansive mid-eighteenth-century demesne at Doneraile.

Neither should the Irish context be ignored. The St Legers were not unknown to Dublin society, as Elizabeth St Leger (wife of Hayes) was daughter to Joseph Deane, Chief Baron of the Exchequer, and niece to the Speaker of the Irish House of Commons [fig. 15].[77] Hayes St Leger was also one of the founding members of the Royal Dublin Society.[78] St Leger was closely related to James Fitzgerald, Earl of Kildare (later 1st Duke of Leinster).[79] Lady Mary O'Brien (1692–1780), mother to James, was the eldest daughter of William O'Brien, 3rd Earl of Inchiquin, born at Doneraile in 1666.[80]

Coote Street (later Kildare Street), Dublin, was purchased by the Kildares in 1744, and the building of Kildare House (Leinster House, as we now know it today) commenced in 1745. Hayes St Leger followed suit in 1746 and started a townhouse, known as Doneraile House, at 45 Kildare Street, in close proximity to the Kildare property.[81] Richard Castle was architect of the Kildare townhouse; John Esnor, his assistant and ultimate successor, was architect of Doneraile House.[82] Lady Mary, James Fitzgerald's mother, finished works on Carton House (also supervised by Richard Castle) in time for his marriage to Emily Lennox in February 1747.[83] Between 1744 and 1749, through some five major land transactions, James and Emily greatly extended the land holding at Carton with the intention of creating a substantive demesne.[84] Given the family relationship between the Fitzgeralds and the St Legers, the proximity of fashionable townhouses in Dublin, and the coeval development of landscape demesnes (of similar scale and disposition), one cannot but surmise a certain alignment of purpose, design and even familial consultation at this time.[85] One should also be aware that the scene had been set for relationships between the Doneralles, Kildares and the Prince of Wales when Frederick leased Cliveden from William O'Brien, 4th Earl of Inchiquin (brother to Lady Mary O'Brien) in 1738.[86]

Eighteenth- and nineteenth-century observers were not slow to record their impressions of the demesne, not least the attractive setting of the River Awbeg, the undulating topography of the north and south parks, and a vast extent of lawns and mature trees, both specimen and in woodland. Charles Smith recorded in 1750 that the gardens were well laid out and of a very considerable extent, including a wilderness, labyrinth, duck decoy and an extensive deer park, well planted and enclosed. The river 'is formed into a fine cascade', with canals adjacent and adorned with 'islands planted with groves of fir, which add an inexpressible beauty to this place'.[87] John Bernard Trotter considered the demesne to be a 'very happy mixture of the antique English and Flemish style and the picturesque of nature' in 1819.[88] Samuel Lewis was content to record in 1837 that the demesne was distinguished for its extent and beauty, while *The Parliamentary Gazetteer* of 1845 positively stated

> 'The demesne around it has a flowing and undulated surface, a profusion of well-arranged and truly ornamental wood, an extensive artificial sheet of

> water, a sinuous and magnificent bisection by the Awbeg, and, in general, a richness, force, and beauty of landscape equal to the majority of the best demesnes in Munster.'[89]

Whilst Doneraile is not a Stowe nor Painshill in terms of architectural eye-catchers or statuary, one cannot say that this eighteenth-century demesne is delinquent in any way. In 1826, James Brewer reflected upon this less superficial aspect when he opined

> 'the whole of the grounds are enriched with a profusion of wood, truly ornamental in growth and arrangement. The surface is varied by fine and graceful swells; and the wide spreads of lawn appear to be of velvety softness. Although these grounds [...] are destitute of grand and commanding objects, with the exception of their venerable wood alone, they are of a stronger character than those, and are decidedly more pleasing, as they evince less obvious efforts of art.'[90]

In keeping with Brewer's sense of 'rural allusion', one can observe today that the deposition of trees and woodlands form the essential natural architecture of this eighteenth-century demesne. Mature specimen trees are located as natural 'eyecatchers' on principal vistas from Doneraile Court and the triumphal arch, a reflection of the 'grave deliberation' that went into the placement of trees here.[91] Phibbs suggests that Doneraile demesne best exemplifies an Irish contribution to the English landscape ideal: 'These layers of formal and natural alternate into the middle in a very un-English manner.'[92]

## Conclusions

There is no doubt that had Edward Villiers, half-brother to George Villiers (1st Duke of Buckingham) and newly minted Lord President of Munster in 1625, not died in September 1626 (creating an unexpected vacancy), the significant landscape heritage at Doneraile – as initiated and promulgated by the St Leger family – might not exist. Beyond this happenstance, it appears that the overweening desire to remain relevant at the English royal court forcibly played out in the garden styles and interventions at Doneraile from the outset and for at least two hundred years thereafter. In this, of course, the *genus loci* of Doneraile, especially its topography and water, were among its most attractive natural attributes, and lent itself foursquare to the endeavours. The arguments promulgated here highlight how central protagonists and their exposure to new fashions can influence garden change and adaptions at key moments. The marriages of Elizabeth St Leger to Murrough O'Brien in 1635, John St Leger to Lady Mary Chichester in 1655, and Lady Margaret Boyle to William O'Brien in 1665 copper-fasten the elite standing of the St Legers. These families were intrinsically linked to the Stuart royal court and the influences of French garden design post-Restoration. Subsequent generations had close links to the Prince of Wales and Burlington circles mid-eighteenth century.

But there were other chances of history which have led to this demesne and its multi-century features to remain substantially intact to this day. The fact that the walled seventeenth-century gardens did not interfere with the principal vista (set out in the eighteenth century) from Doneraile Court across the River Awbeg avoided the need for its grubbing up, and secured the preservation of this unique garden space. Neither did the nineteenth-century melange of haggard, coronation garden and American garden developments to the south of Doneraile Court interfere with the seventeenth-century or eighteenth-century garden layouts. These nineteenth-century developments, and the retrenchments of the twentieth century, will be the subject of part two of this paper in *Irish Heritage Studies*, volume two.

---

**Michael O'Sullivan** holds postgraduate qualifications in science, engineering and law, and has worked as a project manager of multidisciplinary environmental impact assessments and conservation plans for over 30 years. He has lived in Doneraile, co. Cork, for the past 25 years and has taken a close interest in the historical evolution of the extensive parkland demesne of Doneraile Court. He attended the annual historic landscape conferences at Oxford University between 2017 and 2024, and has recently completed a Masters in Historical Studies at Oxford University.

**Endnotes**

1 Vandra Costello, *Irish Demesne Landscapes, 1660–1740* (Dublin: Four Courts Press, 2015). See, for example, seventeenth-century features such as reservoir for cascade (p.132), statuary (p.54) and decoy (p.179). For discussion on seventeenth-century decoy at Doneraile, see Sir Ralph Payne-Gallwey, *The Book of Duck Decoys: their construction, management, and history* (London: John Van Voorst, 1886), pp.189–91; James B. Fox, 'Duck Decoys in North Co. Cork', *Mallow Field Club Journal*, no.2 (1984), pp.111–20; Finola O'Kane, 'The Limits of Brown's Landscape: translations of the landscape garden into Ireland', *Garden History*, vol.44, supplement 1 (Autumn 2016), pp.61–72; Mairéad Dunlevy and E. Charles Nelson, 'Sir William's Irish Lace Gifts from an Irish Viscountess', *Curtis's Botanical Magazine*, vol.12, no.4 (Nov 1995), pp.220–36.

2 Seamus Crowley, 'Doneraile Park: An Historical Note', *Mallow Field Club Journal*, no.1 (1983), pp.109–28.

3 Terry Clavin, 'Sir William St Leger (d.1642), administrator', *Oxford Dictionary of National Biography* (*DNB*) <https://doi.org/10.1093/ref:odnb/24516>.

4 Alexander B. Grosart (ed.), *The Lismore Papers: Autobiographical Notes, Remembrances and Diaries of Sir Richard Boyle, First and 'Great' Earl of Cork*, 2 series, 5 vols each (printed privately, 1886–88), 1st series, vol.3 (1886), p.29.

5 The Doneraile tower house was built in 1402 by William Synan to protect the adjacent crossing of the River Awbeg. Doneraile Castle was sacked by the Confederates in 1645, rebuilt in the 1660s, and sacked again during the Williamite Wars in the early 1690s. The castle is shown as a burnt-out shell on the 1728 Doneraile estate map. No trace of the castle existed by the early nineteenth century. An army barracks was built on the site of the castle by Michael Creagh in 1748; *The Journals of the House of Commons of the Kingdom of Ireland*, 19 vols (Dublin: Printed by Abraham Bradley, 1763–81), VIII: *1749–51* (1763), pp.563–64, 677–79.

6 Grosart (ed.), *Lismore Papers*, 1st series, vol.5 (1886), p.39.

7 Colonel James Grove-White, *Topographical and Historical Notes, etc., on Buttevant, Castletownroche, Doneraile, Mallow, and Places in their Vicinity*, 4 vols (Cork: Guy & Co., 1905–25), III (1913), p.20.

8 Victor Treadwell, *Buckingham and Ireland 1616–1628: a study in Anglo-Irish politics* (Dublin: Four Courts Press, 1998); Philippe Erlanger, *George Villiers, Duke of Buckingham*, trans. Lionel Smith-Gordon (London: Hodder and Stoughton, 1953); Jennifer Potter, *Strange Blooms: the curious lives and adventures of the John Tradescants* (London: Atlantic Books, 2006); Prudence Leith-Ross, *The John Tradescants: gardeners to the rose and lily queen* (London: Peter Owen, 1984).

9 Mea Allan, *The Tradescants: their plants, gardens and museum, 1570–1662* (London: Michael

Joseph, 1964), pp.12–128; Elaine Murphy, 'Sir William St Leger (c.1580–1642)', *Dictionary of Irish Biography* <https://doi.org/10.3318/dib.008226.v1>.

10 See generally, Allan (1964).

11 John Nichols, *The Progresses, Processions, and Magnificent Festivities, of King James the First, his Royal Consort, Family, and Court*, 4 vols (London, 1828), IV, p.880. Of Burley, John Evelyn wrote in 1654 that it was 'worthily reckon'd among the noblest seates in England, situate on the brow of a hill, built a la modern neere a park walled in and a fine wood at the decent'. Some years later he observed 'How godly a sight were it if most of the Demesnes of our County Gentlemen were crown'd and incircl'd with such stately rows of limes, firs, elms and other ample, shady and venerable trees as adorn New Hall.' (William Bray (ed.), *The Diary of John Evelyn*, 2 vols (Ohio: St Dunstan Society, 1901), I, p.295).

12 The 1st Earl of Cork lent the Earl of Barrymore £767 to 'newe bwild his decaied Mannor howse of Castlelyons'. Grosart (ed.), *Lismore Papers*, 1st series, vol.4 (1886), p.208 (3 Oct 1636). For Leamanagh, see Finola O'Kane, *Ireland and the Picturesque: design, landscape painting and tourism 1700–1840* (New Haven and London: Yale University Press, 2013), pp.53–55.

13 Grosart (ed.), *Lismore Papers*, 1st series, vol.2 (1886), p.66 (3 Jan 1622).

14 Ibid., p.206 (10 Jan 1626).

15 Ibid., p.224 (21 Sept 1627).

16 Ibid., 1st series, vol.3 (1886), p.54 (22 Sept 1630).

17 Ibid., 1st series, vol.4 (1886), p.44.

18 Terence Reeves-Smyth, 'The Role of Water in Irish Parks and Gardens, 1600–1750', Northern Ireland Heritage Gardens Trust 30th Annual Conference, 3–5 Oct 2024, Woodenbridge, co. Wicklow, lecture, 4 Oct 2024.

19 Fox, pp.111–20.

20 Lord Inchiquin to Sir Philip Percivall, 1 Feb 1641/42, Historical Manuscripts Commission, *Report on the Manuscripts of the Earl of Egmont*, 2 vols (London: HMSO, 1905–09), I (1905), pp.162–63.

21 C.M. Tenison, 'Cork M.P.'s, 1559–1880 (contd)', *Journal of the Cork Historical and Archaeological Society*, vol.2, no.18 (1896), pp.274–477: 274; John Lodge, *The Peerage of Ireland*, 4 vols (Dublin: J. Leathley, 1754), III, p.190, 'John St. Leger'.

22 J.M. Rigg, 'Arthur Chichester, first earl of Donegal [Donegall] (1606–1675)', *Oxford DNB* <https://doi.org/10.1093/ref:odnb/5275>.

23 See Jill Francis, *Gardens and Gardening in Early Modern England and Wales, 1560–1660* (New Haven and London: Yale University Press, 2018), pp.237–75, ch. 9: 'War and Peace: Gardening in the Mid-Seventeenth Century'; Samuel Hartlib, *Samuel Hartlib his legacy of husbandry* (3rd edn, London: printed by J.M. for Richard Wodnothe, 1655).

24 Toby Barnard, 'Roger Boyle, first earl of Orrery (1621–1679)', *Oxford DNB* <https://doi.org/10.1093/ref:odnb/3138>.

25 Robert Day (ed.), '*Regnum Corcagiense*; or A Description of the Kingdom of Cork, by Sir Richard Cox [cont.]', *Journal of the Cork Historical and Archaeological Society*, 2nd series, vol.8, no.55 (1902), pp.156–79: 176. 'Curious' in the contemporary sense as being 'carefully worked out or prepared; elaborate'; 'Curious', adj., Sense II.8, *Oxford English Dictionary* <https://doi.org/10.1093/OED/1183063189>.

26 Mark Bence-Jones, *Burke's Guide to Country Houses: Volume 1, Ireland* (London: Burke's Peerage, 1978); Keith Lamb and Patrick Bowe, *A History of Gardening in Ireland* (Dublin: National Botanic Gardens, 1995).

27 Dr Gerard Lynch, 'An Overview of the Bricks and Brickwork of the Walled Enclosure of "Moatville House", Charleville and of the Garden Walled Enclosure at "Doneraile Castle, Doneraile, County Cork' (unpublished report, commissioned by CHE Ltd and OPW, 2016).

28 Mizen Archaeology, 'River Awbeg, Doneraile, Co. Cork. Underwater Archaeological Survey' (unpublished report, commissioned by CHE Ltd and OPW, April 2022). Portions of the garden wall were identified upstanding on the riverbed during an investigation conducted by four underwater archaeologists employed by Mizen Archaeology.

29 Ibid. It may be noted here that the vicinity of the village bridge saw considerable economic development in the early 1700s. The 1705 Toll Act of Queen Anne provided for the establishment of a

toll at this bridge crossing of the River Awbeg. This promulgated the establishment of a turnpike road, a fair place and a mill adjacent to the river. The bridge, extant today, is of substantial length and width (70 yards long by 9 yards wide). Examination of the culverts (four in number) demonstrates that the bridge was widened to the west by approximately 9ft at some point in its history. The semi-corbelled downstream arch and radial upstream arch also point to structural change (Rob Goodbody, personal communication). It is considered here that an early eighteenth-century date for this modification, coeval with the tolling of this river crossing, would best fit the evolution of this structure.

30 John McCavitt, 'Arthur Chichester, Baron Chichester (1563–1625)', *Oxford DNB* <https://doi.org/10.1093/ref:odnb/5274>.

31 Patrick Little, 'Murrough O'Brien, first earl of Inchiquin', *Oxford DNB* <https://doi.org/10.1093/ref:odnb/20463>. The earl was restored to his lands by way of the Act of Settlement 1662–67; see *Statutes Passed in the Parliaments Held in Ireland*, 12 vols (Dublin: George Grierson, 1794–1801), I: *From the Third Year of Edward the Second,* A.D. *1310, to the Fourteenth and Fifteenth Years of Charles the Second,* A.D. *1662, inclusive* (1794), p.343. It was while Le Nôtre was working on the reconstruction of the gardens at Saint Germain in 1661 that Louis XIV requested him to commence the building of the gardens at Versailles.

32 Magnus Alexander et al., *Audley End House, Essex – Landscape, Investigation Report*, Historic England research report series no.46–2011 (2015), p.12 <https://historicengland.org.uk/research/results/reports/46–2011>.

33 Paul Drury, *Audley End* (2nd rev. edn, London: English Heritage, 2014), p.39. Charles II purchased Audley End in 1647 for £50,000; see P.J. Drury, 'No Other Palace in the Kingdom Will Compare with It: the evolution of Audley End, 1605–1745', *Architectural History*, vol.23 (1980), pp.1–39: 4, 145–71.

34 The 1st Earl of Cork purchased Broghill and Rathgogan from Mr Thomas Stephens for the price of £3,500 stg on 13 Dec 1622; Grosart (ed.), *Lismore Papers*, 1st series, vol.2 (1886), p.64.

35 Orrery to the Duke of Ormonde, Dublin, 28 Dec 1661, *A Collection of the State Letters of the Right Honourable Roger Boyle the First Earl of Orrery* (London: James Bettenham, 1742), p.31.

36 [Sir] St John Brodrick to Capt. Kenn and Lieut. Greene, Ballyanen, 25 June 1662, 'Concerning work in progress under their supervision, on Orrery's estate [at Charleville]', in Edward MacLysaght (ed.), *Calendar of the Orrery Papers* (Dublin: Stationery Office, 1941), p.22; John Gibney, 'Sir St John Brodrick (1627–1711), *Dictionary of Irish Biography* <https://doi.org/10.3318/dib.000979.v1>; 'J.C.', 'The Old Castles Around Cork Harbour', *Journal of the Cork Historical and Archaeological Society*, vol.21, no.108 (1915), pp.156–75: 162–65.

37 W.W. Webb, 'William O'Brien, second earl of Inchiquin (*c*.1640–1692)', *Oxford DNB* <https://doi.org/10.1093/ref:odnb/20469>.

38 Bodleian Library, Oxford, MS Carte 24, f.483r, letter from Charles II to the Marquess of Ormond, 20 April 1649. For instructions to Lord President of Munster 1660, see British Library, Egerton collection, MS 2542, f.334r, instructions to Roger Boyle, Baron Broghill, 1st Earl of Orrery, as President of Munster, 1660.

39 See Charles Smith, *The Ancient and Present State of the County and City of Cork*, 2 vols (new edn, Cork: J. Connor, 1815), II, p.105.

40 David Jacques, *Tudor and Stuart Royal Gardens* (Oxford: Windgather Press, 2024), p.210.

41 See generally Michael O'Sullivan, 'The Struggles of the Munster Presidency: during and after the wars of the three kingdoms (1641–1672)' (unpublished dissertation submitted for the Postgraduate Certificate in Historical Studies, University of Oxford, 2023).

42 For Ormonde peace, see Bodleian Library, MS Carte 63, f.552v, Lord Jermyn to Marquess of Ormond, 25 Oct 1648; MS Carte 63, f.584v, Marquess of Ormond to Secretary Nicholas, 24 Jan 1648; for support of Irish Catholics, see MS Carte 63, f.541r, Charles R[ex] to Queen Henrietta Maria, St Germain, 13 May 1648; for fleet to Ireland see MS Carte 63, f.552v, Lord Jermyn to Marquess of Ormond, 25 Oct 1648.

43 Bodleian, MS Carte 22, f.343v, Charles R[ex] to Marquess of Ormond, The Hague, 10 Oct 1648.

44 For royal support with fleet, see Bodleian, MS Carte 63, f.562v, Secretary Long to Marquess of Ormond, 12 Dec 1648.

45 Bodleian, MS Carte 63, f.558, Marquess of Ormond to Lord Jermyn, 21 Nov 1648. While the fleet did arrive in Cork in January 1649, Prince Charles was not in attendance. Notwithstanding, for his conspicuous royal support Inchiquin was offered, and accepted, an earldom in 1654. See generally Mark R.F. Williams, *The King's Irishmen: the Irish in the exiled court of Charles II, 1649–1660* (Suffolk: Boydell & Brewer, 2014).

46 Charles Smith, II, p.177.

47 Ibid., p.178.

48 *A Collection of the State Letters*, p.33.

49 James Butler, Duke of Ormonde (Lord Lieutenant of Ireland 1662–68) purchased Moor Hall, Hertfordshire, in 1663 to be close to the court in London. During his short tenure, he planted avenues of trees ending in a semicircle centred on the north side of the old house. He sold the property to Charles II for his son the Duke of Monmouth in 1670. See Paul Drury, Sally Jeffery and David Wrightson, 'Moor Park in the Seventeenth Century', *The Antiquaries Journal*, vol.96 (2016), pp.241–90.

50 For an up-to-date description of Wilton, see Jacques, pp.116–21.

51 David L. Smith, 'Philip Herbert, first earl of Montgomery and fourth earl of Pembroke (1584–1650)', *Oxford DNB* <https://doi.org/10.1093/ref:odnb/13042>; John Newman, 'Inigo Jones, Inigo (1573–1652)', *Oxford DNB* <https://doi.org/10.1093/ref:odnb/15017>. For details of the gardens see Dianne Duggan, 'Pembroke's Arcadia: "Delicious Wilton [...] that Arbour of the Muses"', *British Art Journal*, vol.14, no.3 (2013–14), pp.9–20.

52 Duggan, p.11; Day (ed.), p.176. See n.25 above for meaning of 'curious'.

53 See Toby Barnard, 'Richard Boyle, first earl of Cork (1566–1643)', *Oxford DNB* <https://doi.org/10.1093/ref:odnb/3133>.

54 Grosart (ed.), *Lismore Papers*, 1st series, vol.5 (1886), p.64; Howard Colvin, 'Isaac de Caus [Caux] (1589/90–1648)', *Oxford DNB* <https://doi.org/10.1093/ref:odnb/7406>. De Caus assisted Inigo Jones at Wilton. Duggan (p.9) suggests that de Caus was largely responsible for the design of the garden.

55 John Aubrey, *The Natural History of Wiltshire*, ed. John Britton (London: Wiltshire Topographical Society, 1847), p.83.

56 Charles Smith, I, p.309.

57 Jacques, p.123, figs 7, 9.

58 Patrick Little, 'Murrough O'Brien, first earl of Inchiquin (*c.*1614–1674)', *Oxford DNB* <https://doi.org/10.1093/ref:odnb/20463>. He was High Steward to the Queen Mother's household in exile in the early 1660s; Toby Barnard, 'Richard Boyle, first earl of Burlington and second earl of Cork (1612–1698)', *Oxford DNB* <https://doi.org/10.1093/ref:odnb/3135>; Charles Smith, II, p.186. In passing and as it happened, Orrery had to make do with a visit and tour of Munster by the Duke of Ormond (Lord Lieutenant of Ireland) in August 1666.

59 Wendy Bishop, *Ornamental Lakes: their origins and evolution in England landscapes* (London and New York: Routledge, 2021), pp.47–49.

60 O'Kane (2016).

61 Charles Smith, I, p.309. It is considered here that Doneraile Castle was abandoned following the Williamite Wars in the 1690s. A five-bay, two-storey house is shown adjacent to Fish Pond Lane on the 1728 estate plan. This is likely a mid-seventeenth-century house built by the family following the earlier sacking of Doneraile Castle in 1645, and the site of Doneraile Court as upgraded to a seven-bay, three-storey structure in the 1730s. For general discussion on evolution of Doneraile Court, see Frank Keohane, *The Buildings of Ireland: Cork city and county* (New Haven: Yale University Press, 2020), pp.372–78.

62 Neither Arthur St Leger (1695–1733/34), 2nd Viscount, nor Arthur Mohan (1718–1750), 3rd Viscount, was resident at Doneraile. Hayes St Leger, brother of the 2nd Viscount, was resident from 1727 and elevated upon the death of his nephew, 3rd Viscount, to the position of 4th Viscount Doneraile in 1750; see John Lodge, *The Peerage of Ireland*, 7 vols (Dublin: James Moore, 1789), VI, p.122.

63 Edith Mary Johnston-Liik, *History of the Irish Parliament 1692–1800: commons, constituencies and statutes*, 6 vols (Belfast: Ulster Historical Foundation, 2002), VI, p.225, no.1855 (Rt. Hon. Hayes St Leger).

64 As Brown was head gardener to Lord Cobham at Stowe between 1740 and 1750, and did not begin his own business until 1751, there is no sense that he had any direct participation in the development of the Doneraile demesne; see Jane Brown, *Lancelot 'Capability' Brown: the omnipotent magician, 1716–1783* (London: Pimlico, 2012).

65 The seventeenth-century fish ponds would have acted as a 'proto-canal' analogous to the use of the terminology of Bishop, p.36.

66 Reeves-Smyth, Northern Ireland Heritage Gardens Trust lecture (2024).

67 Charles Smith, I, p.309.

68 Arthur Young, *A Tour in Ireland with General Observations on the Present State of That Kingdom*, 2 vols (London: Printed for T. Cadell and J. Dodsley, 1780), I, p.306.

69 Hayes St Leger was a progressive landowner and one of the inaugural members of the Dublin Society in 1731; Royal Dublin Society, RDS_DO_0268, 'The treasurer's book of the Dublin Society: for the years 1731 to 1739' <https://digitalarchive.rds.ie/items/show/4044> [acc. 27 June 2024]. William Smyth was gardener and park-keeper to the 4th Viscount 1732–66. He was initially paid £10 per annum, rising to £12 after two years. In 1750 he sold excess estate stock, including seeds of beech and hornbeam. In 1758 he was made park-keeper at £15 per annum. The 4th Viscount left him £50 in his will; National Library of Ireland (NLI), Dublin, St Leger MS32,905(2): 1756–58 accounts; Eileen McCracken, 'Notes on Eighteenth Century Irish Nurserymen', *Irish Forestry*, vol.24, no.1 (1967), pp.39–58; NLI, MS 34,112/10, St Leger, Servants Book, unfoliated (cited by Bernard, 2004); National Archives, Kew, PROB 11/928/163, 'Will of the Right Honorable Hayes Lord Viscount Doneraile or Baron of Kilmeaden, 2 May 1767'.

70 Arthur Mohun St Leger, 3rd Viscount (1718–1750) was MP for Winchelsea 1741–47 and MP for Old Sarum 1747–50. Romney R. Sedgwick, 'Arthur Mohun St Leger, 3rd Viscount Doneraile', *The History of Parliament*, member biographies <https://www.historyofparliamentonline.org/volume/1715-1754/member/st-leger-arthur-mohun-1718-50> [acc. 27 June 2024].

71 After his death in 1751, the Prince of Wales 'was described by Peter Collinson, the Quaker draper and botanist, as "the best friend of gardening and planting"', see Alison Hodges, 'Painshill Park, Cobham, Surrey (1700–1800): notes for a history of the landscape garden of Charles Hamilton', *Garden History*, vol.2, no.1 (Autumn 1973), pp.39–68; University of Toronto Libraries, British Armorial Bindings, 'Charles Hamilton (1704–1786)' <https://armorial.library.utoronto.ca/stamp-owners/HAM009> [acc. 27 June 2024].

72 Alexander Corbin Judson, *Spenser in Southern Ireland* (Bloomington, Indiana: Principia Press, 1933); Thomas Herron, *Spenser's Irish Work: poetry, plantation and colonial reformation* (Hampshire: Ashgate Publishing, 2007); Andrew Hadfield, *Edmund Spenser, A Life* (Oxford: Oxford University Press, 2012).

73 William Mason, *The English Garden: A Poem. Book the First* (London: R. Horsfield, 1772); see Michael I. Wilson, *William Kent: architect, designer, painter, gardener, 1685–1748* (London: Routledge & Kegan Paul, 1984), p.207 for discussion.

74 Wilson, pp.211–12.

75 Edmund Spenser, *The Faerie Queene* [...] *Adorn'd with Thirty-Two Copper-Plates, from the Original Drawings of the Late W. Kent* (England: printed for J. Brindley and S. Wright, 1751); see generally, Wilson, pp.148–52. Desmond also suggests that a number of the lifesize figures fashioned by Kent for Queen Caroline at Merlin's Cave, Richmond, were inspired by a number of characters (namely Minerva, Britannia, Bradamante or Britomart) from Spenser's *Faerie Queene*. However, this iconography is not entirely clear; see Ray Desmond, *The History of the Royal Botanic Gardens Kew* (Kew Publishing, 2007), pp.12–13, and Timothy Mowl, *William Kent: architect, designer, opportunist* (London: Pimlico, 2007), pp.199–202 for discussion.

76 For Chiswick, see David Jacques, *Chiswick House Gardens: 300 years of creation and re-creation* (Swindon: Historic England, 2022); For Castlemartyr, see O'Kane (2013), pp.142–49.

77 Elizabeth St Leger died in 1761. Hayes St Leger erected a fashionable monument to her in St Patrick's Cathedral, Dublin, for which see Christine Casey, *The Buildings of Ireland: Dublin* (New Haven and London: Yale University Press, 2005), p.621. It may also be noted that the mother of Elizabeth, Viscountess Doneraile, was Margaret Boyle, daughter of the Roger Boyle, of Castlemartyr, co. Cork, and sister to Henry Boyle, 1st Earl of Shannon, Speaker of the Irish House of Commons 1733–56.

[78] Royal Dublin Society, RDS_DO_0268, 'The treasurer's book of the Dublin Society: for the years 1731 to 1739'.

[79] Eoin Magennis, 'James Fitzgerald, first duke of Leinster (1722–1773)', *Oxford DNB* <https://doi.org/10.1093/ref:odnb/9565>.

[80] See William O'Brien, third Earl of Inchiquin in Lodge (1789), II, pp.58–60.

[81] NLI, Doneraile Papers, MS34,165(1); Leo D. Batt, 'Doneraile House', *Dublin Historical Record*, vol.18, no.4 (Sept 1963), p.127.

[82] For an architectural history of Leinster House, see Casey (2005), pp.498–504. Casey, pp.529–30, records that Doneraile House is of particular significance as it is one of the few terrace houses of the period for which detailed records survive. She notes that 'the house exhibits many features of the Pearce–Castle school and is comparable to houses built on Henrietta Street several decades earlier'. See NLI, Doneraile Papers, MS34,165(1) for reference to John Esnor accounts for Doneraile House. For examples of workmanship quality at Doneraile, see Christine Casey, '"Agreeable to live in": the wainscoted interior in eighteenth-century Britain and Ireland', pp.289–315, and Andrew Tierney, 'A glorious ascent: staircase design, construction and craft in the circle of Richard Castle', pp.316–53, both in Christine Casey and Melanie Hayes (eds), *Enriching Architecture: craft and its conservation in Anglo-Irish building production, 1660–1760* (London: UCL Press, 2023).

[83] Magennis, 'James Fitzgerald'; also Finola O'Kane, *Landscape Design in Eighteenth-Century Ireland: mixing foreign trees with the natives* (Cork: Cork University Press, 2004).

[84] A map prepared by Charles Baylie and John Mooney in 1744 entitled 'Map of the Demeasne of Carrtown together with a map of the adjacent lands intended for a deer-park' served as a master plan to enlarge the demesne to more than double its original size. See also Arnold Horner, 'Land Transactions and the Making of Carton Demesne', *Journal of the County Kildare Archaeological Society*, vol.15, no.4 (1974–75), pp.387–96, and Arnold Horner, 'Carton, Co. Kildare: a case study of the making of an Irish demesne', *Quarterly Bulletin of the Irish Georgian Society*, vol.18, nos 2 and 3 (Apr–Sept 1975), pp.45–103.

[85] Carton demesne runs to *c.*4km squared, Doneraile demesne to *c.*3km squared, per first-edition six-inch-to-one-mile Ordnance Survey maps. The Ryewater bisects the former, the River Awbeg the latter. For a history of Carton demesne, see O'Kane (2004), pp.89–130.

[86] Matthew Kilburn, 'Frederick Lewis, Prince of Wales (1707–1751)', *Oxford DNB* <https://doi.org/10.1093/ref:odnb/10140>.

[87] Charles Smith, I, p.309. Smith recorded that the canal was 370 yards long and 140 yards broad, and well stocked with fish. Site investigation, however, has identified that the canal (which is extant) in two ponds separated by a causeway that delineates the former Fish Pond Lane, which extended to Ryle's Cross to the south-west of the demesne). This suggests that Smith may have acquired his information second-hand, without the opportunity to check measurements on site.

[88] John Bernard Trotter, *Walks through Ireland in the Years 1812, 1814 and 1817* (London: Sir Richard Phillips and Co, 1819).

[89] Samuel Lewis, *A Topographical Dictionary of Ireland*, 2 vols (London: S. Lewis & Co., 1837), I, p.478; *The Parliamentary Gazetteer of Ireland, Adapted to the New Poor-Law, Franchise, Municipal and Ecclesiastical Arrangements, and Compiled with a Special Reference to the Lines of Railroad and Canal Communication, as Existing in 1814–45*, 3 vols (Ireland: A. Fullarton & Co., 1846), III, p.42.

[90] J.N. Brewer, *The Beauties of Ireland*, 2 vols (London: Sherwood, Gilbert & Piper, 1825–26), II (1826), p.434. He continues on the same page to say: 'it is a circumstance particularly gratifying in the disposal of modern pleasure-grounds, that, where extraneous embellishments are introduced, the statues and temples, fashionable a century ago, give place to buildings of the simplest kind, and, generally, to such as have a rural allusion. The Irish excel in such tasteful introductions, as may be instanced by several parts of the demesne at Doneraile.'

[91] Royal Botanic Gardens, Kew, Directors' Correspondence, DC/35/106, Lady Doneraile to Sir William Hooker, 25 Nov 1855.

[92] Ibid., p.153.

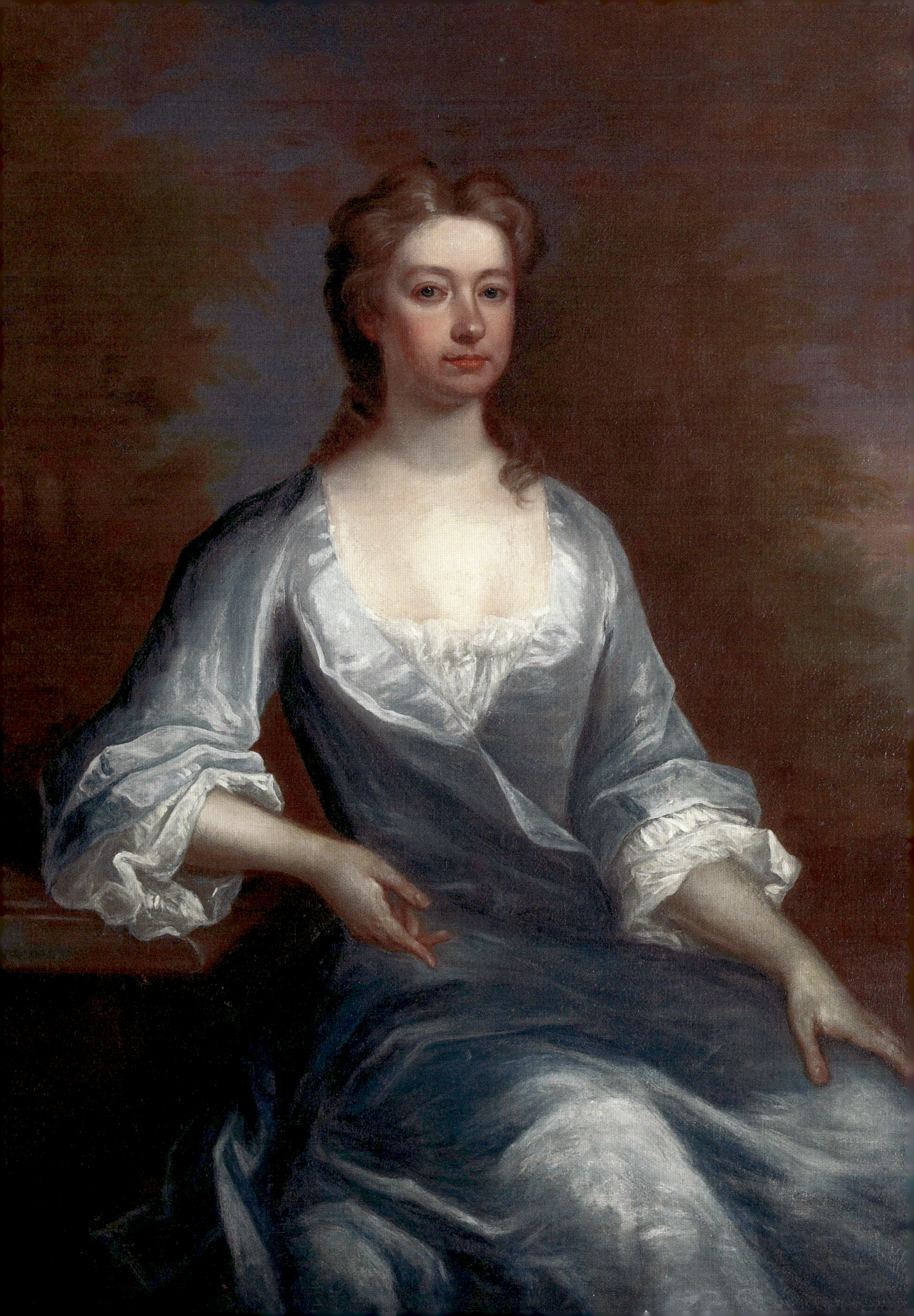

# e Conolly's legacy
# ›e, co. Kildare

.NGLISH TRAVEL WRITER RICHARD TWISS DESCRIBED
s 'the only house in Ireland to which the term
ıd's largest and earliest Palladian-styled coun-
nally built by the Speaker of the Irish House
fe Katherine to 'impress, overawe opponents,
ce of Irish political life' in the early eighteenth
Public Works, the architecture, and the visual
e continue to impress visitors three hundred
'.

ɔlarship on the history and architecture of
significance to acknowledge that much of
ed by architectural and aesthetic improvements
y by successive generations of women.[3] In fact,
es in 1775 can largely be attributed to the influ-
ɔx; 1743–1821), who actively oversaw or par-
cesses of the home and its demesne until her
ı Castletown and its interiors in this capacity
scholarship, and can still be visualised and
om, the dining room and Long Gallery, among
atherine Conolly (*née* Conyngham; *c*.1662–
town's social interiors from the 1720s to the
nparison, despite establishing the home as a
ɔvement' from the early eighteenth century.[5]
midable figure in Castletown's history, Katherine
been largely overshadowed by the life of Lady
'patriot', shrewd political hostess and 'shadow
during her husband's tenure as Speaker from

*erine Conolly)* by Charles Jervas (*c*.1675–1739)
, on loan from the Castletown Foundation, PC36

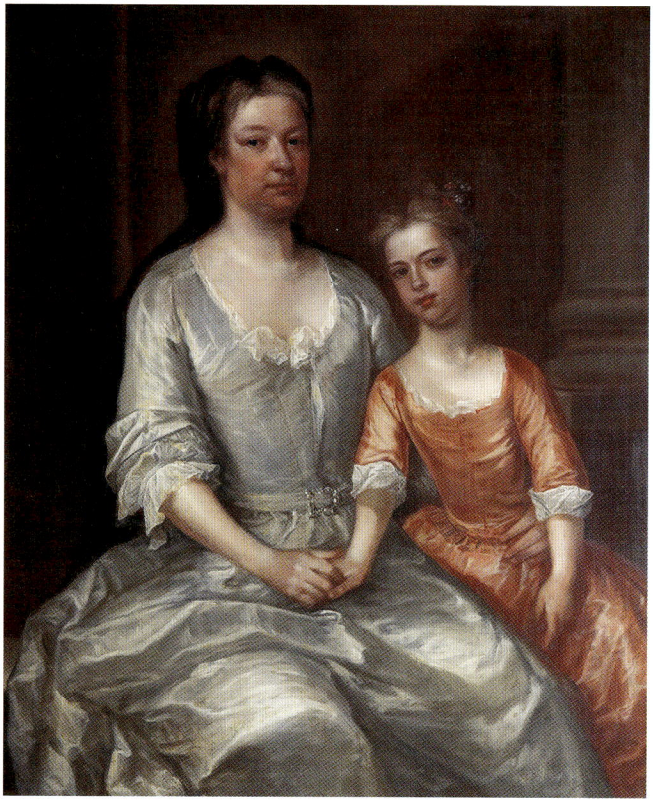

fig. 2 | *Katherine Conolly with Molly Burton* by Charles Jervas c.1730, oil on canvas, 122 x 102 cm, Castletown House, on loan from the Castletown Foundation, PC47

1715 until his death in October 1729.[6] While this can certainly be attributed to the lack of contemporary accounts of Castletown's interiors and building process in the 1720s and 1730s, Katherine's commissions for portraits and furnishings at Castletown deserve further consideration, as they can enrich our understanding of the eighteenth-century domestic sphere and evoke its social ambiance in Ireland's largest Palladian home.[7]

Building upon a diverse and interdisciplinary scholarship, the selected works from Castletown to be discussed will provide a deeper understanding of the role of female portraiture within heritage spaces by addressing the ways in which women's representations were commissioned, displayed and self-fashioned for consumption by Ireland's eighteenth-century elite. While art historian William Laffan has acknowledged that the 'political is inescapable in much Irish portraiture', a political dimension has never complemented an art-historical study of Katherine Conolly's representations and their visual and cultural significance to eighteenth-century Irish audiences within Castletown's domestic ambit.[8] Likewise, while Katherine's extant archive papers include few descriptions of Castletown – being occupied instead with lengthy discussions concerning her family and political affairs – her correspondence in this capacity can inform new perspectives into the emblematic role of her portraits in Ascendancy society.[9] With that in mind, this art-historical paper relies upon a socio-cultural approach to foreground the political and 'pictorial dialogues' of Irishwomen's portraiture and their self-fashioned modes of representation that narratively operated 'beyond the boundaries of individual canvases'.[10] Given Katherine's prominence in elite circles during the formative decades of the Ascendancy, it is important to recognise how her formal representations and commissioned furnishings performed within Castletown's domestic settings as a means to maintain the Conolly family's social legacy, and all the more considering that Katherine's political and cultural influence in Ireland continued independently in the decades following William's death on 30 October 1729.

By reflecting upon the nuanced relationships between portraits, objects and viewers within Castletown's interior spaces, the thematic discussion of this paper demonstrates how Katherine's commissions of artworks and furnishings legitimised her family's legacy in Ascendancy society within the culturally distinctive ethos of 'improvement'.[11] Developing from seventeenth-century English political ideologies of obtaining 'civic perfection', improvement in Ireland by the eighteenth century became socially and visually defined through nuanced patterns of behaviour and display among the Protestant elite. It reflected a shared commitment to economic prosperity and the development of a 'benevolent, independent government' from Westminster with the right to free-trade.[12] This was largely achieved by a collective effort from the elite and middling sorts to support local and charitable initiatives that facilitated agricultural, public and charitable works which benefitted manufacturing and education, alleviated poverty and encouraged political reform. To be seen participating in such acts of 'improvement' from the 1690s onwards was also crucial to being contemporaneously acknowledged as 'patriotic' in society among the Protestant elite, who sought to secure social, religious and political dominance for the ruling Ascendancy minority in post-Restoration Ireland. This was especially important for Anglo-Irish families like the Conollys, who sought to differentiate their social identity from absentee landlords (in addition to Jacobite sympathisers) by choosing to remain in Ireland and 'improve' the country's prosperity following the atrocities of the seventeenth century.[13] However, to be seen as a patriot and improver in visual and material culture required the thoughtful patronage and consideration of Irish artists, architects, designers, tradesmen and local materials to support economic and artistic development.[14] Indeed, it is within these nuanced and complex cultural contexts that Kyle Leyden has argued that the 'Irishness' of Castletown's architecture can be uniquely recognised, despite its stylistic similarities to English estates of the period.[15] The same should also be said of Katherine Conolly's likenesses by Irish-born artist Charles Jervas, which are virtually indistinguishable from English sitters of the period, but were socially significant in Ireland due to Katherine's reputation as a celebrated political hostess and 'improver' in her own right [figs 1, 2].

When considered within the nuanced socio-cultural contexts of the Irish Protestant Ascendancy, Katherine's representations in particular can reveal how self-fashioning and display were crucial to reinforcing the Conolly family's social capital and reputation throughout the eighteenth century as patriots through acts of political theatre within Castletown's social interiors. This is especially important to recognise as the Conollys remained childless throughout their marriage and Katherine became Ireland's wealthiest widow upon William's death in 1729. In this capacity, Katherine's gendered status and agency, which defied conventional modes of womanhood, uniquely shaped the visual narratives of the Conollys' social legacy at Castletown by honouring her and William's shared commitments to Irish 'improvement' and their dedication to family, despite having no progeny of their own.

Likewise, the performative role of Katherine's representations at Castletown can additionally be understood and measured within the sensibilities of female dress and display, which increased in political and patriotic meaning throughout the eighteenth century in Ireland, and were directly influenced by what historian Maxine Berg describes as the 'economy of quality'.[16] The concept of 'quality' that developed during this period in the British Isles was defined both materially and socially through the display and support of local manufacture, and by adhering to specific codes of conduct which were dictated and disseminated by elite culture. Within this socio-economic and cultural context, 'quality' evolved to communicate distinctive patterns of conduct, which 'carried explicit social and cultural connotations' through a 'shared range of activities and familiarity with a shared code of behaviour'.[17] In practice, 'quality' became a societal construct from which the elite and gentry could 'merit admiration' from the public through 'appropriate behaviour', and allowed for the sensibility to manifest itself in unique and particular ways.[18] Within this context, to command respect and maintain social influence, a person of 'quality' had to live and lead by example; in Irish Ascendancy society this referred to an adherence to the Protestant and patriotic causes that could perceivably benefit the welfare of all and would prevent 'the drooping genius of our Isle' in arts and industry.[19]

Historians Ingrid Tague and Toby Barnard, writing about England and Ireland respectively, note that the contemporary didactic use of 'quality' was not only 'ambiguous in its nature', but also shared a noun-like status similar to its 'counterparts, nobility and aristocracy, [which] implied a judgment, and so was not simply a neutral collective'.[20] While outward appearances and 'inner qualities' of virtue were certainly important among elite and middling gendered spheres, it was the close adherence to polite behaviour, a person's genteel status and being seen to support local socio-economic or social improvements which largely dictated ones acceptance into the ranks of 'the quality'.[21]

Such nuanced and gender-based sensibilities of improvement in Ireland arguably resulted in the English visual convention of a 'woman of quality' being adapted in meaning for an Irish audience over the course of the century, which was materially and visually expressed through conservative dress and polite virtues.[22] This conventional style of portraiture, which relied on modest dress and minimal ornamentation, and the ability to convert character to likeness was largely popularised by the influence of English court artist Sir Godfrey Kneller on artists like Charles Jervas, working throughout the British Isles in the early part of the eighteenth century.[23] Women's adherence to these formal styles of dress and display, which were considered 'neat, proportioned and decent', is arguably of particular significance within an Irish socio-cultural context, as gendered patterns of behaviour and dress were subsequently politicised in eighteenth-century Ireland. In fact, the politicisation of dress, which manifested in numerous 'buy Irish' campaigns throughout the Ascendancy period, may be partially traced to the shared patriotic principles of Katherine and William Conolly, whose social and political roles strongly influenced others to display their support of Irish industry as 'improvers' through patterns of behaviour and local consumption.[24] By recognising the Conollys' social capital and 'quality' throughout the period, this brief examination of the role of

Katherine's portraits, commissioned statues and furnishings now on display at Castletown House can provide visitors with new perspectives into her legacy by 'experiencing the reality of its images' through Ascendancy contexts.[25]

## Projecting patriotism

ALTHOUGH THE EXACT DATE WILLIAM AND KATHERINE BEGAN RESIDING AT CASTLETOWN IS unclear, and the home remained unfinished during William's lifetime, it had become a notable site of spectacle in the Kildare countryside from 1725, when the exterior of the main block was completed.[26] Praised in local newspapers for 'stimulating the local economy' due to the Conollys' decision to build with primarily Irish materials, the large construction project served as a 'symbol of economic patriotism' among the Irish elite to encourage similar patterns of behaviour in the effort to 'improve' and stabilise Ireland's socio-economic situation.[27] In commissioning the largest home in the country, the Conollys recognisably distinguished themselves as figures of Irish improvement among their peers by investing in Irish estates built with local materials and tradesmen. They were simultaneously flaunting their wealth and power to incoming English administrations, who frequently visited Castletown as a necessity during the period since the viceregal country residence at Chapelizod, co. Dublin, 'was not suitable for large scale entertainment'.[28] Being an easy day-trip from Dublin, the Conollys' political influence often enticed Irish politicos – in addition to lord lieutenants and their circles – to admire progress or enjoy events at 'the fine house at Castletown', which also advantageously provided a 'discreet location away from [the] spying eyes' of the opposition.[29] This is also particularly noteworthy within gendered contexts, as Katherine's frequent social gatherings of ladies at the Conollys' Dublin residence on Capel Street provided a 'good indicator of which way the political wind was blowing' during Dublin's winter parliamentary sessions. These were characterised as the female equivalent of the 'panels and boards on which her husband, kinsmen, and cronies sat'.[30] However, Katherine was also exceedingly adept and comfortable operating within traditionally masculine social spheres, as she engaged in correspondence with lord lieutenants and their administrators, writing as the Speaker during the 1720s, and acted as a 'channel for people seeking favours from government' or positions at Dublin Castle during William's lifetime.[31] While elite women's participation in formal public life was constricted on the basis of gender during the period, the informal means by which women like Katherine Conolly capitalised upon and expanded their political connections should not always be seen as subordinate to the ways in which their husbands operated. For example, Speaker Conolly's rapid political success following their marriage in 1694 was partially attributed to Katherine, as her brother-in-law James Bonnell served as Ireland's Accountant-General in the 1690s. Additionally, without her large dowry of £2,300 and intimate connections with some of Ulster's most prominent families, historian Toby Barnard suggests that Speaker Conolly's success in the Irish parliament 'would have been unlikely, perhaps impossible'; her actions, within the 'private or domestic province' of the home, 'shaded imperceptibly into the recognisably political arena' that Speaker Conolly inhabited.[32] While her 'shadow' roles in this capacity suggestively informed 'a strong sense of her own importance', Katherine's unique experiences and connections allowed her to retain her influence as a widow throughout the 1730s by demonstratively building upon her husband's legacy through established modes of visual representation and evolving social politics within the domestic space.[33]

To more comprehensively understand the nuanced role of portraiture to Castletown's first visitors, it is important to visualise the home's former spaces, which lacked the detailed damasks, furnishings and artworks associated with Castletown's current rooms. In fact, while the home was described in 1733 by Katherine's English niece-in-law Lady Anne Conolly (*née* Wentworth; 1713–1797) as 'realy [*sic*] a charming one to live in', Lady Anne overall '[did]n't find the place very pleasant', being 'so very unfinish'd without doors' and 'the front without orniments [*sic*] of any sort'.[34] Likewise, Mrs Mary Delany (*née* Granville; 1700–1788) shared similar sentiments, as she acknowledged its 'good furnishings [...] vast deal of room' and 'very fine' situation, but 'not laid out with a very good taste'.[35] Historians Marie-Louise Jennings and Gabrielle M. Ashford have noted that 'perhaps it was Irish taste that dissatisfied the English eye' at Castletown, especially as English responses to the home were comparatively not 'universally favourable' during the period.[36] The nuanced differences between English and Irish 'taste' in this circumstance is perhaps best understood in relation to Castletown's building materials, as expressed by English travel writer and antiquarian John Loveday following his visit to the home in 1732. Declaring that the building was constructed with 'a bastard unfinished marble, quarried locally', and 'too many [windows] either for beauty or strength' on the front façade, the interior rooms were 'large, well-proportioned and well-finished'.[37] While certainly dramatic in tone, Loveday's observations and the perceived inferiority of locally quarried marble would not have been a popularly shared opinion among the Irish Ascendancy, who valued the stone for its significance in supporting the local economy and facilitating artistic development and trade throughout the country.[38] The noted lack of ornamentation in the home during this period can also suggestively be attributed to Irish tastes, as interior designs which displayed local materials favoured simplicity over extravagance, and modes of representation which focused on 'quality' and 'character' were considered essential to shaping social identity and communicating ideals of improvement to contemporary Irish visitors.

However, by the 1730s Castletown's well-received rooms and furnishings would have also included portraits commissioned and collected by the Conollys to visually legitimise their status in Irish society as 'improving landlords'.[39] Indeed, historian Patrick Walsh has suggested that Speaker Conolly was actively commissioning and buying portraits in an effort to ultimately construct a powerful visual lineage in the Long Gallery at Castletown, which concentrated on the Speaker's 'patrons and friends' in lieu of his lack of 'illustrious ancestors' in comparison to established English estates.[40] However, it is also important to note that in the finishing process of country estates in Ireland such as Castletown, portrait galleries – which in England 'were usually used to demonstrate the owner's family pedigree' – were often hung with a 'concentration of patrons and friends instead', as these portraits emphasised 'associational links to notable heroes, military heroes and statesmen, and therefore proclaimed allegiance to the Whig

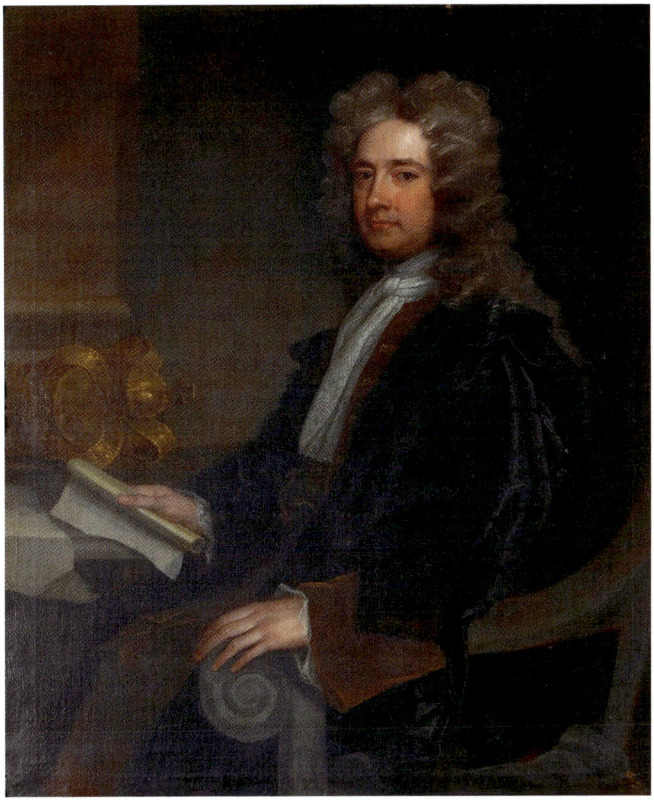

fig. 3 | *William Conolly* by Charles Jervas c.1715–21, oil on canvas, 127 x 94 cm, Castletown House, on loan from the Castletown Foundation, PC46

or Tory cause'.[41] In this capacity, Katherine would have been acutely aware of the impact of the Conollys' collections at Castletown to Irish visitors, with the display of works such as English-born artist Garret Morphy's portrait of William III. However, and more specifically, as Speaker Conolly passed away before being able to fully enjoy Castletown, Katherine's independent role in 'finishing' the home with Charles Jervas's complementary portraits of herself and William, she formatively and performatively communicated their shared social and political ambitions which she visually materialised in Ireland's grandest home.[42] These portraits were to maintain a position of prominence in Castletown for over a century following Katherine's death in 1752, as Castletown's 1898 inventory states that all were displayed in the dining room, a recognised 'showcase' of domestic space during the period that historian Patricia McCarthy has described as 'the stage on which the host and hostess performed'.[43]

Irish-born artist Charles Jervas, who became one of the most popular portraitists in the British Isles in the early years of the eighteenth century, is believed to have completed his portraits of William and Katherine Conolly sometime between 1715 and 1721 when he had returned to Ireland from London to capitalise on his success as one of Kneller's most prodigious pupils [figs 1, 3].[44] The timing of Jervas's visit was especially advantageous for William, who had made a triumphant return to politics in 1715 when he was unanimously elected as the speaker of the Irish House of Commons following his reappointment as the commissioner of revenue in 1714.[45] Conolly's political

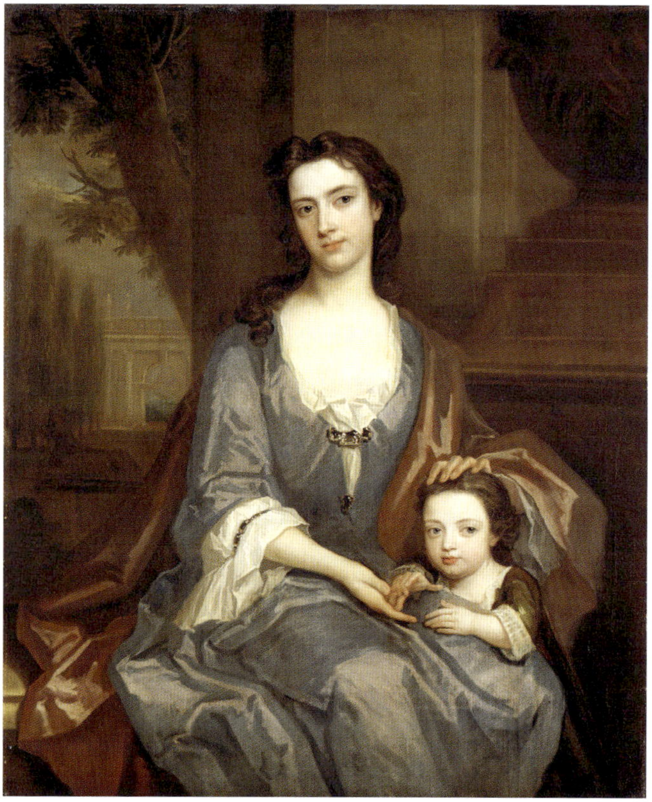

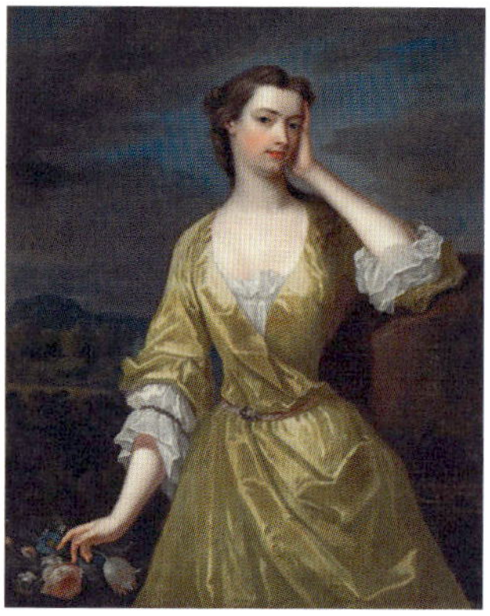

above fig. 5 | *Elizabeth Egerton née Churchill (1687/88–1714), Countess of Bridgewater* by Charles Jervas, pre-1715, oil on canvas, 121 x 95.6 cm (© Christie's Images, 2020)

fig. 4 | *Catherine Harpur née Crewe (1682–1745) and a child* by Charles Jervas, pre-1715, oil on canvas, 125 x 100 cm, Calke Abbey, Derbyshire (© National Trust / Angelo Hornak)

success is recognisably reflected in his portrait, as he confidently meets the viewer's gaze seated in black magisterial robes holding a scroll in his right hand. His robes and voluminously styled grey periwig denote Conolly as a distinguished and sophisticated politician among his peers, while the scroll emphasises his leading role in shaping policy. Costume and emblematic devices were essential to strengthen his visual presence, as they reflected William's political and social standing within Irish society. Additionally, for a contemporary audience, a pair of portraits commissioned from the fashionable Jervas reflected the Conollys' emerging political and social significance in Ireland when originally viewed inside their Capel Street residence, and subsequently at Castletown House. Considering Conolly's political success – which was largely influenced by Katherine's social connections – and their mutually beneficial and happy relationship that was advantageous 'not only for them but also for their brothers, sisters and their children', it is likely that Katherine's portrait was completed by Jervas around the same time in an effort to prominently mark the beginning of the Conollys' political and familial legacy, and visually legitimise their roles in Irish society.[46]

Jervas's *Portrait of a Lady*, in the Castletown collection [fig. 1], is generally accepted as an early portrait of Katherine, and for the purposes of this paper will be understood as such, since her role as Ireland's most influential political hostess during the period suggestively informed a gendered and visual language of 'quality' that was understood by an elite Irish viewership.[47] Katherine's portrait, in both composition and costume, is strikingly similar to two other portraits of women that Jervas completed in England before he travelled to Dublin in 1715.[48] His two portraits of Catherine Harpur (*née* Crewe; 1682–1745) and Elizabeth Egerton (*née* Churchill; 1687/88–1714) depict the sitters in similarly styled informal gowns with conventional poses, gazing directly at the viewer [figs 4, 5]. All three portraits in this capacity, bear the unmistakable influence of Jervas's teacher Kneller, with their 'classical settings, "polite" poses and gestures, and generic clothing'.[49] Art historian Caroline Pegum describes Kneller's – and, by extension, Jervas's – mode of representing costume as being 'composed with a monochrome gown wrapping over plain white linen [...] and absolutely minimal adornment in the forms of jewels, gloves [and] fans'.[50] This style of representation at the beginning of the eighteenth century was considered by contemporary commentators to be 'graceful and timeless', as 'everlasting Drapery of a plain nature was to be admired [since] it focused attention on the sitter's inner character as expressed through the hands and face'.[51] While certainly popular in portraiture of the period, this highly conservative mode of dress was not worn in everyday life, especially as many women depicted in this fashion, like Katherine Conolly, did enjoy accessorising their gowns and wearing fine jewellery. This is important to consider in their likenesses, as this style of portraiture relied upon the act of costuming to visually signal the sitter's virtuous and polite 'qualities'.

Additionally, this style of open robe-dress also performed as a rhetorical pictorial device which 'conscientiously evoked the generic loose gowns' of elite Irish and English female sitters of the seventeenth century, such as the *Duchess of Ormonde* and *Lady Lucy Loftus, Viscountess Lisburne* to visually communicate a Protestant 'social and dynastic continuity' [figs 6, 7].[52] This shared formal style of portrait, which lacked excessive accessories and adornments, was also important to visually differentiating between the Protestant and Catholic elite at the turn of the eighteenth century, as portraits of British and Irish families who remained dedicated to the Jacobite cause often elected to represent themselves in the elaborate French dress associated with the exiled Stuart court at Saint-Germain-en-Laye.[53] For example, the embellished gown in Garret Morphy's *c.*1695 portrait of Anne O'Neill emulated the low décolletage, lace and jewels which were de rigueur in the French courts [fig. 8].[54] Additionally, the distinctively raised and parted hairstyle worn by O'Neill was popular among the French elite throughout the seasons of 1694 to 1695, and subsequently evolved to include decorative ribbons, gems or flowers placed into the hair to reflect the sitter's rank and status. Comparatively, for portraits of prominent Protestant women in Ireland and Britain during this period, the art of 'dressing' was strongly linked to religious and polite virtues that implored young women to 'depend not on vain and affected dress', as 'the true Ornament of a Christian Lady [could] not be the Outward Adorning, or putting on of Apparel, but must be the hidden Dress of the Heart'.[55] While portraits of prominent Irish and English women from this early period, such as Katherine Conolly and the Duchess of Ormonde, are all depicted wearing expensive fabrics to convey their wealth and superiority, it is their lack of adornment, in the forms of ribbons, laces and jewels, which pictorially communicated their social quality and distinguished them from their Jacobite contemporaries.[56] In adhering to this particular mode of representation and costuming, elite women not only reflected their association to Protestant causes and 'qualities', but also

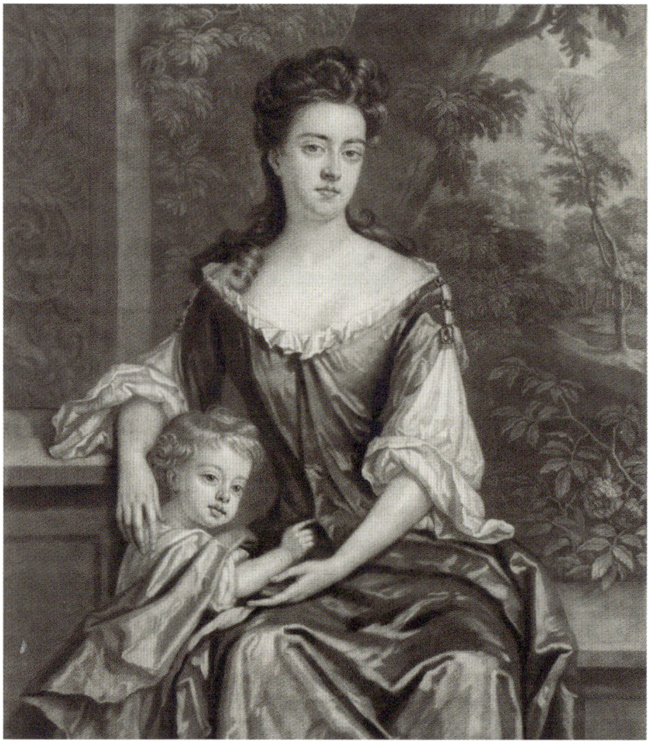

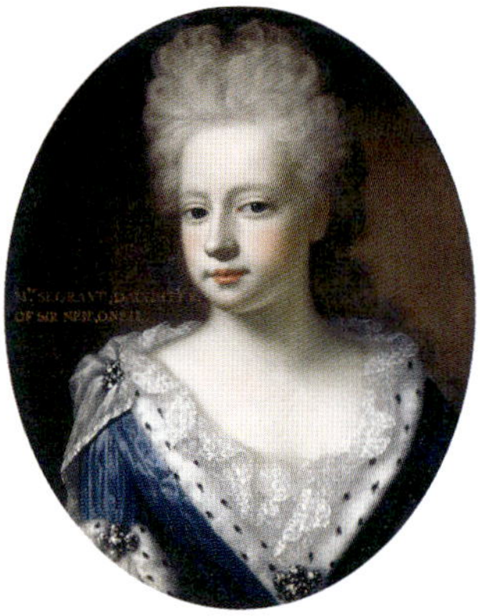

above

fig. 8 | *Anne O'Neill, later Mrs Seagrave*
by Garret Morphy (*c*.1650–1716), *c*.1695, oil on canvas, 45 x 36 cm
National Gallery of Ireland, NGI.4148
(photo: NGI)

left

fig. 6 | *Mary Butler (née Somerset), Duchess of Ormonde, and her son Thomas, Earl of Ossory*
by John Smith (*c*.1652–*c*.1742) after Godfrey Kneller
*c*.1693, mezzotint, 34 x 25 cm
National Portrait Gallery, London, D31316
(© NPG, London)

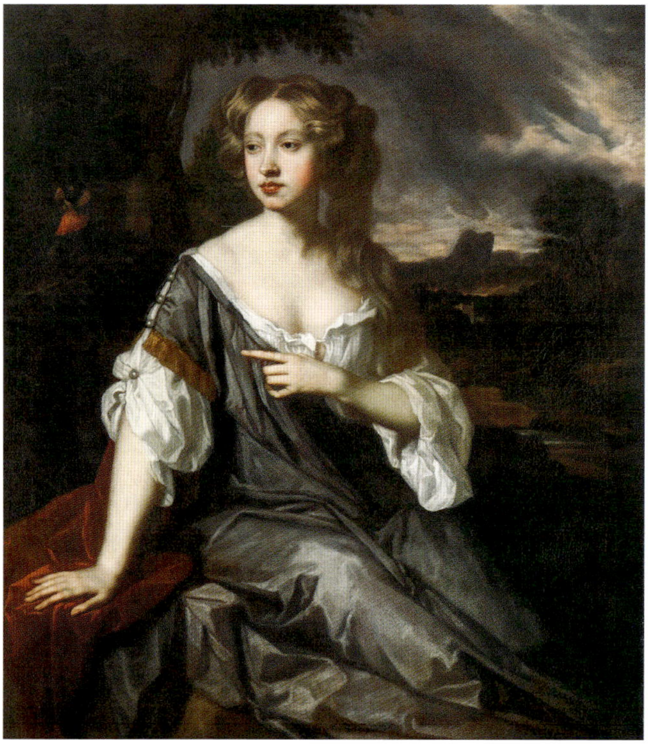

fig. 7 | *Lucy Loftus, Viscountess Lisburne*
by Peter Lely (1618–1680) pre-1689, oil on canvas, 126 x 104.5 cm
Rathfarnham Castle, RMCAS.2010.0030
(OPW / Con Brogan)

shaped the visual language of gendered improvement in Ireland throughout the period.

The popularity of this particular style of representation among women in Ireland can arguably be traced to earlier portraits of the Duchess of Ormonde, whose 'personal Character', inner virtues and patterns of behaviour were recognised as traits to be 'emulated and revered' from imagery during the Ascendancy period.[57] Her likeness by a follower of Michael Dahl, now in the Ormonde Picture Collection at Kilkenny Castle, is remarkably like Dahl's *c*.1695/96 original in the collections of the National Trust, Petworth House, Sussex (NT 486210), and would have been a well-recognised image in Ascendancy Ireland, as similar likenesses of the duchess by Kneller were mass produced for their desirability among collectors in the Irish market.[58] In fact, among the paintings and prints listed in Jonathan Swift's 1742 inventories, Swift had a painting of the duchess in his collection, but only prints of her husband, James Butler, 2nd Duke of Ormonde.[59] Although a revered English court beauty, the duchess's unique social position in Ireland as vicereine (1703–07, 1710–13) and wife of Ireland's first Irish lord lieutenant and highest-ranking peer, distinctively informed her social and visual identity within Ascendancy contexts. During her short residence at Dublin Castle, she had a significant effect on fashion and behaviour in elite and popular culture, as illustrated by instructional guidebooks for young women which were dedicated to her 'illustrious person', and by her active support of the Irish textile industry and charitable patronage of the Dublin workhouse during her tenure as vicereine of Ireland.[60] While Ormonde is certainly not wearing Irish textiles in her portrait, the socio-cultural significance of her likeness to an Irish (Protestant) audience throughout the period would have been informed by her quality – charitable acts of display and improvement.

Likewise, the stylistic continuity between Ormonde and Conolly's likenesses and earlier Anglo-Irish representations in the State collection, such as *Lady Lucy Loftus, Viscountess Lisburne* by Sir Peter Lely [fig. 7], can be explained through the social evolution of religious and moral improvement in self-fashioned dress which signalled a woman's 'qualities' in visual display. For Irish visitors to Castletown in the 1730s, Katherine's portrait by Jervas demonstratively reflected her 'qualities' as one of Protestant Ireland's most influential figures, as she was well recognised for her patriotism and role as a charitable patroness of the textile industry (like Ormonde before her). Similarly, during the period that the portrait would have been viewed within Castletown's domestic space, the linens worn by Katherine would have been politically charged in Ireland due to increasingly restrictive trade legislation imposed by Westminster from the 1690s, which severely impacted the Irish economy up to the 1780s.[61] However, though it cannot be said for certain that Katherine is represented in Irish-made linen, she was strongly associated with the textile in Ireland as she began to publicly support the industry in 1721, and fully 'intended by her purchases to encourage the manufacture of high quality Irish linens which would soon displace other textiles from the tables and persons of the smart, in England as well as Ireland'.[62] Considering her well-known patronage of the linen industry among Ireland's elite, the significance of Katherine's open robe, comprised of a white linen stomacher and *engageantes* (a form of decorative sleeve), with a bodice and overskirt that was often heavily embellished with embroidered designs and placed over a petticoat of expensive fabrics (such as silk or fine linen), has been overlooked.[63] To Castletown's earliest visitors not only was this style of dress associated with social and religious continuity, but also visually representative of Katherine's 'qualities' of improvement associated with the industry itself. In following these formal conventions, Katherine Conolly's portrait becomes a self-fashioned and gendered reflection of quality within Castletown's domestic space through her calm countenance, delicate gestures, and in the performative simplicity of her dress. Crucially, what is not on display is her numerous gold and diamond pendants, as Katherine had a self-professed love of expensive jewellery.[64]

Considering the wide range of contemporary stylistic conventions for female portraiture in Ireland and Britain, which employed myriad allegorical devices and superfluous dress and ornamentation as a means of visually reinforcing elite status, the lack of adornment in Katherine's portrait can be understood as a deliberate and purposeful attempt to visually represent her 'quality' within a politically sensitive milieu. As this particular mode of representation was recognised as 'an appropriate means of portrayal' for elite women to embody the 'Augustan values of sobriety, modesty and reason', it was then a useful masque for Katherine, whose patriotic role in elite Irish society was as well-known as her love of diamonds, gambling and political intrigue.[65]

## Duty and devotion

IN FACT, BY OCTOBER 1733, KATHERINE'S CLANDESTINE EVENINGS OF HIGH-STAKES GAMBLING AT Castletown House had become Dublin's worst-kept secret. With the late-night sessions affording 'the town a great deal of chat', her two sisters, Mrs Mary Jones and Mrs Jane Bonnell, had become excessively worried about the 'crowds of young gay company' indulging in late entertainments hosted by Katherine, including the high-stakes French card game basset, which Jones noted was 'what the Duke [of Dorset, the Lord Lieutenant] does not allow at [Dublin] Castle'.[66] Although Katherine's entertainments – which were attended by politicos and members of Ireland's beau monde – seemed tiresome and indulgent to her sisters, her reputation in this capacity as a respected hostess was crucial for her family to maintain their social superiority and political interests in the years following her husband's death. Katherine's favoured card-playing companion throughout the period – her nephew-in-law Frank Burton, who notoriously kept a 'basset bank at her [Katherine's] house' – also actively benefitted from her political and social standing, as she campaigned on his behalf for the (ultimately successful) position of MP for co. Clare.[67] Similarly, Katherine benefitted from their relationship, as their shared enjoyment of gambling and politics continued a tradition of 'discreet' discourse held away from Dublin Castle. While the conversations of these evenings are mostly unknown, the social atmosphere of Katherine's colourful soirées can be visualised in the current display of an eighteenth-century gaming table on display in the Long Gallery of Castletown [fig. 9].[68] While the maker is unknown, its position within a grand entertaining space, complemented by portraits of the Conollys, provokes past imagery of men and women gossiping with glasses of claret in candlelit rooms. Although the table did not belong to Katherine, its display and significance to visualising Castletown's early social interiors reflects what French philosopher Gaston Bachelard described as the

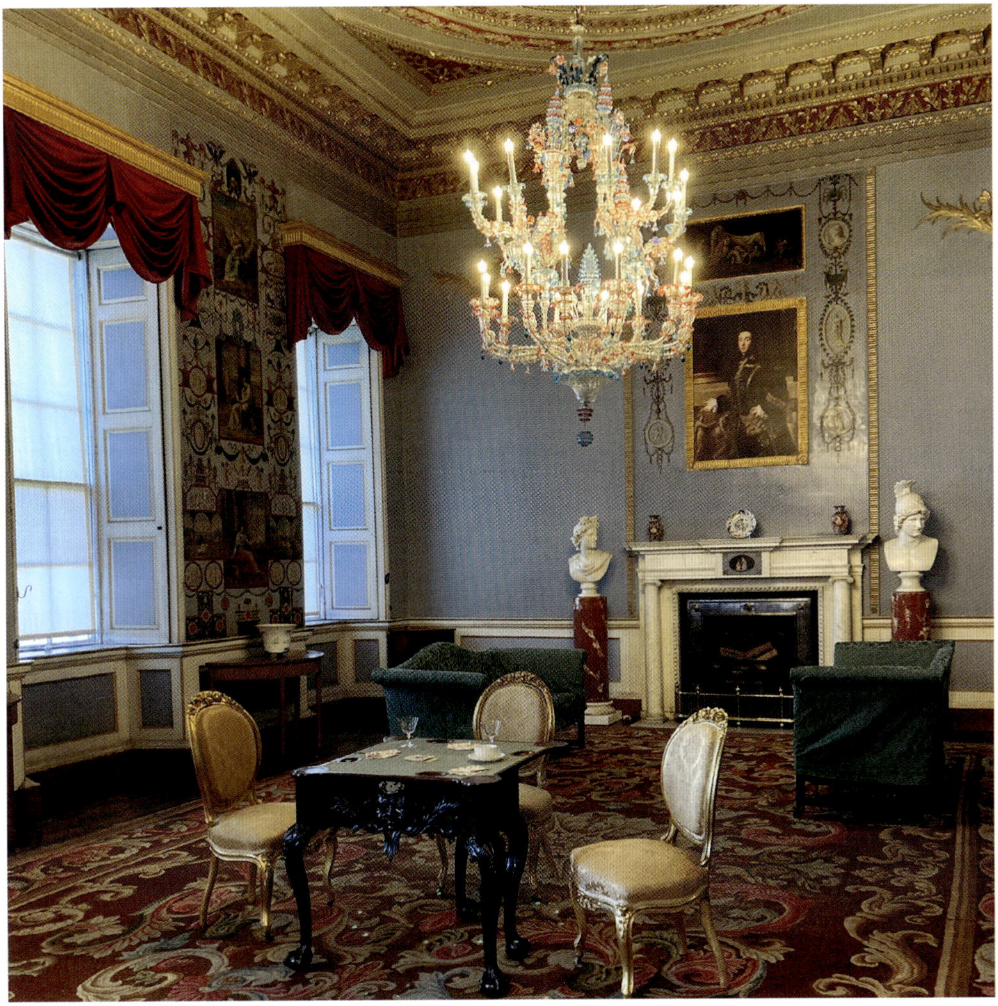

'intimate values of inside space'.[69] By reconsidering the intimate and familiar interactions which occurred within Castletown's eighteenth-century domestic spaces, the gaming table and its associated activities, along with the display of William and Katherine's portraits by Jervas on the walls, can add to our perception of Castletown's history in rooms and objects where 'the personal past adds special colour'.[70]

Katherine's intimate familial connections during her widowhood are also particularly important to emphasise in these contexts. She commissioned from Jervas a portrait of herself with Frank Burton's daughter Molly (1726–1737) in *c.*1730 [fig. 2], and dedicated a bespoke cabinet to the young girl, whom she largely raised [fig. 10]. Katherine also commissioned a pair of funerary monuments representing herself and her husband, completed by London-based sculptor Thomas Carter in 1736 [figs 11, 12].

fig. 9 | View of the Long Gallery, with eighteenth-century Irish gaming table, Castletown House, on loan from the Irish Georgian Society
(photo: the author, 2022)

Considering Katherine's elevated and unique social status at the time of these commissions, her representations strongly reflect her dedication to pictorially acknowledging herself as a woman of duty, family and 'quality'. For such wealthy and well-connected widows, historian Amanda Vickery states that 'chastity was an essential condition of virtuous widowhood, as was loyalty to the dead, but an inflexible retirement or nun-like renunciation of worldly goods was not demanded by propriety'.[71] Additionally, for wealthy widows like Katherine who chose not to remarry, their widowhood was considered to be 'a dignified condition' when 'staged with decorum [...] and if combined with prosperity could be a period of unique independence and self-expression'.[72] Katherine's commissions of a double portrait with her grandniece and bespoke cabinet, together with the funerary monuments of herself and her late husband, strongly reflect her role as a virtuous and independent widow in Irish society, whose familial devotion could be visually and materially measured. Vickery also notes that throughout the period, 'glamourous noble widows might project themselves in paintings, surrounded by their progeny, but with the dead husband still present in a portrait in the background', which was 'an ingenious device that asserted the survival [and] endurance of the marriage bond even in death, and perhaps continuity of the blood'.[73] Within these conventional contexts Katherine's commissions are unique and significant to her circumstances, as the Conollys had a childless marriage and the 'continuity' of the family was the ideological and 'patriotic' legacy of Speaker Conolly, which strongly relied on Katherine's ability to support socio-economic improvements through political theatre. As Katherine's careful management of his legacy at Castletown and her 'continued access to ministers on both sides of the Irish Sea helped perpetuate the late speaker's influence and memory' through the 1730s, her instrumental role in independently supporting improvements well into her widowhood (such as the textile industry) firmly established the Conolly family's reputation as 'patriotic landlords' which lasted throughout the century.[74] Additionally, Katherine's decision to represent herself with her young grandniece is also notable, reflecting her maternal 'qualities' and social status as a wealthy widow who could independently and financially support extended family.

The double portrait of Conolly and her grandniece Molly Burton was likely completed during Jervas's sojourn to Ireland between 1729 and 1734.[75] Although Katherine's dress is strikingly similar to his earlier portrait, her widowhood is subtly revealed through the emblematic use of a black linen veil, which is pinned to the crown of her head and cascades behind her shoulders. Distinctively, there is one significant deviation from the dress in her earlier portrait, which is the inclusion of a small gold and diamond belt buckle. The buckle not only reflects her love of jewellery, but also her active involvement with creating heirloom pieces in gold and diamonds to gift and commemorate her family.[76] Despite her grandniece not wearing any adornments except for the small sprig of flowers in her hair, Conolly was known to excessively dote on Molly and her family, and even commissioned a pair of diamond combs to replace a pair Katherine had loaned to Molly's mother, 'Missy' Burton, to 'make the figure in co. Clare'.[77] As a favourite of Katherine, and a beloved family member, Molly was a sensical choice for a double portrait, but also a narrative departure from depictions of wealthy matriarchs with male successors. It is important to note this distinction considering

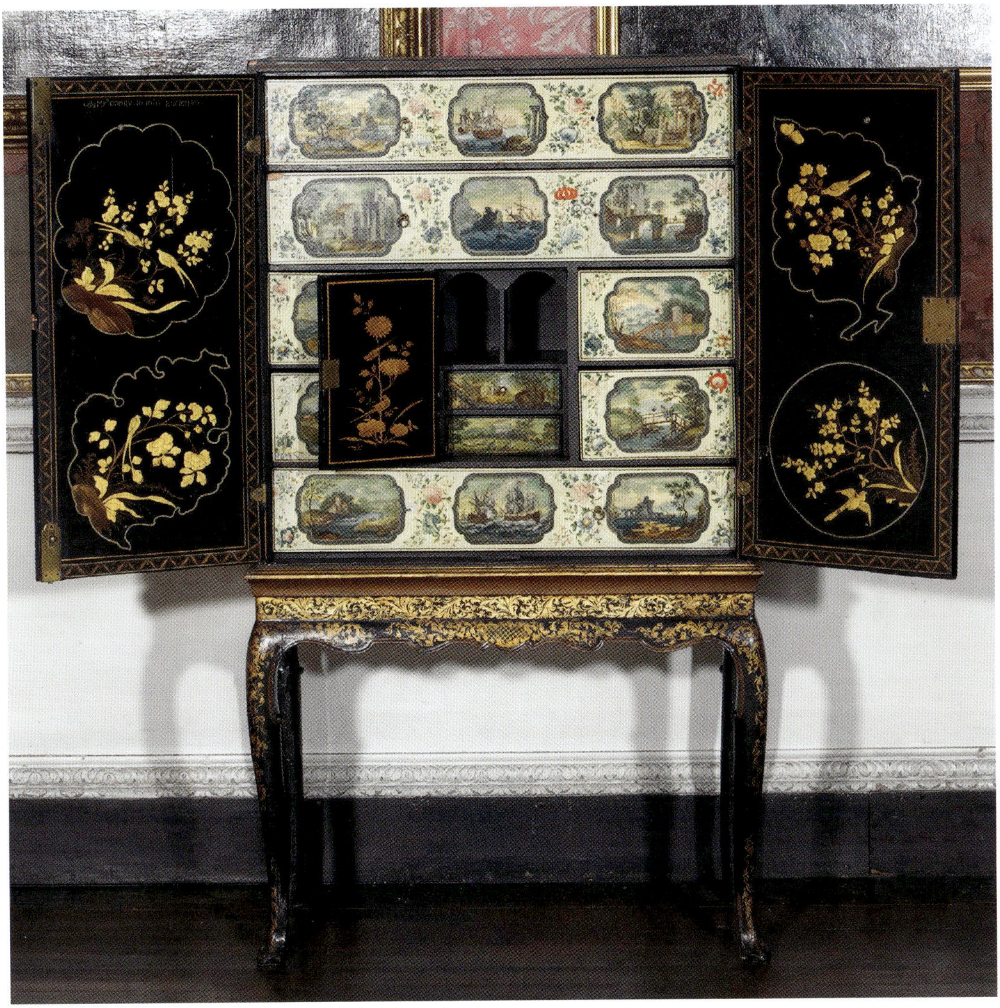

Conolly's unique situation and highly unusual influence, since she continued to receive political visitors after her husband's death in 1729.[78] However, this portrait, with its tender interaction between herself and her grandniece, expresses Katherine's compassionate and gendered qualities which were intimately known within her private sphere. Similarly, it is remarkably alike in style to Jervas's earlier portrait of Catherine Harpur who is posed with (presumably) one of her eight children [fig. 4].[79]

Conolly was particularly devoted to Molly, and often referred to her as 'my child' or 'my girll' in correspondence with her sisters, and she remained a prominent maternal figure in the child's life.[80] Due to Molly's fragile disposition, which Katherine described as being affected by 'esterick [hysteric] fits', she felt herself responsible for the young girl's protection from illness or harm, and often cared for her before Molly's

fig. 10 | Chinese cabinet with later (Irish?) painted additions, early eighteenth century, pine and lacquer, on Irish stand, Castletown House, on loan from the Castletown Foundation, FC55

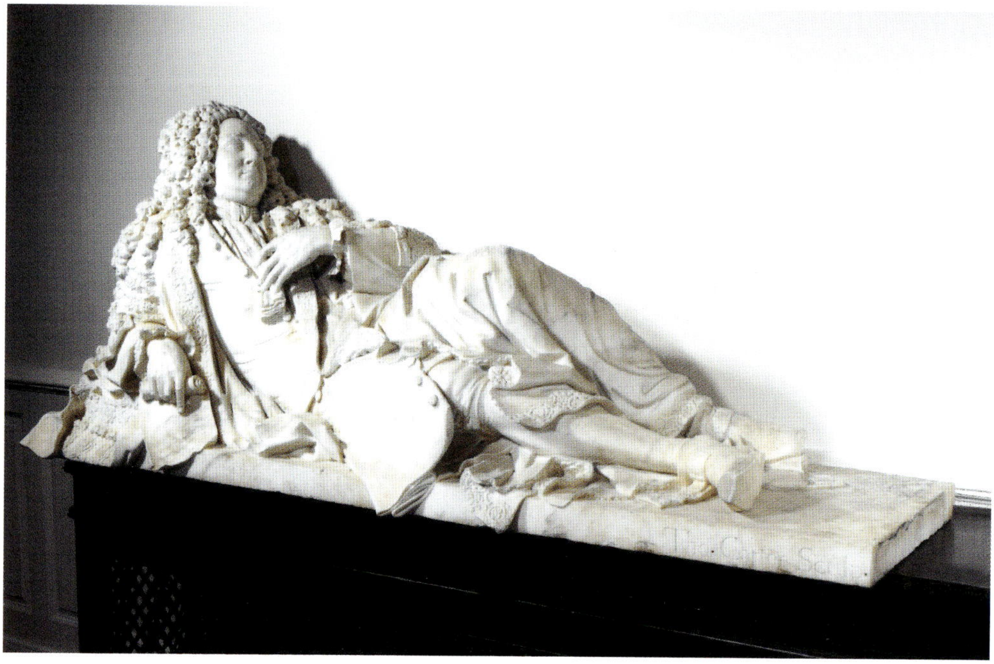

untimely death at the age of eleven in 1737.[81] Although Burton was often unwell, Katherine allowed her to 'play and gallop about' at Castletown and provided her with books and cross-stitch to make her comfortable when she fell ill.[82] It is likely that the portrait was completed during one of Burton's stays with Conolly, who personally tended to her care throughout the 1730s. This close relationship is reflected in their portrait, as Katherine delicately wraps her arm around the young girl's waist as if to pull her closer as they hold each other's hands in Conolly's lap. This connection is also reflected in the material of their gowns, as Katherine took great interest in showing off fabric samples intended for Burton to her female friends, and enjoyed dressing Burton in silks and linens despite her acknowledgment that 'she durtys and wears her co[a]tes out soe fast [they] will not last long'.[83] Additionally, the modest linens represented in their garments remained Katherine's primary 'patriotic' cause, as she also sent her sister, Jane Bonnell, samples of 'Ierish cloth', along with Burton's silks in 1732.[84] Considering Katherine's influential role in society, and more particularly in Molly's life, this self-fashioned and conventional portrait provided Conolly with the ability to visualise her maternal and matriarchal status in Ascendancy Ireland.

Katherine's subsequent commission of two funerary monuments from Thomas Carter in 1736, of herself and her late husband, also reflects the continuity of their marriage bonds in death and their patriotic legacy [figs 11, 12].[85] The monuments depict William and Katherine in 'tragic pose', with each lying on their side and holding

figs 11, 12 | Funerary monuments for William Conolly and Katherine Conolly by Thomas Carter (d.1756), c.1736, marble, 201cm and 183cm long respectively, Castletown House, FS11
(OPW)

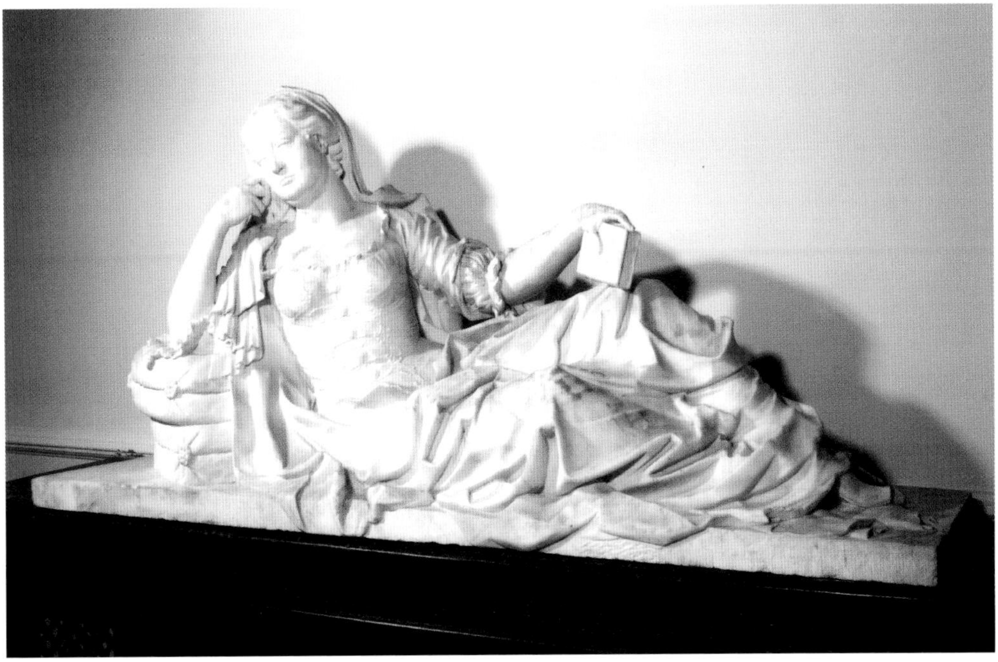

emblematic devices to denote their gendered and complementary roles in elite society. Together, they represent a cohesive visual narrative of politics and polite Christian virtues, as William is depicted firmly holding a scroll in reference to his political career, and Katherine's role as a virtuous Protestant woman of quality is reflected in the prayer book she holds. The monuments, which are now displayed at Castletown House, were originally placed in the so-called 'Death House', a mausoleum connected to the church of Kildrought in nearby Celbridge, which contained a 'marble plaque describing William Conolly's virtues and achievements'.[86] The commemorative project cost Katherine £2,000, as she employed local Irish and English artists to visually express her devotion to family, marriage and religion. Their marble likenesses are remarkably similar to Jervas's earlier representations, with Speaker Conolly in his periwig and dress coat, and Katherine wearing a draping veil; however, the intricate detail captured by Carter in the lace, folds and embellishments of their dress further emphasises their elite status and suggestively reflects Katherine's keen interest in textiles.[87] Her matriarchal role during and after the Speaker's lifetime is further reflected in the original placement of the monuments, in which she is elevated and positioned above her husband. Within this context, she is narratively overseeing the legacy of the late Speaker, who lies with his face turned affectionately towards her, his eyes closed and his left hand placed above his heart. Considering that Katherine commissioned these pieces specifically to honour his memory in the mausoleum, this subtle positioning also reflects her role in overseeing its construction and design to reflect both the Speaker's and the family's socio-cultural achievements. The project also provided Katherine with the opportunity to further reinforce the family's 'patriotic' legacy by hiring local artists. For example, while the sculptures were imported from London, the striking doric tabernacle, which originally framed the figures of William and Katherine, is attributed to Irish-based artist William Kidwell (1662–1736), who created similar pieces for other members of the Ascendancy elite, such as Viscount Duncannon (d.1724) at Fiddown, co. Kilkenny, and Sir Donal O'Brien (d.1717) at Kilnasoolagh, co. Clare.[88] Just as the Conollys had supported Irish builders and materials for Castletown in the 1720s, Katherine's choice of Kidwell reflects how she independently continued with this socially and politically astute pattern of behaviour to visually reflect her dedication to local 'improvements'.

In conclusion, the 'palatial' environs of Castletown House were uniquely experienced by eighteenth-century Irish audiences through Katherine's agency in finishing the home and continuing to independently and recognisably build on its legacy as a site of 'improvement' in widowhood. Approaching her commissions and representations for display at Castletown within the socio-cultural nuances of the Protestant Ascendancy not only informs previously overlooked narratives of inherent Irish patriotism, but also reveals further insights into her impact on the home's earliest collections and the convivial domestic atmosphere enjoyed by friends and family. As Castletown has certainly evolved since Katherine's lifetime, it is important to reflect upon the social significance of her representations in its collections, and in particular their ability to broadly enrich our understanding of how women have shaped the experiences and perceptions of visitors past and present in the OPW's historic properties.

---

**Dr Priscilla Sonnier** completed her PhD in the History of Art from University College Dublin in 2023. Her research focuses on the socio-cultural evolution of elite female portraiture in eighteenth-century Ireland in response to Anglo-Irish Protestant 'improvement', with broader interests in gendered architectural and design processes among Irishwomen and their social networks. She is a former tour guide of Farmleigh House and Estate (OPW), and currently the executive officer for the Royal Society of Antiquaries of Ireland.

**Endnotes**

1 Richard Twiss, *A Tour in Ireland in 1775* (London: J. Robson, 1776), p.65.

2 Patrick Walsh, *The Making of the Irish Protestant Ascendancy: the life of William Conolly 1662–1729* (Suffolk: Boydell Press, 2010), p.184.

3 It is also important to mention Lady Anne Conolly (*née* Wentworth), who married William's nephew Thomas, and, like Katherine, influenced Castletown's earliest social interiors. For an insightful study on the impact of Lady Anne on Castletown's collections see, Nicola Figgis, 'Lady Anne Conolly (1713–97): context and collection', *Irish Architectural and Decorative Studies*, vol.20 (2017), pp.142–55.

4 For more on the life of Lady Louisa and her architectural improvements see: National Library of Ireland (NLI), Conolly Papers; Irish Architectural Archive (IAA), Castletown Papers; University of Nottingham, Marlay Collection; Brian FitzGerald, *Lady Louisa Conolly, 1743–1821: an Anglo-Irish biography* (London: Staples Press, 1950); Ruth Johnstone, 'Lady Louisa Conolly's Print Room at Castletown', in Elizabeth Mayes (ed.), *Castletown, Decorative Arts* (Dublin: OPW, 2011), pp.67–77; Joseph McDonnell, 'The Lafranchini Stuccowork at Castletown' in Mayes (ed.), pp.51–55; Ann Keller, '"In Great Vogue": the Long Gallery of Castletown House', in Mayes (ed.), pp.57–65, and Finola O'Kane, 'Design and Rule: women in the Irish countryside 1715–1831', *Eighteenth-Century Ireland, Iris an dá chultúr*, vol.19 (2004), pp.56–74: 59, 65–72.

5 Outside of comprehensive biographical and socio-cultural research by Marie-Louise Jennings, Gabrielle M. Ashford and Rachel Wilson, there has been relatively little written

about Katherine throughout scholarship. For more see, Marie-Louise Jennings and Gabrielle M. Ashford (eds), *The Letters of Katherine Conolly 1707–1747* (Dublin: Irish Manuscripts Commission, 2018), and Rachel Wilson, *Elite Women in Ascendancy Ireland, 1690–1745: imitation and innovation* (Woodbridge: Boydell and Brewer, 2015), pp.120–40.

6 Kyle Leyden, 'Substance over Style: Castletown and the protean politics of Irish "improvement"', *Irish Architectural and Decorative Studies*, vol.20 (2017), pp.14–39.

7 Jennings and Ashford (eds), p.xiv; David Griffin, 'An Architectural History of Castletown', in Mayes (ed.), pp.29–45: 30; Terence Dooley and Christopher Ridgway (eds), *Country House Collections: their lives and afterlives* (Dublin: Four Courts, 2021).

8 While the political nuances of Katherine's portraits have been overlooked in scholarship, Castletown's domestic spaces and their visual impact are well documented in Mayes (ed.), (2011). William Laffan, 'Portraits and Pantheons', in William Laffan and Christopher Monkhouse (eds), *Ireland, Crossroads of Art and Design, 1690–1840* (Chicago: Art Institute of Chicago, 2015), pp.39–62: 39.

9 NLI, Smythe of Barbavilla Papers; IAA, Castletown Papers.

10 Mark Hallett, 'Reading the Walls: pictorial dialogue at the eighteenth-century Royal Academy', *Eighteenth-Century Studies*, vol.37, no.4 (Summer 2004), pp.581–604.

11 Ibid., p.581.

12 Leyden, p.17.

13 For more on the significance and impact of absenteeism in Ireland, see: NLI, LO 388. *1742 Irish Register: or a list of the duchess dowagers, countesses, widow ladies, maiden ladies, widows, and misses of large fortunes, in England, as register'd by the Dublin Society, for the use of their members*. See A.P.W. Malcomson, *In Pursuit of the Heiress: aristocratic marriage in Ireland, 1740–1840* (Belfast: Ulster Historical Foundation, 2006); Walsh, 2010; Michael Brown, *The Irish Enlightenment* (Cambridge: Harvard University Press, 2016); John Turpin, *A School of Art in Dublin since the Eighteenth Century: a history of the National College of Art & Design* (Dublin: Gill & Macmillan, 1995).

14 For additional reading on economic improvement and its impact on visual and material culture, see Turpin (1995); Toby Barnard, *Making the Grand Figure: lives and possessions in Ireland, 1641–1770* (New Haven and London: Yale University Press, 2004); Sarah Foster, '"An honourable station in respect of commerce, as well as constitutional liberty": retailing, consumption and economic nationalism in Dublin, 1720–85', in Gillian O'Brien and Finola O'Kane (eds), *Georgian Dublin* (Dublin: Four Courts, 2008), pp.32–44.

15 Leyden, pp.14–39.

16 Maxine Berg, *Luxury and Pleasure in Eighteenth-Century Britain* (Oxford: Oxford University Press, 2005), p.27.

17 Ingrid Tague, *Women of Quality: accepting and contesting ideals of femininity in England, 1690–1760* (Woodbridge: Boydell Press, 2002), p.13.

18 Toby Barnard, *A New Anatomy of Ireland: the Irish Protestants, 1649–1770* (New Haven and London: Yale University Press, 2003) pp.41–42.

19 Ibid., pp.55–56, 71–72; Amy Prendergast, *Literary Salons across Britain and Ireland in the Long Eighteenth Century* (London: Palgrave Macmillan, 2015), p.117.

20 Tague, p.13; Barnard (2003), pp.41–42.

21 Tague, pp.13, 140–48; Barnard (2003), pp.41–43.

22 Tague, pp.12–17, 49–71.

23 Caroline Pegum, 'A new contribution to the oeuvre of Garret Morphy (*c*.1650–1716)', *British Art Journal*, vol.15, no.3 (Spring 2015), pp.85–92.

24 Foster (2008), pp.32–44; François de Salignac de la Mothe Fénelon, *Instructions for the Education of a Daughter*, trans. George Hickes (London: Jonah Bowyer, 1708), p.207; Toby Barnard, *Irish Protestant Ascents and Descents 1641–1770* (Dublin: Four Courts, 2004), pp.266–89.

25 Gaston Bachelard, *The Poetics of Space*, trans. Maria Jolas (New York: Penguin, 2014), p.53.

26 Griffin (2011), pp.29–30.

27 Walsh, pp.184–85.

28 Jennings and Ashford (eds), p.xv.

29 Ibid.; Griffin (2011), p.30.

30 Barnard, *Ascents and Descents*, p.276; Walsh, p.182; Wilson, p.108; Barnard, *Grand Figure*, p.353.

31 Extant correspondence was respectively given to Charles Fitzroy, 2nd Duke of Grafton, Lord Lieutenant 1720–24, and Thomas Clutterbuck, Chief Secretary of Lord Cartaret's administra-

tion 1724–30. IAA, Castletown Papers, A/3; Jennings and Ashford, (eds), pp.xix.

32 Barnard, *Ascents and Descents*, p.270; Barnard (2003), p.119.

33 Jennings and Ashford (eds), p.xii; Walsh, pp.103–24; Barnard, *Ascents and Descents*, p.278; Wilson, p.281.

34 IAA, Castletown Papers, J/3/1/3, Receipt of 26 March 1735, George Ewing to Lady Ann Conolly; Castletown Papers IAA/9/1–24, letters of Mrs Katherine Conolly to Lady Anne Conolly; Jennings and Ashford (eds), p.xiv.

35 Jennings and Ashford (eds), p.xiv.

36 Ibid.

37 John Loveday, *Diary of a Tour in 1732 through parts of England, Wales, Ireland and Scotland* (Edinburgh: W. Blackwood, 1890), p.48.

38 The socio-cultural and economic circumstances in Ireland that shaped such decisions of 'taste' are further discussed in Foster (2008), pp.32–44; Sarah Foster, 'Buying Irish: consumer nationalism in 18th-century Dublin', *History Today*, vol.47, no.6 (June 1997), pp.44–50; Walsh, pp.181–99; Turpin (1995); Padhraig Higgins, 'Consumption, Gender, and the Politics of "Free Trade" in Eighteenth-Century Ireland', *Eighteenth-Century Studies*, vol.41, no.1 (2007), pp.87–105; Martyn J. Powell, *The Politics of Consumption in Eighteenth-Century Ireland* (New York: Palgrave, 2005); Mary O'Dowd, 'Women and Patriotism in Eighteenth-Century Ireland', *History Ireland*, vol.14, no.5 (Sept/ Oct 2006), pp.15–38; Priscilla Sonnier, '"A Taste for Building": domestic space in elite female correspondence', in Conor Lucey (ed.), *House and Home in Georgian Ireland: spaces and cultures of domestic life* (Dublin: Four Courts, 2022), pp.175–84: 177–81.

39 Walsh, pp.181–99.

40 Ibid., p.190.

41 Kate Retford, *The Art of Domestic Life: family portraiture in eighteenth-century England* (New Haven and London: Yale University Press, 2006), pp.166–67.

42 Walsh, pp.190–91.

43 IAA, Castletown Papers, J/11; Patricia McCarthy, 'A Male Domain? The Dining Room Reconsidered', in Lucey (ed.), pp.51–53.

44 Mayes (ed.), pp.147–49.

45 Conolly had been in government since his election as an MP for co. Donegal in 1692, and by 1709 was appointed as Commissioner of Revenue. However, he was dismissed in 1710 for his Whig politics, only to be reappointed in 1714 following the succession of George I; Walsh, pp.25–125.

46 Mayes (ed.), p.179; Jennings and Ashford (eds), p.xviii.

47 Mayes (ed.), pp.147–49.

48 Ibid.; Anne Crookshank and the Knight of Glin, *Ireland's Painters: 1600–1949* (New Haven and London: Yale University Press, 2002), p.31.

49 Pegum, p.90.

50 Ibid.

51 Joseph Addison, *The Spectator*, no.129, 28 July 1711. Quoted in Pegum, p.90.

52 Pegum, p.90.

53 Ibid., pp.85, 89–90.

54 Morphy was also a preferred portraitist of Jacobite and Catholic families in Ireland following his arrival from London in 1694. Pegum, pp.85–86.

55 Fénelon, p.207.

56 Ibid.; Pegum, pp.85, 89–91.

57 Anon., *A Short Memorial and Character of that most Noble and Illustrious Princess Mary Dutchess of Ormonde* (London[?]: 1735); Samuel Madden, *Reflections and Resolutions Proper for the Gentlemen of Ireland* (Dublin: R. Reilly, 1738); Higgins, pp.87–92.

58 For a broader consideration of the desirability of popular eighteenth-century figures such as the Duchess in Irish print collections, see Rosalind M. Elmes, *Catalogue of Engraved Irish Portraits mainly in the Joly Collection and of Original Drawings* (Dublin: Stationery Office, 1937).

59 St Patrick's Hospital Archives, Dublin, Jonathan Swift Papers, A/23. I would to thank Scott Hayes for sharing these inventories with me.

60 Anonymous (1735); Fénelon (1708); Myles Campbell (ed.), *Vicereines of Ireland: portraits of forgotten women* (Newbridge: Irish Academic Press, 2021), pp.224–26.

61 Barnard (2003), p.63; Higgins, pp.87–105; Foster (1997), pp.44–50; [Margaret Bingham, Countess of Lucan], *Verses on the Present State of Ireland* (Dublin: Wogan, Bean and Pike, 1768).

62 Barnard, *Ascents and Descents*, pp.270, 278.

63 *Engageants* were decorative sleeves, often made from linen, cotton, silk or lace, and underpinned at the elbow for a fashionable look. For more on Irish dress and fabrics, specifically *engageants* in portraiture, see Mairead Dunlevy, *Pomp and Poverty: a his-*

*tory of silk in Ireland* (New Haven and London: Yale University Press, 2011), p.53; Mairead Dunlevy, *Dress in Ireland* (New York: Holmes & Meier, 1989), pp.90–129; Pegum, p.90.

64 For more, see the transcriptions in Jennings and Ashford (eds), pp.73, 85–93, 95–97, 105–06, 269, 273, 281, 287.

65 Pegum, p.90. Following her widowhood, Katherine's letters reveal her enjoyment in commissioning fine jewellery for herself and close family members. In fact, her numerous commissions of gold and diamond pieces led to her assuring her sister's jeweller in 1732 'to trust her' on payment as she had not yet received her rental income for the year. For more, see the transcriptions in Jennings and Ashford (eds), pp.85–87, 92–93.

66 NLI, Smythe of Barbavilla Papers, MS 41,577/2, letter from Mary Jones to Jane Bonnell, 16 Oct 1733. For more on the rules of basset, see Jean-Baptiste le Rond d'Alembert, 'Basset' in *The Encyclopedia of Diderot & d'Alembert Collaborative Translation Project*, trans. Richard J. Pulskamp (Ann Arbor: University of Michigan Library, 2009) <https://quod.lib.umich.edu/d/did/did2222.0001.11?view=text;rgn=main> [acc. 26 Feb 2025]; trans. of *Bassette, Encyclopédie ou Dictionnaire raisonné des sciences, des arts et des métiers*, vol.II (Paris, 1752).

67 Ibid., MS 41,577/2, letter from Jane Bonnell to Mary Jones, 16 Oct 1733.

68 There are also two gaming tables made of walnut listed in Castletown's 1898 inventory which were located in the billiard room and first-floor corridor. IAA, Castletown Papers, J/11.

69 Bachelard, p.25.

70 Ibid., p.53.

71 Amanda Vickery, *Behind Closed Doors: at home in Georgian England* (New Haven and London: Yale University Press, 2009), p.220.

72 Ibid., pp.220–28.

73 Ibid.

74 Walsh, p.198.

75 Crookshank and Glin, p.31.

76 For more, see the following transcriptions in Jennings and Ashford (eds), pp.73, 85–93, 95–97, 105–06, 269, 273, 281, 287.

77 Katherine's vested interests in the Burtons are evident throughout her extensive correspondence with her sister, Mrs Jane Bonnell, as frequent topics of conversation.

78 Wilson, p.109; Barnard, *Ascents and Descents*, p.281.

79 I would like to thank Caroline Pegum for information on Harpur's portrait.

80 Molly is a frequent subject of conversation (along with her family) throughout the young girl's lifetime (1726–1737). For more, see the following transcriptions in Jennings and Ashford (eds), pp.70–146.

81 NLI, Smythe of Barbavilla Papers, MS 41,578/2, letter of 6 June 1721, Katherine Conolly to Jane Bonnell; MS 41,578/2, letter of 12 July 1722, Conolly to Bonnell; MS 41,578/4, letter of 6 June 1726, Conolly to Bonnell; MS 41,578/6, letters of 12 April 1731 and 30 September 1732, Conolly to Bonnell; MS 41,578/7, letter of 29 July 1734, Conolly to Bonnell.

82 Ibid., MS 41,578/6, letter from Katherine Conolly to Jane Bonnell, 30 Sept 1731.

83 Ibid., MS 41,578/7, letter from Katherine Conolly to Jane Bonnell, 29 May 1733.

84 Ibid., MS 41,578/5, letter from Katherine Conolly to Jane Bonnell, 23 Feb 1729; MS 41,578/6, letter from Conolly to Bonnell, 30 Sept 1732.

85 Katherine may have also commissioned two other statues of herself and the Speaker which were not intended for the mausoleum. While the Castletown catalogue states that the funerary monuments were commissioned from Thomas Carter (Katherine's possibly being completed by his son, Thomas Carter Jn.) and were being shipped from London in August 1736, the *Dublin Journal* of 7 September mentions two other statues which were 'curiously carved in fine Italian Marble [...] to be sett up in the Gardens at Celbridge'; Mayes (ed.), pp.204–05.

86 Ibid.

87 Additionally, Carter was intimately acquainted with Jervas, who had loaned Carter funds for the extension of his London studio. The likenesses between Carter's sculptures and Jervas's paintings may have been on account of this relationship, in addition to the commission itself, as Jervas had an established a working relationship with Conolly by this time. Celine Hanratty, 'William Conolly's Funeral', Castletown House website <https://castletown.ie/remembering-and-william-conollys-funeral/> [acc. 9 May 2024].

88 Mayes (ed.), pp.204–05.

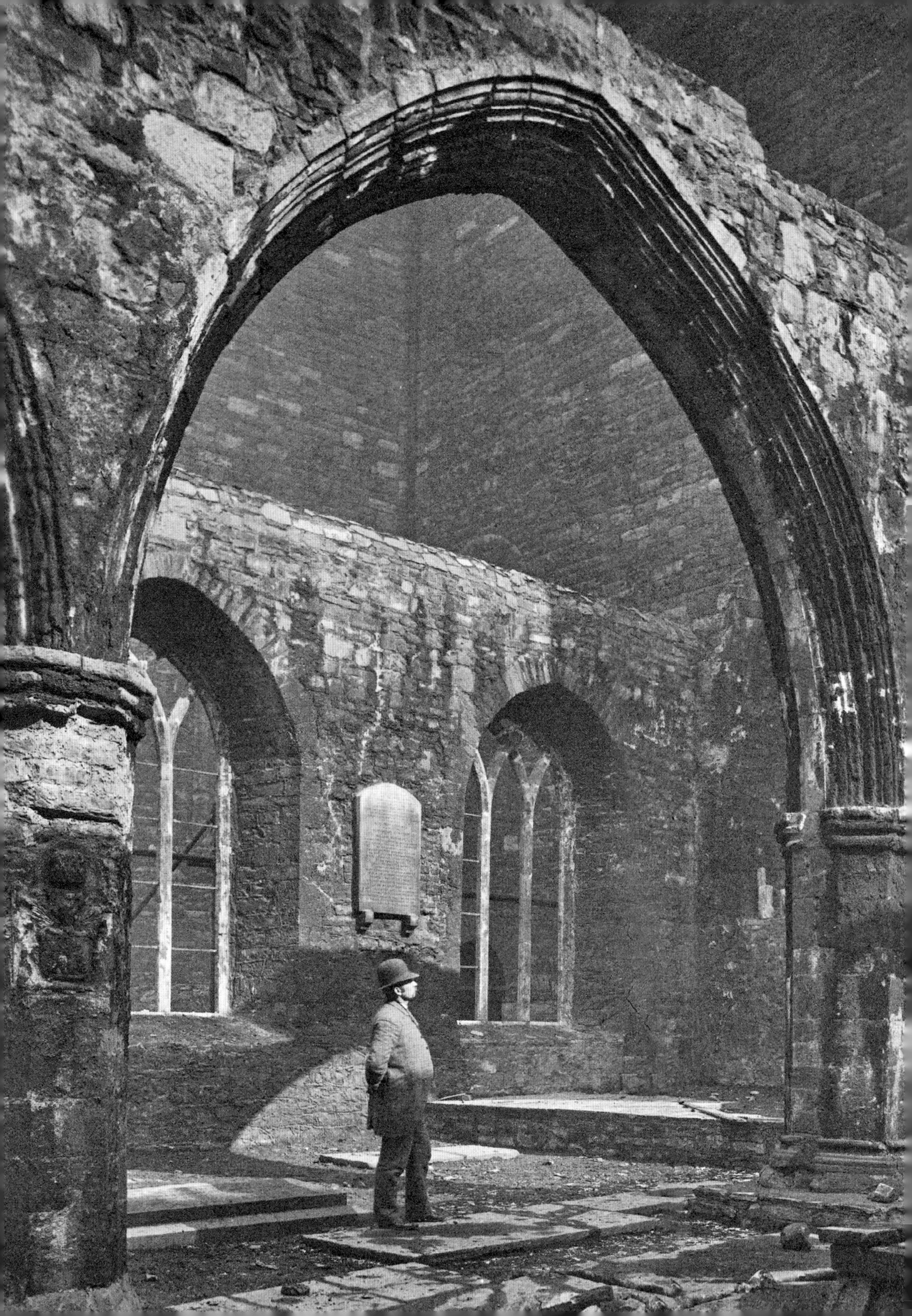

# St Audoen's Church, Dublin: a century in limbo

NEIL MOXHAM

'THAT THE CHURCH OF ST AUDOEN, IN THE CORN MARKET, IS SO LITTLE KNOWN OR CARED for by archaeologists – and more especially by architects – is perhaps scarcely so strange as its being found there at all in any state of preservation, however mutilated.' So wrote architect Thomas Drew (1838–1910) in 1867.[1] For decades, Drew made the care of St Audoen's Church [fig. 1] something of a personal mission, keeping those responsible for the building under his very close scrutiny. He was among the first to recognise the full historical significance of this ancient church which had stood at the western edge of Dublin's medieval walled city. Uniquely, the building still retained architectural elements dating back to the twelfth century, while its contemporaries had all been either rebuilt or abandoned in the post-Reformation era. It was only when local and national events placed the very survival of the site in jeopardy that a lifeline was presented in the form of the OPW. However, that intervention was far from simple. For the parish church, the transfer of an ancient site of Christian worship and interment to the strictly secular control of the State was not an easy step to take. For the OPW, the complexities of sharing a National Monument with an active church led to some pragmatic but necessary compromises which continued right up until the site was revitalised in the 1990s.

## The ancient church

BUILT BY THE FIRST GENERATION OF NORMANS TO OCCUPY DUBLIN, AND NAMED IN HONOUR of a seventh-century French saint whom they venerated, St Audoen's Church is among the oldest built structures in continuous regular use anywhere in Ireland. The church's commonly accepted foundation date of 1190 is inferred from an ecclesiastical grant the following year.[2] Excavations have confirmed multiple extensions to the church right up to the time of the Reformation – a crucial turning point in the history of both the building and its congregation. These extensions, and the addition of a bell-tower, saw the building grow to more than four times its original size, always retaining parts of its twelfth-century fabric [fig. 3].[3] As Drew suggests in his preceding

fig. 1 | St Audoen's, Dublin, photographed by Thomas F. Geoghegan, c.1887
National Library of Ireland, ALB8
(© National Library of Ireland)

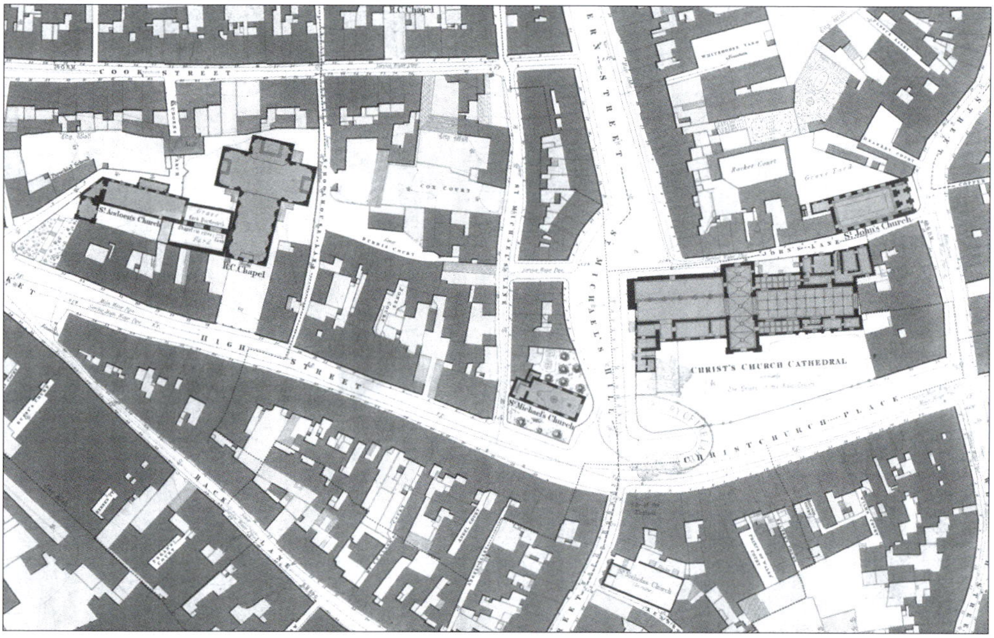


quote, the ongoing survival of any of this fabric has owed as much to luck as to providence. In the post-Reformation period, St Audoen's had a high degree of Roman Catholic recusancy among its nominally Protestant congregation, creating a stand-off in which funding could not be secured for any major renovations. The era of the Penal Laws tilted the balance firmly in favour of the Protestant Ascendancy, but this coincided with an economic decline in this once-exclusive part of Dublin. As the size and wealth of the congregation shrank, the parish allowed slightly under half of the medieval building – the chancel and the Portlester Chapel – to be unroofed and left open to the elements in 1773. The former St Anne's Chapel was similarly unroofed in 1820–21. Though ruined, the parish church retained ownership of these areas, principally because they included subterranean burial vaults in which the descendants of some

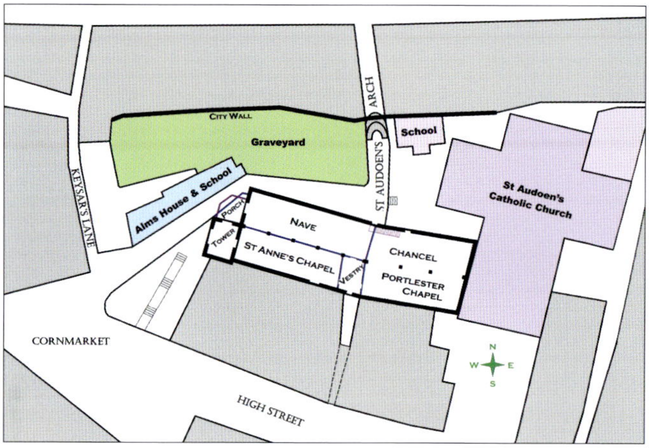


fig. 2 | Detail of 1847 OS map showing (L to R) St Audoen's, St Michael's, St Nicholas Within, Christ Church Cathedral and St John's (© Tailte Éireann – Surveying, permit no. CYAL50441786; courtesy of UCD Digital Map Library)

fig. 3 | Plan of St Audoen's Church, Dublin, in 1869 (digital drawing by the author, 2024)

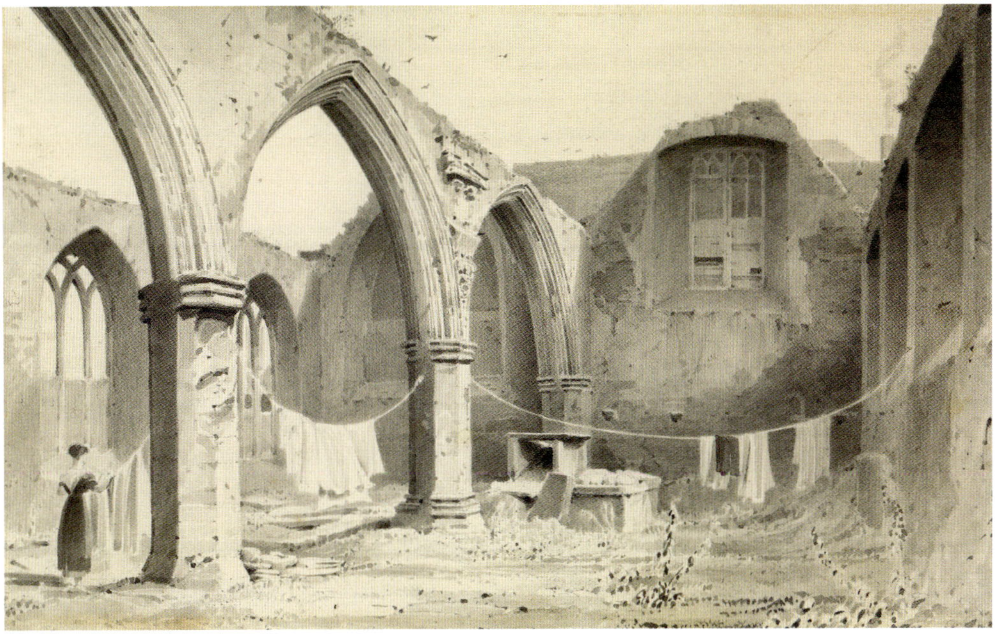

of Dublin's most prominent Anglo-Norman families had continuing rights of interment.

It was also good fortune which saw the church survive long enough to provide a rare example of authentic Gothic architecture during a nineteenth-century revival of all things medieval. The earliest-known illustrations of St Audoen's Church are to be found in Thomas Bell's *Origin and Progress of Gothic Architecture* (1825/1829).[4] George Petrie's famous drawing of a woman hanging laundry across the Portlester Chapel (*c.*1829) [fig. 4] focused on the decaying grandeur of the church ruins, and gothic novelist J. Sheridan Le Fanu (1814–1873) similarly used the crumbling memorials of St Audoen's as a symbolic metaphor in two of his earliest stories.[5] In appreciation of this legacy, Sir William Betham and Dr William Wilde of the Celtic Society spearheaded a campaign against plans to reduce the size of the active church still further in 1848.[6] Their intervention saved the rare Jacobean-style plaster wall monuments to the Sparke and Duffe families, which survive to the present day, but also pointed towards a new role for the church. St Audoen's would now be regarded not just as an active parish church, but as a place of sanctuary for the city's ancient heritage.

Reverend Alexander Leeper (1814–1893) became rector of St Audoen's in 1859, and during his long incumbency the role of the parish church would be completely redefined. Leeper clearly had an appreciation for the historical legacy he inherited, even if it was sometimes expressed eccentrically.[7] His first months saw the conservation of seventeenth-century stained-glass window fragments, the restoration of the late twelfth-century baptismal font, and the relocation of three particularly ancient

---

fig. 4 | *Hanging Washing in Lord Portlester's Chapel, Saint Audeon's* [sic], *Dublin* by George Petrie (1790–1866), *c.*1829, graphite and wash on paper, National Gallery of Ireland, NGI.6002

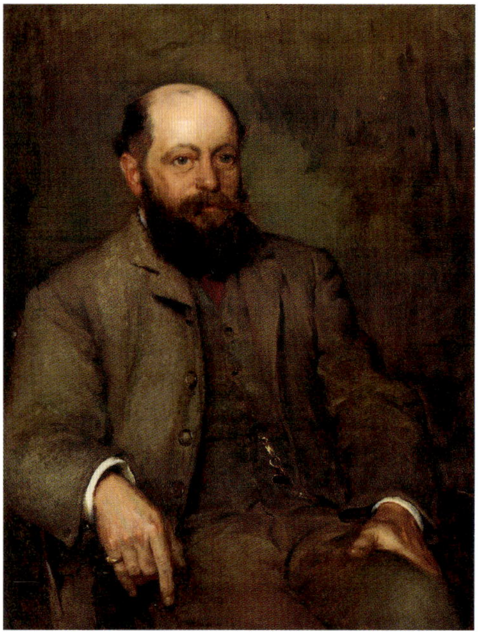

funerary monuments from the unroofed Portlester Chapel to the safety of the bell-tower.[8] These were the ledger tombstone of John Burnell (1495) and the effigies of Lord and Lady Portlester (1482) and of an unidentified figure (early fourteenth century).[9] There were suggestions that these monuments had been damaged not just by exposure to the elements, but by falling debris from the construction of the neighbouring Roman Catholic St Audoen's Church during the 1840s.[10] In any case, the movement of these monuments indoors undoubtedly spared them from further erosion, and it is unfortunate that nothing could be done to salvage the plaster memorials attached to the walls of the ruins. With the endorsement of parish authorities, Thomas Drew – then a young, Belfast-born architect, newly resident in Dublin – undertook a case study of St Audoen's Church in 1866, earning him the Fitzgerald Silver Medal from the Royal Institute of the Architects of Ireland [fig. 5]. Although Drew's study was limited to a description of the visible structure and some conjecture about a forgotten underground passageway, it was the first professional examination of the site and was subsequently published in pamphlet form, complete with architectural plans.[11] This, finally, brings us to the point where the Board of Works (as the Office of Public Works was consistently referred to during this period) becomes involved in the story of St Audoen's Church.[12]

## Disestablishment and National Monument status

THE CHURCH OF IRELAND UNDERWENT A PERIOD OF FUNDAMENTAL REORGANISATION IN THE late nineteenth century. As the 'established' State religion of Ireland since the 1530s, it had a formal role in local government, with, at times, powers over everything from levying tithes to policing and fire-fighting. However, a State religion which represented only eight percent of the Irish population (according to the 1861 census) was impossible to justify. Additionally, the parishes in Dublin city centre – once a cornerstone of the Church of Ireland – were shrinking as those parishioners who could afford to, moved to the suburbs. The parish of St Nicholas Within was merged with St Audoen's in 1867, as was that of St Michael in 1872, and most of the remaining city-centre

---

fig. 5 | *Portrait of Sir Thomas Drew (1838–1910) Architect* by Walter Frederick Osborne (1859–1903) 1891, oil on canvas, 68 x 51 cm, National Gallery of Ireland, NGI.931
(© National Gallery of Ireland)

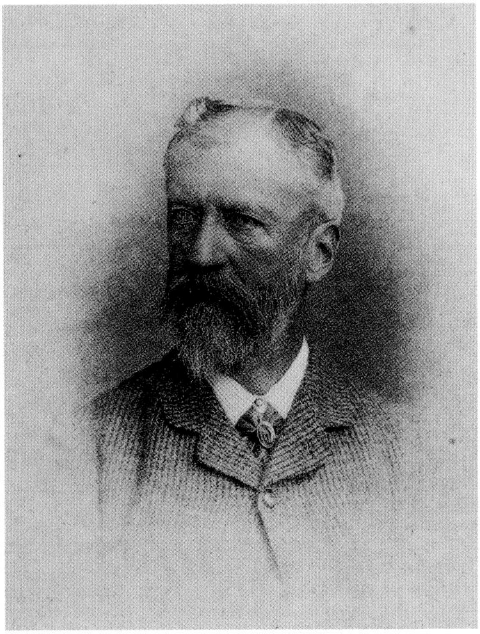

churches would close over the following century [fig. 2].[13] The Gladstone government's Irish Church Act of 1869 disestablished the Church of Ireland, placing it on an equal footing with other religions, but also removing its privilege of public funding. One unavoidable consequence of this was the inability of the Church of Ireland to financially sustain the unused but historically significant sites in its property portfolio. In recognition of this, Section 25 of the Act enabled the Church of Ireland to divest itself of 'any church or ecclesiastical building or structure' which was no longer in use, and was unlikely to be put back into use, but which was worthy of preservation because of its 'architectural character or antiquity'. The inclusion of this clause was strongly promoted by the antiquarians of the Royal Irish Academy and the Historical and Archaeological Association of Ireland (now the Royal Society of Antiquaries of Ireland), who had already carried out private conservation projects at sites like Clonmacnoise and Jerpoint Abbey. This provision would see such properties transferred to the Commissioners of Church Temporalities, who were, in turn, authorised to vest certain of these properties to the Board of Works after careful consideration. These properties were to be designated as 'National Monuments' – a newly coined term intended to class them as now being of historical rather than religious significance. Intervention with these structures was to be strictly limited to preservation rather than restoration. The Commissioners of Church Temporalities would cover most of the preservation and maintenance costs for the properties through the establishment of a £50,000 fund.[14]

The early years of the National Monuments scheme involved detailed studies of potential sites under the supervision of James H. Owen (1822–1891), Architect to the Board of Works.[15] This initial phase of the scheme did not meet universal approval, however, and antiquarians such as John Ribton Garstin, John G.A. Prim and Robert Young intensely debated its merits before it had even been put into effect. While they all welcomed the State's involvement in preserving Ireland's heritage (albeit limited to sites of Christian heritage), they disagreed on the extent of preservation work which should be applied to these ancient structures. More specifically, they all had some reservations about Owen's lack of experience with medieval buildings, and there were calls for an advisory committee of recognised experts to be formed.[16] Prim's *Kilkenny Moderator* newspaper, for example, cautioned against any unsympathetic restoration

fig. 6 | *T.N. Deane, RHA, Architect of National Museum Dublin* by Messrs Werner & Son, *c.*1890 (reprinted from *Building News*, 28 February 1890)

of the Rock of Cashel, warning that, should it happen, 'it will not be an ancient National Monument, but simply a modern Board of Works monument'.[17] At the other extreme, a rejected 1873 amendment to the Irish Church Act would have allowed the Rock of Cashel to be fully restored as an active Roman Catholic cathedral.[18] Nevertheless, in October 1874 the Rock of Cashel was scheduled as Ireland's first National Monument. This was followed just seven weeks later by a further thirteen structures. Unsurprisingly, these first monuments included high-profile sites already identified by the antiquarian community, such as Monasterboice and Glendalough, with the focus on ancient ruined churches, round towers and high crosses. Responding to perhaps justified concerns, the Board of Works appointed Thomas N. Deane (1828–1899) as Superintendent of National Monuments in March 1875 [fig. 6]. In this new role, Deane would supervise the preservation work at the existing National Monuments whilst also taking over Owen's responsibilities of inspecting further potential sites.[19] Deane was also an architect, but his previous work on the medieval cathedrals at Tuam and Kilkenny gave reason for some optimism. Ultimately, Deane proved to have a boundless enthusiasm for his task. The beautiful architectural drawings of medieval stonework which accompanied his detailed updates were worthy of a better home than the back pages of the Board of Works' very dry annual reports, but at least there they were in the public domain.

The fourteenth- and fifteenth-century ruins at St Audoen's Church were an obvious candidate for vesting as a National Monument, but this may not have initially been the desired outcome for the parishioners. In line with the terms of the Irish Church Act, the entire building and the adjoining parish graveyard were transferred to the Commissioners of Church Temporalities on 1 January 1871, pending a final decision. In an article published just a few months later, Rev. Leeper referenced the uncertainties brought by disestablishment, whilst also identifying the ruins of St Audoen's as an ideal project for the contemporary philanthropic church-builder or restorer: 'When we think of what a Guinness, a Roe and a Findlater have done, we cannot but think that the day is not far distant when all who are interested in the disendowed church will see St Audoen's rise again in beauty.'[20] His article was adapted and published in pamphlet form two years later in what would appear to be a campaign to avoid the carving-up of the ancient church site.[21] No wealthy benefactor came forward, however, and only the active church, the porch, the tower and the graveyard were transferred to the Representative Church Body (RCB) in 1873. The RCB was another body established in the wake of disestablishment, responsible for active Church of Ireland churches, schools and rectories. Assistant Secretary of the RCB for its first forty-three years was Rev. Christopher T. McCready (1837–1913), who was simultaneously curate of St Audoen's Church and a meticulous historian of the parish. That the chancel, Portlester and St Anne's chapels ruins remained in the hands of the Commissioners of Church Temporalities indicated that their status was still under consideration.

There were a number of complicating factors which set St Audoen's apart from other National Monument candidate sites. The active church was still using a portion of the medieval structure for worship, which ruled that section out for state ownership, but it meant that they would have to share partitioning walls and windows. A brick vestry had been built right across the east end of the ruined St Anne's Chapel in 1848,

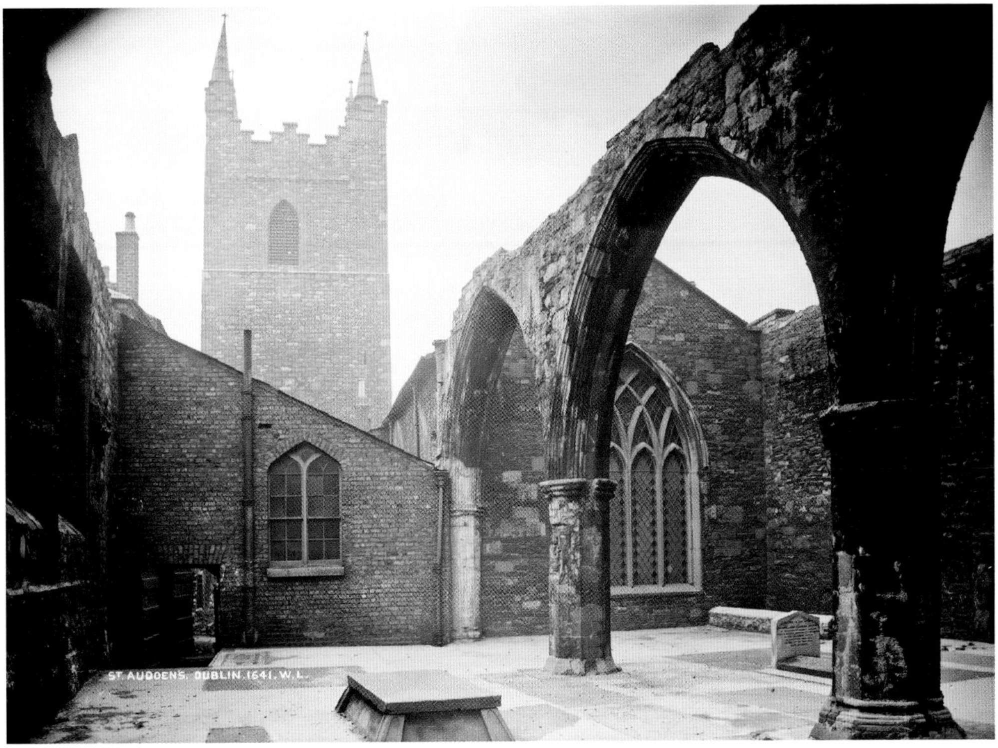


providing a convenient side entrance from High Street, but leaving the western end of that chapel cut off from the other ruins [fig. 7]. With the church and vestry still in use, there was no easy access to the Portlester Chapel and chancel ruins except through church property. Another potential problem was access to the burial vaults beneath the ruins. There were provisions for ongoing burial rights within National Monuments, but in practice the Board of Works discouraged burials on its sites.[22] The last specified use of the burial vaults beneath the eastern ruins had been the interment of Sir Capel Molyneux in the Ussher family vault in 1832, but the presence of later gravestones in the ruins strongly hints at subsequent burials there.[23] At least one of the burial vaults under St Anne's Chapel was probably still earmarked for future use.[24] A memorial to the noted scientist William Molyneux (d.1698) was affixed to the wall of the chancel ruins in 1869 – something which the Board of Works' strict regulations about protected structures would not have permitted. For many reasons, then, the creation of a National Monument was not a forgone conclusion, and the parish continued to see the entire building as their responsibility. As late as January 1877, the Select Vestry (the decision-making committee of Church of Ireland parishioners) had noted that 'the old arches in the churchyard [surely meaning the Portlester Chapel] having been for a long time threatening to fall, it was resolved that they should be repaired'.[25]

---

fig. 7 | St Audoen's, Dublin (showing brick vestry) by Robert French (1841–1917) *c.*1887–1914, glass plate photograph, National Library of Ireland, NLI, L_ROY_01641 (© National Library of Ireland)

On 12 December 1877, under the guidance of Deane, a third tranche of National Monuments was scheduled for vesting to the State. With 105 new additions, this represented a massive acceleration of the scheme, but it was a reflection of public support.[26] Number thirty on the new schedule was 'The Portlester Chapel, with Ruins adjoining the same'.[27] Intentionally or otherwise, this description was vague; the 'Portlester Chapel' name has been variously applied to just the south-east corner of the church or to the entire eastern end, and so the 'Ruins adjoining' could be interpreted in different ways, but it would be a few more years before any further clarification was needed. Deane had, by now, gathered a team of skilled craftsmen to work on his preservation projects. In consequence, National Monuments were worked on in rotation by his expert team rather than having simultaneous projects staffed by hired local builders. It made for slow, methodical, but economical and, above all, highly professional progress.[28] In the meantime, the ruins at St Audoen's lay dormant. Ultimately, it was decided in February 1879 to hand St Anne's Chapel back to the care of the parish church, most likely because of the practical difficulties of access.[29] Reverend Leeper gave the scheme a positive public endorsement in May 1880, when Dublin Corporation proposed the demolition of St Audoen's Arch, the last surviving gateway in the medieval city walls. As part of a widespread public backlash, Leeper suggested that the arch should be taken into the care of the Board of Works, 'as the ruined arches in the neighbouring church of St Audoen's are'. He described the arch rather poetically as 'a kind of landmark on the road of time, a link between the present and the past'.[30] Less poetically, the Select Vestry pointed out that the wall of the graveyard might collapse were the arch to be demolished.[31] By the following month the Corporation had relented, and the arch still stands today. On 30 October 1880, the Commissioners of Church Temporalities issued a further vesting confirmation order, consolidating the previous three transfers into one new list and adding a further twenty or so sites, to bring the total number of National Monuments to 137. The Portlester Chapel (and 'Ruins adjoining') was number thirty-four on the new schedule; this number was assigned by alphabetical order within each county rather than reflecting any hierarchy of importance.[32] The National Monuments programme has gone through enormous changes since then – adding 'Ancient Monuments' (broadly, pre-Christian sites) after 1882, and navigating the splitting of Ireland into two jurisdictions – but the National Monument at St Audoen's remains number thirty-four.[33]

## Preservation of the National Monument

During the extended delay in starting preservation work at St Audoen's, *The Irish Builder* architectural journal began a serialised history of the church, which would appear twice-monthly from January 1886 until December 1888. This mammoth collection was published anonymously, but was almost certainly the work of Rev. McCready, whose enormous collection of personal research is now housed in Marsh's Library.[34] The launch of this series kicked off almost a decade of intense activity in and around the old church. In February 1886 Thomas Drew returned to St Audoen's to offer his architectural services free of charge.[35] Drew had previously made a similar

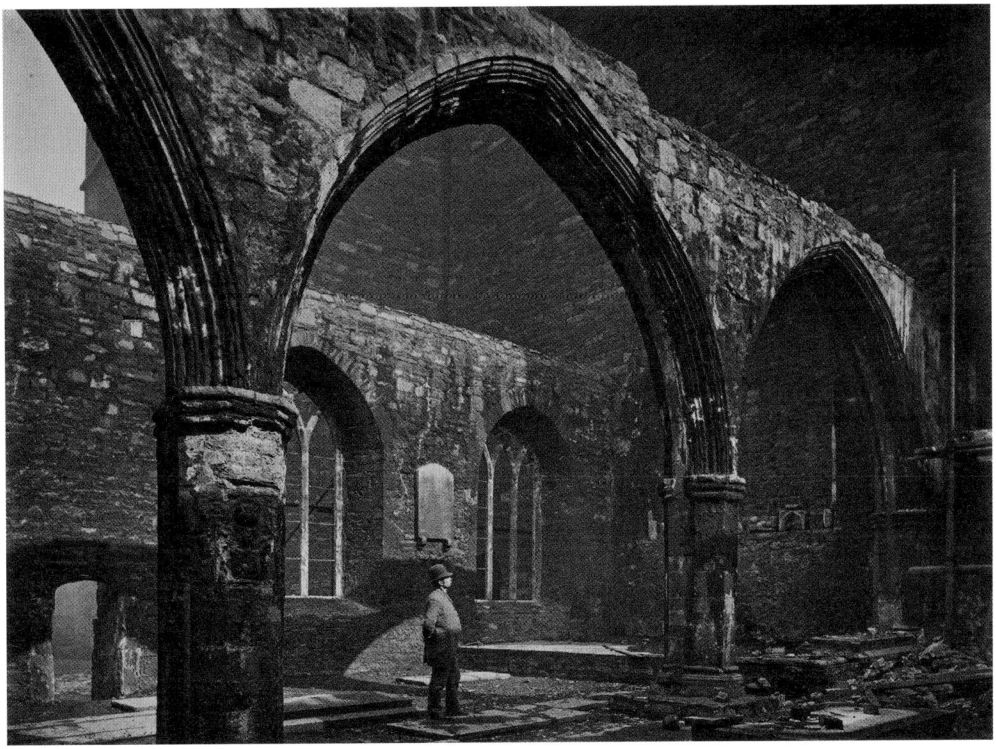

offer at St Francis' Abbey in Kilkenny, and a later Board of Works memo suggests, rather dismissively, that Drew had hoped to be appointed to oversee the preservation of the ruins at St Audoen's, which he had studied twenty years earlier.[36] True or not, Drew displayed an enduring affection, even protectiveness, towards St Audoen's Church, and his sincerity can be in little doubt. His offer may have put some pressure on the Board of Works because, by April, Deane had acknowledged the lack of progress and had hastily drawn up a plan for the church ruins.[37] The actual work didn't commence until 27 January 1887, under the direction of Deane as superintendent and James H. Owen as architect, but it would be the prime focus of Deane's team for the rest of that year [fig. 8].[38] *The Irish Builder* reported that the first actions were to open up the two large windows and the Tudor-era sandstone doorway in the north wall of the chancel, each of which had been blocked up.[39] Attention then turned to opening up the blocked windows of the south and east walls of the ruins (although, intriguingly, all of these windows appear open in Petrie's drawing of just a few decades earlier). Those on the southern wall had to be immediately blocked again with a shallow course of red brick because they formed the back walls of adjoining houses.[40] The flat 'ledger' gravestones on the floor were levelled and set in a bed of concrete in February, although it was noted that the gravestone of the Knox family (1687) 'unfortunately fell to pieces' while attempting

fig. 8 | St Audoen's, Dublin, photographed by Thomas F. Geoghegan, c.1887
National Library of Ireland, ALB8
(© National Library of Ireland)

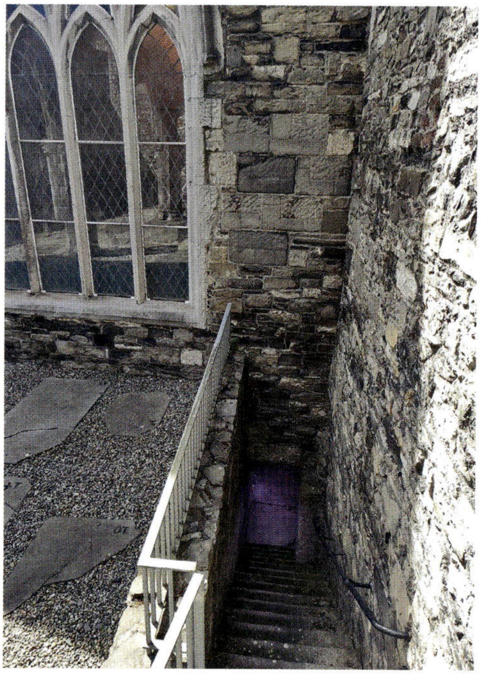

to move it.[41] Hundreds of medieval floor tile fragments were discovered during the work, of which about ninety were set into concrete on window sills in the south walls of the ruins.[42]

It was hoped that the passageway beneath the working church, theorised by Drew in 1866, could be found and converted into a new means of public access to the Portlester and Chancel ruins. A significant volume of Board of Works registered paperwork from this time alludes to the problems and progress of creating a suitable site entrance. Unfortunately, although indexed, the actual papers themselves cannot be located today, so whether any evidence of the passageway was found is not known.[43] Some excavations did occur, however, because in March 1887 a doorway and a narrow, steep granite stairwell were tunnelled under the north-east corner of the working church, linking the ruins to the laneway at St Audoen's Arch (the arch being at considerably lower ground level than the church, due to a sharp incline in the topography). Some form of agreement must have been reached with the Church of Ireland parish to permit breaking through the base of the thirteenth-century wall and potentially disturbing burial vaults beneath their floor, but this was a much lighter intervention than excavating a tunnel under the full breadth of the church. The stairwell remains in place today [fig. 9]. At precisely the same time as Deane was carrying out his work in the chancel and Portlester Chapel, the parish authorised Drew to supervise their own archaeological project in the unroofed part of St Anne's Chapel. Multiple arched outlines in the stonework of the south wall were investigated, leading to some extraordinary medieval finds. Two piscinas (niches which housed water bowls for the washing of communion vessels) and a doorway were revealed close to ground level, along with three 'squint windows' (hagioscopes) high in the wall, the middle of which had been repurposed as a fireplace for an adjoining Georgian building. Most impressive of all was an early fifteenth-century fresco painting discovered in a blocked-up recess and still somewhat intact [fig. 10]. More paintings of a similar age were found at the edges of a partially uncovered window arch, but the presence of the sixteenth-century plaster monument to the Malone family across this space prevented a fuller investigation.[44] The extent to which Deane and Drew collaborated during this process can only be speculated upon; most newspaper reports of the discoveries specified that these were two simultaneous but separate projects, but when Deane gave an account and sketch of the fresco in the Board of Works' annual report he did not acknowledge Drew's involvement.[45]

With Drew as their advisor, the parish met with the Board of Works in April

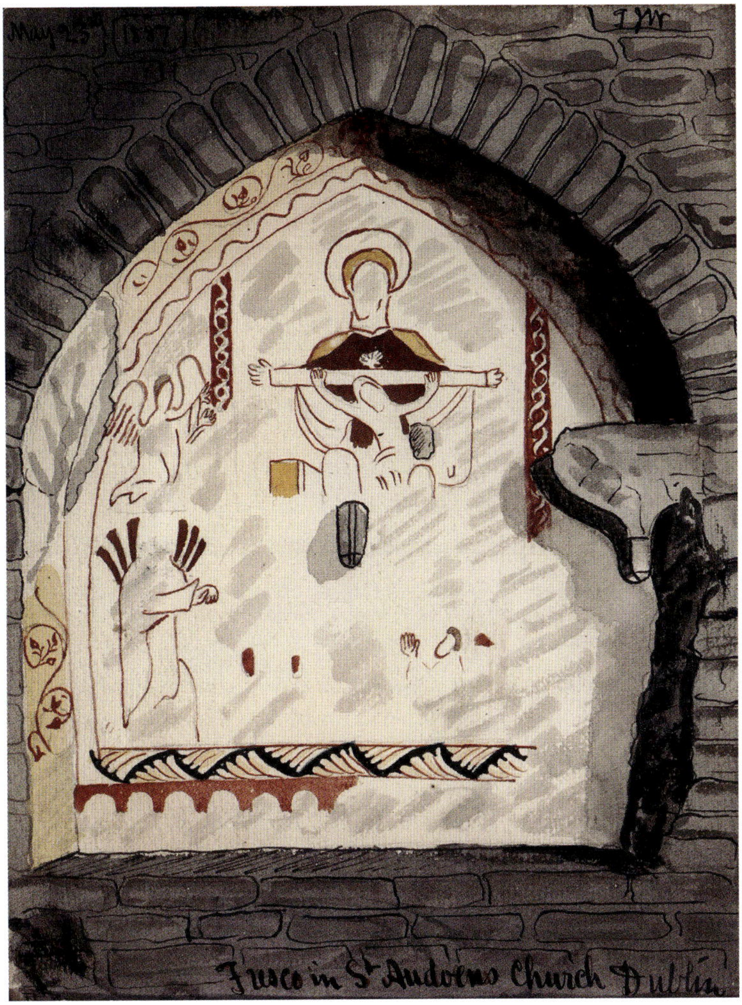


fig. 10 | *Fresco in St Audoen's Church, Dublin* by Thomas Johnson Westropp (1860–1922) 1887, watercolour, Royal Irish Academy, RIA C/24/6/C box 1: sheet 47,184 (© Royal Irish Academy)

opposite

fig. 9 | The Board of Works stairwell, constructed in 1887 (photo: Benedetta Bruno, 2024)

1887 to discuss the next steps in public access and supervision of the National Monument ruins. The parish was starting from a strong bargaining position because the new stairwell was running through (or rather, beneath) their property, and technically they could refuse access if they were unhappy with the Board's decisions. Their main demand related to the appointment of a caretaker – a position mandated for each National Monument site – insisting that it should be a person nominated by the Select Vestry and that the caretaker's annual salary should be increased from the proposed ten shillings to £5. With limited options, the Board accepted the terms about appointing a caretaker, but capped the salary at £1 per year. In return, the RCB granted a right-of-way under the church to the Commissioners of Public Works for the nominal sum of one shilling, taking effect from 23 June 1887.[46] A gate at the bottom of the stairwell was to be kept locked, and all visits to the ruins were to be supervised by the caretaker. An 'accident' on 29 June, the details of which are not recorded, necessitated railings to be installed to prevent unsupervised access, and this may have delayed the planned

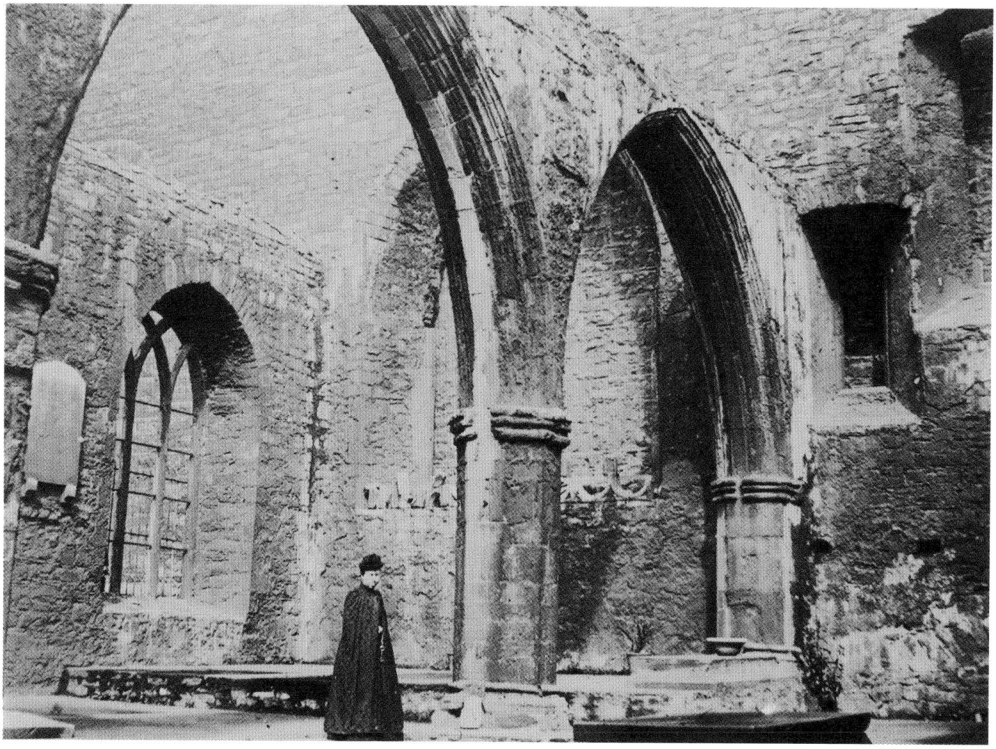

opening of the site to the public.[47] In November 1887 the Select Vestry appointed Miss Margaret Stewart (1849–1905) to succeed her father, David Stewart, who had served as sexton of the parish church for forty years. They also nominated her as caretaker of the National Monument.[48] The sexton was essentially the caretaker for the active church, so it made practical sense to have Stewart perform similar duties for the 'inactive' church [fig. 11]. In fact, the Board of Works generally took a pragmatic approach to the appointment of caretakers of these early National Monuments. It was not uncommon for a landowner to be appointed if the monument was located within their property, nor was it uncommon for a woman to hold the post. A standard form, titled 'Instructions for the guidance of the Caretaker', was issued to all National Monument sites. The instructions specified that the caretaker, as keyholder, should admit visitors at all reasonable hours, keep the space 'in neat and proper order' (all necessary implements being supplied by the Board), prevent any alteration to the structure, and report any damage.[49] In contrast to the agreed £1 per annum for her Board of Works caretaking duties, Stewart received £20 per annum as parish sextoness.[50]

The reprieve of St Audoen's Arch and the opening of the Portlester Chapel ruins probably spurred on the next phase of redevelopment in the area. Dublin Corporation's 'Open Spaces Committee' had been formed in 1886 in response to the

---

fig. 11 | St Audoen's Church by A. Harris
c.1894, gelatin silver photograph, National Library of Ireland, ALB30
(© National Library of Ireland)

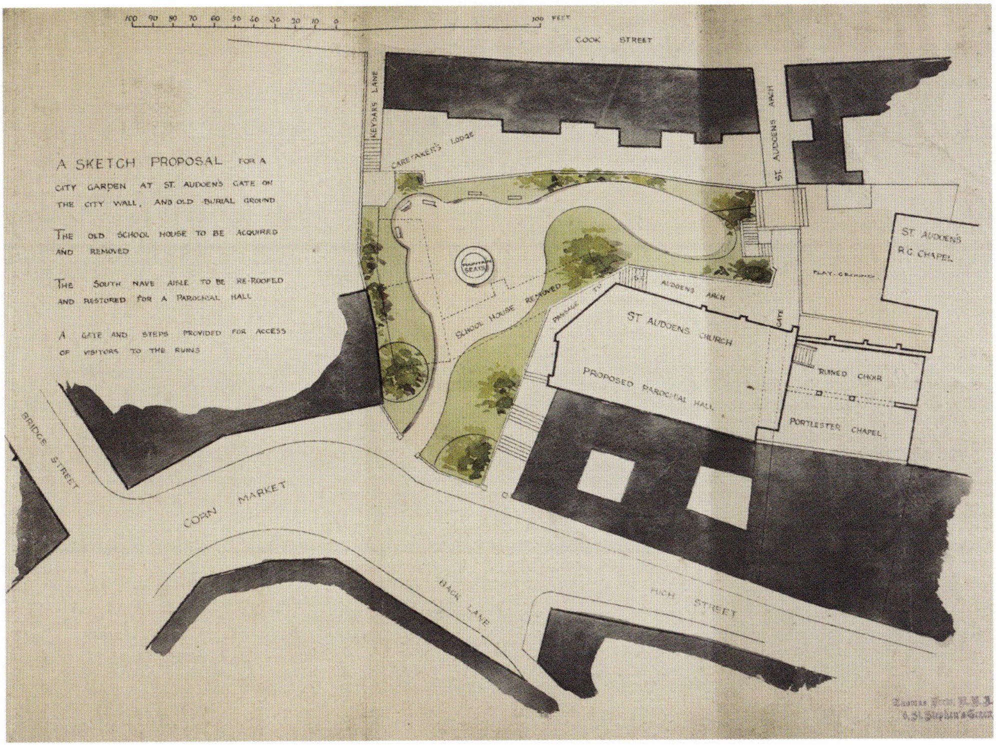


congestion and pollution of Dublin's inner city. Its specific task was to identify disused burial grounds which could be used for public recreation, and one such site was at St Audoen's Church. The parish graveyard was situated just inside the medieval city wall, separated from the church itself by the laneway leading to St Audoen's Arch and some derelict parochial buildings running alongside it. The graveyard was likely to have been in use since medieval times and, as such, estimates of anywhere up to 30,000 interments sound plausible, but it was also a very small plot of ground. There were very few burials after 1860, as the ground was essentially full. In February 1888 the Open Spaces Committee, under the direction of lawyer Thomas W. Bell, approved a plan to convert St Audoen's Graveyard.[51] Drew was involved in the project from the early stages; an undated watercolour plan shows Drew's design for the new public park, including the passageway beneath the church which he anticipated would be found and opened up [fig. 12]. The same plan includes a new parochial hall built within a re-roofed St Anne's Chapel. In this context it would appear that the 1887 investigations of St Anne's Chapel may have been part of an intended restoration project, but that there was a subsequent change of plans. Another drawing by Drew, dated 5 May 1888, shows a less ambitious park layout and makes no reference to any new parochial hall. The graveyard was formally closed from 1 November 1888, and landscaping work began.[52] The committee

---

fig. 12 | *Sketch Proposal for a City Garden at St Audoen's* by Thomas Drew (1838–1910) c.1887, watercolour over architectural plan, RCB Library, P.0116.05.02, item 7

initially pledged to preserve the gravestones and arrange them upright along the city wall and church walls, but just weeks later the Select Vestry gave Bell permission to use the gravestones instead as rubble for rebuilding the wall along the laneway, where fragments of broken memorial inscriptions can still be spotted today.[53] As few as five gravestones were salvaged and moved inside the church ruins, while the rest were reportedly left *in situ* and (along with the human remains of thousands) buried beneath new layers of soil.[54] With hindsight, it seems extraordinary that the parish church agreed to such mistreatment of graves, but they may have seen it as a quid pro quo.

In February 1890, work on the new Open Space came to a complete standstill as relations between the church and the committee broke down. The church authorities were under the impression that they would be allowed to build a new parochial hall on the footprint of the abandoned buildings, but the committee strongly contended that they were promised the entire area for conversion into a park.[55] This impasse lasted for three years, during which time there was renewed interest in restoring St Anne's Chapel as an alternative parochial hall site. Reverend Leeper enquired whether the Board of Works needed to be consulted in any restoration work, to which Deane replied that the wording 'Portlester Chapel, with Ruins adjoining' could be taken to mean that St Anne's Chapel was part of the National Monument.[56] This response was not to the liking of Rev. McCready, who followed up with a tetchy reply:

> 'Your Board has never laid out a penny on S. Anne's Aisle. Your Inspector never inspects S. Anne's Aisle – your local caretaker does not regard herself as placed by your Board in charge of S. Anne's Aisle. When some frescoes were believed to be buried in S. Anne's Aisle some years ago, we picked away at the plaster without fancying that we had to ask your leave. You have no key or method of entry in S. Anne's Aisle.'[57]

The Land Commission, now drawn into the dispute, opined that there was 'no record to show St Anne's Aisle was not vested in Bd. with Portlester Church [*sic*]'. Drew subsequently wrote to the Board in defence of the parish church, arguing simply that 'St Anne's Aisle does not adjoin Portlester Chapel' (which, because it was separated by the vestry building, was true).[58] This seems to have been the final word on the matter, with St Anne's now definitively under direct Church authority, but such disputes did nothing to improve relations between the Church, the Open Spaces Committee and the Board. Eventually, an alternative site for the parochial hall was secured at the far side of the proposed Open Space, and work finally resumed.[59] St Audoen's Park was officially opened in May 1895, complete with the new and appropriately nicknamed '40 Steps' in granite and concrete, and a mock-medieval palisade added to the top of the ancient city wall.[60] Initially less than one acre in size, the park remained legally the property of the RCB until 1971, with Dublin Corporation again paying for a caretaker nominated by the Select Vestry.[61]

Meanwhile, the opening of the Portlester Chapel National Monument got off to a bumpy start. Thomas Drew was no less critical of the Church and the Corporation than he was of the Board, and as early as June 1889 he wrote to James H. Owen complaining that the ruins were practically inaccessible to the public. The new entrance stairwell was always locked and was strewn with rubble, the approach from St Audoen's Arch was poorly maintained by 'the Corporation scavengers', and the sextoness/caretaker was hard to find: 'Many complaints are made to me that when the Sexton of St Audoen's can be hunted up the only access is by favour through St Audoen's Church & the coal hole door under the vestry stairs.' Drew recommended that a notice board should be erected at the stairwell gate advertising Miss Stewart's home address in Back Lane, to which Owen agreed.[62] In advance of the opening of St Audoen's Park in 1895, Drew again took issue with the neglect of the National Monument and suggested alternative arrangements; entry to the ruins should be through the new park, across the top of St Audoen's Arch (recently restored by the Corporation, he writes, at a cost of £250), through the playground of the Catholic National School and through the restored 'Tudor doorway'. The current caretaker should be dismissed, he added, and St Audoen's Catholic Church be given the right to nominate future caretakers.[63] This time, Deane sided with Drew, ordering, 'High level doors should be made the usual entrance. New gate required'.[64] Work on adapting the 'Tudor doorway' as a public entrance began in July 1895 and brought an instant and furious response from the new rector, Rev. David Anderson (1849–1922):

> 'Someone without my sanction has taken away the gate leading into the ruins of St Audoen's, shattering the Norman [*sic*] doorway and injuring the wall [...] I think it was rather high-handed business to send a rough individual to take down the gate in the first instance without any supervision or without consulting the Rector of the Parish.'[65]

Anderson's major worry was that the new entrance would not be supervised, that the ruins would become a playground for the schoolchildren, and that the east window of the working church would be 'altogether exposed to the young pups' who had frequently broken the other windows of his church. He threatened legal action unless the previous situation was restored.[66]

The administrative paper trail becomes somewhat sparse after this point in the history of the National Monument at St Audoen's, coinciding with the departure of some of the key figures involved in its establishment. Alexander Leeper, James H. Owen and Thomas N. Deane all died in the 1890s. Deane and Thomas Drew had been occasional rivals, most notably in the design of the National Library and National Museum buildings on Kildare Street, for which Deane was knighted, but in a glowing obituary Drew commended Deane's 'genuine and patriotic devotion to his charge [...] for a mere nominal salary, visiting assiduously remotest [*sic*] places and exposed coasts and islands, and facing western seas in any seasons'.[67] Margaret Stewart married in 1897, and within a few years her husband, Thomas Pearson, had taken over her duties as sexton and caretaker of the National Monument. Stewart died in December 1905, and Pearson was dismissed from his duties just four months later.[68] Thomas J. McKnight, caretaker of St Audoen's Park since its opening, took on these additional duties, and the three roles were generally combined for most of the twentieth century.[69] Reverend Christopher McCready remained curate until his death in 1913, but in his later years he spent less time on parish or historical matters. Thomas Drew was himself knighted in 1900 and he devoted his final years to designing a new cathedral in his native Belfast, but he continued to argue that St Audoen's deserved greater appreciation until his death in 1910.[70]

By some metrics, the establishment of the National Monument at St Audoen's

Church was not a great success. The best intentions of the above-mentioned people quickly gave way to petty squabbles, poor public access and, according to Drew, a poor standard of conservation. On the other hand, Deane's preservation work stabilised not just the Portlester and chancel ruins, but the heritage of St Audoen's Church itself. The protection afforded by National Monument status guaranteed the survival of the ruins through to better times, and probably had some bearing on the survival of the active church too. On at least two occasions (1922 and 1959) the parish church was earmarked for closure only to be reprieved; the fate of its sister churches, St Luke's in the Coombe (dereliction and fire) and St Peter's on Aungier Street (demolition), present sobering examples of what might have followed.[71]

## Difficulties of maintaining the National Monument

From the turn of the century through to the 1980s, the National Monument at St Audoen's had a comparatively unremarkable existence, accessible only to those few who knew who to ask and to those who did not seek permission. Trespass in the ruins and vandalism to the working church and vestry were a constant feature throughout the twentieth century. Reverend Anderson complained to the Board of Works in 1904 and 1905 that the stairwell gate had been broken open several times, people were sleeping rough in the ruins, all sorts of filth was deposited there, the east window of the church had been broken several times (on one occasion twenty-five panes were smashed) and the vestry had been broken into. He requested that the stairwell, the 'Tudor doorway' and the windows of the National Monument should all be 'built up' to prevent trespass.[72] Luckily, from a conservation perspective, this was not acted upon, but the minutes of the Select Vestry show that serious incidents continued right up to the late 1990s, including damage to the twelfth-century font in 1925, the destruction of the stained-glass east window at Christmas 1966, and the theft of an eagle lectern and a seventeenth-century painting of regimental arms in 1992.[73] Barbed wire along the top of the ruined walls was replaced in 1935 by bespoke metal security railings.[74] A more unusual incident was the breaking-through of the red-brick fill within the Portlester Chapel's south windows in 1915. The Board's inspector reported that the adjoining premises at number 17 High Street were 'occupied by somewhat irresponsible people – the Irish Transport and General Workers Union', who had a meeting hall at the back of the building and had improvised a window opening into the medieval ruins.[75]

The division of responsibilities for maintenance was once again raised by Rev. Anderson in 1912–13. The church's bell-tower was in such perilous condition that ringing the full peal of six bells was stopped in 1898 because it was considered unsafe; the 'fifth' bell alone would sound for ten minutes each Sunday morning.[76] After one of the four cast-iron pinnacles had fallen from the top of the tower, Anderson attempted to convince the Board that they had an obligation to contribute towards the repair of the tower. Ignoring the actual timeline of events, he argued that:

> 'The monuments from the Portlester Chapel under your care were transferred to a shelter beneath the tower to save them from wear and weather [...] you

> are legally bound to preserve them [...] Ladies and Gentlemen, priests and parsons, archaeologists and interested persons come to view the ruins and are conducted through the tower by our sexton and your caretaker, so you are the users much more than we are.'

The Board firmly and repeatedly rejected Anderson's claims, and the parish itself eventually funded limited stabilisation work on the tower in 1916.[77] The biggest disruption to the business of the parish church was the death of Rev. Anderson in March 1922. With the continuing decline of the congregation, the Church of Ireland opted not to replace him, but rather to amalgamate the parish with that of St Peter's Church.[78] St Audoen's was demoted to the status of a secondary parish church for the first time in its long history. St Peter's Church itself closed in 1975, after which St Audoen's was linked to the Church of St Catherine & St James on Donore Avenue, South Circular Road.

The automatic appointment of the church sexton as caretaker of the National Monument (and the park) continued, but the practice was problematic. The parish had some difficulty in retaining a sexton, and they were unfortunate in some of their choices for appointment. A further issue was that they often failed to notify the Board of Works of a change in personnel. Thomas McKnight was replaced in late 1918 by Robert McDonnell, but the Board only became aware of McDonnell's death in January 1922 when his quarterly wage payment was returned to them by his widow. Frederick Whittle next became acting sexton, but the Board became suspicious a few months later when a 'James Whittle' presented himself as caretaker.[79] The church apologetically explained that Frederick had joined the new Free State Army and had been replaced by his brother.[80] By the 1920s the Board's annual salary for the caretaker had been increased to £2, but compared to the £20 earned for the combined role of sexton, bellringer and organ-blower, and £60 as caretaker of the park, this low income may have influenced the level of care given to the National Monument ruins.[81] James Whittle was dismissed as sexton in 1929, and once again the Board was only alerted to this when his pay order was returned to them. The next sexton was dismissed after a year for being 'not satisfactory', his successor was dismissed in 1937 because he 'left the church unattended and was associated with an unruly gang which frequented the church and park', and subsequent sextons were dismissed for poor conduct and for embezzlement.[82] Harold G. Leask, the Superintendent of National Monuments, complained about the phenomenon of the Board's caretaker being dismissed without the Board being notified. As a pragmatic exception, he suggested that instead of paying a sexton/caretaker directly, the Board should – 'for the time being' – appoint the church's Select Vestry as collective caretakers of the National Monument. In May 1930, the Board of Works confirmed the Select Vestry as caretakers of 'the ancient choir and the Portlester Chapel of St Audoen's Church', with the salary to be forwarded by them to whoever they have tasked with the work.[83] In practice, the previous arrangement continued, as confirmed by the specific advice given in 1948 to those wishing to visit the ruins: 'The sexton will generally be found in or near the church from 11 to 1 and from 2 to 5, except on Wednesday afternoons.'[84] The sexton/caretaker's other responsibilities included opening the park at 11am every day, but eventually the sexton's position became vacant and caretaking duties fell into abeyance. In a 1970 catalogue of National Monuments, the site was found to be open only occasionally, but 'otherwise closed, and the key is not available locally. Not signposted.' There was no public access at all by the 1980s.[85]

In light of this obscurity, it is no surprise that the site did not receive frequent care and attention from the Board of Works. By the early twentieth century, the medieval floor tiles which had been embedded into concrete in the window sills were by now in very poor condition because they were not water-resistant.[86] When inspections were carried out in 1934 and 1935, it was discovered that the metal 'guard bars' inserted into the windows by Thomas N. Deane some fifty years earlier had rusted to the extent that they had expanded and shattered stones in the medieval wall. 'It is many years since a really thorough overhaul of this monument has been carried out [...] the structure looks very bad. The walls are covered with what might be called soot "stalagmites" and look ugly and uncared for.'[87] Some degree of renovation to the ruins must have occurred shortly thereafter, because two highly unusual ceramic pots were placed in the care of the National Museum in 1936, having been found concealed inside the north wall of the ruined choir at St Audoen's Church [fig. 13]. These are potentially extremely rare Irish examples of fifteenth-century 'acoustic vases' – intended to resonate and carry the frequencies of liturgical singing voices – but a lack of documentation about their discovery makes conclusions difficult.[88] In fact, the survival rate for Board of Works paperwork relating to St Audoen's is pitiful; of sixty-four registered papers logged in the official index books before 1935, a meagre four were lodged with the National Archives and one is noted as having been destroyed. The remaining fifty-nine papers are unaccounted for, although ten of them were discovered in OPW hands and transcribed in recent years before disappearing once again. There is no publicly available index of registered papers after 1935, and the OPW is unable to locate any administrative documents in its custody for St Audoen's prior to 1987. These missing records would allow a much

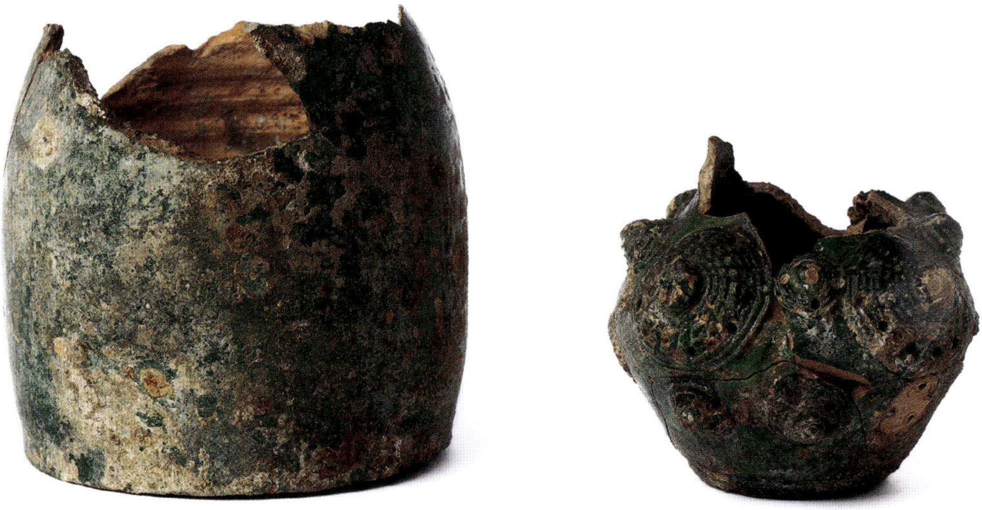

fig. 13 | Portions of two jugs (possibly 'acoustic vases'), found built into the wall of St Audoen's Church, fifteenth century, green glazed pottery, National Museum of Ireland, DC:1936.12, DC:1936.13
(© National Museum of Ireland)

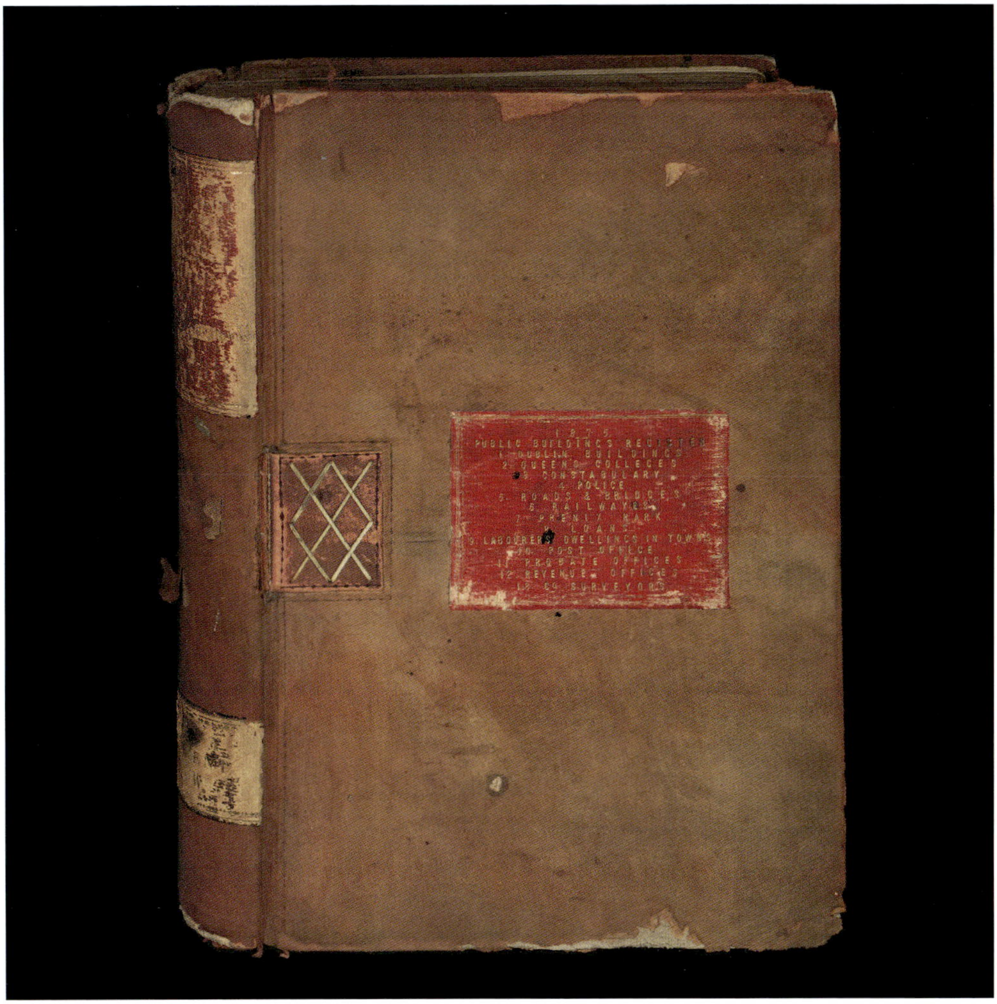

more comprehensive story to be told, and there is reason to hope that some of them may remain in uncatalogued limbo rather than being altogether lost, but the Board's index book summaries and the Select Vestry's minute books go some way to bridging the gap [fig. 14]. The earliest series of architectural photographs, dating from 1951, shows the ruins in good order, albeit with walls stained by the soot which affected all city-centre buildings at that time. In contrast, a subsequent series of photographs from the 1950s or 1960s shows the site badly overgrown and one of the burial vaults broken open [fig. 15].[89] Later work saw Deane's concrete floor removed and replaced with the less-stark gravel surface found today. Conversely, having again briefly floated the idea of re-roofing the area, the parish church set the ledger gravestones in St Anne's Chapel into a bed of concrete in early 1934. Acknowledging that access to the burial vaults

fig. 14 | Board of Works Public Buildings Register 1875, National Archives of Ireland, OPW/5/3/43

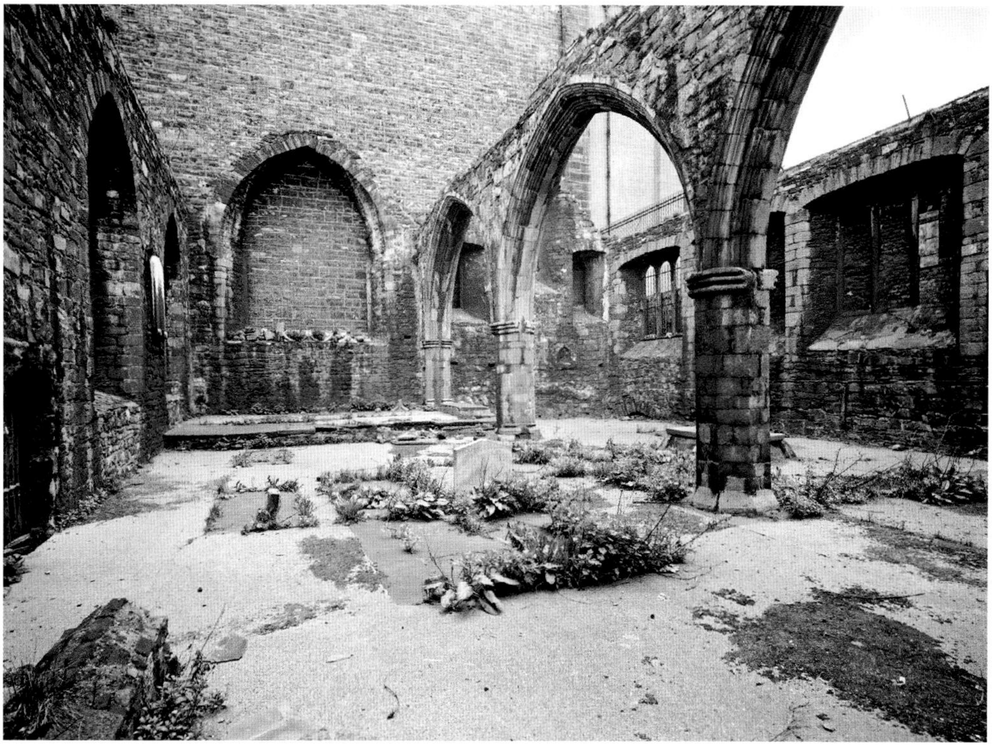

would not be needed again, these gravestones were first lifted and some of the vaults opened and reinforced with sheets of galvanised iron and rubble before the floor was sealed.[90] In about 1952 the Victorian-era vestry building was demolished, joining up the two ruined areas as a continuous space, and further blurring the division between Church and State property [fig. 16].

## Renewal of the National Monument

THE EVENTS WHICH LED TO THE REVIVAL OF THE NATIONAL MONUMENT CAN ARGUABLY BE traced back to 1961 when Dublin Corporation passed a resolution requesting that St Audoen's Park should be cleaned up, especially around the medieval gate, and Bord Fáilte enquired whether St Audoen's Church could be opened daily as a tourist attraction.[91] It appears that the active church was indeed opened to visitors in early 1963, but this arrangement did not last.[92] It was three separate but simultaneous processes during the 1980s which led to a more sustained exhibition of the historic site. The first of these was an ambitious series of renovations to the parish church between 1979 and 1998 which saw the restoration of the bell-tower, the roof, the east window

fig. 15 | Portlester Chapel and Chancel by unknown photographer, c.1950s/60s, National Monuments Service, 34.26
(© Photographic Archive, National Monuments Service, Government of Ireland)

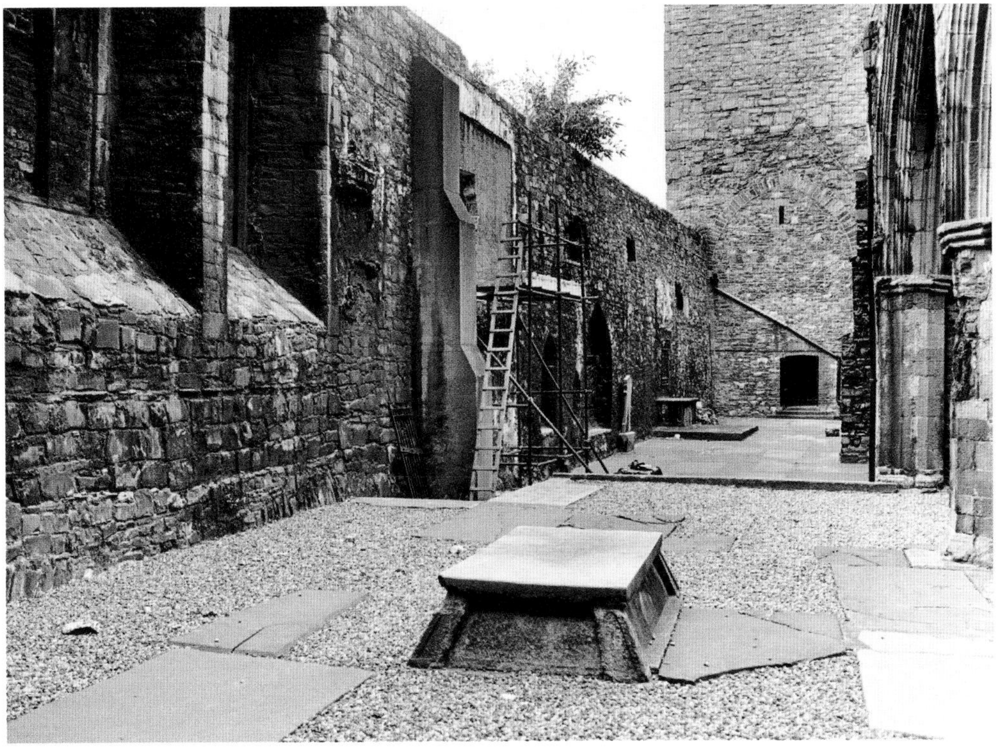

and the Sparke and Duffe memorials. In conjunction with this, the vicar, Canon John Crawford, wrote a booklet on the history of St Audoen's, published in 1986.[93] This built upon the short but colourful introductory pamphlets published by Rev. Leeper (1873) and churchwarden Alex Donovan (1929), each of which was part of similar fund-raising initiatives. Mention should also be made of a mischievously humorous pamphlet written by Rev. McCready in 1887 for circulation among the 'Band of Hope' youth temperance movement.[94] Canon Crawford followed up with another booklet about the memorial inscriptions of the church, and the site's first visitor guide leaflets and postcards were produced in advance of the church's 800th anniversary in 1990. In the late 1980s/early 1990s the parish began opening their newly renovated building to the public on Saturday and Sunday afternoons during the summer months, overseen by volunteers from the congregation.[95]

A second process was the renovation of the area by Dublin Corporation. St Audoen's Park had expanded to almost double its original size when it reopened to the public in June 1982. In April 1984 the Corporation demolished the remaining properties along High Street, which had hidden all except the church tower from public view for centuries. However, the resulting build-up of debris against the wall of St Anne's Chapel gave rise to very serious concerns that this wall could collapse. A drawn-out dispute

---

fig. 16 | Portlester Chapel and St Anne's Chapel by unknown photographer, c.1989, RCB Library, MS 465/2

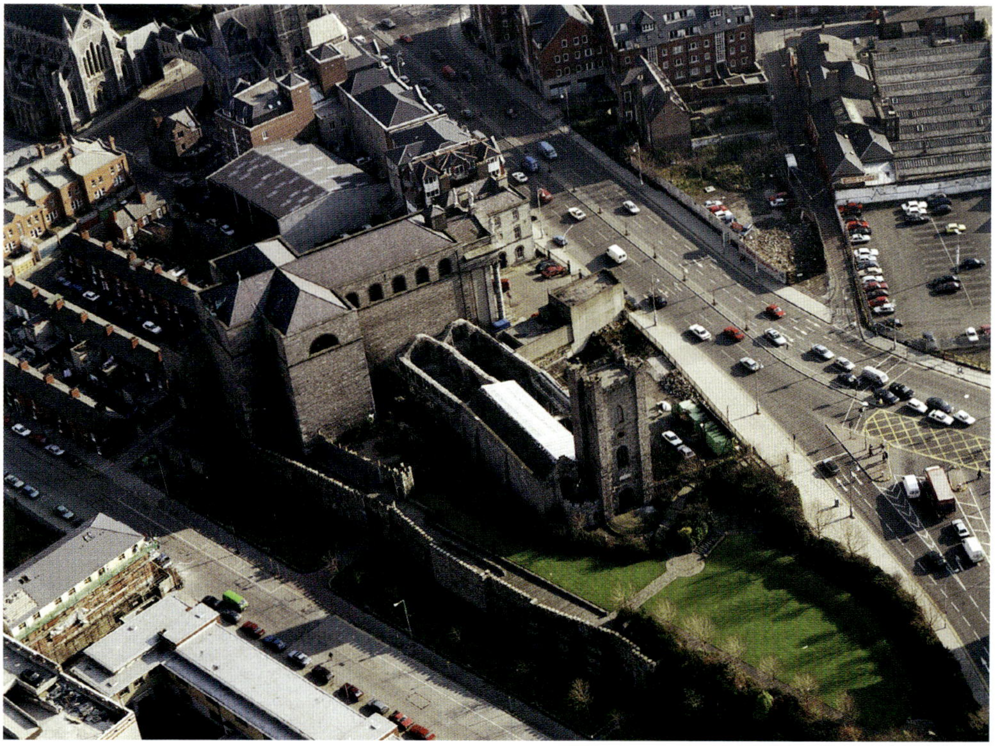

between the church and the Corporation prompted a brief archaeological study by Mary McMahon in 1986 and excavations of the vault beneath the Malone/Pentony tomb by a building contractor in 1986/1987.[96] One consequence of this was a greater appreciation of the church's place in history by Dublin Corporation and the OPW. The third ongoing process was a broader re-evaluation of Dublin's medieval past. In the aftermath of the hugely unpopular redevelopment of Wood Quay (1973–86), 1988 was selected as a year of celebration of the foundation of Dublin one thousand years earlier (more or less), and the oldest surviving structures in the city, therefore, took on extra relevance. The celebrations would include a 'Viking Adventure' housed in the vaults beneath St Audoen's Catholic Church, providing another boost to the locality. In October 1986, Canon Crawford wrote to the OPW about the neglected National Monument ruins and the importance for the site to be in good repair for the upcoming Millennium festivities and church anniversary celebrations. The OPW agreed to tidy up and repair the ruins, and the Select Vestry further suggested that the ruins of St Anne's Chapel should be placed in the care of the OPW too.[97] This transfer was formalised by the RCB on 16 December 1987, and so, in short order, the working church was renovated, the National Monument was refreshed and expanded, and the entire site emerged from behind a centuries-old veil of tenement buildings.[98]

In September 1989 the OPW announced an ambitious programme of works

---

fig. 17 | St Audoen's Church by an unknown photographer, 1994, National Monuments Service, N2.43 (© Photographic Archive, National Monuments Service, Government of Ireland)

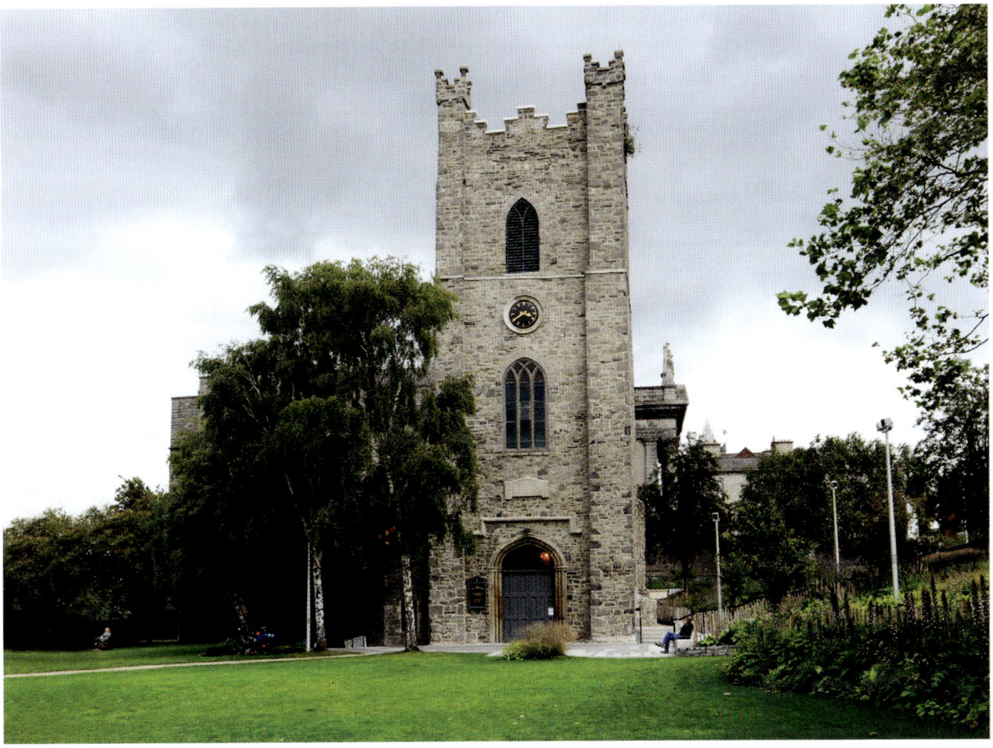

at St Audoen's Church. Starting the following May and anticipated to last about two years, remedial repairs and excavations would be followed by the re-roofing of St Anne's Chapel and the opening of the entire National Monument as an accessible public resource [fig. 17].[99] The excavations of the eastern end of St Anne's Chapel and the area directly outside its south wall were carried out between 1991 and early 1992 under the direction of Mary McMahon, and uncovered a trove of church and secular artefacts relating to Dublin's medieval past. The excavations also reassessed the accepted wisdom about the order in which the various parts of the church were built, and appeared to finally disprove Drew's notion of a lost tunnel under the church.[100] The task of re-roofing St Anne's Chapel with a traditional slate exterior and installing a modern visitor centre inside stretched into 1999, overseen by OPW senior architect William Cumming and project architect Kevin Blackwood. During this period, responsibility for National Monuments passed to Dúchas, the new State heritage agency initiated in 1995. St Audoen's Church Visitor Centre opened its doors to the public on 7 July 1999, and offers free admission to the general public during summer seasons. The relaunch was marked by a much more harmonious relationship between the various stakeholders than existed a century earlier. The support of the parish for the new enterprise was demonstrated by an agreement to allow access to the active church for guided tours (under certain conditions), and the use of items of church silverware and of Canon Crawford's archival

fig. 18 | St Audoen's Church today
(Alamy / Boaz Rottem, 2019)

photographs in the OPW exhibition.[101] As one veteran parishioner comments today about the re-roofed St Anne's Chapel, 'they took it over on the premise that they would clean it up and look after it [...] And it's great to have the visitor centre there [...] It must be an improvement to have [guides] there interested in showing the people around.' Another adds, 'it's nice to see it opened, very nice to see it opened, and long may it last' [fig. 18].[102] The success of the visitor centre is as much a testament to the dogged determination of Thomas Drew and the conscientious preservation of Thomas N. Deane as it is to any of the people who finally brought their project to completion 122 years after the initial scheduling of the National Monument.

---

**Neil Moxham** is a native of Abbeyshrule, co. Longford, living in Dublin for over thirty years. He has studied and written extensively on local history, oral history and genealogy. For ten years he worked as a seasonal tour guide with the OPW at sites including St Audoen's Church, the National Botanic Gardens, the Custom House and Dublin Castle. Neil now works as an archivist with the IFI's Irish Film Archive.

**Author's acknowledgements**

I am very grateful to the advisory board of the *Irish Heritage Studies* journal for giving me the opportunity to write about one of my favourite subjects, and to Caroline Pegum in particular for her support and encouragement during this project. I am indebted to the Office of Public Works Registry, the Office of Public Works Library, the National Monuments Service Archive, the National Monuments Service Photographic Archive, the National Archives of Ireland, the National Museum of Ireland Irish Antiquities Division and to Dr Clare McCutcheon for their assistance and patience in my search for the historical records and artefacts of St Audoen's Church.

Particular thanks are due to Dr Susan Hood and the staff of the Representative Church Body Library for their generosity in helping me to find and make copies of historical parish records, and to Canon Mark Gardner for allowing me access to the current records. I am also very grateful to Cecil Pakenham and James Kilbey for sharing their invaluable personal recollections of St Audoen's Church over the last fifty years.

I am extremely grateful to Catherine O'Connor for having the foresight to transcribe century-old OPW documents when they were temporarily placed in her custody, without which this paper would be a much, much shorter work. I must also commend the staff of the National Archives of Ireland's production department for their kindness in going above and beyond the call of duty to help when my research had hit a dead-end. My colleagues at St Audoen's Church OPW visitor centre were exceptionally tolerant of my shirking my tour-guiding duties for endless research. I hope you will think it was worthwhile. Thank you to all.

**Endnotes**

1 Thomas Drew, *St Audoen's Church, Corn Market, Dublin* (Dublin: Peter Roe, 1867), p.2.

2 Mary McMahon, 'The Architecture and Archaeology of St Audoen's Church, Cornmarket, Dublin' (unpublished M.Litt thesis, Trinity College Dublin, 2001), pp.6–7.

3 Ibid., pp.48–83.

4 The Royal Irish Academy holds a handwritten manuscript version of Bell's book, dated 1825 (RIA MS 12 O 11), which includes a different illustration of the Portlester ruins to that featured in the official 1829 publication (Dublin: W.F. Wakeman).

5 'The Fortunes of Sir Robert Ardagh' (1838) and 'The Cock and Anchor' (also called 'Morley Court'; 1845).

6 'Irish Antiquities', *Dublin Evening Post*, 20 May 1848.

7 Representative Church Body Library, Dublin (RCBL), MS 465, Canon John Crawford Papers, Box 2. In private correspondence with John Ribton Garstin, Rev. McCready flatly rejected some of the fanciful stories Rev. Leeper had published in his 1873 pamphlet about St Audoen's. (See also *Church of Ireland Gazette*, 23 Dec 1871, in which Rev. Leeper claimed to have found the lost 'Lucky Stone'

of St Audoen's Church – a granite cross-slab, long associated with spiritual protection, which had been located at the church since the fifteenth century but had been missing for forty-five years – only for the real Lucky Stone to be rediscovered elsewhere within months).

8 *Irish Ecclesiastical Gazette*, 15 Sept 1860, pp.407–08.

9 Brian and Moira Gittos, 'Irish Purbeck', *Church Monuments*, vol.13 (1998), pp.5–14: 11–12.

10 'St Audoen's Church – Preservation of the Antiquities', *Dublin Evening Post*, 6 June 1848.

11 Drew (1867).

12 Rena Lohan, *Guide to the Archives of the Office of Public Works* (Dublin: Stationery Office, 1994), pp.1–2.

13 Stephen Hilliard, 'Too Many Churches in Centre of Dublin', *Church of Ireland Gazette*, 4 Feb 1977.

14 Lohan, pp.85–87.

15 Ibid.

16 Robert Young, 'The Duty of Preserving National Monuments', *The Irish Builder*, 1 and 15 May 1872; 'Protection of National Monuments', *The Irish Times*, 1 March 1873; James Graves, 'The National Monuments', *The Kilkenny Moderator*, 19 August 1874.

17 'The Board of Works and the National Monuments', *The Kilkenny Moderator*, 12 Aug 1874.

18 'Imperial Parliament – House of Lords', *Downpatrick Recorder*, 31 May 1873.

19 Lohan, pp.90–92.

20 'Saint Audoen's Church, Dublin', *Irish Ecclesiastical Gazette*, 22 May 1871.

21 RCBL, MS 465, Canon John Crawford Papers, Box 2.

22 Lohan, pp.104–06.

23 The memorials to Lieutenant Roger Coghlan (1834) and Colonel John Staunton Rochfort (1844) both rise above ground level, unlike the flat 'ledger' tombstones which surround them.

24 The final entry in the church's burial register was for Mrs Anna Whitfield Cornwall in 1885, a daughter of Isaac Tyndall, who had a burial vault beneath St Anne's Chapel.

25 RCBL, P.0116.05.01, 'Vestry Minutes of the Parish of St Audoen 1870–86'.

26 'The National Monuments of Ireland', *Londonderry Journal*, 21 Nov 1877; 'Irish National Monuments', *Sligo Chronicle*, 24 Nov 1877.

27 'Report of the Commissioners of Church Temporalities in Ireland, 1877', p.22.

28 'Irish National Monuments', *Northern Whig*, 16 Aug 1876.

29 OPW Registry, D94/437/2, 'High Street, Dublin, St Audeon's [*sic*], The Portlester Chapel and adjoining ruin', 1987.

30 'St Audoen's Arch, Dublin', *The Irish Builder*, 1 May 1880, pp.130–31.

31 Ibid.

32 'Report of the Commissioners of Church Temporalities in Ireland, 1869–80', p.136.

33 John Scarry, *Monuments in the Past: photographs 1870–1936* (Dublin: Stationery Office, 1991), pp.vii–ix.

34 Marsh's Library, Dublin, 'Memorials of St Audoen's Parish, Dublin', MS Z2.2.24.

35 McMahon (2001), pp.3–4.

36 Scarry, p.vii; Catherine O'Connor (transcriber), 'Report by Mr Cochrane of the Board of Works', 1905; transcribed *c.*2017 (held at St Audoen's visitor centre) from a document now untraced.

37 National Archives of Ireland, Dublin (NAI), OPW 5/2/22, 'Board of Works Numerical Register, 1886'.

38 *Fifty-Sixth Annual Report of the Commissioners of Public Works in Ireland [...] for the year 1887–88* (Dublin: Alexander Thom & Co. / HMSO, 1888), p.29.

39 'Reparations at the old Church of St Audoen', *The Irish Builder*, 1 Feb 1887, p.33.

40 'St Audoen's Church', *Freeman's Journal*, 17 March 1887.

41 'St Audoen's Church, Corn Market', *The Irish Builder*, 1 March 1887, p.70.

42 O'Connor, 'Report by Mr Cochrane of the Board of Works'.

43 NAI, OPW 5/2/24, 'Board of Works Numerical Register, 1887'.

44 'St Audoen's Church', *Freeman's Journal*, 17 March 1887; 'Interesting Discoveries at St Audoen's Church', *The Irish Times*, 19 March 1887. The fresco, once exposed to the elements, soon disappeared completely. At least two black-and-white photographs were taken of the fresco (see Mary McMahon, *St Audoen's Church, Cornmarket, Dublin: archaeology and architecture* (Dublin: Stationery Office, 2006), pp.46–47), and one detailed sketch (*Fifty-Fifth Annual Report of the Commissioners of Public Works in Ireland [...] for the year 1886–87* (Dublin: Alexander Thom & Co./HMSO, 1887),

pp.62–69; *The Irish Builder*, 15 Dec 1887, p.349). In May, Thomas Johnson Westropp made a painting which was not architecturally accurate but gives the only indication of the colour scheme [fig. 8]. Intriguingly, Thomas Mason, an optician of 21 Parliament Street, notified the public (see *The Irish Builder*, 15 Jan 1888, p.24) that he had taken lantern slides of the fresco the day after its discovery, and would show them by appointment. It is unknown whether these were identical to the two surviving photographs.

45 *Fifty-Fifth Annual Report of the Commissioners of Public Works*, 1887, op. cit., pp.62–69.

46 RCBL, P.0116.05.02, 'Vestry Minutes of the Parish of St Audoen 1887–1913'; RCBL, Diocesan box for St Audoen's Parish, 1805–1942.

47 NAI, OPW 5/2/24.

48 RCBL, P.0116.05.02.

49 Lohan, p.121; NAI, OPW 5/8066/30, 'National Monument no. 34, St Audoen's Church, The Portlester Chapel with ruins adjoining same', 1930.

50 RCBL, P.0116.05.02. It's quite possible that David Stewart served as Board of Works caretaker in the months before his retirement, but no surviving documentation confirms this. As sexton prior to the vesting of the National Monument, he would already have looked after the ruins before 1877.

51 Dublin City Library and Archive (DCLA), 'Dublin City Council Minutes', Item 56, 1888.

52 RCBL, P.0116.05.02; DCLA, 'Dublin City Council Minutes', Item 297, 1888.

53 RCBL, P.0116.05.02.

54 *Belfast News-Letter*, 5 Nov 1897. A handful of the gravestones found today in the floor of the National Monument were recorded by Sir William Betham and *The Irish Builder* as having previously been located in the graveyard; National Library of Ireland, Dublin (NLI), microfilm P.529, 'Genealogical collections of Sir W. Betham, relating to English and Irish families and containing pedigrees, monumental inscriptions, collections for a peerage and baronage of Ireland, etc. 19th c.', pp.320–23; *The Irish Builder*, 1 and 15 Nov and 1 Dec 1886.

55 NLI, EPH D69, 'St Audöen's Open Space', 1890.

56 NAI, OPW 5/2/34, 'Board of Works Numerical Register, 1892'.

57 O'Connor, 'St Audoen's. Re. "St Ann's Aisle"', 1892; transcribed *c.*2017 from OPW 5/19662/92 (now untraced).

58 NAI, OPW 5/3/53, 'Public Buildings Subject Register, 1893'.

59 RCBL, P.0116.05.02.

60 DCLA, Dublin City Council Public Health Committee Report 76, vol.ii, 1895, p.511.

61 RCBL, P.0045.05.12, 'Select Vestry Minutes of the Parish of St Peter and St Audoen 1957–71'.

62 NAI, OPW 5/8095/89, 'St Audoen's. Difficulty of access. T. Drew.', 1889.

63 O'Connor, 'St Audoen's Church vested Bdgs', 1893; transcribed *c.*2017 from OPW 5/2217/93 (now untraced).

64 NAI, OPW 5/3/55, 'Public Buildings Subject Register, 1895'; DCLA, 'Dublin City Council Minutes', Item 233, 1895.

65 O'Connor, 'St Audoen's', 1895; transcribed *c.*2017 from OPW 5/11001/95 (now untraced).

66 Ibid.

67 Thomas Drew, 'The Late Sir Thomas Deane, R.H.A.', *Journal of the Royal Institute of British Architects*, 3rd series, vol.7 (1899), pp.48–49.

68 General Register Office, Registers of Births, Marriages & Deaths, marriage registration of Margaret Stewart and Thomas Pearson, 11 Oct 1897; death registration of Margaret Pearson, 9 Dec 1905 (available via <https://www.irishgenealogy.ie>); the latter, as well as census returns, identify Margaret as the 'wife of a sexton'.

69 NAI, OPW 5/3/65, 'Public Buildings Subject Register, 1906'; RCBL, P.0116.05.02.

70 'Athlone Bridge and "Sir" Peter Lewys, Architect', *The Irish Times*, 25 April 1905. Drew managed one more dig at the 'Board of Works men' in 1905, accusing them of the wanton destruction of medieval floor tiles at St Audoen's.

71 RCBL, P.0045.05.12.

72 O'Connor, 'St Audeon's [*sic*] Church, Dublin', 1904, and 'St Audeon's [*sic*] Church – Portlester Chapel', 1905; transcribed *c.*2017 from OPW 5/16187/04 and OPW 5/386/05 (both now untraced).

73 'Boys Break into City Church', *Irish Independent*, 7 Oct 1925; 'Vandals in old Dublin church', *The Irish Times*, 21 Dec 1966; RCBL, P.0512.05.03, 'Vestry Minutes of the Parish of St Catherine and St James with St Audoen 1991–2003'.

74 NAI, OPW 5/8066/30, 'National Monument no.34, St Audoen's Church, The Portlester

Chapel with ruins adjoining same', 1930.

75 O'Connor, 'Report by M.J. Bourke', 1915; transcribed *c.*2017 from document now untraced.

76 NAI, OPW 5/3/71, 'Public Buildings Subject Register, 1912'; RCBL, P.0045.25.12, *St Peter's Parish Magazine*, 1923–24.

77 O'Connor, 'St Audeon's [*sic*] Church Tower', 1913, and 'St Audeon's [*sic*] Church', 1913; transcribed *c.*2017 from OPW 5/13709/13 and OPW 5/13780/13 (both now untraced).

78 RCBL, P.0116.05.03, 'Vestry Minutes of the Parish of St Audoen 1913–22'.

79 Ibid.; O'Connor, 'St Audeon's [*sic*] Church. Caretaker', 1919, and 'Fredk. Whittle acting caretaker and sexton', 1922; transcribed *c.*2017 from OPW 5/146/19 and OPW 5/4498/22 (both now untraced).

80 O'Connor, 'Jas. Whittle new caretaker', 1922; transcribed *c.*2017 from OPW 5/12251/22 (now untraced). This is a surprisingly rare and brief acknowledgement of the profound political changes happening in Ireland at this time, although the index books of the Board of Works do indeed show a sharp downturn in National Monument activity during the independence struggle.

81 RCBL, P.0045.05.09, 'Select Vestry Minutes of the Parish of St Peter and St Audoen 1919–36'.

82 NAI, OPW 5/8066/30; RCBL, P.0045.05.11, 'Select Vestry Minutes of the Parish of St Peter and St Audoen 1937–57'.

83 NAI, OPW 5/8066/30. Thomas N. Deane was succeeded as Superintendent of National Monuments by Robert Cochrane in 1899, followed by Andrew Robinson in 1916 and by Harold G. Leask in 1923. It only became a full-time position in 1930.

84 H.A. Wheeler and M.J. Craig, *The Dublin City Churches of the Church of Ireland* (Dublin: Association for Promoting Christian Knowledge, 1948), pp.12–15. Henry Wheeler was later employed by the National Monuments Service and Maurice Craig became one of Ireland's foremost architectural historians; see McMahon (2001), pp.3–4.

85 RCBL, P.0116.05.03; Peter Harbison, *Guide to the National Monuments of Ireland* (Dublin: Gill & Macmillan, 1970), p.73; interviews by the author with parishioners Cecil Pakenham and James Kilbey, June 2024; the paid position of sexton of St Audoen's Church was discontinued in the 1970s, and, because of safety concerns, only members of the parish congregation had access to the ruins thereafter.

86 O'Connor, 'Report by Mr. Cochrane', 1905; transcribed *c.*2017 from document now untraced.

87 NAI, OPW 5/8066/30.

88 In just two sentences, Wheeler and Craig (1948) provide the only available information about these artefacts, whose connection to St Audoen's might well otherwise have been forgotten. Having been brought back under the spotlight on foot of recent enquiries by the visitor centre staff, they are currently being examined by the National Museum and medieval ceramics expert Clare McCutcheon. It is to be hoped that further details might survive in uncatalogued OPW documents.

89 National Monuments Service Photographic Unit, 34.26.

90 RCBL, MS 465, Box 2.

91 DCLA, 'Dublin City Council Minutes', resolution, 15 May 1961.

92 RCBL, P.0045.05.12. The sexton was to be paid £4 per week to supervise tourist visits, and the scheme was to be reviewed in June, but there are no further references until late 1969 when the parish enquired about whether the Irish tourist board would pay for the church to be opened to the public.

93 RCBL, P.0512.05.01, 'Vestry Minutes of the Parish of St Catherine and St James with St Audoen 1970–83'; P.0512.05.02, 'Vestry Minutes of the Parish of St Catherine and St James with St Audoen 1983–91'; P.0512.05.03.

94 RCBL, P.0116.05.03; RCBL, MS 465, Box 2; Rev. McCready's pamphlet playfully contrasted the youth of his intended readers with the 'old Rector', 'old Curate' and 'old Sexton' of 'old St Audöen's'.

95 RCBL, P.0512.05.02; RCBL, P.0512.05.03.

96 'Vestry Minutes of the Parish of St Catherine and St James with St Audoen 2004–24', unpublished documents courtesy of Canon Mark Gardner; RCBL, MS 465, Box 2.

97 RCBL, P.0512.05.02.

98 OPW Registry, D94/437/2, 'High Street, Dublin, St Audeon's [*sic*], The Portlester Chapel and adjoining ruin', 1987.

99 RCBL, P.0512.05.02.

100 See McMahon (2006).

101 RCBL, P.0512.05.03.

102 The author's interviews with parishioners Cecil Pakenham and James Kilbey, June 2024.

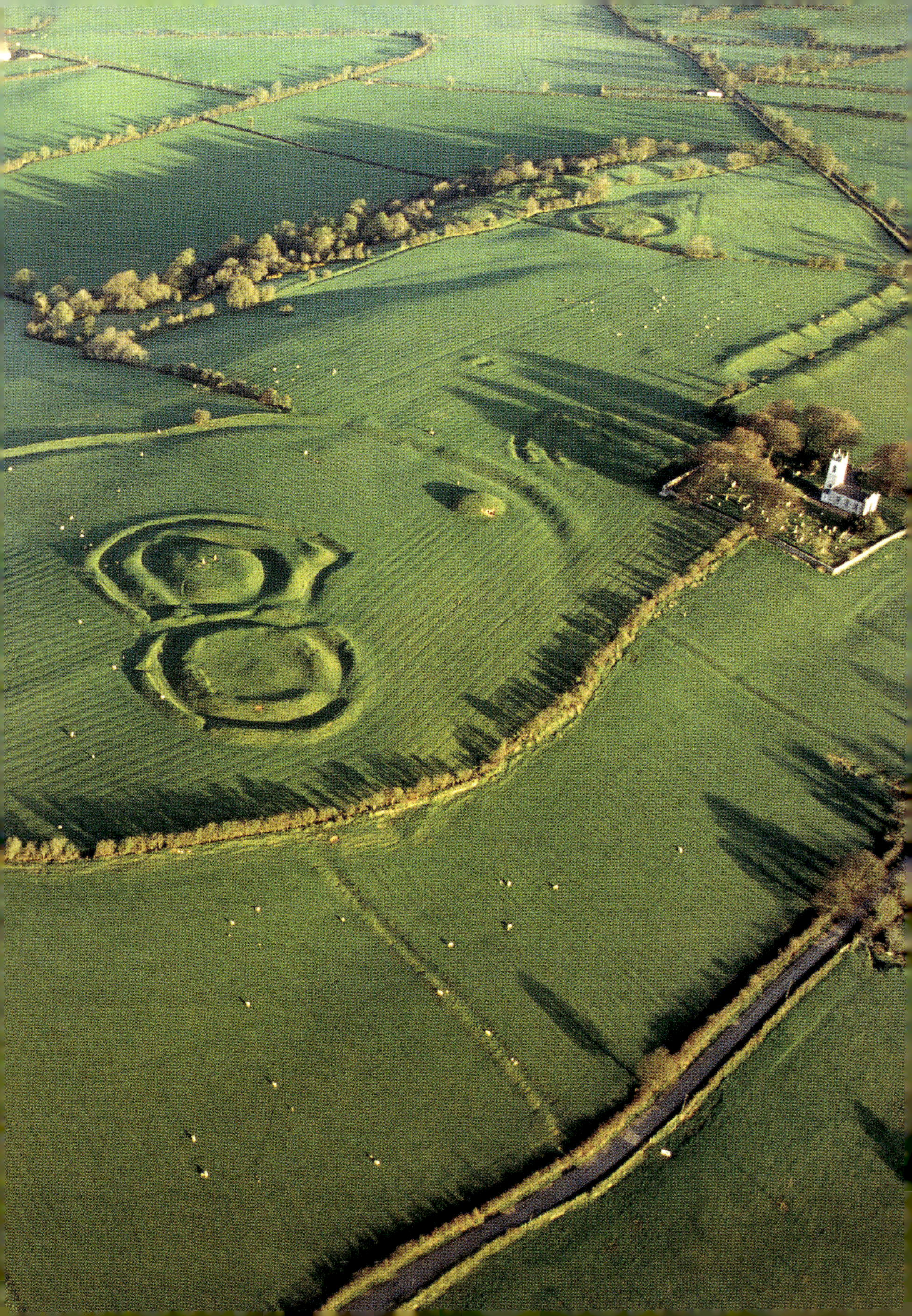

# The study of Tara by R.A.S. Macalister (1870–1950), antiquarian and Professor of Celtic Archaeology

MAIRÉAD CAREW

Tara is an important prehistoric burial site in co. Meath and the traditional seat of the high kings of Ireland [fig. 1]. It was studied by Robert Alexander Stewart Macalister (1870–1950) during his tenure as Professor of Celtic Archaeology at University College Dublin, from 1909 to 1943 [fig. 2]. During that period, Macalister was the only academic archaeologist in Ireland writing about Tara. Papers on his life and career have been published, but an archaeological historiography of Tara has not been written to date, and Macalister's contribution to it has not been adequately explored and evaluated.[1] This paper charts his influence – both as an antiquarian and as an archaeologist – in the development of the academic study of Tara. It traces the evolution of his ideas and their impact on subsequent generations of scholars, including modern archaeologists, and provides an overview of his work in the context of the archaeological historiography of Tara. It situates Macalister in the context of his times, and includes consideration of his academic background, his training in archaeological field work, his published research which was influential in scholarship on Tara, and the reception of his writings by his contemporaries at home and abroad. Finally, his innovative means of engaging popular interest in and understanding of Tara's archaeological significance is explored.[2]

Macalister first wrote about Tara when the British Israelites dug the site between 1899 and 1902 in an effort to recover the biblical Ark of the Covenant.[3] They believed that the royal site of Tara was the 'transplanted Jerusalem' in a new Israel, which they identified as the British Empire.[4] Macalister, then working in Palestine, wrote to the newspaper *Fáinne an Lae* outlining his objections to the dig. Published on 28 October 1899, his letter lamented the fact that Tara, 'the site of the palace of the kings of Ireland', had fallen into the hands of British Israelites, that it was a 'national calamity', and that their unscientific diggings were 'an object-lesson in the danger of neglecting scientific truth'.[5] As far as Macalister was concerned, they were pulling to pieces 'the most important and interesting site in all Ireland'.[6] Other cultural nationalists, including Arthur Griffith, Maud Gonne, W.B. Yeats, Douglas Hyde and George Moore, were

---

fig. 1 | Aerial photograph of Tara, co. Meath
[© Photographic Archive, National Monuments Service, Government of Ireland)

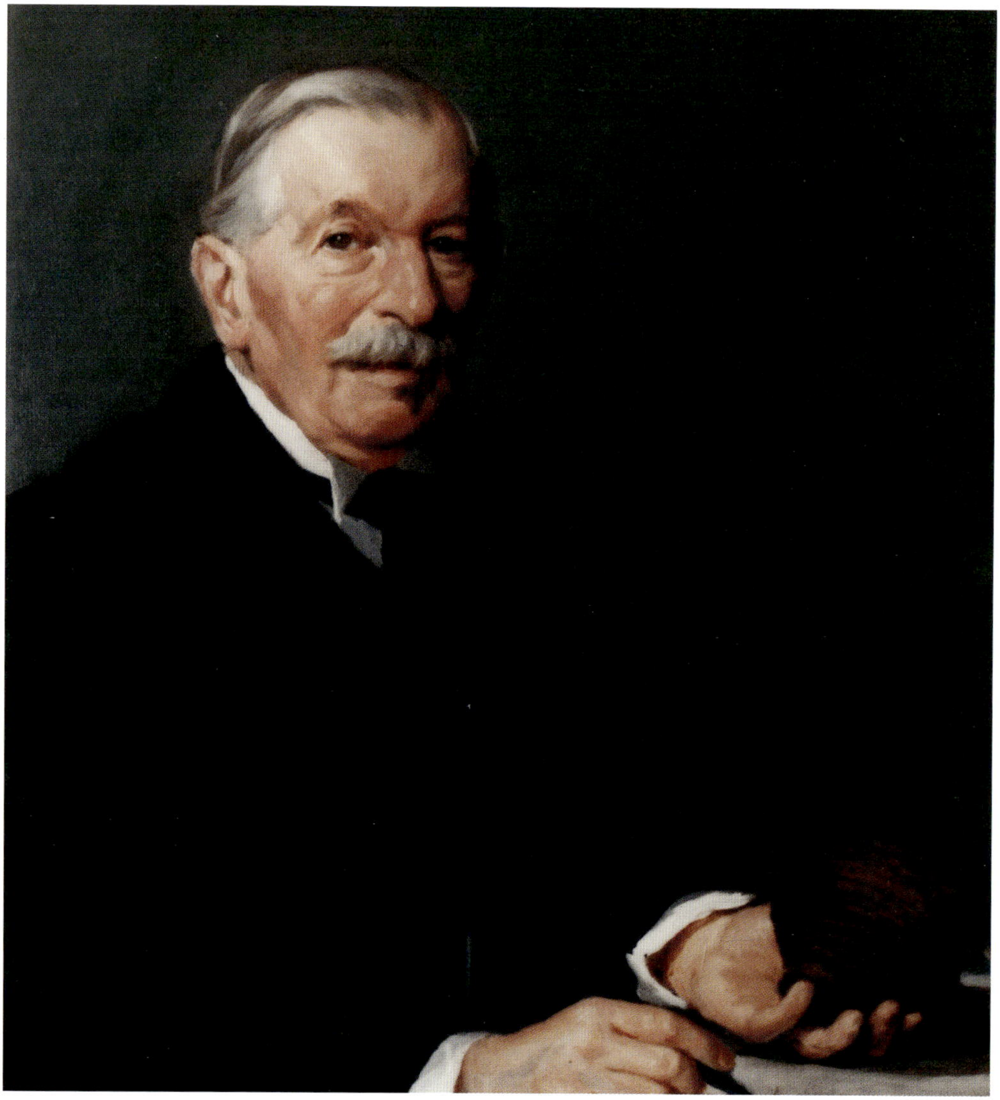

involved in an effective media campaign, and succeeded in getting the unorthodox diggings on Tara stopped. They believed that Tara was the capital of independent ancient Ireland and 'probably the most consecrated spot' in the country.[7] The idea of Tara as sacrosanct in the cultural and political sphere was relevant in terms of the potential for its scientific excavation by Macalister. Conor Newman's comment about Tara being 'as much an evolving concept as a physical reality' is pertinent to the understanding of the role of Tara in the national psyche, as well as Macalister's approach to the study of it.[8]

The history of investigation of Tara reflects the history of archaeology in Ireland

fig. 2 | *R.A.S. Macalister* by Dermod O'Brien, PRHA (1865–1945), oil on canvas, 64 x 50 cm approx., Royal Irish Academy
(by permission of the Royal Irish Academy, © RIA)

and its development from an antiquarian pursuit to a scientific endeavour. Macalister was central to this process. It also reflects the cultural-political milieu in which Irish archaeology was practiced in his lifetime. According to Muiris O'Sullivan, Macalister 'bridged the gap from antiquarianism to modern archaeology'.[9] He did this by developing a more modern approach to scientific archaeology while simultaneously being involved in antiquarianism. Recent studies have revised the understanding of the work of antiquarians and their role in society. Kelsey Jackson Williams described an antiquarian as 'a dynamic, interdisciplinary, questioning scholar whose work stretched across many disciplines and fields of enquiry and whose scholarship lay at the centre of humanist and enlightenment projects to recover and understand the human past'.[10] Guy Beiner, in his study of the antiquarian roots of interdisciplinary scholarship, stated that antiquarians were polymaths, a term suited to Macalister.[11] His interests encompassed Irish, European and Near Eastern archaeology, Celtic epigraphy, languages including Irish and Arabic, Irish and European history, music and ecclesiastical vestments.[12]

Macalister held several leadership positions in the realm of archaeology during his time at UCD: he was president of the Royal Society of Antiquaries of Ireland 1924–28, president of the Royal Irish Academy 1926–31, and chairman of the National Monuments Advisory Council 1930–43. These key positions enabled him to have influence and a prominent role in two important cultural initiatives in the Irish Free State, which had far-reaching consequences for the future interpretation and protection of Irish archaeology. These were the Lithberg Report (1927), the first cultural policy document for Irish archaeology in the Irish Free State, and the National Monuments Act (1930) which defined a 'national monument' for the first time.[13] This legislation, spearheaded by Macalister on behalf of the Royal Society of Antiquaries of Ireland, was crucial to the management and protection of archaeological sites, including Tara.[14]

## Training and fieldwork

Macalister studied at St John's College, Cambridge, graduating with a degree in mathematics in 1892. He studied geology and carried out research in the Sedgwick Museum of Geology. He also taught prehistoric archaeology in Cambridge before the archaeological and anthropological tripos was established. He trained in archaeological techniques and methodology under the auspices of the Palestine Exploration Fund between 1898 and 1900 [fig. 3]. Macalister was an assistant to Frederick Jones Bliss (1859–1937), and together they excavated sites in the southern Shephelah region of Palestine between 1898 and 1900. He took over from Bliss and became director of excavations at Gezer during the years 1902–05 and 1907–09.[15] These excavations were very ambitious at the time in Palestine, and Macalister's work influenced the understanding of the sites he excavated. His work in the region was the subject of a workshop at the Albright Institute of Archaeological Research in Jerusalem in 2013, and the published proceedings reassessed Macalister's contribution to the field.[16] While his shortcomings were acknowledged, Baruch Brandl considered Macalister to be an 'outstanding scholar' who was ahead of his time and whose

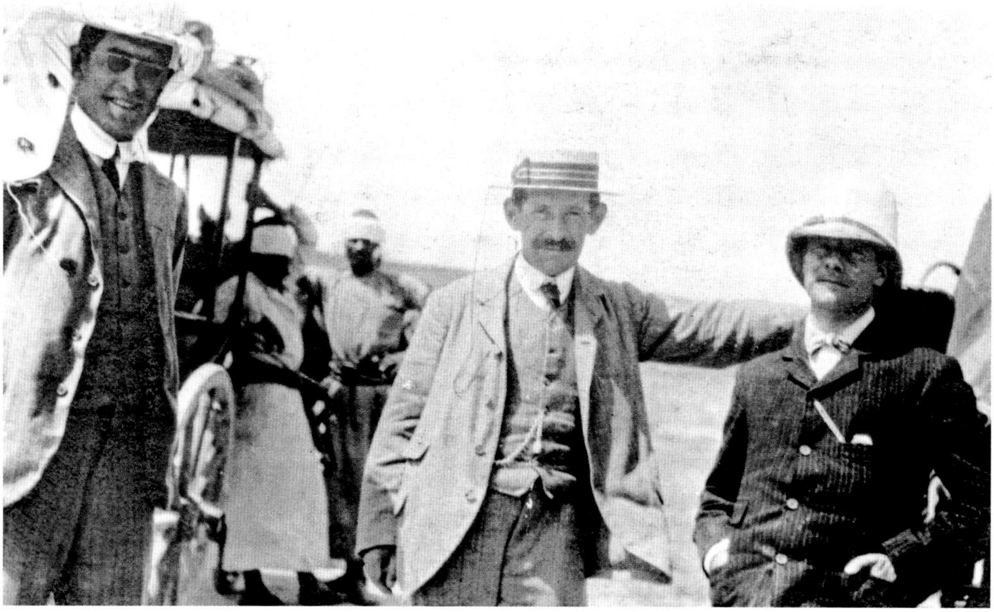

achievements 'should be judged in retrospect and not in comparison with current norms'.[17] This is the theme of this workshop's publication, whereby Macalister is defined as much by his achievements as by his errors, and is placed in the context of his times.[18]

The excavation of Tell ej-Judeideh – carried out by Macalister and Bliss in 1899 – has been re-examined by Shimon Gibson, who concluded that the quality of their records was sufficiently good 'to reconstruct the archaeological history of the site'.[19] Gibson also praised Macalister for his extremely good drawing skills and his use of photography as a major tool for recording excavated features and artefacts.[20] Macalister's survey of the hinterland at Gezer, in which the site was placed in the context of its broader setting, was innovative for its time, and Eric Mitchell acknowledged that 'Macalister deserves praise for attempting one of the first, if not the first, serious surveys of a major tell's hinterland'.[21] Macalister also discovered one of the largest and possibly oldest water systems in the ancient Near East at Gezer. His work was described as 'spot-on' by Warner, Tsuk and Parker who wrote that 'we have nothing but the highest respect for Macalister's work'.[22] Previously, in 1971, the renowned archaeologist Kathleen Kenyon described Gezer as having been 'excavated [by Macalister] with the greatest care and the results very fully published'.[23]

In October 1923, during his time at UCD, Macalister went to Jerusalem to direct excavations in the area of the Ophel (City of David).[24] An aerial photograph of the City of David was one of the first of its kind in an excavation report. Macalister was to become a pioneer in the use of aerial photography in Irish archaeology and, in partic-

fig. 3 | left to right: Dr Ernest William Gurney Masterman (1867–1943), secretary of the Palestine Exploration Fund, R.A.S. Macalister and his brother George Hugh Kidd Macalister (1879–1930) at Nablus in Palestine, 1907
(Palestine Exploration Fund, London)

ular, in his research on Tara. This is discussed in more detail later in this paper. Macalister published *A History of Civilization in Palestine* in 1912 and *A Century of Excavation in Palestine* in 1925. Brian G. Scott commented that Macalister 'did advance significantly the cause of archaeology in the Levant'.[25]

Macalister, 'a cultured and widely read intellectual', was appointed to the position of Professor of Celtic Archaeology at UCD (one of the first university chairs of prehistoric archaeology in Western Europe) in 1909.[26] His skillset as a notable antiquarian and experienced excavator equipped him to carry out his new role effectively, and 'a great stimulus was given to archaeological work in Ireland'.[27] He was influential in the shaping of archaeology as an academic subject and instrumental in setting up a professional school of archaeology in UCD.[28] Muiris O'Sullivan described him as 'the pioneer whose interpretation of the role set an ambitious standard for those who followed'.[29] The first scientific excavation which Macalister carried out in his new role was at Carrowkeel, co. Sligo in 1911.[30] Later, this was described by Adolf Mahr in 1937 as 'almost the only really very successful and important (also from the international viewpoint) excavation undertaken for many years' in Ireland.[31] When the Carrowkeel excavation was reviewed by archaeologists in 2014, the methodology was criticised, but it was acknowledged that 'we are still dependent on the 1911 excavation report for information on the monuments and finds'.[32] Macalister was also involved in a number of other scientific excavations on a variety of archaeological sites in Ireland during his time at UCD, including crannógs, forts, Bronze Age barrows and the well-known sites of Newgrange, Knowth and Uisneach.[33]

Macalister is regarded as 'the founding father of modern ogham studies'. Drawing on extensive fieldwork, he published *Studies in Irish Epigraphy* in three volumes between 1897 and 1907, and later a two-volume inventory *Corpus inscriptionum insularum Celticarum*, in 1945 and 1949.[34] His reports and books reflect an antiquarian tradition side by side with a burgeoning scientific consciousness in the discipline of archaeology. Macalister published important monographs on Irish and European archaeology in the 1920s and 1930s. These included *Ireland in Pre-Celtic Times* (1921); *A Textbook of European Archaeology* (1921) – 'an excellent summary of the Palaeolithic and Mesolithic' – and *The Archaeology of Ireland* (1928; revised 1949), which became the model for later syntheses up to and including *The Prehistoric Archaeology of Ireland* by John Waddell, published in 1998.[35]

Macalister brought an intellectual rigour, scientific mindset, literary gifts, imagination and an international perspective to the study of Tara. His interdisciplinary approach was a non-invasive one, and included archaeological survey, photographs of monuments and artefacts, aerial photography and analysis of literary and historical sources.

## Temair Breg

MACALISTER PUBLISHED A SUBSTANTIAL PAPER, 'TEMAIR BREG' IN THE *PROCEEDINGS OF the Royal Irish Academy* in 1919, which explored topography, origin, kingship, gods and cults, the Lia Fáil (Stone of Destiny) and the place of Tara in

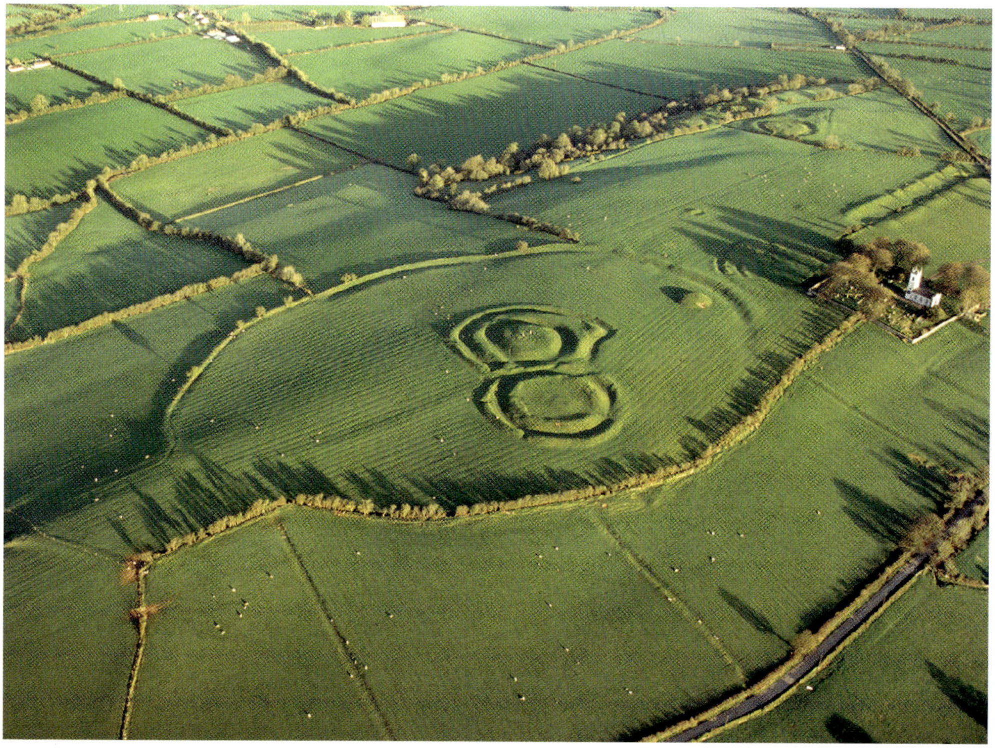

European culture [fig. 4].[36] He was later to argue that Tara was one of the most important historical sites in Europe, and of world significance.[37] His paper was based on the medieval topographical tract, Dindshenchas Érenn, consisting of literary compositions in prose and verse about the prominent places of Ireland. Dindshenchas Érenn is extant in multiple manuscripts dating to the eleventh and twelfth centuries. The material relating to Tara consists of five poems and two pieces of prose. Edel Bhreathnach considered that the prose tract 'Dindgnai Temrach' ('The remarkable places of Tara') 'is so detailed that it is tantamount to a medieval survey of the Hill of Tara'.[38]

In the nineteenth century, a survey of the Hill of Tara based on the Dindshenchas had been carried out by the antiquarian George Petrie (1790–1866) and published in the *Transactions of the Royal Irish Academy* in 1839.[39] His paper, 'On the History and Antiquities of Tara Hill', was a correlation of information gleaned from Dindshenchas Érenn, and the observation and measurements of the monuments. Sites that had disappeared by the time Petrie came to carry out his survey – but were referred to in the Dindshenchas Érenn – were also included. Petrie believed that the key to the understanding of the antiquities of Tara was to be found in ancient Irish texts.[40] He used the work of Captain Thomas Larcom and Lieutenant Bordes, John O'Donovan, Edward O'Reilly and Eugene O'Curry in his paper.[41] A polymath, Petrie saw himself as an 'antiquarian investigator' or 'antiquary'.[42] While he was given the

fig. 4 | Aerial photograph of Tara, co. Meath
(© Photographic Archive, National Monuments Service, Government of Ireland)

accolade of 'father of the modern school of Irish archaeology' at his death, there is no evidence that he excavated any archaeological sites himself.[43] Perhaps it would have been a more fitting accolade for Macalister?

Macalister acknowledged the work of Petrie and wrote that his 1839 essay 'still stands as a model of industry and archaeological insight'.[44] However, it was his opinion that a new study was required to review the whole subject after eighty years of research, since more ancient texts had been published, a more rigid historical criticism of the documents used by Petrie could be applied, and the science of anthropology had come into being.[45] Macalister was very interested in the subject of anthropology and its complementary use in the discipline of archaeology. Later, in 1927, in an address to the Royal Irish Academy, he called for an anthropological committee in the academy and the establishment of archaeological schools within the universities, because at that time archaeology as a discipline was 'simply an appendage to the Celtic School'.[46] In his 'Temair Breg' paper, Macalister wrote about the place of Tara in European culture and believed that a knowledge of Irish tradition and Irish archaeology was essential to an understanding of European Antiquity.[47]

While Macalister had confidence in the knowledge of Dindshenchas Érenn's author about the topography of Tara, he also had reservations about its use for archaeological purposes. He wrote that 'this document, with its wild folklore, may well seem a perilous quicksand on which to found what is intended to be sober historical investigation'.[48] Macalister's nascent scientific leanings when it came to the study of the past meant that he was dubious about the literary sources but he didn't have alternative material or technologies at his disposal at the time. A contemporary reviewer of Macalister's paper, published in *The Irish Monthly* in 1919, was impressed that the author 'shows such ingenuity joined to erudition in the piecing together of details gathered from far-separated sources'.[49] Conor Newman criticised both Petrie and Macalister for devoting too much time in their papers to literary conundrums, including discussions about the origin of the name of Tara, 'at the expense of objective description and critical archaeological analysis'.[50] However, he aptly comments that the papers on Tara authored by Petrie and Macalister were 'works of their time and it would be facile to criticise them without taking into account the historical milieu in which they were written'.[51]

## *Tara: A Pagan Sanctuary of Ancient Ireland*

MACALISTER'S BOOK *TARA: A PAGAN SANCTUARY OF ANCIENT IRELAND* WAS PUBLISHED simultaneously in New York and London in 1931 [fig. 5]. It was an expanded version of his paper 'Temair Breg' with the addition of new research.[52] It was in two parts, the first a descriptive study of the actual archaeological remains based on the medieval Dindshenchas, and the second a discussion of the mythology and legends associated with the site. He acknowledged the value of the Dindshenchas to the study of Tara, referring to it as 'a sort of historico-geographical dictionary of the Ireland of its day', which 'serves the purpose of a guide-book quite as well as any modern compilation'.[53] The Irish antiquarian and eminent historian Goddard H. Orpen, in his review in

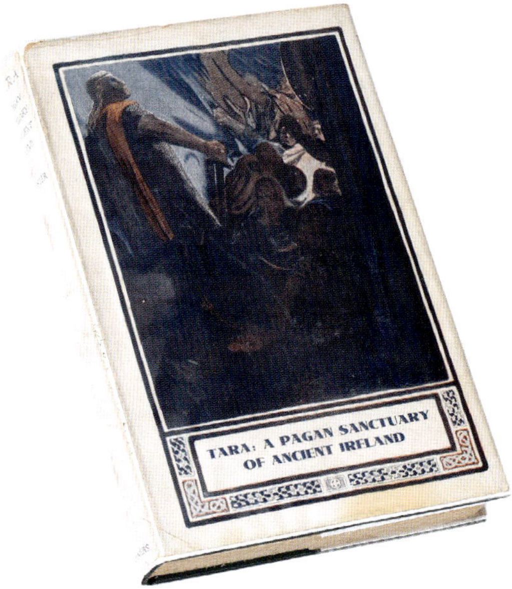


*The English Historical Review*, considered Macalister to be a competent guide on Tara and praised the latter's 1931 publication as 'a handy book which can be read anywhere and could be carried on to the hill itself'.[54] George Grant MacCurdy, assistant Professor of Archaeology at Yale University, in his review of Macalister's book viewed the Dindshenchas as 'indispensable for the topography of Tara'.[55] However, Macalister himself had reservations about the Dindshenchas, and warned that 'what it professes to report of the history of the site has no historical value'.[56] He was aware of its limitations in terms of scientific investigation of Tara despite acknowledging its importance in terms of the location of its monuments.

In a review in the influential London science magazine *Nature*, the Dindshenchas was described as a 'guide-book' of the ninth century.[57] In this review Macalister's book was fittingly judged 'a study in archaeology and traditional history combined, such as would be possible nowhere but in Ireland'.[58] It was referred to as 'a work which might well be regarded as a national duty'.[59] This is a very insightful review reflecting archaeology as it was practiced in Ireland at the time, accommodating a newly developing scientific archaeology within a framework of legendary history. Macalister's book was also reviewed by Thomas F. O'Connor, a member of the Department of History in Saint Louis University, Missouri. He put Macalister and his work in the context of the author's scholarly achievements to date, and described him as being 'the most celebrated of living Irish archaeologists' whose book was 'a ground-study of one of the most celebrated localities in Irish song and story'.[60]

O'Connor lauded Macalister for his use of aerial photography: 'The utility, at least in initial survey work, of that new auxiliary of archaeology, air photography, is convincingly demonstrated in Professor Macalister's investigation of the topography of the vicinity of Tara' [fig. 6].[61] The photographs of Tara were provided by the Air Corps of the Irish Free State. Macalister was the first to use aerial photography as a tool of archaeological research in Ireland. Its value lay in recovering new archaeological features on the site, recording the relationship between the site and the surrounding landscape, the defining of the contours of features that were often difficult, or even impossible, to see on the ground, and the confirmation of features known from literary sources.[62] O'Connor also reminded the reader that Macalister was working in a field 'in which archaeology and authentic history have as yet done little to banish the mists of legend and folklore'.[63] In *Modern Language Notes*, published by John Hopkins University Press, the book was described by the reviewer as an 'authoritative monograph', and praised for its historical and descriptive detail. The book was recommended

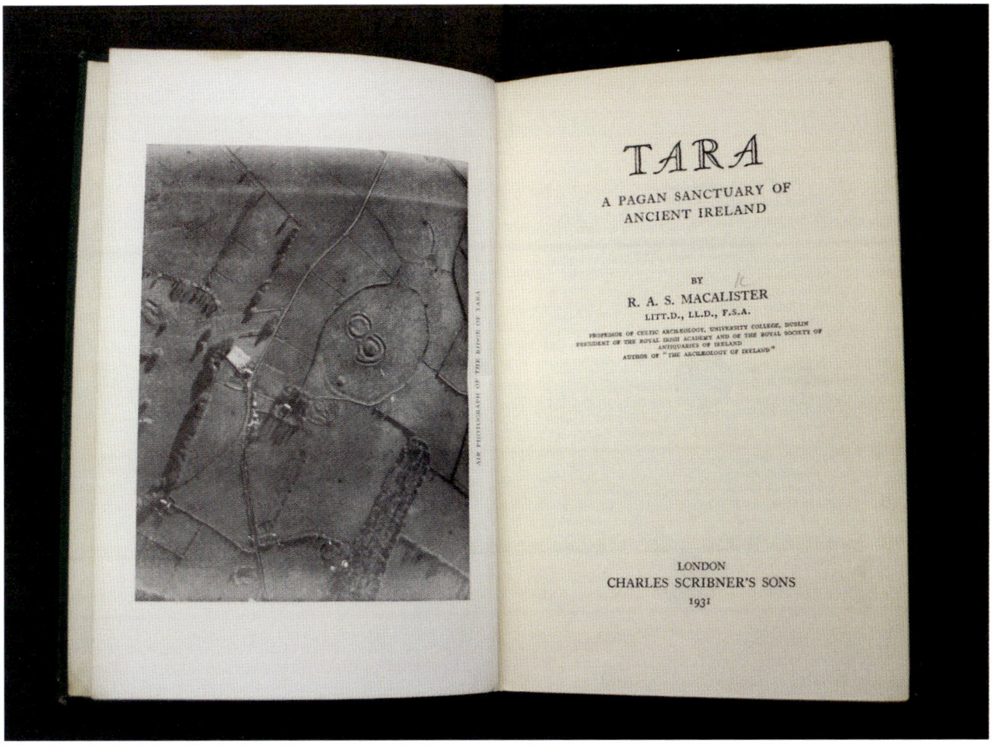


because of its 'eminently readable narrative, attractive to lay and learned alike'.[64]

In *Tara: A Pagan Sanctuary of Ancient Ireland*, Macalister repeatedly expressed his wish to carry out scientific excavations on Tara, and stated that a systematic investigation was very important to Irish archaeology.[65] Despite being an experienced fieldworker, and acknowledging that research questions about Tara could only be answered by archaeological excavation, Macalister did not dig at Tara during his tenure as UCD professor. After the founding of the Irish Free State, this complex and enigmatic site was highly symbolic as Ireland's ancient capital, and attempts at excavation had the potential to be mired in tense cultural politics.[66] Orpen suggested in his review that 'the excavations could best be done under the experienced eye of Dr. Macalister himself'.[67] Eoin MacNeill, in his review of Macalister's book, agreed with the author, and argued that 'it remains to be ascertained by archaeological investigation of the site what is the antiquity of Tara as a centre of human activities'.[68] While MacNeill disputed some of the details in the book, he agreed with Macalister's main thesis that aside from being a great political and social centre, Tara was also a great religious centre in pre-Christian Ireland.[69] In 1998, Chris Lynn commented that 'Macalister was not far wrong' when he described Tara in 1931 as 'a pagan sanctuary of ancient Ireland'.[70]

Macalister's book was generally well received by his contemporaries in

---

figs 5, 6 | Front cover, frontispiece and title page of *Tara: A Pagan Sanctuary of Ancient Ireland* by R.A.S. Macalister (New York and London: Charles Scribner's Sons, 1931)
(cover photo: Ross's Auctioneer, Belfast; frontispiece/title page photo: British Library Collection: 07709.cc.54)

Ireland. His use of photography was praised by a reviewer in *The Irish Monthly*: 'Many mounds and earthworks invisible to the ordinary observer are shown in clear outline on the photographs.'[71] In the opinion of the reviewer in the *Journal of the Royal Society of Antiquaries of Ireland*, Tara was 'a disappointing site to the unprepared visitor', but Macalister's book would make it possible to discover much of what had almost disappeared.[72] His book was described as one 'written for the general reader rather than for specialists, which shows that this university professor, who has done much important scientific work in Ireland, and twice acted as director of excavations in Palestine, does not scorn the part of the *vulgarisateur* [populariser].'[73]

In a review of Macalister's book in the *Journal of the County Louth Archaeological Society*, it was noted that 'Prof. Macalister has given the general public what they have long sought – an authoritative and convenient modern account of the palaces and halls which once stood where now are the low grassy mounds of Tara.'[74] The reviewer praised Macalister for bringing the visitor by the hand and 'bringing story and meaning to the folds and hollows' of Tara.[75] In *The Irish Monthly* review it was recommended that 'every Celtic student should read these two hundred and eight pages of painstaking research'.[76]

These reviews reflect the transitional nature of the text – Macalister's intellectual roots in antiquarianism side-by-side with a maturing scientific archaeological sensibility – and the book was deservedly praised at the time. At that stage, Macalister had earned an international reputation as a prehistorian. But the practice of archaeology was about to change in Ireland. *Tara: A Pagan Sanctuary* was published in 1931, the year the American archaeologist, Hugh O'Neill Hencken (1902–1981), came on a reconnaissance trip to Ireland to see which sites the Harvard Archaeological Mission to Ireland would excavate.[77] The Harvard Mission sprang from a successful academic tour of US universities by Eoin MacNeill in 1930 to attract funding for Celtic research in Ireland and to promote Celtic studies in American universities.[78] On 3 July 1931, Hencken had a meeting with Macalister about the proposed archaeological project.[79] At the time, Macalister was professor, president of the RIA and also chairman of the National Monuments Advisory Committee. While Hencken was satisfied that he was prepared to help rather than to hinder, he was also dismissive of Macalister and his role as Professor of Celtic Archaeology: 'As the name of the chair which he holds might suggest, he is not an archaeologist in the modern sense but a 19th century antiquary.'[80] This intended derogatory comment may reflect the fact that Adolf Mahr had commandeered the Harvard Archaeological Mission, which was to work under the auspices of the National Museum of Ireland, sidelining Macalister and the universities in the process. Hencken referred to an academic feud between Mahr and Macalister because 'each feels that by virtue of his position he is State Archaeologist of Saorstát Éireann'.[81] Mahr acted as administrator and advisor to the American archaeologists during the course of their five-year research project. The Harvard Mission excavated eighteen sites in the Irish Free State and Northern Ireland, and published all their results. This was a turning point in Irish archaeology in terms of new scientific methodologies and techniques, and the reports are used to this day. Tara was considered to be under the remit of Macalister and was, therefore, not included in the Harvard Mission research project. This was, perhaps, an opportunity lost.

## Leabhar Gabhála Éireann

MACALISTER'S SKILLSET AS A POLYMATH AND ANTIQUARIAN ENABLED HIM TO COMPLETE HIS magnum opus – the translation and editing of the eleventh-century text Leabhar Gabhála Éireann (LGÉ), 'The Book of the Taking of Ireland', commonly known as 'The Book of Invasions'. He published it in five volumes between 1938 and 1956, the last being posthumous.[82] It is a foundational text for Irish historiography which places Irish history in the context of the biblical history of the world.[83] It is considered to be essential to Celtic scholarship, and served as a primary text and backdrop for legend, historiography, poetry and political thought in subsequent centuries.[84] Macalister tackled this 'bewildering textual labyrinth' in order to make it accessible to the public.[85] A 'titanic project', it influenced subsequent writings on Tara and was important, in particular, to the study of Tara and kingship.[86] The concept of the high kingship of Ireland was crucial to the chronology of LGÉ.[87] John Carey described Macalister's discussion of the text as demonstrating the latter's 'broad learning, enormous energy, and lively and relentless curiosity'.[88] While Carey did not deny Macalister's errors in his edition of LGÉ – pointed out by a variety of scholars – he did acknowledge that Macalister's version was a generally faithful presentation of all of the medieval versions of LGÉ.[89] R. Mark Scowcroft also acknowledged Macalister's errors in his edition, but accepted that the latter brought 'great industry and erudition' to his task.[90]

LGÉ also influenced generations of Irish archaeologists in terms of 'invasion hypotheses' to explain the archaeological record. Stories about a sequence of invasions served as the basic framework of Irish legendary history in the LGÉ. A new artefactual assemblage recovered from an archaeological site was interpreted as the material culture of invaders.This thinking continued to be evident in the writings of Irish archaeologists down to the 1970s.[91] It was not questioned until 1978 when John Waddell published his paper, 'The invasion hypothesis in Irish prehistory'.[92] Macalister's intellectual feat of scholarship in providing a translation of the only existing complete edition of LGÉ has not been matched since, as no other scholar has attempted to tackle the text on such a monumental scale. He certainly achieved his aim of providing an accessible edition of LGÉ, and a text which is continually used by scholars today.[93] While it is essential to scholarship on Tara, it is beyond the scope of this paper to analyse it in any depth.

## Public engagement

IN 1997, GEORGE EOGAN COMMENTED ABOUT TARA THAT 'THE MONUMENTS THEMSELVES CAN be an anti-climax', but that they are also 'archaeologically, quietly spectacular'.[94] Macalister had also understood this to be the case, and made valiant efforts to explain Tara to the public through lectures, newspaper articles, the first Irish radio broadcast from an archaeological monument and a guidebook. He was an intellectual who wrote scholarly works but was always willing to use popular media to communicate his knowledge in an accessible way. His earliest lectures on prehistory and early history were published in instalments in *The Irish Monthly*, an Irish Catholic magazine founded in 1873.[95] Other contributors to *The Irish Monthly* included members of Irish cultural and nationalist circles of the time, such as Charles Gavan Duffy, Dora Sigerson and Katharine Tynan. Macalister wrote some of the earliest guidebooks on National Monuments, which included Clonmacnoise (1911), Newgrange (1929) and Monasterboice (1944).[96] He published *Teamhair: Tara* (official handbook) in 1935, a pamphlet giving very brief descriptions and history of each monument on Tara.[97] Macalister was described by Estyn Evans as 'the warm-hearted and exuberant champion of a subject which he did more than anyone else in Ireland to popularise by his fluent and far-ranging pen'.[98]

Macalister the 'intellectual giant' was also a 'deservedly popular lecturer, a ready-speaker, lucid, humorous and always interesting'.[99] He was involved in the first-ever radio broadcast from an Irish archaeological site in 1937. This consisted of an interview by Liam Price, a district justice and antiquarian [fig. 7].[100] The broadcast took place on the Mound of the Hostages, and was the first time that a radio interview had been conducted with an Irish archaeologist who attempted to explain an archaeological site to a public listenership. According to Corlett, 'It is appropriate that their [the broadcaster 2RN] first choice should be Tara', and it was significant because 'for the first time in history people heard an oration from Tara without having to leave the comfort of their own hearth'.[101] Macalister stated that Tara and its traditions could only be explained as 'a religious site of very high antiquity' and 'takes its place among the great sanctuaries of the world'.[102]

When the thorny issue of excavating Tara arose, and Macalister was asked about the possibilities, he replied that 'Tara is one of the most important historical sites in Europe, and its proper excavation should be a national undertaking of the highest importance.'[103] Two of the monuments he expressed interest in excavating were the Banqueting Hall and the Mound of the Hostages. The excavation of Tara was, according to Macalister, 'for the present [...] only a dream of the future'.[104] This sentiment probably reflected his perception of cultural politics and archaeology in the Irish Free State and

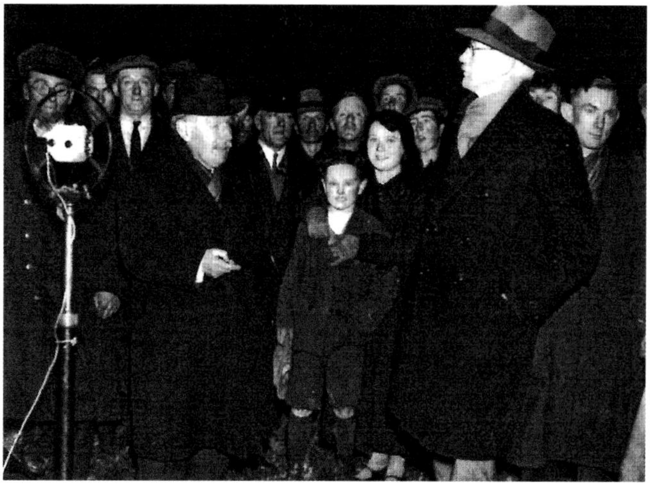

fig. 7 | 'Broadcast from the Hill of Tara', *The Irish Press*, 9 April 1937. Macalister is centre left, near the microphone, and the interviewer, District Justice Liam Price, is on the right. (National Library of Ireland)

opposite

fig. 8 | The excavation of Tara was initiated by Macalister's successor at UCD, Professor Seán P. Ó Ríordáin in the 1950s. (© Photographic Archive, National Monuments Service, Government of Ireland)

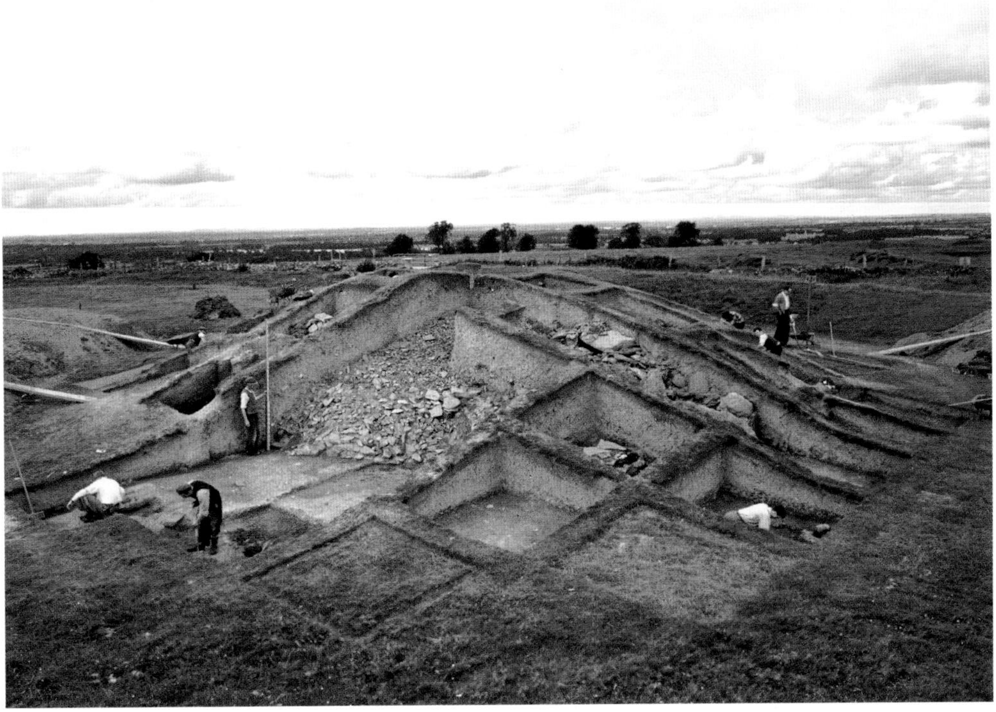

the sensitivities surrounding the excavation of the capital of ancient Ireland (considered by nationalists to be a 32-county Ireland). His own background and social position in the new state may also have been a factor.

### Legacy of research on Tara at UCD

RESEARCH ON TARA WAS TO CONTINUE AT UCD WHEN MACALISTER RETIRED IN 1943 AND the professorial post was filled by the talented fieldworker and academic, Seán P. Ó Ríordáin (1904–1957).[105] An over-sensitivity about the excavation of Tara continued into the post-war era. It was again to become the subject of media controversy in the 1950s.[106] Eoin MacWhite (1923–1972), Irish diplomat, archaeologist and scholar, started the controversy with an article titled 'Should Hill of Tara be excavated?' published in *The Irish Times* on 2 February 1952. MacWhite suggested that no Irish archaeologist was qualified by 'experience or achievement' to excavate such an important complex. Maud Gonne, who had campaigned against the British-Israelites diggings at the turn of the century, wrote in 1952 that 'If Tara is be excavated it must be done only by experts and for the nation.'[107] Ó Ríordáin ably took up the challenge and began the excavation at the Rath of the Synods (the monument the British-Israelites had extensively damaged) in 1952. He excavated the Mound of the Hostages during 1955/56 [fig. 8]. His premature death in 1957 halted the excavations, but they resumed two years later under his successor at UCD, Ruaidhrí de Valera (son of Éamon de Valera). The results, however, were not published until many decades later.[108] Research on Tara continued at UCD under Professor Muiris O'Sullivan with the publication of *Tara, From the Past to the Future: towards a new research agenda*, a wide-ranging review of the significance of Tara and its environs. Contributors to the volume included specialists from Ireland, Britain, Europe and the United States.[109]

## Discovery Programme: Interdisciplinary research on Tara

MACALISTER'S LEGACY OF INTERDISCIPLINARY RESEARCH ON TARA IS EVIDENT IN THE WORK of the Discovery Programme, an archaeological research institute set up in 1991 by Taoiseach Charles J. Haughey of Fianna Fáil. The core period prioritised for research was the Late Bronze Age/Iron Age, or Celtic Period, and Tara was one of the sites selected for study.[110] An archaeological survey of the monuments was carried out using cutting-edge technology at the time by Conor Newman, Director of the Tara Project. A select bibliography of literary sources on Tara was prepared, and research on the historical, cultural and political context of the British-Israelite excavations was carried out. The results of all three strands were published by the Discovery Programme.[111]

George Eogan noted in his foreword to Conor Newman's book *Tara, An Archaeological Survey* that 'the enduring popularity of Tara derives more from its prominence in Irish mythology and the tradition that it was the seat of the high-kings of Ireland than from any in-depth scientific understanding of its monuments'.[112] Newman lamented the fact that 'the monuments have, to some extent, become hidden beneath a deep stratigraphy of oral and literary accretions'.[113] It was the case that Tara had acquired considerable standing in Irish archaeology even though relatively little was known about its archaeology.[114] At the time of the Discovery Programme survey, the excavations carried out in the 1950s by Seán P. Ó Ríordáin and Ruaidhrí de Valera had yet to be published.

Like Macalister before him, Newman carried out a non-invasive survey of Tara. While Macalister relied on literary sources, Newman carried out a ground-breaking geophysical survey, asserting that 'the starting point of any survey of Tara must be the archaeological analysis of its monuments'.[115] However, there are twelve references to Dindshenchas Érenn included in the book, and Newman explains that the description of the monuments on Tara 'follows the precedent established in the Dindshenchas and the progression is ordered from south to north'.[116] Also, he retained the medieval nomenclature for the monuments. Innovative methods were used – a Total Station electronic distance-measuring instrument to capture topographic survey data, and resistivity and geomagnetic surveys. Topographical data was presented as wire-mesh models and hill-shaded digital terrain models. Like Macalister, he used aerial photography as a research tool. Newman concluded that 'there is no evidence that [Tara's] elevated mythological and historical status is a reflection of any national supremacy it might have enjoyed during most of the prehistoric period'; Tara was 'a palimpsest of prehistoric ritual activity'.[117] The survey was very successful and the number of individual sites recognised at Tara was increased significantly. Further research included four large-scale geophysical surveys undertaken by the Discovery Programme in collaboration with the National University of Ireland, Galway, between 2002 and 2010. A detailed and extensive helicopter-based Light Detection and Ranging (LiDAR) survey was carried out in 2007. In 2014, a joint research project in partnership with the Römisch-Germanische Kommission, a branch of the German Archaeological Institute (Deutsches Archäologisches Institut), was established.[118]

In 1997, George Eogan had written that the promise of ongoing State financial support for the Discovery Programme 'allows us now to consider for the first time a focused campaign of excavation at Tara itself'.[119] However, only one small excavation was carried out by the Discovery Programme at Rath na Ríogh that same year.[120] Barry Cunliffe, at the Tara Symposium in UCD in 2009, argued strongly for selective excavation of Tara in the future.[121]

## Conclusion

MACALISTER, WHO WAS BORN IN THE NINETEENTH CENTURY, WAS A TRANSITIONAL FIGURE in Irish archaeology, and in many instances his work was innovative for its time. While his methodology was often flawed in comparison to archaeology as it is practiced today, it has to be remembered that he was a scholar of his times. Antiquarianism, as a cultural and scholarly pursuit – and those who practised it – has been reassessed in recent years. A more generous approach to Macalister's work is increasingly evident with a re-evaluation of his archaeological practice in Palestine and at Carrowkeel in Ireland, and his study of ogham inscriptions. His work on LGÉ has also been judged in a more positive light. Macalister can be commended as the only archaeologist in Ireland to tackle the complex site of Tara during an important cultural and political era. Estyn Evans, who was also critical of Macalister, conceded that 'Irish archaeology is fortunate in having been led for so long by a man of his wide scholarship and European outlook'.[122] Macalister's distinction as an archaeologist was recognised during his lifetime by the awarding of honorary doctorates by Cambridge, Dublin and the universities of Wales and Glasgow. Whether he is admired or derided,[123] Macalister has earned his place in the archaeological historiography of Tara.

---

**Mairéad Carew** is an archaeologist, author and OPW tour guide. Her publications include *Tara and the Ark of the Covenant: a search for the Ark of the Covenant by British Israelites on the Hill of Tara, 1899–1902* (Royal Irish Academy, 2003), *Tara, The Guidebook* (Discovery Programme, 2016) and *The Quest for the Irish Celt: the Harvard Archaeological Mission to Ireland, 1932–1936* (Irish Academic Press, 2018).

### Endnotes

1 Muiris O'Sullivan, 'The Life and Legacy of R.A.S. Macalister: a century of archaeology in UCD', in Gabriel Cooney et al. (eds), *Relics of Old Decency: archaeological studies in later prehistory. Festschrift for Barry Raftery* (Dublin: Wordwell, 2009), pp.521–29; Muiris O'Sullivan, 'R.A.S. Macalister', in Próinséas

Ní Chatháin and Siobhán Fitzpatrick (eds), with Howard Clarke, *Pathfinders to the Past: the antiquarian road to Irish historical writing, 1640–1960* (Dublin: Four Courts Press, 2012), pp.161–71; Hilary Richardson, 'Robert Alexander Stewart Macalister', *Dictionary of Irish Biography,* https://doi.org/10.3318/dib.005093.v1; David Pilgrim Godden, 'Robert Alexander Stewart Macalister: a paradox in the scientific discipline of archaeology' (unpublished MA thesis, Saor-Ollscoil na hÉireann, 1993).

2 It is outside the remit of this paper to analyse Macalister's work on other archaeological sites and time periods.

3 Mairéad Carew, *Tara and the Ark of the Covenant: a search for the Ark of the Covenant by British-Israelites on the Hill of Tara, 1899–1902* (Dublin: Royal Irish Academy (RIA) / Discovery Programme, 2003).

4 They also referred to Tara as 'the spiritual birthplace of the Anglo-Saxon Nation'; Carew (2003), p.20.

5 R.A.S. Macalister, 'A menace to the Irish language: a letter from Palestine', *Fáinne an Lae*, 28 Oct 1899, p.134. The letter also discussed philology and archaeology.

6 Ibid.

7 Carew (2003), p.88.

8 Conor Newman, *Tara, An Archaeological Survey* (Dublin: RIA / Discovery Programme, 1997), p.241.

9 O'Sullivan (2012), p.169.

10 Kelsey Jackson Williams, 'Antiquarianism: a reinterpretation', *Erudition and the Republic of Letters*, vol.2, no.1 (2017), pp.56–96: 95.

11 Guy Beiner, 'Irish Historical Studies avant la Lettre: the antiquarian genealogy of interdisciplinary scholarship', in Reneé Allyson Fox, Mike Cronin and Brian Ó Conchubhair (eds), *Routledge International Handbook of Irish Studies* (London: Routledge, 2021), pp.47–58: 52.

12 Mary Lou Brennan, 'Robert Alexander Stewart Macalister 1871–1950', *Journal of the Royal Society of Antiquaries of Ireland (JRSAI)*, vol.103 (1973), pp.167–76; Siobhán de hÓir, 'R.A.S. Macalister 1871–1950', *JRSAI*, vol.123 (1993), p.170; Samuel R. Wolff, 'R.A.S. Macalister's bibliography pertaining to Palestinian archaeology, epigraphy and ethnography', in Samuel R. Wolff and Philip R. Davies (eds), *Palestine Exploration Fund Annual XII: Villain or Visionary? R.A.S. Macalister and the archaeology of Palestine. Proceedings of a workshop held at the Albright Institute of Archaeological Research, Jerusalem, on 13 December 2013* (Jerusalem: Palestine Exploration Fund, 2015), pp.1–4.

13 Mairéad Carew, '"The Glamour of Ancient Greatness": the importance of the 1927 Lithberg Report to Irish archaeology', *Archaeology Ireland*, vol.22, no.1 (Spring 2008), pp.20–22; Christiaan Corlett 'The Royal Society of Antiquaries of Ireland and the protection of monuments: Part II', *JRSAI*, vol.141 (2011), pp.167–89; Christiaan Corlett, 'The Royal Society of Antiquaries of Ireland and the protection of monuments: Part III', *JRSAI*, vol.142–43 (2012–13), pp.166–83.

14 The term 'national monument' was defined for the first time in Section 2 of the National Monuments Act (1930): 'the preservation of which is a matter of national importance by reason of the historical, architectural, traditional, artistic or archaeological interest attaching thereto.'

15 R.A.S. Macalister, *The Excavation of Gezer: 1902–1905 and 1907–1909*, 3 vols (Cambridge: Cambridge University Press, 1912).

16 Wolff and Davies (eds).

17 Baruch Brandl, 'Are the finds from Macalister's Gezer I-III still relevant for current research a century later?' in Wolff and Davies (eds), pp.50–55: 50.

18 Samuel R. Wolff, the editor of the volume, commented that 'his achievements were numerous, as were his errors in judgement and in the field': Samuel R. Wolff, 'Preface', in Wolff and Davies (eds), p.vii. For criticism of Macalister's work at Gezer, see William G. Dever, 'R.A.S. Macalister at Gezer: a response to Jonathan Tubb', in Wolff and Davies (eds), pp.20–23.

19 Shimon Gibson, 'The disputed legacy of R.A.S. Macalister's archaeological explorations in Palestine', in Wolff and Davies (eds), p.37. In the Near East and south-east Europe, a 'tell' is an artificial mound or hill resulting from the accumulation of debris over a long period of time. Successive phases of settlement were constructed upon the ruins of their predecessors and then, in turn, levelled to provide a platform for succeeding structures.

20 Ibid., p.31.

21 Eric Mitchell, 'The Gezer Survey: an assessment of Macalister's work', in Wolff and Davies (eds), p.72.

22 Daniel A. Warner, Tsvika Tsuk and Jim Parker, 'The Gezer water system re-examined', in Wolff and Davies (eds), p.62.

23 Kathleen Kenyon, Royal Cities of the Old Testament (London: Barrie and Jenkins, 1971), p.68.

24 Shimon Gibson, 'The Palestine Exploration Fund and the search for the "City of David"', in Eyal Meiron (ed.), *City of David: studies of ancient Jerusalem* vol.4 (Jerusalem: Megalim Institute, 2009), pp.45–61; Garth Gilmour (ed.), *Palestine Exploration Fund Annual IV: final report of excavations on The Hill of The Ophel by R.A.S. Macalister and J. Garrow Duncan 1923–1925: catalogue and examination of the finds in the collections of the Palestine Exploration Fund* (London: Routledge, 2024).

25 Brian G. Scott, review of Wolff and Davies (eds), *Journal of Irish Archaeology*, vol.31 (2022), pp.142–43: 143.

26 Jonathan N. Tubb, 'R.A.S. Macalister: villain or visionary?', in Wolff and Davies (eds), p.5. Macalister was not the first choice for the position of Professor of Celtic Archaeology, as Eoin MacNeill was recommended to the Dublin Commission by the governing authority of the National University of Ireland in 1909. See UCD Archives, University College Dublin Minute Book Governing Body, 19 Oct 1909. See also Michael Tierney, *Eoin MacNeill: Scholar and man of action 1867–1945* (Oxford: Clarendon Press, 1980), p.86.

27 Michael Herity and George Eogan, *Ireland in Prehistory* (London: Routledge & Kegan Paul, 1977), p.13.

28 Richardson, 'Robert Alexander Stewart Macalister', *Dictionary of Irish Biography*.

29 O'Sullivan (2009), p.521.

30 R.A.S. Macalister, E.C.R. Armstrong and R.L. Praeger, 'Report on the Exploration of Bronze-Age Carns on Carrowkeel Mountain, Co. Sligo', *Proceedings of the Royal Irish Academy* (*PRIA*), vol.29 (1911–12), pp.311–47.

31 Adolf Mahr, *New Aspects and Problems in Irish Prehistory: Presidential Address for 1937. Paper no.11, reprinted from the Proceedings of the Prehistoric Society for 1937 (July–Dec)*, p.267.

32 Robert Hensey and others, 'A Century of Archaeology: historical excavation and modern research at the Carrowkeel passage tombs, county Sligo', *PRIA*, vol.114C (2014), pp.57–87: 58.

33 Brennan, pp.167–76.

34 Katherine Forsyth, 'R.A.S. Macalister, A Life', *OG(H)AM: Harnessing digital technologies to transform understanding of ogham writing, from the 4th century to the 21st*, 6 July 2023 <https://ogham.glasgow.ac.uk/index.php/2023/07/06/r-a-s-macalister-a-life/> [acc. 23 May 2024].

35 Herity and Eogan, p.13; O'Sullivan (2012), p.167.

36 R.A.S. Macalister, 'Temair Breg: a study of the remains and traditions of Tara', *PRIA*, vol.34C (1917–19), pp.231–404. 'Temair Breg' means 'Tara of Brega', a medieval Irish kingdom stretching from the River Liffey to the River Boyne, including parts of counties Meath, Dublin and Louth.

37 Christiaan Corlett, 'The Tara Broadcast', *Ríocht na Midhe: records of Meath Archaeological and Historical Society*, vol.14 (2003), pp.5–21: 21.

38 Edel Bhreathnach, *Tara, A Select Bibliography* (Dublin: RIA / Discovery Programme, 1995), p.27.

39 George Petrie, 'On the History and Antiquities of Tara Hill', *Transactions of the Royal Irish Academy*, vol.18 (1839), pp.25–232.

40 Paul Walsh, 'George Petrie: his life and work', in Ní Chatháin and others (eds), pp.44–71: 54–55.

41 Edel Bhreathnach, 'In Retrospect: introduction to George Petrie's "On the History and Antiquities of Tara Hill"', *PRIA*, vol.106C (2006), pp.409–16: 410.

42 William Stokes, *The Life and Labours in Art and Archaeology of George Petrie* (London: Longmans, Green & Co., 1868), pp.82–83.

43 W.F. Wakeman, 'George Petrie LLD', *Dublin Saturday Magazine*, vol.27 (1866), p.58; Walsh (2012), p.46, n.17.

44 Macalister (1917–19), p.231.

45 Ibid., p.232.

46 R.A.S. Macalister, 'Some Unsolved Problems in Irish Archaeology: an address delivered to the Academy, 28th February 1927', *PRIA*, vol.37 (1924–27), pp.245–62: 254, 258.

47 Macalister (1917–19), p.398.

48 Ibid., p.232.

49 Anon., *Irish Monthly*, vol.47, no. 553 (July 1919), pp.404–05.

50 Newman, p.5.

51 Ibid.

52 R.A.S. Macalister, *Tara: A Pagan Sanctuary of Ancient Ireland* (New York and London:

Charles Scribner's Sons, 1931).

[53] Ibid., p.4.

[54] Goddard H. Orpen, review of Macalister (1931) in *English Historical Review*, vol.48, p.106.

[55] George Grant MacCurdy, review of Macalister (1931) in *American Journal of Archaeology*, vol.36, no.2 (Apr–June 1932), pp.215–16: 215.

[56] Macalister (1931), p.82.

[57] Anon., review of Macalister (1931) in *Nature*, vol.129, no.3264, p.745.

[58] Ibid.

[59] Ibid.

[60] Thomas F. O'Connor, review of Macalister (1931) in *Catholic Historical Review*, vol.18, no.1 (April 1932), pp.102–03: 102.

[61] Ibid.

[62] D.L. Swan, 'The Hill of Tara, County Meath: the evidence of aerial photography', *JRSAI*, vol.108 (1978), pp.51–66: 51.

[63] O'Connor, p.103.

[64] Kemp Malone, review of Macalister (1931), in *Modern Language Notes*, vol.48, no.3 (March 1933), pp.205–06: 206.

[65] Macalister (1931), pp.16, 20, 26, 61, 85.

[66] For general discussions on cultural politics and archaeology, see Peter Woodman, 'Who Possesses Tara: politics in archaeology in Ireland', in Peter J. Ucko (ed.), *Theory in Archaeology: a world perspective* (London and New York: Routledge, 1995), pp.278–97; Gabriel Cooney, 'Building the Future on the Past: archaeology and the construction of national identity in Ireland', in Margarita Díaz-Andreu and Timothy Champion (eds), *Nationalism and Archaeology in Europe* (London: Routledge, 1996), pp.146–63.

[67] Orpen, p.107.

[68] Eoin MacNeill, review of Macalister (1931) in *Studies: An Irish Quarterly Review*, vol.20, no.80 (December 1931), pp.665–68: 665.

[69] Ibid., p.668.

[70] Chris Lynn, review of Newman (1997) in *Archaeology Ireland*, vol.12, no.1 (Spring 1998), pp.36–37: 37.

[71] 'T.B.', review of Macalister (1931) in *Irish Monthly*, vol.59, no.702 (Dec 1931), pp.785–87: 786.

[72] Anon., review of Macalister (1931) in *JRSAI*, vol.1, no.2 (31 Dec 1931), pp.204–05: 205.

[73] Ibid., p.204.

[74] 'H.G.T.', review of Macalister (1931) in *Journal of the County Louth Archaeological Society*, vol.7, no.3 (Dec 1931), pp.438–39: 438.

[75] Ibid.

[76] 'T.B.', p.786.

[77] Mairéad Carew, *The Quest for the Irish Celt: the Harvard Archaeological Mission to Ireland, 1932–1936* (Kildare: Irish Academic Press, 2018), pp.40–47.

[78] Ibid., p.3.

[79] Ibid., p.23.

[80] Ibid., p.34.

[81] Ibid., p.40.

[82] R.A.S. Macalister, *Lebor Gabála Érenn*, 5 vols (London: Irish Texts Society, 1938–56).

[83] R. Mark Scowcroft, 'Leabhar Gabhála. Part II: the growth of the tradition', *Ériu*, vol.39 (Dublin: Royal Irish Academy, 1988), pp.42–43.

[84] John Carey, *The Irish National Origin-Legend: synthetic pseudohistory*, E.C. Quiggin Memorial Lectures (Cambridge: Cambridge University Press, 1994), p.4.

[85] Ibid., p.23.

[86] Bhreathnach (1995), p.16; John Carey, *A New Introduction to Lebor Gabála Érenn: the Book of the Taking of Ireland, edited and translated by R.A. Stewart Macalister* (Dublin: Irish Texts Society, 1993), pp.18–19.

[87] Edel Bhreathnach, 'Cultural Identity and Tara from Lebor Gabála Érenn to George Petrie', *Discovery Programme Reports No. 4: project results* (Dublin: RIA / Discovery Programme, 1996), pp.85–98: 85.

[88] Carey (1993), p.16.

[89] Ibid. In a review of vol.4, D.A. Binchy wrote that Macalister had 'failed lamentably' to provide a reliable text and translation of LGÉ' (D.A. Binchy, *Celtica*, vol.2, pt.1 (1952), pp.195–209). Paul Walsh reviewed vols 1 and 2 in *Irish Historical Studies*, vol.2, issue 5 (March 1940), pp.89–91. The same journal published Macalister's response to the review in vol.2, issue 6 (Sept. 1940), pp.208–10.

[90] R. Mark Scowcroft, 'Leabhar Gabhála. Part I: the growth of the text', *Ériu*, vol.38 (Dublin: Royal Irish Academy, 1987), pp.82–83.

[91] See for example Séamus Caulfield, 'Celtic problems in the Irish Iron Age', in Donnchadh Ó Corráin (ed.), *Irish Antiquity: essays and studies presented to Professor M.J. O'Kelly* (Cork: Tower Books, 1981), p.4; Peter Harbison, 'Celtic Migrations in Western Europe,' in Antonio Tovar (ed.), *Actas del II*

*Coloquio sobre Lenguas y Culturas Prerromanas de la Peninsula Iberica* (Salamanca: Ediciones Universidad de Salamanca, 1979), p.229.

92 John Waddell, 'The Invasion Hypothesis in Irish Prehistory', *Antiquity*, vol.52 (1978), pp. 121–28.

93 Bhreathnach confirms 'I use Macalister's text, despite its many inaccuracies [it] is the most accessible'. Bhreathnach (1996), p.86, n.4.

94 Newman, p.ix.

95 Herity and Eogan, p.13.

96 R.A.S. Macalister, *Cluain Maccu Nois (Clonmacnois)* (Dublin: Catholic Truth Society of Ireland, 1911); *Newgrange, Co. Meath* (Dublin: Stationery Office, 1929); *Guide to Monasterboice* (Dundalk: Dundalgan Press, 1944).

97 R.A.S. Macalister, *Teamhair: Tara* (Dublin: Stationery Office, 1935). Two guidebooks on Tara have since been published by the Discovery Programme – Edel Bhreathnach and Conor Newman, *Tara* (1995) and Mairéad Carew, *Tara, The Guidebook* (2016).

98 E. Estyn Evans, 'R.A.S. Macalister and the Archaeology of Ireland', *Ulster Journal of Archaeology*, vol.14 (1951), pp.2–6: 5–6.

99 Tubb (2015), p.17; H.G. Leask, 'Robert Alexander Stewart Macalister', *JRSAI*, vol.80, p.270.

100 Corlett (2003).

101 Ibid., p.7.

102 Ibid., pp.13, 16.

103 Ibid., p.18.

104 Ibid., p.19.

105 Glyne Daniel, 'Professor Seán Ó Ríordáin: An Appreciation', *University Review*, vol.2, no.1 (Spring 1960), pp.59–61; Gabriel Cooney, 'The Legacy of Seán P. Ó Ríordáin', *Archaeology Ireland*, vol.11, no.4 (Winter 1997), pp. 30–31.

106 Muiris O'Sullivan, 'Tales from the trenches at Tara', *JRSAI*, vol.140 (2010), pp.15–21; Patrick Wallace, '"These gentlemen" – an old row over who should excavate Tara', in Cooney et al. (eds), pp.549–53.

107 O'Sullivan (2010), p.16.

108 Muiris O'Sullivan, *Duma na nGiall: Tara, the Mound of the Hostages* (Dublin: Wordwell and UCD School of Archaeology, 2005); Eoin Grogan, *The Rath of the Synods, Tara, Co. Meath: excavations by Seán P. Ó Ríordáin* (Dublin: Wordwell, 2008).

109 Muiris O'Sullivan, Chris Scarre and Maureen Doyle (eds), *Tara, From the Past to the Future: towards a new research agenda* (Dublin: Wordwell, 2013).

110 *The Discovery Programme: strategies and questions* (Dublin: Discovery Programme, 1992), p.5.

111 Newman; Bhreathnach (1995); Carew (2003).

112 Newman, p.ix.

113 Ibid., p.237.

114 Ibid., p.6.

115 Ibid., p.xiii.

116 Ibid., p.3.

117 Ibid., pp.242, 237.

118 Roseanne Schot et al., 'A Renewed Programme of Discovery at Tara,' *Archaeology Ireland*, vol.30, no.1 (Spring 2016), pp.18–21.

119 George Eogan, *The Discovery Programme: initiation, consolidation and development* (Amsterdam: Nederlands Museum voor Anthropologie en Praehistorie, 1997).

120 Helen Roche, 'Excavations at Ráith na Ríg, Tara, Co. Meath, 1997', *Discovery Programme Reports No. 6: project results* (Dublin: RIA / Discovery Programme, 2002), pp.19–127. The purpose of the excavation was to re-open and expand two cuttings originally excavated by Seán P. Ó Ríordáin, and to record and sample the stratigraphy in an effort to extract evidence for dating purposes. It is not possible to date monuments and features on the basis of geophysical survey.

121 Barry Cunliffe, 'Postscript: A review of the Tara Symposium 2009', in O'Sullivan et al. (eds) pp.578–79.

122 Evans, p.6.

123 Hugh O'Neill Hencken wrote that 'his British origin and lack of ability combined with his small stature and strict Methodism' had put Macalister at a 'grave disadvantage in Dublin'; Carew (2018), pp.34–35. Macalister was, in fact, born in Dublin. William G. Dever, director of the Harvard Semitic Museum–Hebrew Union College excavations at Gezer in 1966–71, 1984 and 1990, described Macalister as an 'incompetent buffoon'; see Wolff (2015), p.20. Dever wrote that George Eogan, Professor of Celtic Archaeology at UCD, 1979–95, told him that 'Macalister was widely regarded in Ireland as an egotistical buffoon.' Dever also condemned Macalister for having 'a Napoleonic complex'; see Wolff (2015), p.20.

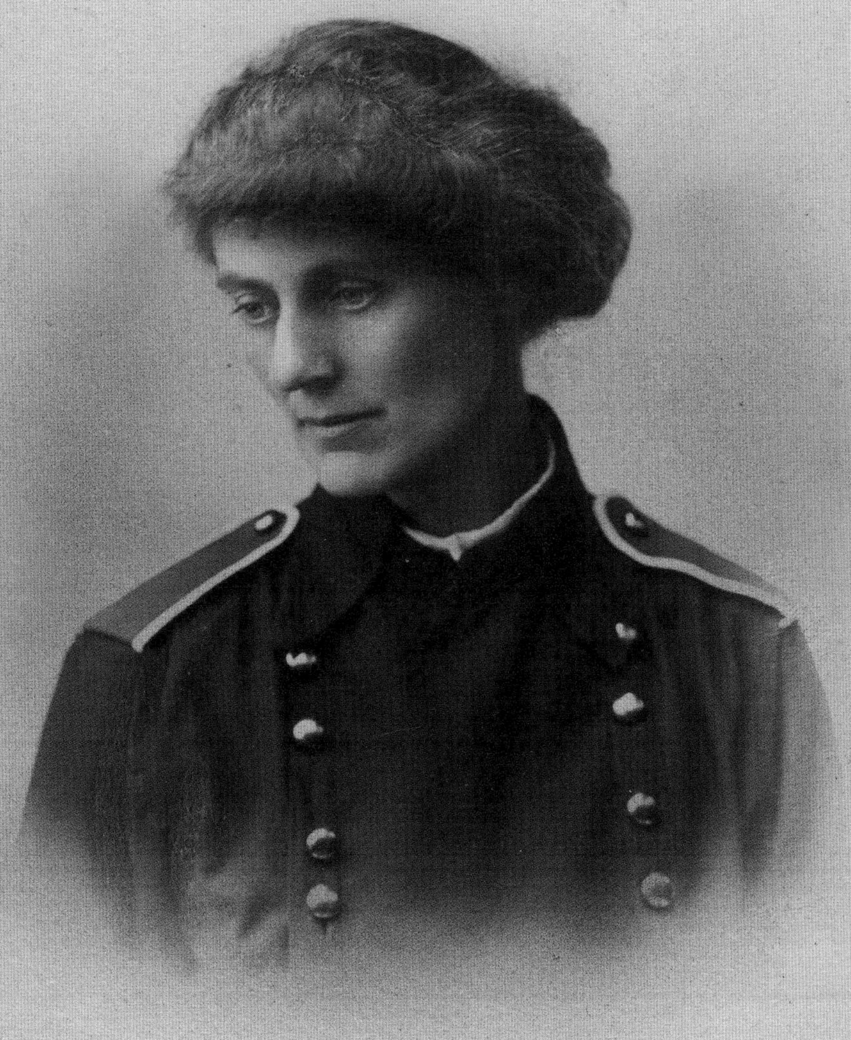

# 'I find it hard to believe that Madame would glue newspaper cuttings to her prayer-book': Constance Markievicz's creation of a War of Independence memorial in the pages of her prison prayer book

BRIAN CROWLEY

COUNTESS CONSTANCE MARKIEVICZ WAS A PRISONER FOR MORE THAN HALF THE DURATION of the Irish War of Independence [fig. 1]. From June to October 1919, she was held in Cork Gaol, and from September 1920 to July 1921 she was held in Mountjoy Prison in Dublin. While a prisoner in Cork, she was presented with a Catholic prayer book, *The Augustinian Manual* by the Rev. Richard A. O'Gorman, which now forms part of the collection of Kilmainham Gaol Museum [fig. 2].[1] Over the course of her incarceration, Markievicz used the prayer book to record the deaths of friends and comrades killed in the struggle for Irish independence. She carefully cut images, articles and poems from contemporary newspapers and pasted them onto the pages of this prayer book to create a unique and deeply personal memorial to the dead. This private act of remembrance also offers an insight into Markievicz's spiritual life and her very personal brand of Catholicism, in which her religious faith was inseparable from her political beliefs. This aspect of the prayer book has been largely unknown, as few who have viewed it on exhibition in Kilmainham Gaol since its donation in 1963 have been aware of this aspect of its history. For much of this time, it has been presented closed alongside two notes it contained written to Markievicz by Patrick Moran and Thomas Whelan in Mountjoy Prison the night before their executions on 14 March 1921. This paper seeks to open up this prayer book and examine the ways it can enhance our understanding of how Markievicz coped with her imprisonment, and the ways in which her political and spiritual beliefs became inextricably enmeshed in the wake of her conversion to Catholicism following the 1916 Rising. With the exception of Sari Oikarinen's

fig. 1 | Countess Constance Markievicz in her Irish Citizen Army uniform, *c.*1917, photograph, Kilmainham Gaol Museum, KMGLM.18PO-1B14-28
(all images OPW / Kilmainham Gaol Museum unless otherwise stated)

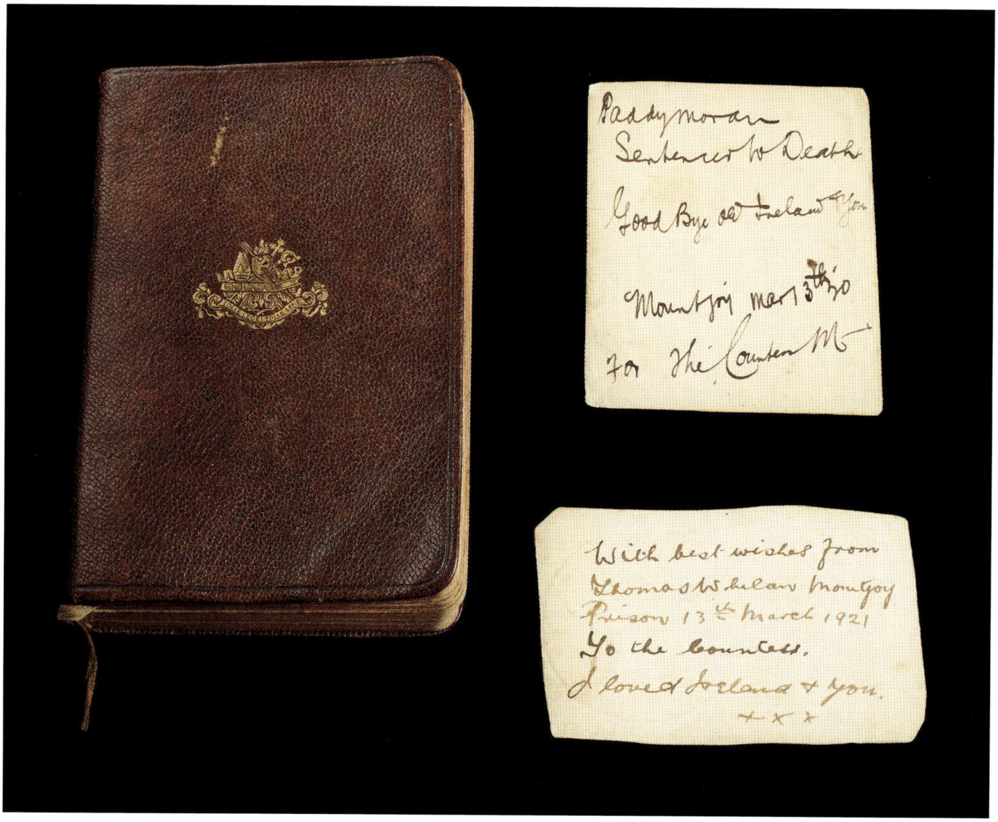


1998 monograph on Markievicz's political career, and Lauren Arrington's 2015 study of Markievicz and her husband Casimir,[2] Markievicz's biographers have not explored her conversion in any great depth, presenting it primarily as a political act of solidarity with her comrades. Little consideration has been given to its longer-term impact on Markievicz and her subsequent revolutionary career. However, within the pages of the prayer book is evidence of the ways in which Markievicz's distinctive Catholicism sustained her during one of the most challenging periods of her remarkable life.

## Incarceration

Markievicz came to national and international prominence as a result of the 1916 Rising. Although she was born into the wealthy Anglo-Irish land-owning Gore-Booth family of Sligo, she ultimately rejected her privileged upbringing and embraced radical socialism and Irish separatism. She became a senior member of the Irish Citizen Army (ICA), a paramilitary organisation formed by Irish trade unionists.

fig. 2 | Prayer book given to Countess Constance Markievicz in Cork Gaol in 1919 accompanied by two notes sent to her from Patrick Moran and Thomas Whelan before their execution in Mountjoy Prison on 14 March 1921. Kilmainham Gaol Museum, KMGLM.2021.0003.01–20

It was her membership of the ICA which ultimately led to her playing a leading role in the 1916 Rising, during which she was second-in-command at the rebel outpost in St Stephen's Green. Following the defeat of the rebels, Markievicz was arrested and spent a brief period in Kilmainham Gaol and Mountjoy Prison before being transferred to Aylesbury Gaol, a women's prison in Buckinghamshire. It was in Kilmainham Gaol that she announced her intention to convert to Catholicism, but she was only formally received into the church following her release from Aylesbury in June 1917. She was arrested again in May 1918, and this time was sent to Holloway Prison in London. While still a prisoner in December 1918, she stood in the general election as a Sinn Féin candidate for St Patrick's Ward in Dublin and became the first woman ever elected to a British parliament. However, following her release in March 1919 she did not take up her seat in Westminster. Instead, she joined her fellow Sinn Féin MPs (who had adopted the Irish title of Teachta Dála or TD) in the Irish Dáil, which had met for the first time in the Mansion House in Dublin on 21 January. She was appointed Minister for Labour, reflecting her long commitment to workers' rights and the trade union movement.

On the same day as the inaugural Dáil meeting, the first military engagement of the Irish War of Independence took place. Members of the Irish Volunteers (henceforth known as the Irish Republican Army, or IRA) led an attack on a group of Royal Irish Constabulary (RIC) policemen who were escorting a delivery of gelignite to a quarry north-west of Tipperary town. The increasingly unsettled state of the country led the British administration to introduce a series of repressive measures and the frequent banning of public meetings. On 17 May 1919, Markievicz spoke at a public meeting in Newmarket in co. Cork, despite the fact that it had been prohibited by the authorities. A month later she was arrested in Dublin on a charge of participating in an unlawful assembly.[3] Accompanied by a police and military guard, she was transported by train to Mallow in co. Cork, where she was sentenced to four months without hard labour in what was then Cork's women's prison.

Built in the 1820s, Cork's female gaol was located in the Sunday's Well area of the city.[4] Markievicz was given special privileges as a political prisoner and was very positive about the prison and its elevated south-facing location.[5] She wrote to her sister Eva Gore-Booth on 14 June that 'This is the most comfortable jail I have been in yet. There's a nice garden, full of pinks, and you can hear the birds sing. I have heaps of friends here, who send me lots of very good food – in fact, all my meals' [fig. 3].[6] In a letter to Kathleen Clarke written on 15 June 1919, Markievicz mentioned a visit she received the previous Saturday from Mrs Mina O'Hegarty, wife of the Cork-born Irish republican P.S. O'Hegarty, and Nora Wallace, who brought her 'strawberries and other nice things'.[7] Nora Wallace (1893–1970) and her sister Sheila (1887–1944) ran a newsagents at 13 Brunswick (now St Augustine) Street in Cork, which was used as a secret headquarters by the Cork No.1 Brigade of the IRA during the War of Independence; during this time both women acted as intelligence officers [fig. 4]. In a letter to Nora Connolly O'Brien on 26 June, Markievicz asked that if anyone was planning to visit her they should contact Nora Wallace or Mary MacSwiney[8] in advance as she was only allowed a set number of visits.[9] Based on her surviving letters, Markievicz always seems to have adapted well to prison life. She kept herself remarkably busy, and

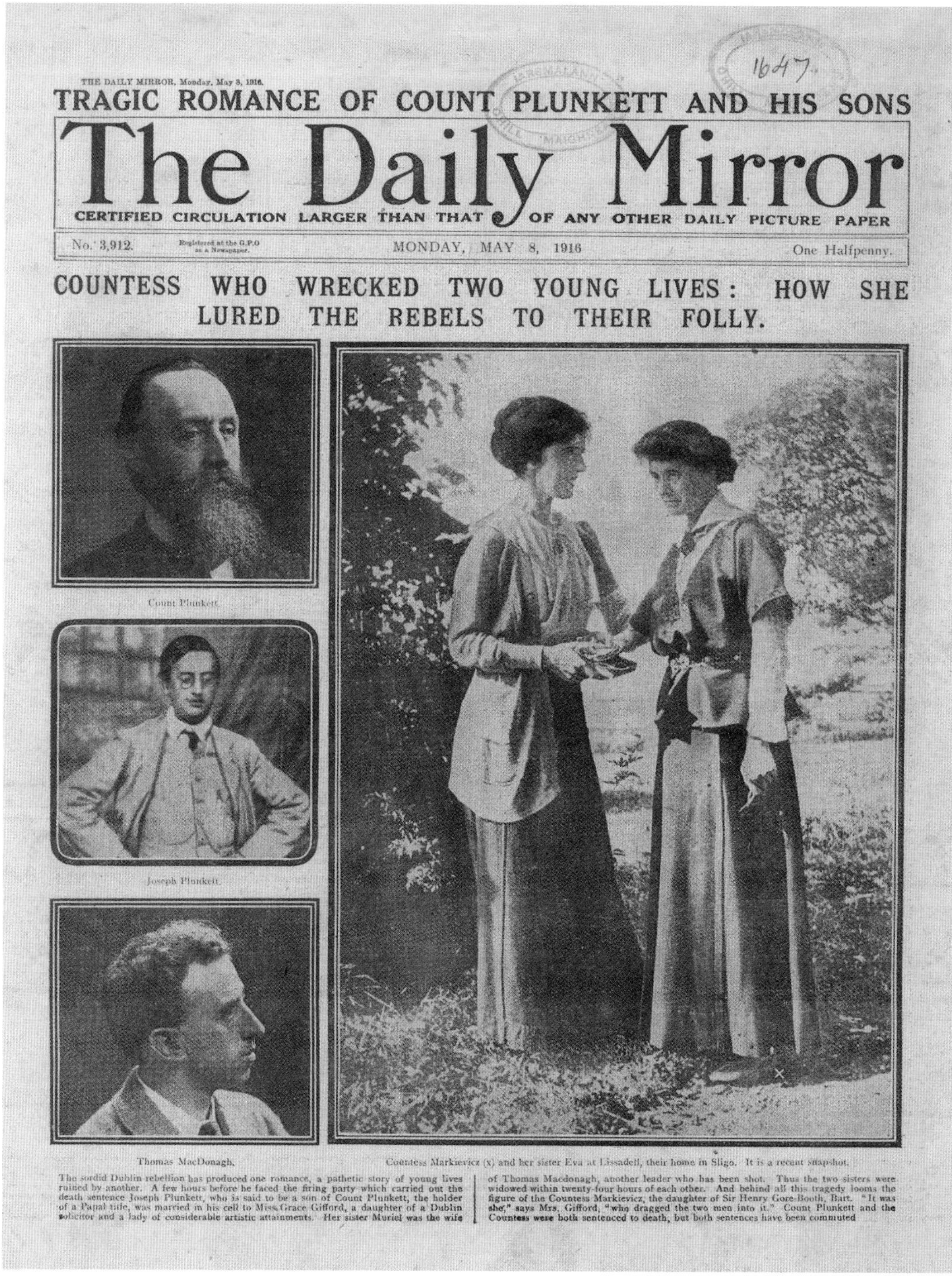

THE DAILY MIRROR, Monday, May 8, 1916.

TRAGIC ROMANCE OF COUNT PLUNKETT AND HIS SONS

The Daily Mirror

CERTIFIED CIRCULATION LARGER THAN THAT OF ANY OTHER DAILY PICTURE PAPER

No. 3,912. Registered at the G.P.O as a Newspaper. MONDAY, MAY 8, 1916 One Halfpenny.

COUNTESS WHO WRECKED TWO YOUNG LIVES: HOW SHE LURED THE REBELS TO THEIR FOLLY.

Count Plunkett

Joseph Plunkett.

Thomas MacDonagh.

Countess Markievicz (x) and her sister Eva at Lissadell, their home in Sligo. It is a recent snapshot.

The sordid Dublin rebellion has produced one romance, a pathetic story of young lives ruined by another. A few hours before he faced the firing party which carried out the death sentence Joseph Plunkett, who is said to be a son of Count Plunkett, the holder of a Papal title, was married in his cell to Miss Grace Gifford, a daughter of a Dublin solicitor and a lady of considerable artistic attainments. Her sister Muriel was the wife of Thomas Macdonagh, another leader who has been shot. Thus the two sisters were widowed within twenty-four hours of each other. And behind all this tragedy looms the figure of the Countess Markievicz, the daughter of Sir Henry Gore-Booth, Bart. "It was she," says Mrs. Gifford, "who dragged the two men into it." Count Plunkett and the Countess were both sentenced to death, but both sentences have been commuted

fig. 3 | Markievicz (right) and her sister Eva Gore-Booth on the cover of *The Daily Mirror* on 8 May 1916 in the wake of the Easter Rising. Eva was Markievicz's main correspondent during her many periods of imprisonment. Kilmainham Gaol Museum, KMGLM.2015.0144.

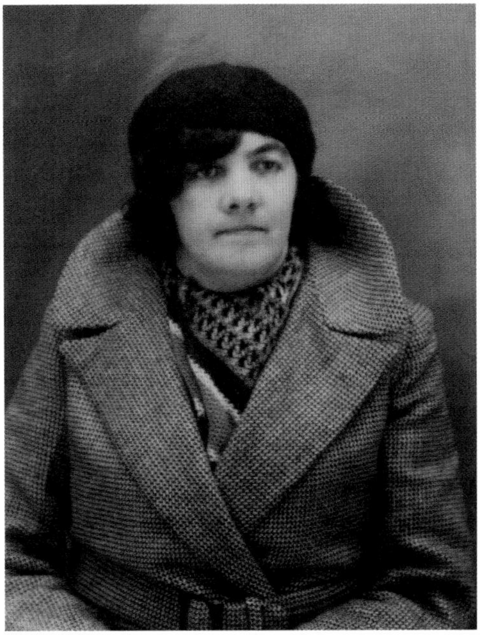

her prison letters were filled with references to books and newspaper stories she was reading as well as art and craft projects she was working on. As a young woman she had trained as an artist in the Slade School in London before going on to the Académie Julian in Paris. While in Holloway Prison in 1918 she asked Eva to send her watercolours and other art supplies,[10] and her fellow-prisoner Kathleen Clarke later recalled that she devoted much of her time to painting.[11] Clarke was the widow of the 1916 leader, Thomas J. Clarke, and despite a sometimes fractious relationship when they were prisoners together, Clarke invited Markievicz to move into her home in Fairview in Dublin and store her possessions there. Markievicz was actually living in the Clarke family home when she was arrested in June 1919. In a letter to Clarke written in Cork Gaol on 2 July 1919, Markievicz mentions that she will write later with a specific list of paints she wants Clarke to send to her. However, she goes on to say that 'at present I'm spending all my energy on studying'.[12] In a later letter written to Clarke on 28 August, she expands on this:

> 'Do you remember suggesting to me in Holloway that I should work out schemes of government? I could never put my mind to it there; but I remembered and started on it directly I got in here. I am absolutely absorbed in it now and have learnt a lot and thought a lot. One is a bit held up by not always being able to get the books one wants, but even so, that throws one back on one's imagination. So here I am from day to day trying to build up an ideal Republic in my mind.'[13]

This project seems to have influenced her choice of reading, which was very much focused on history, politics and economics. She located a copy of Martin Haverty's *History of Ireland* (published 1860) in the prison library,[14] and also referenced books such as George O'Brien's *The Economic History of Ireland in the Eighteenth Century* (1918),[15] *The Skilled Labourer 1760–1832* by J.L. and Barbara Hammond (1919),[16] and *Human Nature in Politics* (1908) by the Fabian and socialist Graham Wallas.[17] She seems to have had good access to newspapers, including left-wing publications like *The Workers' Dreadnought*, the *Daily Herald* and *The Irish Citizen*. She also read for pleasure, particularly poetry, and took a keen interest in her sister Eva's poetry. Markievicz wrote verse herself but was very dismissive of it, describing it as 'doggrel'.[18]

---

fig. 4 | A portrait photograph of Nora Wallace (1893–1970), *c.*1930s
(courtesy of the Wallace family collection)

## *The Augustinian Manual* (1915)

ONE BOOK WHICH DOES NOT GET A MENTION IN MARKIEVICZ'S PRISON CORRESPONDENCE is her copy of *The Augustinian Manual*. The source of the manual, like many other aspects of its history, is something of a mystery. On the front free endpaper is an inscription that reads: 'With kindest wishes to one who has suffered may you always be well & happy from a friend' [fig. 5]. When it was donated to Kilmainham Gaol in 1963, Nora Wallace recalled that in Cork the book could only be obtained from the Augustinian Priory.[19] Located on Washington Street, the priory backed onto Brunswick (now St Augustine) Street where the Wallace sisters ran their shop. Wallace said she remembered being given a copy of the manual herself and that, as far as she recalled, hers had a dedication written in the same handwriting as Markievicz's. While she believed it was possible she had been given a copy to give to Markievicz as well, she had no memory of this.[20]

The manual was published by R. & T. Washbourne Ltd, a well-known London-based publisher that specialised in Catholic publications. The author was the New Ross-born Rev. Richard A. O'Gorman who is described as the prior of Hythe in Kent on the title page [fig. 6]. In the same year as the book's publication, O'Gorman was appointed as prior of the Augustinian Order in Cork.[21] The sacred nature of the book is reflected in the high-quality materials used in its production. Bound in brown leather with limp covers, the pages are gilt-edged with a silk ribbon bookmark. It features a number of illustrations of religious subjects, and the emblem of the Augustinian order is embossed in gold on the front cover. Based on an advertisement taken out by R. & T. Washbourne in *The Tablet* on 3 March 1917, it seems the manual was available in a number of different bindings, which commanded different prices from 2*s*. 6*d*. for the cloth-bound version up to 6*s*. for finest morocco leather.[22] Despite being pocket-sized and easily portable – it measures just 9 by 13.3 cm – the book contains approximately 800 tissue-thin pages.

The prayer book's full title was *The Augustinian Manual, comprising a prayer book for the use of the faithful in general with special instructions and devotions for such as worship in churches of the Order of St. Augustine, or who belong to any confraternity or sodality established in these churches*. Its purpose was to direct and guide every aspect of a Catholic's devotional life. Among its contents were the orders of service for high and low Masses, as well as special feast days such as Good Friday and Palm Sunday. The Mass liturgy is given in parallel Latin and English, allowing the congregant to follow the ceremony. It includes the text of prayers to be recited every day, including morning and evening prayers, the Angelus, and grace before and after meals, as well as the Litany of the Dead, prayers for the sick and the dying, and a whole section devoted to the Rosary. An introductory section on 'Christian Faith and Practice' outlines the key tenets a Catholic must believe in, as well as the actions they should take and the rules

---

fig. 5 | Inscription on the front free endpaper written by an unidentified friend. The page opposite features a newspaper image of Terence MacSwiney and the date of his death, 25 October 1920.

fig. 6 | Title page of *The Augustinian Manual* by the Very Rev. Richard A. O'Gorman, which was published by R. & T. Washbourne Ltd, London, in 1915

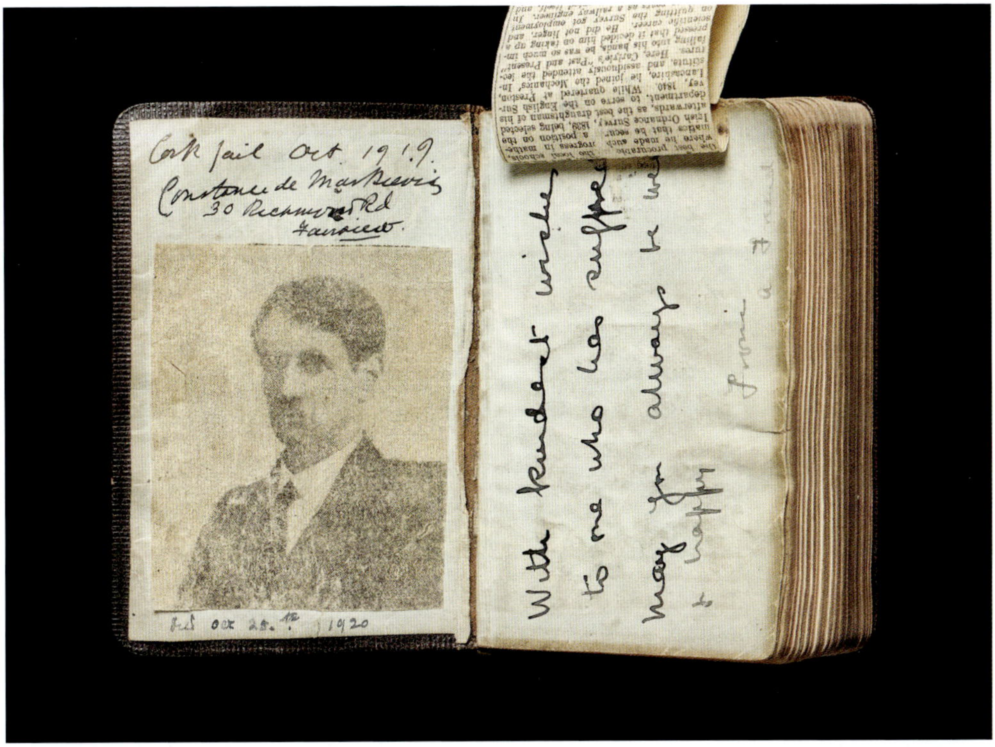
Cork Jail Oct. 1919.
Constance de Markievicz
30 Richmond Rd
Fairview.
With kindest wishes

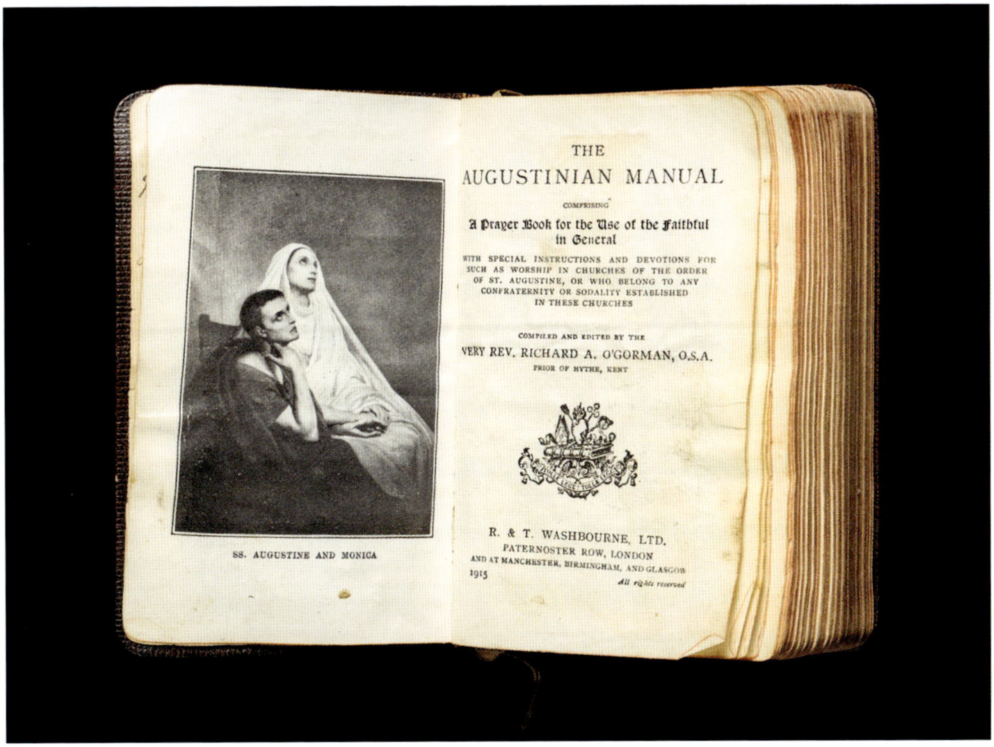
SS. AUGUSTINE AND MONICA
THE
AUGUSTINIAN MANUAL
COMPRISING
A Prayer Book for the Use of the Faithful in General
WITH SPECIAL INSTRUCTIONS AND DEVOTIONS FOR SUCH AS WORSHIP IN CHURCHES OF THE ORDER OF ST. AUGUSTINE, OR WHO BELONG TO ANY CONFRATERNITY OR SODALITY ESTABLISHED IN THESE CHURCHES
COMPILED AND EDITED BY THE
VERY REV. RICHARD A. O'GORMAN, O.S.A.
PRIOR OF HYTHE, KENT
R. & T. WASHBOURNE, LTD.
PATERNOSTER ROW, LONDON
AND AT MANCHESTER, BIRMINGHAM, AND GLASGOW
1915
All rights reserved

they should follow in daily life. A Calendar of the Saints lists the saint to whom each day of the year is dedicated, while a separate part gives details of special days of obligation on which Catholics were obliged to attend Mass and abstain from servile work. Details are also provided about what fast days are to be observed and what kinds of food may not be consumed. As alluded to in the title, there are also sections of the book devoted to practices and devotions particularly associated with the Augustinian Order, such as the rites of the Archconfraternity of the Cincture and the Pious Union of Genazzano, as well as the indulgences available to those who wore the Augustinian White Scapular.

The emergence of items like this manual must be seen in the context of what Emmet Larkin described as the 'devotional revolution' that swept through Irish Catholicism in the years after the Famine. This movement introduced new devotional practices into the Irish Church, mainly of Roman origin, which were

> 'organized in order to communalize and regularize practice under a spiritual director and included sodalities, confraternities such as the various purgatorian societies, the Society of St. Vincent de Paul, and Peter's Pence as well as temperance and altar societies. These public exercises were also reinforced by the use of devotional tools and aids: beads, scapulars, medals, missals, prayer books, catechisms, holy pictures, and Agnus Dei, all blessed by priests who had recently acquired that privilege from Rome through the intercession of their bishops.'[23]

In her essay on the material culture of the devotional revolution in Ireland, Lisa Godson states:

> 'Irish Catholics were not unique in adopting new forms of material piety in the nineteenth century. A tide of ultramontanism altered the political and authority structures of the Church worldwide and, as it did so, it both encouraged the building of new institutions and transformed popular devotional practice. However, it is contended that the pace and durability of change in Ireland was particularly notable.'[24]

By the time of Markievicz's conversion in the early twentieth century, Irish Catholicism was often characterised by a rigid formality, an emphasis on devotional orthodoxy, and a highly regulatory approach when it came to ensuring that members met their religious obligations in the manner prescribed by the Church authorities.

## Family and faith

PROTESTANTISM WAS CENTRAL TO THE PRIVILEGE INTO WHICH MARKIEVICZ WAS BORN, AS ONE of the Gore-Booths of Lissadell. The family estate, largely located in co. Sligo, consisted of 32,000 acres centred on Lissadell House, a Greek-revival mansion built in the early 1830s. The founder of the family's fortune was Paul Gore, an Elizabethan soldier and adventurer who came to Ireland in 1599. He was one of the beneficiaries of the Crown's appropriation of lands previously held by the native Gaelic Catholic ruling families, and was created a baronet in 1622 in recognition of his loyal service to James I.[25] The Gore (later Gore-Booth) family's further rise in the centuries which followed was inextricably linked with the legal, political and economic advantages brought by their Protestant faith. Although it was disestablished in 1869, the Anglican Church of Ireland was still the official state church in Ireland at the time of Markievicz's birth, despite the fact that it represented just one-eighth of the population.[26] Markievicz appears to have had a relatively traditional religious upbringing, though her grandfather and parents had an interest in Spiritualism and arranged a number of séances in both Lissadell and their London home.[27] At the time of her marriage to the Polish-Catholic Count Casimir Markievicz in 1900, Lauren Arrington describes her as 'a Protestant by birth and an atheist by disposition'. She resisted the pressure from both the Russian authorities and Casimir's family to marry in a Catholic church as she felt this would require a commitment to bring up her children as Catholics and she was hostile to the notion of a marriage 'recognized by Rome with PAPISH babies'.[28]

Despite her earlier suspicions of Catholicism, in 1916, while a prisoner in Kilmainham Gaol following the Rising, Markievicz expressed a desire to convert to Catholicism.[29] *The Catholic Bulletin* from February 1917 featured an article which quoted extensively from an unnamed priest who said he had the 'privilege of making her acquaintance last May, while she awaited in Kilmainham Prison the result of her court-martial'. When asked by a prison official when she had converted to Catholicism, the priest reported that her reply was 'I became a Catholic at the College of Surgeons'. In a later conversation with the priest, she explained 'it was Michael Mallin and Councillor Partridge made me a Catholic'.[30] Markievicz served under Michael Mallin (1874–1916) at the Irish Citizen Army outpost in St Stephen's Green during the Easter Rising. By the Tuesday of Easter Week, a decision was made to retreat into the College of Surgeons on the west side of the square. The College proved a relatively impregnable location, where Markievicz and her comrades could hole up for the next few days.[31] It was there that the trade-unionist William Partridge (1874–1917) led the garrison each evening in saying the Rosary.[32] Clearly this act of communal prayer and the sense of comradeship it created had a great effect on Markievicz, and may explain why she was attracted to the rosary in particular. When presented with a set of rosary beads in Kilmainham Gaol by her priest friend, he reported that 'she expressed the greatest pleasure', and she explained to him that 'we said the Rosary regularly at the College of Surgeons'. The priest also noted that she wore the beads around her wrist and that the 'consolations of religion' gave her the 'strength and solace' to withstand the unbearable strain of hearing the sound of executions by firing squad of the leaders of the rebellion, Michael Mallin among them.[33] The article also reproduced an extract from a poem she wrote inspired by Partridge's recital of the rosary:

> One hope, one prayer,
> Filled all our hearts, one perfect holy faith
> Lifted our souls. As we knelt humbly there
> Your silvery voice, soft as a dying breath,
> Was answered by a hundred strong and clear,
> Craving a grace from her whom all hold dear:
> 'Mary, be with us at the hour of death.'

While there is no doubting the sincerity of Markievicz's conversion, it is also clear that it had little to do with an interest in Catholic doctrine. It stemmed almost entirely from a sense of solidarity and spiritual connection with her comrades, living and dead. In nearly every way she was set apart from her revolutionary comrades: she was the only woman in a major leadership role, she was a member of the upper class, and she was a Protestant. While many of Ireland's revolutionary leaders, such as Wolfe Tone and Robert Emmet, had been Protestants, and there were many Protestants who fought in the 1916 Rising, it was still a marker of difference with the majority of her fellow rebels. Catholicism and the practices of the devotional revolution had also assumed a central position within the identity of Irish nationalists. To quote Larkin,

> 'The devotional revolution [...] provided the Irish with a substitute symbolic language and offered them a new cultural heritage with which they could identify and be identified and through which they could identify with one another. This is why, for example, Irish and Catholic have become almost interchangeable terms in Ireland, despite the attempts of Nationalists to make Irish rather than Catholic the inclusive term.[34]

As Oikarinen points out, Markievicz's conversion may in part have also developed out of a sense of estrangement from the Protestant ascendency class. Her decision to join the Catholic church was in many ways a final break from the life she was born into and the values of her family back in Lissadell.[35]

While Markievicz was genuine in her conversion, the doctrinal intricacies of Catholicism seem to have been of little interest to her. In her biographical sketch of Markievicz, Esther Roper quotes Hannah Sheehy-Skeffington's views on Markievicz's Catholicism. Sheehy-Skeffington recalled meeting the Rev. Fr McMahon, a chaplain in Mountjoy Prison, in 1916. He had been tasked with preparing Markievicz to enter the church:

> 'He said to me "I can't understand Countess Markievicz at all. She wants to be received into the Church, but she won't attend me when I try to explain Transubstantiation and other doctrines. She just says 'Please don't trouble to explain. I tell you I believe all the Church teaches. Now, Father, please tell me about the boys!'." From another source I heard that she shocked the padre by defending Lucifer as a "good rebel", but that, I think, was part of her habit of leg-pulling of authority."[36]

Sheehy-Skeffington maintained that Markievicz 'belonged to the Church of St. Francis of Assisi, rather than that of St. Paul',[37] and that it was

> 'The ritual and the ceremonies, the music and the beauty of the Catholic Church, its art and cultural background attracted the mystic in her. She defended the socialist Connolly against an attack by a Jesuit, Fr McKenna. She held Socialism to be possible within the Church. Individual clerics she often sharply disagreed with. Over her bed was a picture of Da Vinci's Christ.'[38]

Markievicz seems to have formed a particular bond with Fr Albert Bibby from the Franciscan Capuchin Friary on Church Street in Dublin's north inner city. He and some of his fellow Capuchins ministered to her and the other prisoners held in Kilmainham Gaol following the Rising. They became firm friends, and Fr Albert even agreed to help smuggle out some of Markievicz's prison writings from Kilmainham Gaol.[39] On 30 March 1917 he wrote to Eva Gore-Booth and mentioned that he planned to send a copy of a book entitled *Mysteries of the Mass in Reasoned Prayer* to Markievicz in Aylesbury Prison.[40] While the prayers it contains are written in continuous prose, they were presented like poetry in broken lines in the hope that the reader would pause and contemplate the meaning of the words as they read them.[41] Bibby also wrote to Markievicz about the book on 4 April 1917:

> 'I am sending a little book on the mass to the Deputy Governor for you. I hope you'll get it. When reading it, read it slowly & thoughtfully & prayerfully & if you do you'll like it. It would be grand if you could read it in the chapel. Love of the mass is Irish: only a Catholic devotion but a very Irish one also. Should you want any other books of this kind, or Rosaries, perhaps the Deputy Governor would allow me to send them to you, if so tell Miss Eva as I know you can't write.'[42]

After a year of conversations and correspondence, Fr Albert clearly had quite an insight into Markievicz's character. He knew that *Mysteries of the Mass*'s poetic approach toward prayer would appeal to her literary tastes, but he was also aware that she could be impatient and her enthusiasm often led her to quickly skim over books and potentially miss out on their deeper meanings. This is reflected in his advice that she read the book slowly and contemplatively, preferably in the prison chapel where she could focus without distraction on the meaning of the liturgy. He clearly also had a very good sense of the motivation behind her conversion, and, significantly, makes reference to his belief that there was something particularly Irish about the love the Mass.

## Markievicz's adaptation of her prayer book

THE PRAYERS CONTAINED IN *THE AUGUSTINIAN MANUAL* ARE PRESENTED IN A MUCH MORE conventional way, but it seems likely that Markievicz would have appreciated its handsome appearance and welcomed it as a useful reference work for any questions she had about her relatively new religious affiliation. As she makes no reference to it in her surviving letters, we do not know how Markievicz used the prayer book during her time in Cork Gaol. No doubt she found it helpful if she wished to follow the Latin Mass or if she was called upon to lead a rosary. Beyond the dedication from the unknown person who sent it to her, the only physical interventions that can be dated to that time are her signature on the endpaper which is dated 'Cork Jail Oct.1919'. She also wrote her address at the time, '30 Richmond Rd, Fairview', where she lodged with the Clarke family. The prayer book does contain one other souvenir of her time in Cork Gaol. Placed between its pages was a photograph of Dulcibella Barton (1879–1956) with Markievicz's dog Poppet, which was taken outside Barton's family home, Glendalough House in co. Wicklow [fig. 7]. Nora Wallace remembered being sent the photograph and the pleasure it brought Markievicz when she passed it on to her in Cork Gaol. In her witness statement submitted to the Bureau of Military History in 1954, Barton wrote, 'whenever Con Markievicz went to gaol her dog, a brown spaniel, always came to me'.[43]

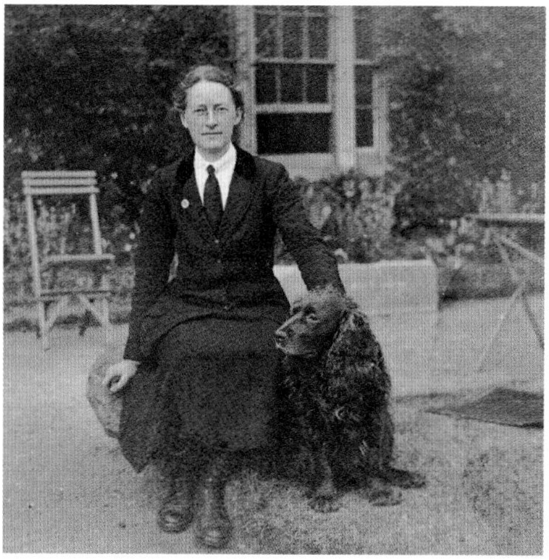

fig. 7 | Nora Wallace remembered passing on this photograph to Markievicz in Cork Gaol in 1919. It shows Markievicz's spaniel Poppet in the care of Dulcibella Barton at Glendalough House in Wicklow.

fig. 8 | Blossom preserved in the pages of Markievicz's prayer book

fig. 9 | Markievicz recorded the date of her imprisonment in Mountjoy Prison on 27 September 1920, followed by the names and death dates of Michael Fitzgerald, Terence MacSwiney, Joe Murphy and Kevin Barry. Among the pasted items are two memorial poems entitled 'For Sean' by Alice Ffrench, and 'Terence MacSwiney' by Katharine Tynan.

Markievicz's use of the prayer book was to change significantly during her next prison sentence. She was arrested in Terenure on 26 September 1920 while travelling with Seán MacBride and a French journalist, Maurice Bourgeois.[44] They were pulled over for a broken tail light, were recognised by the police and were brought to the Bridewell station. Markievicz and MacBride were subsequently transferred to Mountjoy Prison. As usual, Markievicz set about a number of different projects. Her letters to Eva were full of references to her determination to use her time in prison to learn the Irish language. A keen horticulturalist, she also began working in the prison garden, and in a letter written on 8 June 1921 she wrote about the pleasure it gave her to see her peas, pansies and carnations in bloom.[45] Indeed, a dried blossom still preserved between the pages of the prayer book may well be a souvenir of the prison garden in either Cork or Mountjoy [fig. 8]. One of her other projects centred on her prayer book, which presumably had been sent in to her in the prison. Her prison sentence coincided with a significant escalation of violence in the War of Independence, and it was over the course of her time in Mountjoy in 1920–21 that the process of transforming the prayer book into a personal memorial to her fallen comrades took place. On the flyleaf verso she recorded the date of her arrival in Mountjoy, 27 September 1920. Beneath that, she wrote the names of Michael Fitzgerald, Terence MacSwiney, Joe Murphy and Kevin Barry. Michael Fitzgerald died on hunger strike in the male prison in Cork[46] after sixty-seven days on hunger strike on 17 October 1920 [fig. 9]. Joe Murphy died on the same hunger strike after seventy-six days on 25 October.

On the same day, Terence MacSwiney died in Brixton Prison. MacSwiney had joined the hunger strike in Cork Prison but was subsequently transferred to London. One of the most prominent of the interventions Markievicz made to the prayer book was to paste a newspaper photo of Terence MacSwiney inside of the front cover [fig. 5]. His death made international news at the time, in part due to his status as the Lord Mayor of Cork.[47] MacSwiney's compelling political writings were infused with religious symbolism and captured the imagination of the Irish public. This combination of the political and the religious is reflected in a poem dedicated to MacSwiney's memory by

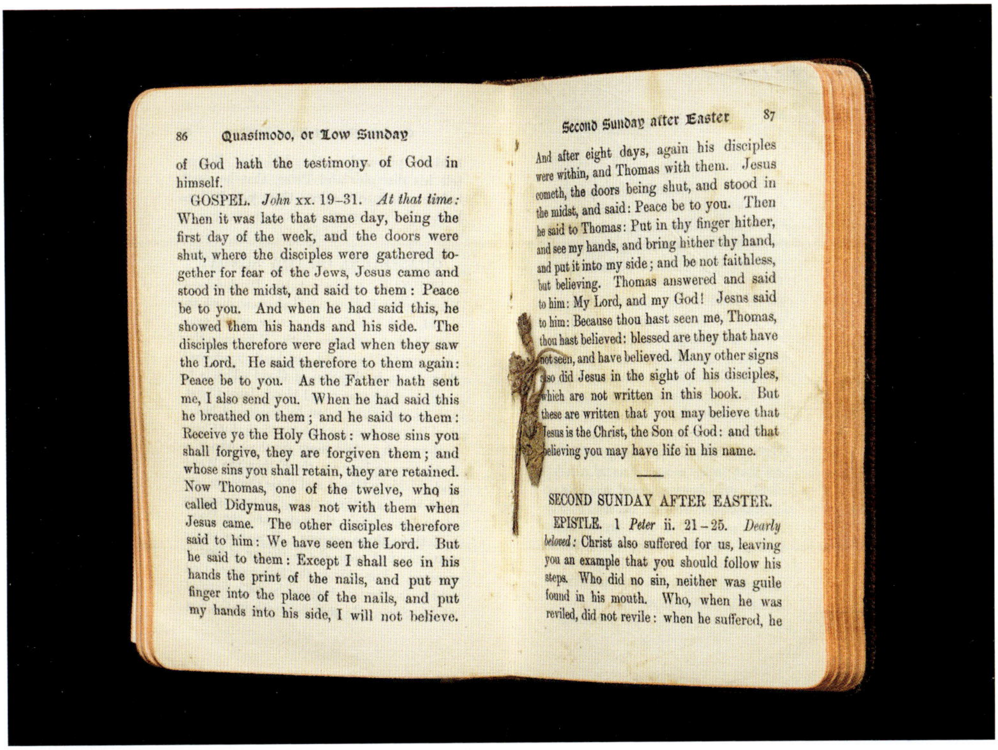
86 Quasimodo, or Low Sunday
of God hath the testimony of God in himself.
GOSPEL. John xx. 19–31. At that time: When it was late that same day, being the first day of the week, and the doors were shut, where the disciples were gathered together for fear of the Jews, Jesus came and stood in the midst, and said to them: Peace be to you. And when he had said this, he showed them his hands and his side. The disciples therefore were glad when they saw the Lord. He said therefore to them again: Peace be to you. As the Father hath sent me, I also send you. When he had said this he breathed on them; and he said to them: Receive ye the Holy Ghost: whose sins you shall forgive, they are forgiven them; and whose sins you shall retain, they are retained. Now Thomas, one of the twelve, who is called Didymus, was not with them when Jesus came. The other disciples therefore said to him: We have seen the Lord. But he said to them: Except I shall see in his hands the print of the nails, and put my finger into the place of the nails, and put my hands into his side, I will not believe.
Second Sunday after Easter 87
And after eight days, again his disciples were within, and Thomas with them. Jesus cometh, the doors being shut, and stood in the midst, and said: Peace be to you. Then he said to Thomas: Put in thy finger hither, and see my hands, and bring hither thy hand, and put it into my side; and be not faithless, but believing. Thomas answered and said to him: My Lord, and my God! Jesus said to him: Because thou hast seen me, Thomas, thou hast believed: blessed are they that have not seen, and have believed. Many other signs also did Jesus in the sight of his disciples, which are not written in this book. But these are written that you may believe that Jesus is the Christ, the Son of God: and that believing you may have life in his name.
SECOND SUNDAY AFTER EASTER.
EPISTLE. 1 Peter ii. 21–25. Dearly beloved: Christ also suffered for us, leaving you an example that you should follow his steps. Who did no sin, neither was guile found in his mouth. Who, when he was reviled, did not revile: when he suffered, he

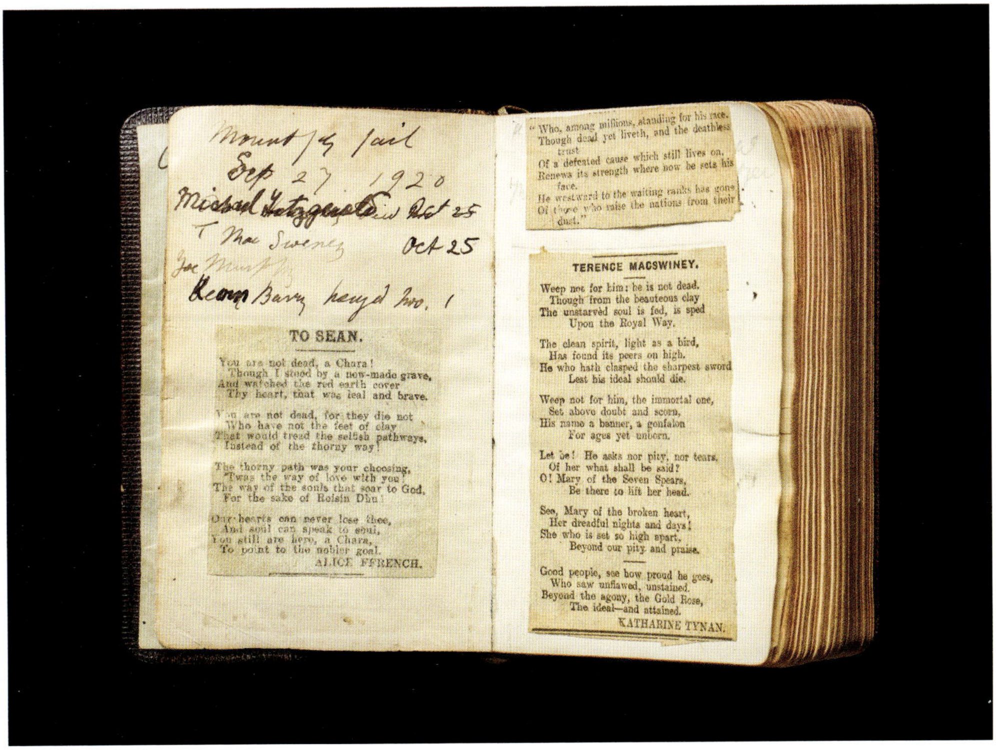
TO SEAN.
You are not dead, a Chara!
Though I stood by a new-made grave,
And watched the red earth cover
Thy heart, that was leal and brave.
The thorny path was your choosing,
For the sake of Roisin Dhu!
ALICE FFRENCH.
"Who, among millions, standing for his race,
Though dead yet liveth, and the deathless trust
Of a defeated cause which still lives on,
Renews its strength where now he sets his face.
He westward to the waiting ranks has gone
Of those who raise the nations from their dust."
TERENCE MACSWINEY.
Weep not for him: he is not dead.
Though from the beauteous clay
The unstarved soul is fed, is sped
Upon the Royal Way.
The clean spirit, light as a bird,
Has found its peers on high.
He who hath clasped the sharpest sword
Lest his ideal should die.
Weep not for him, the immortal one,
Set above doubt and scorn,
His name a banner, a gonfalon
For ages yet unborn.
Let be! He asks nor pity, nor tears,
Of her what shall be said?
O! Mary of the Seven Spears,
Be there to lift her head.
See, Mary of the broken heart,
Her dreadful nights and days!
She who is set so high apart,
Beyond our pity and praise.
Good people, see how proud he goes,
Who saw unflawed, unstained,
Beyond the agony, the Gold Rose,
The ideal—and attained.
KATHARINE TYNAN.

the writer and poet Katharine Tynan which Markievicz pasted onto a page at the front of the prayer book. In Tynan's poem she tells her readers that they need not weep for MacSwiney's 'clean spirit, light as a bird / has found his peers on high'. Tynan references 'Mary of the Seven Spears' and seems to link the sorrows of MacSwiney's sister Mary and those of the Virgin Mary. The prayer book also contains a loose clipping featuring a memorial poem dedicated to MacSwiney entitled 'Mac Suibhne', which is attributed to 'W. Hope'. It too encourages its readers to 'weep no tears' as his 'grave is a pulsing fire / To quicken the seeds grim toilers have sown'. A further pasted news clipping containing a description of some of MacSwiney's last words was attached to the back free endpaper.[48]

In his essay on ephemera and personal responses to the 1916 Rising, Jack Elliot describes the creation of scrapbooks at this time as a way for individuals to shape their own narrative of historical events they were living through.[49] This is undoubtedly true for Markievicz, who appears to have been creating a kind of personal pantheon in which she could honour those who were sacrificing their lives for Irish independence. While her prayer book undoubtedly became a form of scrapbook, its pre-existing status as a prayer book brought with it a powerful aura of sanctity. Pasting these images and memorial poems onto its holy pages becomes an act of beatification, and the sacrifice and death of those she places in it becomes bound up with the sacrifice of Christ. The news clippings, which were previously just pieces of ephemera, were transformed and elevated to the status of devotional objects.

The fourth name on Markievicz's handwritten list was Kevin Barry who was hanged in Mountjoy Prison on 1 November 1920. There was a total of ten hangings of political prisoners during Markievicz's time in Mountjoy, placing her in direct proximity with some of the most notable and tragic events of the War of Independence. Barry was arrested on 20 September following an attack on a detachment of British soldiers on Church Street in central Dublin. Barry's fate caught the public imagination as he was just eighteen years old and was the first person to be tried and executed under the Restoration of Order in Ireland Act, 1920, which had been passed just twelve weeks before. Markievicz pasted an image of Barry in her book which retained its somewhat misleading newspaper headline 'The School-Boy Who Died' (Barry was a medical student in UCD at the time of his arrest). Markievicz displayed the fruits of her Irish language studies by adding the handwritten inscription, *'Do ċum glóire Dé, agus Onóra na h-Éireann'* ('For the glory of God and the Honour of Ireland') along with the date of his execution [fig. 10]. Although Markievicz would have been in an entirely different section of the prison, all of the prisoners in Mountjoy would have been acutely aware of what was happening. Markievicz wrote a poem in memory of Barry, and it seems likely that the first verse was based on her real experiences in Mountjoy:

'We knelt in Mass with sobbing hearts,
Cold, in the dawn of day.
The dawn for us, for him the night
Who was so young and gay.'

The poem also reflects Markievicz's increasing conflation of Catholicism with the national struggle as she concludes the poem by comparing Barry's sacrifice with Christ's:

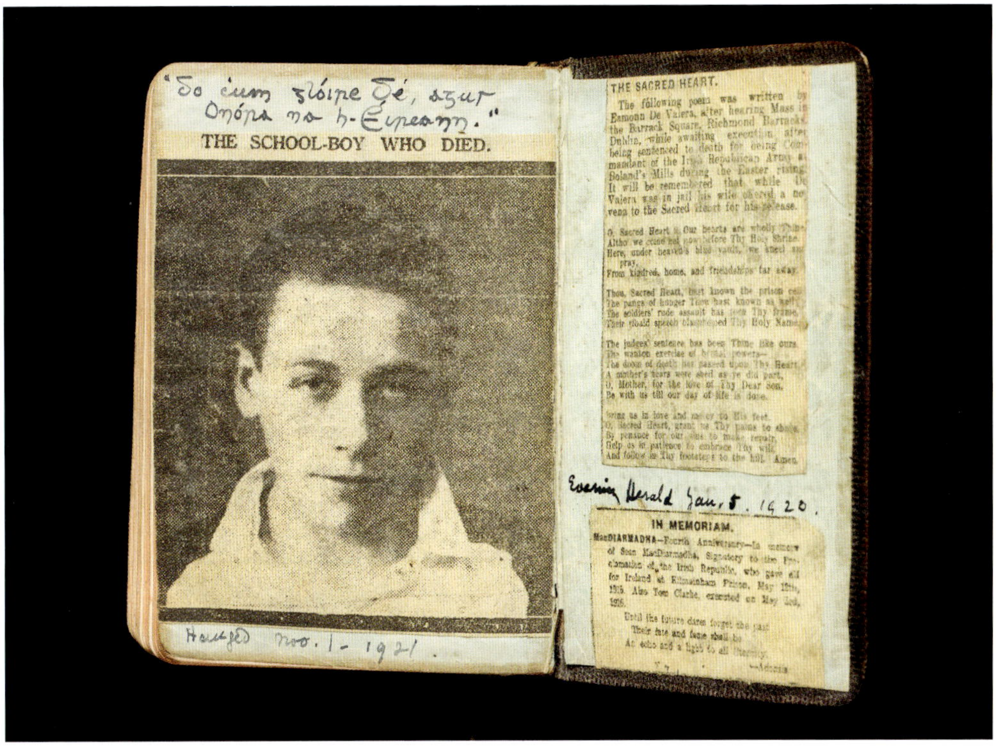


'And Christ who died for love of us,
Tortured and bruised and shamed,
Gives courage to such hero souls,
Unbending and untamed.'[50]

It is not always possible to establish definitively who some of the clippings commemorate. Just beneath the first list of War of Independence casualties, Markievicz pasted a poem by a woman named Alice Ffrench entitled 'To Sean'. It gives little specific information about its subject other than the fact that he gave his life for Ireland. It could possibly be Seán Treacy, who was killed in a shootout with British forces on Talbot Street in Dublin on 14 October 1920. He was one of the key figures behind the Soloheadbeg Ambush in 1919 and became one of the main leaders of the Third Tipperary Brigade of the IRA. However, the poem may commemorate another Seán. Seán Doyle was a member of the 4th Batt. Dublin Brigade of the Irish Volunteers who was shot in the Dublin Mountains on 19 September 1920. It is possible that Markievicz had a personal connection with Seán Doyle as he had been a former member of the Inchicore branch of Na Fianna Éireann. Markievicz co-founded Fianna Éireann in 1909 as a nationalist organisation for boys, and remained very close to many of its members. Both Seán Treacy and Seán Doyle are mentioned in a separate clipping pasted elsewhere in the book. It was a public notice about a Mass which was to be said by the Rev. W. Landers

fig. 10 | Pasted image of Kevin Barry inscribed by Markievicz with the words, *'Do ċum glóire Dé, agus Onóra na h-Éireann'* ('For the glory of God and the Honour of Ireland') in St Andrew's Church on Westland Row in memory of 'Kevin Barry, Terence MacSwiney, Michael Fitzgerald, Joseph Murphy, Sean Treacy, William O'Connell, Sean Doyle and all those who have recently died in the fight for Ireland'.

While it would seem that the majority of the items pasted in the prayer book date from Markievicz's time in Mountjoy, there are items which may predate the start of her sentence in September 1920. On the inside of the back endpaper she pasted a copy of 'The Sacred Heart', a devotional poem written by Éamon de Valera in Richmond Barracks when he was under sentence of death following the 1916 Rising. Underneath it she wrote 'Evening Herald, Jan. 5, 1920'. Attached to the same page is an 'In Memoriam' notice to mark the fourth anniversary of the execution of the 1916 leader Seán Mac Diarmada, which occurred on 12 May 1920. She may have pasted them in before her arrest, or possibly she had cut these items from a newspaper and kept them in the prayer book for safekeeping before deciding to paste them in while in prison.

Mountjoy Prison's location on the bank of the Royal Canal in Dublin's north inner city meant that Markievicz could hear some of the violent events of the War of Independence happening outside its walls. In a letter to Eva written on 6 December 1920 she mentioned hearing the shooting in nearby Croke Park sports ground on Bloody Sunday, 21 November 1920.[51] That morning, IRA members killed fifteen men as part of a co-ordinated series of attacks on suspected British Army intelligence officers around Dublin. British forces retaliated later that day by firing into a crowd attending a Gaelic football match in Croke Park, killing fourteen people. In a further act of retribution two senior members of the IRA who had been arrested the previous evening, Dick McKee and Peadar Clancy, were shot in Dublin Castle along with Conor Clune, a young man from Clare, who was arrested with them in the mistaken belief he was also a senior member of the IRA. Markievicz managed to secure images from a newspaper of McKee and Clancy which she pasted together on the same page.[52]

A number of arrests were made in connection with the killing of the British agents on the morning of Bloody Sunday. Among them were Patrick Moran and Thomas Whelan, who were both subsequently sentenced to death by a British military court and were sent to Mountjoy to await their execution. They were hanged on 14 March 1921 along with four other men – Frank Flood, Thomas Bryan, Patrick Doyle[53] and Bernard Ryan. These four men were captured following a failed ambush in Drumcondra in Dublin on 21 January 1921. Eithne Coyle, one of the women imprisoned with Markievicz in Mountjoy, recalled the devastating effect the executions had on her and the other prisoners in her Bureau of Military History witness statement in 1952. She also remembered running away from the wardress one day during exercise so she could wave over at the condemned men in their enclosure.[54] Markievicz dedicated a page of her prayer book to the six men. It featured images of Flood and Bryan and a poem

---

fig. 11 | Leo Fitzgerald was killed in a British Army raid on Great Brunswick Street on 14 March 1921. Markievicz was very close to him and his family, and had known him since he joined Fianna Éireann as a boy.

fig. 12 | List of the nine men hanged in Mountjoy Prison in 1921. Markievicz was a prisoner in Mountjoy at the time for all these hangings.

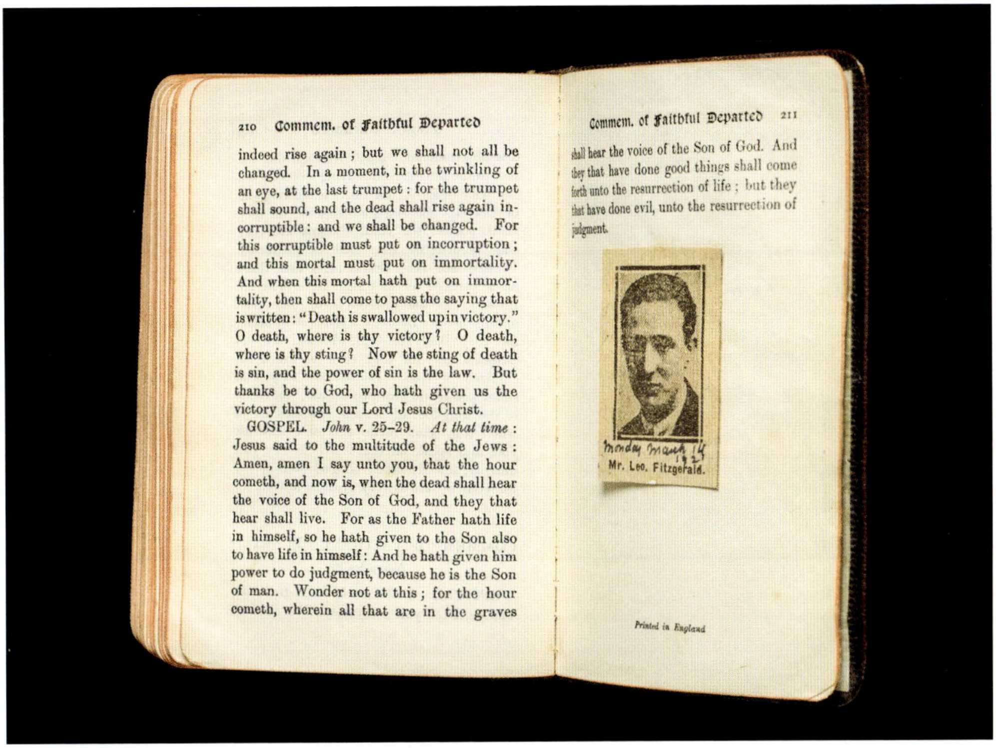

210 Commem. of Faithful Departed

indeed rise again; but we shall not all be changed. In a moment, in the twinkling of an eye, at the last trumpet: for the trumpet shall sound, and the dead shall rise again incorruptible: and we shall be changed. For this corruptible must put on incorruption; and this mortal must put on immortality. And when this mortal hath put on immortality, then shall come to pass the saying that is written: "Death is swallowed up in victory." O death, where is thy victory? O death, where is thy sting? Now the sting of death is sin, and the power of sin is the law. But thanks be to God, who hath given us the victory through our Lord Jesus Christ.

GOSPEL. *John* v. 25–29. *At that time*: Jesus said to the multitude of the Jews: Amen, amen I say unto you, that the hour cometh, and now is, when the dead shall hear the voice of the Son of God, and they that hear shall live. For as the Father hath life in himself, so he hath given to the Son also to have life in himself: And he hath given him power to do judgment, because he is the Son of man. Wonder not at this; for the hour cometh, wherein all that are in the graves

Commem. of Faithful Departed 211

shall hear the voice of the Son of God. And they that have done good things shall come forth unto the resurrection of life; but they that have done evil, unto the resurrection of judgment.

Monday March 14 1921

Mr. Leo. Fitzgerald.

Printed in England

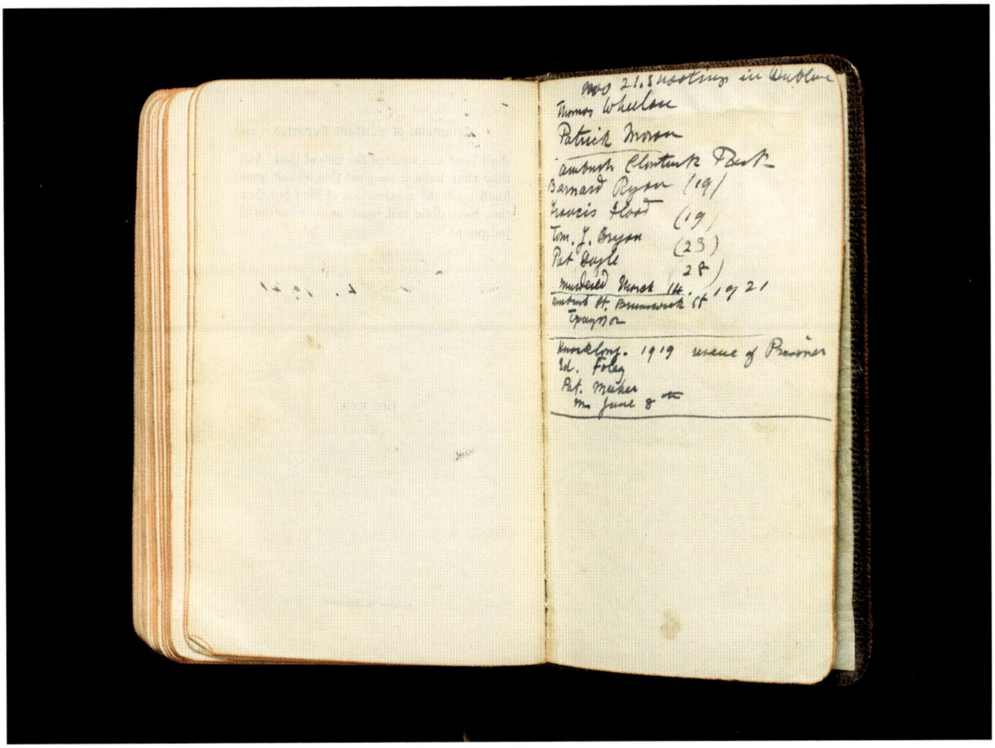

21 Shooting in Dublin
Thomas Whelan
Patrick Moran
ambush Clontarf Park
Bernard Ryan (19)
Francis Flood (19)
Tom. J. Bryan (23)
Pat Doyle (28)
murdered March 14. 1921
ambush at Brunswick St
Traynor
Knocklong. 1919 rescue of Prisoner
Ed. Foley
Pat. Maher
June 8th

entitled 'Calvary', which had the subtitle 'To the Six Martyrs, Hanged in Mountjoy'. Written by a nineteen-year-old woman named Eibhlín de Paor, from Chorley in Lancashire, like many of the poems Markievicz pasted in the book it invoked Catholic religious imagery in describing their sacrifice for the national cause. Markievicz pasted a second poem dedicated to the men executed on 14 March at the front of the book. 'The Gallows Tree' by the poet and nationalist Alice Furlong appeared in *The Sunday Independent* on 20 March 1921. In her poem, Furlong describes how 'Death was hovering like a hawk, / O'er Dublin town forlorn' when the Virgin Mary, dressed all in white, descended on the city and made her way to the 'gallows tree'. Referencing the six men who were hanged, Furlong described how the Virgin plucked 'Blossoms, three and three' and carried them with her into the clouds.[55]

While Markievicz did not secure images of Whelan and Moran, the prayer book contained two remarkable mementoes of them both. The night before their executions they each sent Markievicz short farewell notes written on the back of prayer cards. These messages indicate a significant personal connection between Markievicz and the two men, and the existence of channels of communication between them and Markievicz while they were in Mountjoy. In his note to Markievicz, Thomas Whelan wrote, 'With best wishes from Thomas Whelan Mountjoy Prison 13th March 1921. To the Countess. I loved Ireland & you. XXX', while Moran's note read: 'Paddy Moran Sentenced to Death. Good Bye old Ireland & you. Mountjoy, Mar 13th 20 [*sic*]. For the Countess M.' It is significant that Markievicz chose not to paste these notes into the prayer book. While the news clippings were only made sacred by attaching them to the pages of the prayer book, these notes were themselves a form of holy relic and far too precious to be interfered with in any way.

Seventeen-year-old Dermot O'Sullivan was arrested with the other men involved in the Drumcondra Ambush and sentenced to death, but this was commuted due to his age. He was the only living person whose image was pasted into the book. He knew Markievicz personally as he had joined the Fianna when she was co-leader along with the executed 1916 leader Seán Heuston in 1913.[56] While the survival of O'Sullivan may have been of some comfort to Markievicz, her losses on 14 March 1921 were further compounded by events outside the prison that evening. British forces led a raid on a building being used by the IRA on Great Brunswick (now Pearse) Street. Among the casualties was a twenty-eight-year-old house painter named Leo Fitzgerald. Like O'Sullivan, he and his brother Theo had been members of Fianna Éireann as young boys, and Markievicz was very close to both of them. She made a number of references to members of the Fitzgerald family in her prison letters.[57] In 1963 Nora Wallace described him as a personal friend of Markievicz and remembered being in his family home with her.[58] Markievicz obtained a small, black-bordered image of him which she pasted on a blank space on the last page of the prayer book and inscribed the date of his death beneath his name [fig. 11].[59]

There were three more executions while Markievicz was in Mountjoy. Thomas Traynor was arrested during the Great Brunswick Street ambush on 14 March and was hanged on 25 April. Edmond Foley and Patrick Maher were arrested in September 1919 on suspicion of helping in the rescue of an IRA prisoner at Knocklong train station in

Limerick which resulted in the deaths of two policemen. Markievicz did not obtain images of those men, but on one of the back pages she wrote a list of the nine men hanged in 1921 [fig. 12]. She also included the date of their executions and the event which had led to their arrest. In the case of the young men executed for their part in the Drumcondra Ambush, she also added their ages. One of the last items to be pasted in the prayer book during Markievicz's imprisonment in Mountjoy was a newspaper photo of Thomas Patrick O'Reilly, one of five men killed during the attack on the Custom House on 25 May 1921.

In addition to the notes from Whelan and Moran, the prayer book contained a number of loose items, including several news clippings which presumably had been kept there for safekeeping. Markievicz makes several references in her correspondence to news stories she had clipped from the papers either to keep or send to friends. These other clippings reinforce the sense that Markievicz was very deliberate in what she decided to paste in the prayer book. The loose clippings tend to relate to general news stories; for example, one from late 1920 references the fact that de Valera continued to evade the authorities. Another featured an image of Alderman Kathleen Clarke and related to her appointment on 16 March 1921 as the first female president of Dublin Corporation's Court of Conscience [fig. 13].[60] There is also a clipping featuring the text of 'England's Choice', a poem by Sir William Watson. While it is a poem written in support of Irish independence, its lack of any religious content or imagery may have rendered it unsuitable for inclusion in the prayer book.[61] Similarly, a clipping about a meeting of Wicklow Urban Council which was adjourned as a mark of respect and sympathy following the deaths of MacSwiney, Fitzgerald, Murphy and Barry may have seemed too purely secular to have a permanent place in the prayer book. Other items include five prayer cards, among them a 'Litany of Irish Saints', 'A Prayer for Ireland' and a guide to the 'Medal of The Immaculate Conception, called Miraculous Medal' issued by the Orphanage of St Vincent on North William Street, Dublin. She also kept a small handwritten note from 23 December 1920 in which 'Dick' thanks her for some roses she sent him and 'Mrs. D.'.

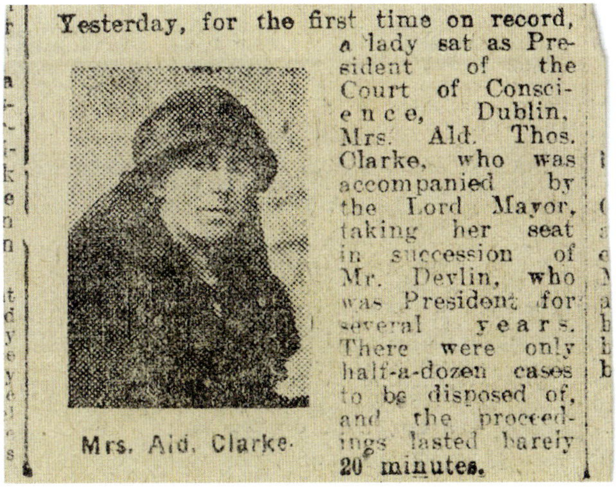

Yesterday, for the first time on record, a lady sat as President of the Court of Conscience, Dublin, Mrs. Ald. Thos. Clarke, who was accompanied by the Lord Mayor, taking her seat in succession of Mr. Devlin, who was President for several years. There were only half-a-dozen cases to be disposed of, and the proceedings lasted barely 20 minutes.

Mrs. Ald. Clarke.

fig. 13 | Among the loose items in the prayer book was a clipping relating to the appointment of Kathleen Clarke as president of Dublin Corporation's Court of Conscience in March 1921.

## The prayer book's presentation to the Kilmainham Jail Restoration Society

There are just two Civil War period items in the book which date from after her release from Mountjoy. The first is a memorial card for Harry Boland, who died on 1 August 1922 as a result of wounds sustained in a raid by Irish Free State forces. The second card commemorates the executions of Rory O'Connor, Liam Mellows, Richard Barrett and Joseph McKelvey in Mountjoy Prison on 8 December 1922. Based on this, Markievicz must have been separated from it sometime after December 1922. There is nothing to suggest she had it with her during her last-ever period of imprisonment in the North Dublin Union in November–December 1923. It resurfaced forty years later in April 1963 when Seamus Brennan, the chairman of the Kilmainham Jail Restoration Society (KJRS), received a package from the office of the then President of Ireland, Éamon de Valera, containing the prayer book. A letter accompanying it, written on the President's behalf by his private secretary Máire Ní Cheallaigh, explained that it had been presented to de Valera by Major Florence 'Florrie' O'Donoghue on a recent trip to Cork.[62] Ní Cheallaigh also forwarded a copy of a letter she had received from Major O'Donoghue in which he explained that his wife Josephine had been given the prayer book by a man living in Cork whose name O'Donoghue decided not to reveal. O'Donoghue wrote that the man was 'rather vague and evasive as to how it came into his possession; all he would say was that it was found in a drawer of some furniture which had been sent to an auction room in the city from a house on the South Douglas Road.' O'Donoghue said his efforts to verify this story had failed, and mentioned that there was an unconfirmed suggestion that the prayer book had been found in a raid during the Civil War.[63] Both O'Donoghues had played active roles during the revolutionary period. Florence (1897–1967) had been a leading member of the Irish Volunteers during the War of Independence and served as the adjutant and intelligence officer of the 1st Southern Division. Although he was appointed the Adjutant-General of the anti-Treaty IRA from March to June 1922, he ultimately stepped away from this role as part of an attempt to reunite the pro- and anti-Treaty factions of the IRA. He later wrote a number of histories related to the 1916–23 period, was an adviser to the Bureau of Military History and a leading light in the cultural life of Cork city in the mid-twentieth century. Josephine O'Donoghue had also been an important covert intelligence agent during the War of Independence.[64] It was she who made contact with Nora Wallace, as she knew of her connection with Markievicz. Wallace provided a memorandum vouching for the authenticity of the book, which was also forwarded to the KJRS, and Florrie O'Donoghue asked that the book be donated in Wallace's name.

At the conclusion of her April 1963 memorandum about the prayer book, Nora Wallace said that she found it 'hard to believe that Madame would glue newspaper cuttings to her prayer-book and [I] am inclined to think that was done in Cork. That these cuttings refer to Terry MacSwiney confirms this.'[65] Wallace's refusal to believe that Markievicz had made these interventions gives a sense of how unorthodox, and potentially sacrilegious, her actions would have seemed to those who had been raised in the Catholicism of post-Devotional Revolution Ireland. In essence, she had taken a Church-sanctioned manual designed to regulate and control her religious practice and physically imposed her own unique Catholicism upon it instead.[66] She essentially made her own devotional tool for her own specific and very personal belief system. In her biography of Markievicz, Lauren Arrington argues that, by the time of the War of Independence, there had been a gradual shift in her politics from 'a purely socialist discourse of class warfare to a language of spiritual struggle that reflects Irish republicanism more broadly'. She attributes this in part to Markievicz's conversion to Catholicism, but she also believes that 'the deaths of friends and political comrades had a profound effect on her psyche; during her imprisonments, she reflected on these losses, and one way of combating depression was to focus on spiritual redemption.'[67]

Her prison prayer book is in many ways a physical manifestation of this process. A close and detailed examination of the prayer book, and her additions to it, reveals the significant amount of care and thought she invested in creating this personal memorial. While her very particular use of the prayer book reinforces the consensus among Markievicz's biographers that her conversion was not driven by an attraction to or interest in Catholic doctrine, it does also suggest that it went far beyond a desire to make a grand political gesture during her imprisonment after the 1916 Rising. Ultimately the prayer book should be seen as a profound and deeply moving catalogue of tragedy and loss experienced by Markievicz during the War of Independence, which offers us a significant insight into the complexity of her political, spiritual and emotional life during a key moment in Irish history.

---

**Brian Crowley** is employed by the OPW as Curator of Collections for Kilmainham Gaol and the Pearse Museum. As well as curating exhibitions in both venues, he also had curatorial responsibility for the most recent redisplay of the collections in Derrynane House, co. Kerry. He has published several historical essays and an illustrated biography of Patrick Pearse entitled *Patrick Pearse: A Life in Pictures* (Cork: Mercier Press, 2013).

**Endnotes**

1 Kilmainham Gaol Museum collection, KMGLM.2021.0003.01–20.

2 Lauren Arrington, *Revolutionary Lives: Constance and Casimir Markievicz* (Princeton: Princeton University Press, 2020 pb); Sari Oikarinen, *'A Dream of Liberty': Constance Markievicz's vision of Ireland, 1908–1927* (Helsinki: Suomen Historiallinen Seura, 1998).

3 *Weekly Irish Times*, 21 June 1919.

4 The women's prison in Cork was designed by Sir Thomas Dean in the Georgian Gothic style and was originally built as the city gaol. In the 1870s, when Irish prisons were centralised under the General Prisons Board, it was designated as a women's prison.

5 Lindie Naughton (ed.), *Markievicz: prison letters & rebel writing* (Newbridge: Merrion Press, 2018), p.138.

6 Ibid., p.107.

7 Ibid., p.108.

8 In 1917, Mary MacSwiney (1872–1942) had been elected to the national executive of Cumann na mBan, a female auxiliary to the IRA. She later came to national prominence following the death of her brother, the Lord Mayor of Cork, Terence MacSwiney, who died in Brixton Prison on 25 October 1920 on the seventy-fourth day of his hunger strike.

9 Naughton (2018), p.111.

10 Ibid., pp.72, 101.

11 Helen Litton (ed.), *Kathleen Clarke: revolutionary woman* (Dublin: O'Brien Press, 2008), p.213.

12 Naughton (2018), p.113.

13 Ibid., p.138.
14 Ibid., p.113.
15 Ibid., p.122.
16 Ibid., p.143.
17 Ibid., p.136. Kathleen Clarke was somewhat scornful of Markievicz's reading while they were in Holloway together: 'She ordered a lot of books on economics, labour, socialism, and other topics. She never had patience to read through a book, she would skim through it, trying in her quick way to get the sense of it.' Litton (ed.), p.215.
18 Naughton (2018), pp.123–24.
19 Kilmainham Gaol Museum, Dublin, Kilmainham Jail Restoration Society Papers, Nora Wallace Memorandum, 7 April 1963. While Nora Wallace remembered that in Cork it was only sold in the Augustinian Priory, it appears to have been widely available for purchase, and was frequently advertised for sale in the British Catholic press in particular.
20 In a letter written to Kathleen Clarke on 20 July 1919, Markievicz mentioned that two monks 'with white beards' had been to visit her but did not specify the Order to which they belonged or if they gave her a prayer book. Naughton (2018), p.122.
21 *New Ross Standard*, 15 October 1915.
22 *The Tablet*, 3 March 1917.
23 Emmet Larkin, 'The Devotional Revolution in Ireland, 1850–75', *The American Historical Review*, vol.77, no.3 (June 1972), pp.625–52: 644–45.
24 Lisa Godson, 'Charting the material culture of the "Devotional Revolution": the Advertising Register of the Irish Catholic Directory, 1837–96', *Proceedings of the Royal Irish Academy: archaeology, culture, history, literature*, vol.116C (2016), pp.265–94: 269.
25 Sonja Tiernan, *Eva Gore-Booth: an image of such politics* (Manchester: Manchester University Press, 2012), p.1.
26 Malcolm M.A. Marcourt, 'The Religious Inquiry in the Irish Census of 1861', *Irish Historical Studies*, vol.21, no.82 (Sept 1978), p.168.
27 Tiernan, pp.18–19.
28 The Russian authorities initially said they would only recognise a marriage between a Catholic and a Protestant if the marriage was a Catholic ceremony. Arrington, pp.25–26.
29 Although she declared herself a Catholic following her arrest in 1916, she was formally received into the church in Clonliffe College, Dublin, on 24 June 1917 when she took the baptismal name of Anastasia. See Lindie Naughton, *Markievicz: a most outrageous rebel* (Newbridge: Merrion Press, 2016), p.198.
30 'The Events of Easter Week', *The Catholic Bulletin*, February 1917, pp.129–30.
31 Ronan Kelly, *Every Branch of the Healing Art: a history of the Royal College of Surgeons in Ireland* (Dublin: Eastwood Books, 2023), pp.194–203.
32 Interestingly, Partridge was the son of a Protestant father and Catholic mother. Although baptised into the Church of Ireland, the influence of a teaching nun led to him adopting the Catholic faith at age eleven. See Lawrence William White, 'William Patrick ('Bill') Partridge (1874–1917)', *Dictionary of Irish Biography* <https://doi.org/10.3318/dib.007221.v1>.
33 *The Catholic Bulletin*, Feb 1917, pp.129–30.
34 Larkin, p.649.
35 Oikarinen, p.100. Markievicz's mother, Lady Georgina Gore-Booth, seems to have remained suspicious of Catholicism. While Markievicz was in Mountjoy in the summer of 1921, her sister Eva was on a visit to Italy and appears to have had a papal audience. Markievicz wrote 'Gaga [Lady Gore-Booth] must have been shocked at your seeing the Pope'; Naughton (2018), p.190. Eva also rejected her privileged background and became an activist in feminist, socialist and pacifist politics and attended a Unitarian church before becoming an active member of the radical Labour Church with her partner, Esther Roper; Tiernan, p.62.
36 Esther Roper, 'Biographical Sketch', in *Prison Letters of Countess Markievicz* (London: Virago Press, 1987), p.74.
37 St Francis of Assisi, the founder of the Franciscan order, was a medieval saint particularly associated with the care of the poor, and led a life of poverty. St Paul was a Christian apostle who converted

to Christianity in the years immediately after the death of Jesus Christ; his writings shaped many of the core tenets of Christian doctrine and theology.

38 Ibid., p.75.

39 Arrington, p.144.

40 Roper, p.32–33.

41 William Roche, *Mysteries of the Mass in Reasoned Prayer* (London: Longmans, Green & Co., 1915), p.v.

42 Kilmainham Gaol Museum, KMGLM.2015. 0023, letter from Fr Albert Bibby to Constance Markievicz, 4 April 1917.

43 Military Archives, Dublin, Bureau of Military History, 1913–1921, Witness Statement no.936.

44 Seán MacBride was the son of Maud Gonne and the executed 1916 leader John MacBride.

45 Naughton (2018), p.192.

46 This was a separate prison to the one in which Markievicz was held in 1919. Built as the Cork County Prison, it became male-only in 1878. The original entrance front and part of the walls were later incorporated into the campus of University College Cork.

47 He was in fact the second lord mayor of Cork to die in the conflict; his predecessor Tomás MacCurtain had been killed in a police raid the previous March.

48 Headlined 'Dark Rosaleen', the clipping reads: 'Even in his ravings, "Dark Rosaleen" seemed to occupy the Lord Mayor's thoughts, for he muttered, in Irish:

'Béad dílis duit, a chailin [*sic*] deas, béad dilís duit go deo.'

Which rendered in English reads: I shall be true to my fair colleen, I shall be true to thee for aye.'

49 Jack Elliott, 'Ephemera and personal responses to the Easter Rising', in Lisa Godson and Joanna Brück (eds), *Making 1916: material and visual culture of the Easter Rising* (Liverpool: Liverpool University Press, 2015), pp.96–97.

50 *Wolfe Tone Annual*, 1935 (Brian O'Higgins, publisher, Dublin)

51 Naughton (2018), p.171.

52 A clipping on the opposite page contains details of a series of devotions to be said as part of an 'Appeal to the Sacred Heart and Our Heavenly Mother Mary for Our Beloved Country Ireland', but there is nothing to suggest that it is specifically related to Clancy and McKee.

53 Patrick Doyle named his eldest daughter Catherine Constance after Markievicz; see Tim Carey, *Hanged for Ireland: 'The Forgotten Ten' executed 1920–21, a documentary history* (Dublin: Blackwater Press, 2001), p.101.

54 Military Archives, Dublin, Bureau of Military History, 1913–1921, Witness Statement no.750.

55 The Sunday Independent, 20 March 1921

56 Military Archives, Dublin, Bureau of Military History, 1913–1921, Witness Statement no.508.

57 Naughton (2018), pp.118–19, 138, 154–55.

58 Nora Wallace Memorandum, 7 April 1963.

59 Nora Wallace seems to have misremembered this detail, and she described the book as containing a mortuary card for Leo Fitzgerald.

60 The Court of Conscience was run by Dublin Corporation and dealt with small debts. It was abolished in 1923.

61 Although sympathetic to Irish independence, Watson was also still very much part of the British establishment and Markievicz may not have wanted to have his poem pasted in the prayer book alongside the heroes of the War of Independence.

62 Kilmainham Gaol Museum, Dublin, Kilmainham Jail Restoration Society Papers, Máire Ní Cheallaigh to Seamus Brennan, 11 April 1963.

63 Ibid., Florence O'Donoghue to Máire Ní Cheallaigh, 4 April 1963.

64 Marie Coleman, 'Florence ('Florrie') O'Donoghue (1897–1967)', *Dictionary of Irish Biography* <https://doi.org/10.3318/dib.006706.v1>.

65 Nora Wallace Memorandum, 7 April 1963.

66 Interestingly, while Markievicz generally found blank spaces in the prayer book on which to paste her clippings, one page of text she did largely cover was that recording the official imprimatur of the Vicar-General of the Archdiocese of Westminster, opposite the foreword.

67 Arrington, pp.206–07.

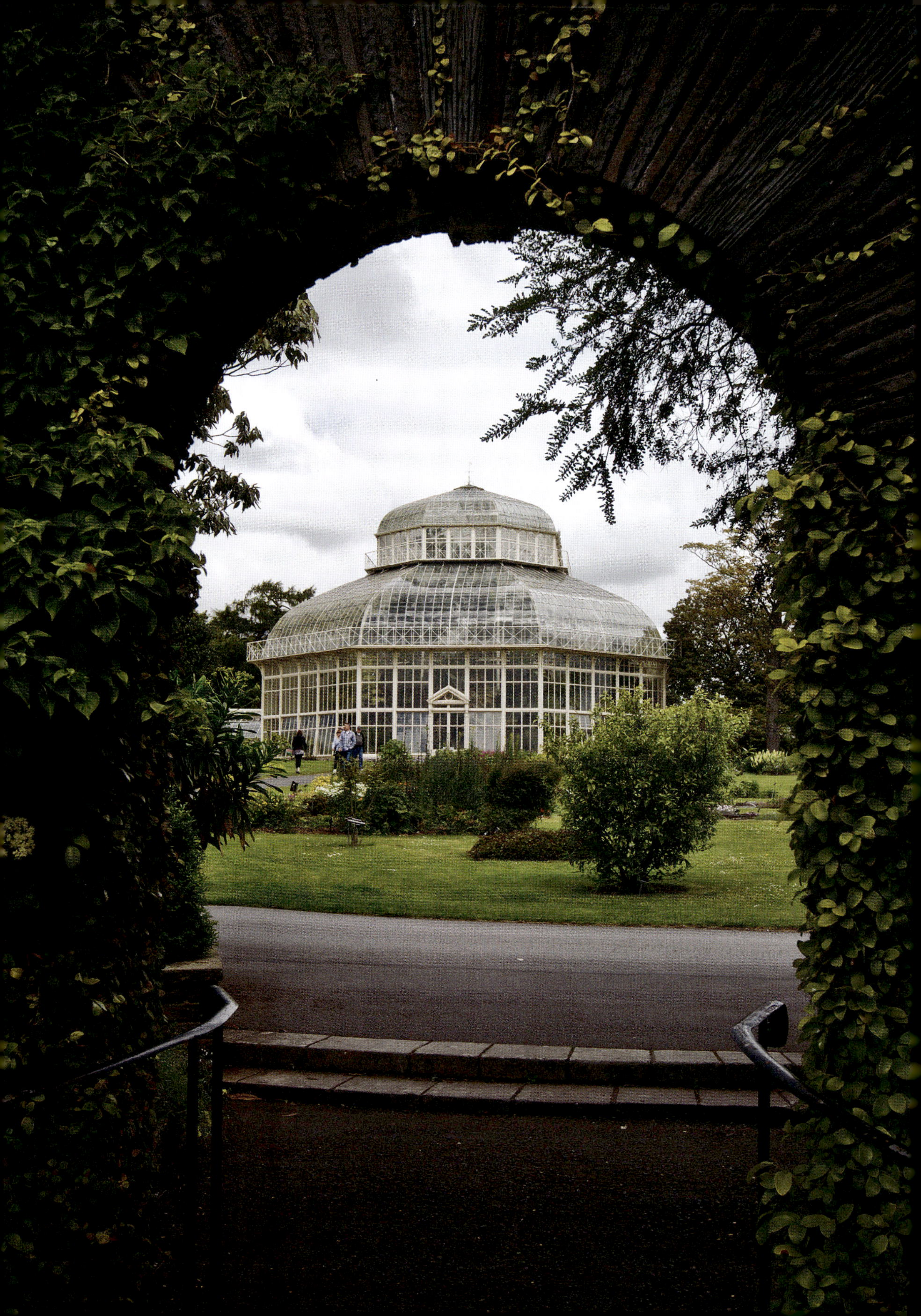

# Decolonising and reinterpreting national collections: the case for the National Botanic Gardens, Dublin

AUDREY WALSHE

A RESEARCH TRIP IN 2023 TO THE NATIONAL BOTANIC GARDENS IN GLASNEVIN WAS THE prompt for this paper [fig. 1]. When taking an official tour of the site, the information disseminated to visitors was historically and scientifically focused and naturally engaging. It was, however, obvious that certain aspects of the Gardens' history have not been foregrounded, reflecting priorities of the times in which the tours were first established. This article argues that there is now an opportunity to expand our understanding of the historical and colonial contexts of the Gardens and settings, while also addressing more contemporary concerns such as climate change and the biodiversity crisis. That visit prompted the present consideration of how the historic collections in Glasnevin could be reinterpreted by applying a more critical lens of decolonisation, looking at who created the collections on the site and where the specimens originated from, as well as investigating Irish involvement in colonial practices in the development of scientific knowledge more broadly.

The public garden space is a perfect place to interrogate the complex relationship between humans and plants. Prior to the opening of formal botanic gardens as scientific institutions in the late eighteenth and early nineteenth centuries, botanising was mainly conducted by those involved in the study of medicine. The National Botanic Gardens were initially concerned with the development of modern Irish agricultural science but were also deeply linked to colonialism and imperial expansion from the Victorian period onwards. The Economic Botany Collection contains 20,000 samples of plant products, including fruits, seeds, wood, fibres, plant extracts and artefacts, with specimens used for studying economic potential and purposes. This collection preserves tangible and intangible bio-cultural heritage for the Irish State. Together with botanic gardens, economic botany collections work to show the connections between plants and products. The herbarium is a reference centre, a data storehouse and a research institution documenting Irish and international botany.[1] Viewing the gardens and herbarium in Glasnevin as a location of historical colonial power and a symbol of Irish involvement in the imperial project, it becomes apparent that not only is the Botanic Garden in Glasnevin truly the OPW's 'brightest jewel',[2] but also a gem that has the potential to engage new audiences.

fig. 1 | The Great Palm House, National Botanic Gardens, Glasnevin
(Tourism Ireland / Brian Morrison)

It is here argued that it, and comparable institutions, have the potential to demonstrate an awareness of contemporary issues of urban deprivation in relation to green spaces, race and gender inequalities, social and environmental justice matters relating to horticulture and botany as well as land access, biodiversity and climate change.

## National Botanical Collections

THE NATIONAL BOTANICAL COLLECTIONS ARE MADE UP OF SEVERAL GARDENS AND PLANT collections owned and cared for by the State. These range from the National Botanic Gardens and Herbarium at Glasnevin and at Kilmacurragh, co. Wicklow, to publicly owned estate parklands such as those at Castletown House in co. Kildare, Oldbridge Estate in co. Meath, Doneraile Court and Annes Grove in co. Cork, while also including a variety of memorial gardens such as the Garden of Remembrance and the Irish National War Memorial Gardens in Dublin. Gardens created as war memorials and dedicated to the memory of 'all those who gave their lives in the cause of Irish freedom' are clear in their intention and function.[3] A guide titled *Ireland's Historic Gardens in the care of the OPW* launched in June 2023 notes a remarkable and historic array of gardens dating from the formal seventeenth-century Italian renaissance gardens at Portumna Castle, co. Galway, the eighteenth-century great parks such as Castletown, the nineteenth-century Paradise Gardens of Altamont, co. Carlow, to the Victorian splendour of the People's Garden in the Phoenix Park in Dublin.[4] The guide emphasises the importance of the OPW in recording and preserving these collections, gardens and places for future generations, and serves as a promotional publication with the stated hope that it will encourage future visitors. However, while it specifies the diversity of spaces to visit, it is less specific about the diversity of visitors it welcomes. Noticeably, the photographic images it uses are not of a culturally diverse public, OPW employees are not presented as multiracial, and the guide includes a photograph showing a back profile of the late queen of England. Despite significant progress in terms of the recognition of cultural diversity and cultural differences in society, Irish institutional cultural heritage guides have inconsistent outcomes which is exemplified in this guide.

To make meaningful progress on inclusivity and accessibility, institutions are required to reflect on their sites and the artefacts held in their collections; to address the inequalities of wealth, poverty and power that may have created these collections; to question who shapes the meanings of how we think now; and to discuss and implement plans to conserve, preserve and display such collections while highlighting awareness of outdated and unacceptable modes of systemic behaviour.

## Colonial public heritage

IRELAND'S STATUS AS A FORMER COLONY HAS SOMETIMES MUTED THE DISCUSSIONS ON THE INHERent coloniality of our public heritage, a position considered by Dr Dónal Hassett in his recent project 'Decolonizing Irish Public Heritage', based at University College Cork.[5] Our national collections, civic spaces (including gardens) and country houses were often the products of the exploitation not just *of* Ireland, but also *by* Ireland of colonies throughout the British empire.[6] In post-independence Ireland, the removal or alteration of the most blatant symbols of the colonial past resulted in a limited decolonisation of the Irish public space. In fact, the renaming of the Royal Botanic Gardens to the National Botanic Gardens is an example, a name change introduced into common use but never legally implemented.

The newly independent State also largely ignored the ways in which the participation of many Irishmen and women in the administration and oppression of other colonial territories has always shaped public heritage here,[7] although historians have recognised that the experience of empire was very central in the formation of new nation states.[8] For centuries, professional and political networks linked Ireland to London and the wider empire, and its opportunities.

## Botanical collections

FOCUSING ON THE COLLECTIONS AND PEOPLE ASSOCIATED WITH THE NATIONAL BOTANIC Gardens in Glasnevin in the nineteenth century, it is argued here that now is a good time to critically evaluate its collecting methodologies into the early twentieth century. That time period is relevant, given that political and social factors in the context of empire were at play, as well as scientific enquiry.[9] The make-up of the collections and their interpretation in a culturally sensitive manner is equally relevant to other institutions today. In July 2023 Trinity College Dublin returned thirteen human skulls to Inishbofin Island off the coast of Galway, the skulls having been stolen in 1890 and held in the Anatomy Department ever since.[10] Their return to and reburial on the island aligns with the international ethical concerns about the treatment of inappropriate acquisitions in public collections and places of education in particular.

Dr Martha Fleming of the Natural History Museum of Denmark argues that botanical archives are archives of human as well as natural history, and that an herbarium must be viewed as a place of individual and collective memory formed on three levels – collectors' memories, plant memories and place memories. She continues that an herbarium has the potential to be approached as an archive that provides us with unexplored sources with which to create new environmental histories. The language used in herbaria is economic, yet often one person's economic plant and commodity is another's cultural plant. Collection histories are valuable in helping us to understand local peculiarities, and often the only way to link a botanical artefact to what was a living plant is to use oral history and testimony.[11] The dominant global narrative now tends to characterise contemporary ethnographic collections as colonial 'loot', but this only displays half the story: items were also gifted, bought or traded. The problem in these instances is that the power dynamic between the buyer and seller was unequal. Additionally, items could be adapted to meet consumer expectations, transforming objects of cultural significance into souvenirs.

As botanists worked to 'master' natural history in the nineteenth century, they worked in tandem with Europe's drive to acquire overseas territories, with botanic gardens

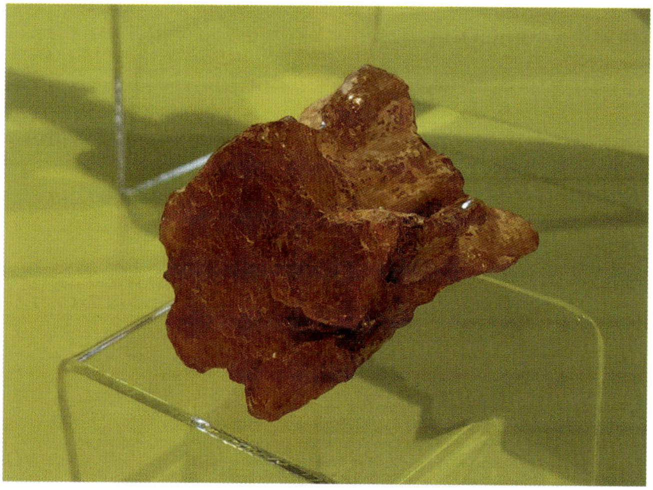

fig. 2 | A piece of gum copal from Upper Congo, deposited in the Science & Art Museum (now NMI) by Roger Casement on 25 June 1904. National Botanic Gardens Herbarium, DBN-M-006056 (photo: Colin Kelleher)

opposite fig. 3 | *Prospectus of the arrangements in the Dublin Society's Botanical and Agricultural Garden, at Glasnevin* (RDS, 1818) National Library of Ireland (photos by the author, unless otherwise stated)

being an intrinsic part of the European imperial project and experience. Critical scholarship about the history of Irish natural science collections is not extensive, particularly in relation to colonial collections [fig. 2].[12] Much remains to be done in terms of critically examining and contextualising Ireland's role in collection-gathering, which will build our understanding of Ireland's contribution to British colonialism. It will also highlight public institutions and collections which carry ideologies and narratives which would benefit from decolonisation. A complication presented by Ireland is the web of social and political histories shared with Britain where Irish people took on both subaltern and dominant roles within the imperial system, often taking advantage of their European ethnicity and English-language fluency.

In June 2020, in light of public debates worldwide, Alexandre Antonelli, Director of Kew Science, wrote an article titled, 'It's time to re-examine the history of botanical collections', and explained why Kew Gardens must address 'our colonial legacy'.[13] Antonelli's comments (published on Kew's website) refer to the institution's role in the nineteenth century which often focused on the movement of plants and many other commodities around the British Empire. Statements like this do not acknowledge Ireland as either part of the Union at that time or a former colony of Britain, or even consider Irish involvement at all. Antonelli continued by observing, however, that in his own field of research, an imperialist view still prevails: 'Scientists continue to report how new species are "discovered" every year, species that are already known and used by Indigenous people in different regions who remain unnamed, unrecognised and uncompensated for their contribution to scientific knowledge.'[14] This invisibility in history is something which could also be applied to Irish people who took part in the work of empire, which ranges from complete obscurity to being minimised in Irish national heritage due to lack of archival information and the cultural amnesia of nationalism.

The Royal Botanic Gardens at Glasnevin mirrored its sister organisations in other colonial cities – from Calcutta to Belfast – by being interested in botanical enquiry. But it differed in having been founded by the Dublin Society to advance agriculture in Ireland for commercial purposes, as will be explained in more detail below. However, botanic gardens globally, including Dublin, were more usually a colonial construct, designed to bring 'nature' from tropical climes and present them to European publics. They represented how Europe would control, classify and impose taxonomic order on the globe, and turn plants into global commodities. They were places with a human-centred set of values, and now present ideal sites to dismantle this thinking.

## Historical context

IN 1790 THE IRISH PARLIAMENT, WITH THE SUPPORT OF THE SPEAKER OF THE HOUSE JOHN FOSTER (1740–1828), granted funds to the Dublin Society (now Royal Dublin Society) to establish a public botanic garden. Foster had represented constituencies in co. Louth in the Irish parliament since 1761, and did so until his elevation to the peerage in 1821. He was opposed to the Act of Union which saw Ireland's direct control over its own affairs removed to London in 1801. Foster also believed that Dublin should have a public garden of equal status to the Kew and Edinburgh botanic gardens, maintaining that Ireland was an equal partner within the new United Kingdom. Foster was well-regarded outside politics as a horticulturist and botanist, and he was acknowledged by J.C. Loudon as one who 'introduced by far the greatest number of trees into Ireland' during the eighteenth century and that the Botanic Gardens 'owes its origin, in 1797, to the late Lord Oriel'.[15]

In 1795, the Royal Botanic Gardens Dublin was founded on lands at Glasnevin to promote a scientific approach to the study of agriculture. In the early years, the living and archival specimens were collected and studied for the purpose of researching foods and medicines, along with plants that promoted an understanding of systematic botany or were simply beautiful or interesting in themselves.[16] The Dublin Society published a prospectus in 1818 containing information relating to the usefulness of the Gardens [fig. 3]. The prospectus generated an air of expectation, and appealed not only to the 'real botanist', but the 'botanophilist',[17] an early indication that the Gardens were to be an inclusive space for recreation and science alike. The prospectus categorised who the Gardens could assist, ranging from the dyer wishing to be acquainted with certain vegetables which would yield colouring materials; the medical student who may wish to be acquainted with herbs used in the care of disease; those interested in rural affairs (the hay garden contained the plants which a farmer should either encourage or eradicate); and the exotics in the greenhouses, hothouses

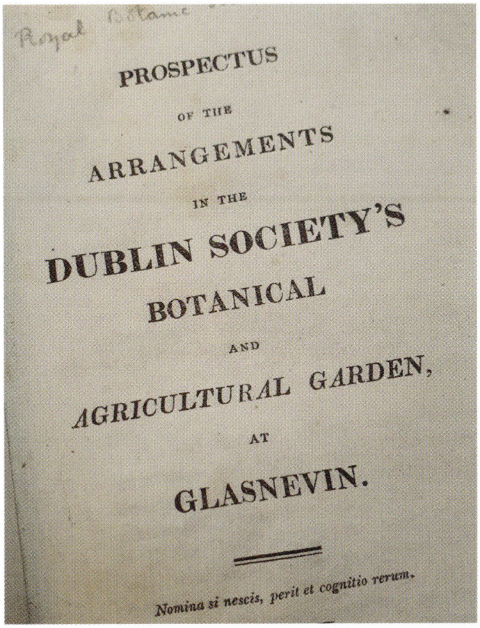
PROSPECTUS
OF THE
ARRANGEMENTS
IN THE
DUBLIN SOCIETY'S
BOTANICAL
AND
AGRICULTURAL GARDEN,
AT
GLASNEVIN.

*Nomina si nescis, perit et cognitio rerum.*

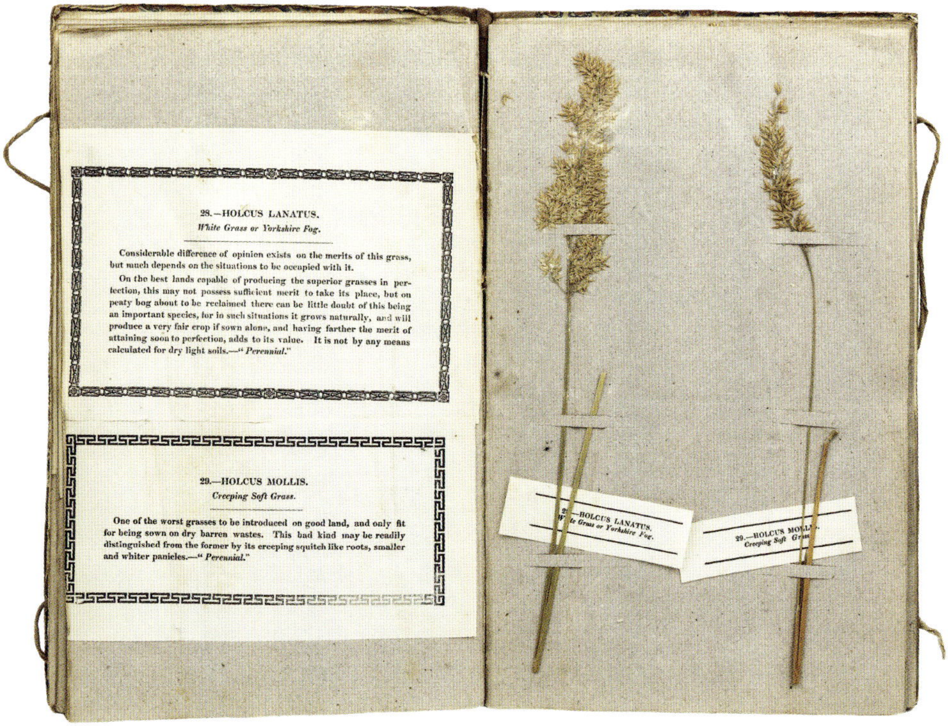


and conservatories were to appeal to the 'true florist' and provide an embellishment and 'finish to the whole botanical establishment'. The front page of the pamphlet is inscribed *'Nomina si nescis, perit et cognito rerum'*, meaning that in losing the names of things, we lose the knowledge attached to them – thus affirming the value of the Linnean system of binomial nomenclature. In this case, the pamphlet was endorsing a globalising botanical language, overlooking the fact that plants would lose their origin names, including native Irish plans with Gaelic names.

Carl Linnaeus (1707–1778) is most famous for creating the system of naming plants and animals still in use today.[18] The binomial approach assigned each species of plant and animal a genus name followed by a species name, both being in Latin. In deciding that 'man' was an animal like any other, and placing *Homo Sapiens* in the animal kingdom, he foreshadowed Darwin's evolutionary thesis a century later. Linnaeus subdivided mankind into four different 'varieties', based on skin colour and geographic origin: 'European white', 'American reddish', 'Asian tawny' and 'African black'.[19] The Glasnevin gardens' director in the mid-nineteenth century, Dr David Moore (1808–1879) [fig. 4], was among those who did not subscribe to the Darwinian theory, and even gave an anti-evolution lecture in Rosemary Street Presbyterian church in Belfast in December 1874, demonstrating a conflict with his religious beliefs.[20] While the adoption of the Linnean system at Glasnevin is not significant in itself, in the context of who is welcomed to contemporary publicly funded botanical gardens it is incumbent upon institutions to show that these were the subtexts underpinning the study and promotion of botanical sciences, and consider how to address them now.

Barry Crosbie has demonstrated that after the Act of Union of 1801, Irish scientific institutions played a decisive role in the emergence of colonial strategies and the construction of British imperial rule.[21] At the same time, Irish migrants (both Catholic and Protestant) were at the forefront of exporting systems of scientific knowledge and practice to different parts of the empire, where they were adopted and used.[22] Crosbie is here referring to geology and the Ordnance Survey in India, but one can include botanical knowledge in which there were benefits that flowed from Irish imperial postings. This mapped with the RDS's intention for the Botanic Gardens to serve a profitable role for Ireland. However, that involved the adoption of a coloniser mindset – a fact that is often overlooked. Irish botanical gardens and individuals connected to them were part of a global network of botanical collecting and, on a more local level, part of social circles connected by these interests.

Ninian Niven (1799–1879), superintendent of the Gardens in 1838, produced another publication called *The Visitor's Companion to the Botanic Garden* [fig. 5].[23] This was written and presented in the style of an instructional manual with a focus on vegetable growing and agricultural specimens, with a section on nursery growing and landscape gardening. He referred to God being the ultimate Creator in several instances, stating 'how wisely arranged and counterbalanced are all the works of that Omnipotent Being, who in their creation pronounced all things "very good"'.[24] Niven noted the economic possibilities of the Erica heather plant in assisting honey bees to produce the purest honey, and how a tea plant could survive if planted in a sheltered location in the south of Ireland.[25] He continued by advising the reader that by first directing attention to the botany of their native country they will be better prepared to take up positions among men of science, studying the botany of the world.[26] In 1885, a *Guide to the Royal Botanic Gardens, Glasnevin* was published, the work of the late director David

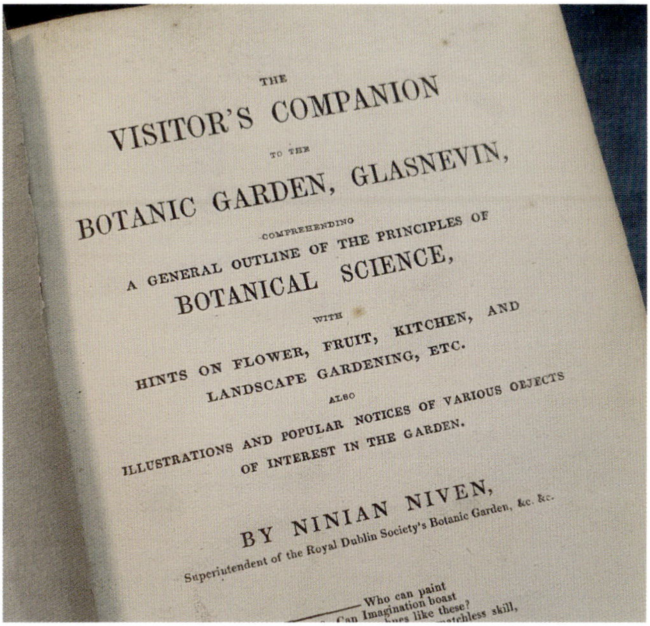
THE
VISITOR'S COMPANION
TO THE
BOTANIC GARDEN, GLASNEVIN,
COMPREHENDING
A GENERAL OUTLINE OF THE PRINCIPLES OF
BOTANICAL SCIENCE,
WITH
HINTS ON FLOWER, FRUIT, KITCHEN, AND
LANDSCAPE GARDENING, ETC.
ALSO
ILLUSTRATIONS AND POPULAR NOTICES OF VARIOUS OBJECTS
OF INTEREST IN THE GARDEN.
BY NINIAN NIVEN,
Superintendent of the Royal Dublin Society's Botanic Garden, &c. &c.
—— Who can paint
Can Imagination boast

fig. 5 | Ninian Niven,
*The Visitor's Companion to the Botanic Garden, Glasnevin*
(William Curry Jun. & Co., 1838)
National Library of Ireland

opposite

fig. 4 | David Moore, *Concise Notes of the Indigenous Grasses of Ireland, best suited for agriculture, with dried specimens of each kind*
(Glasnevin, 1843)
National Botanic Gardens
(OPW / Mike Brown, 2019)

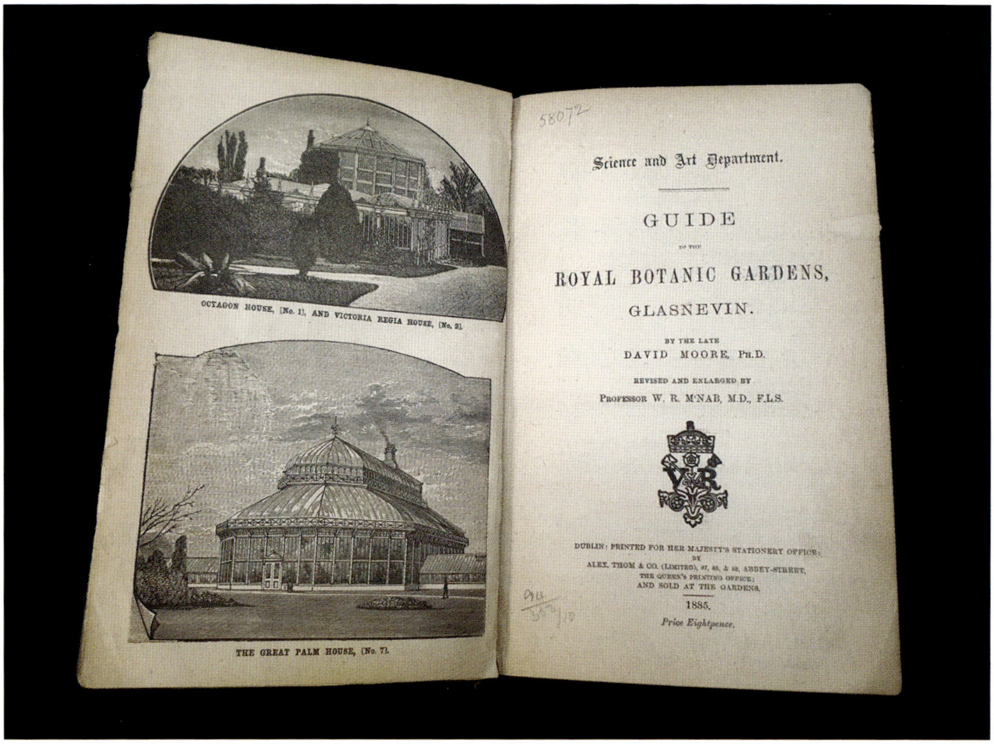


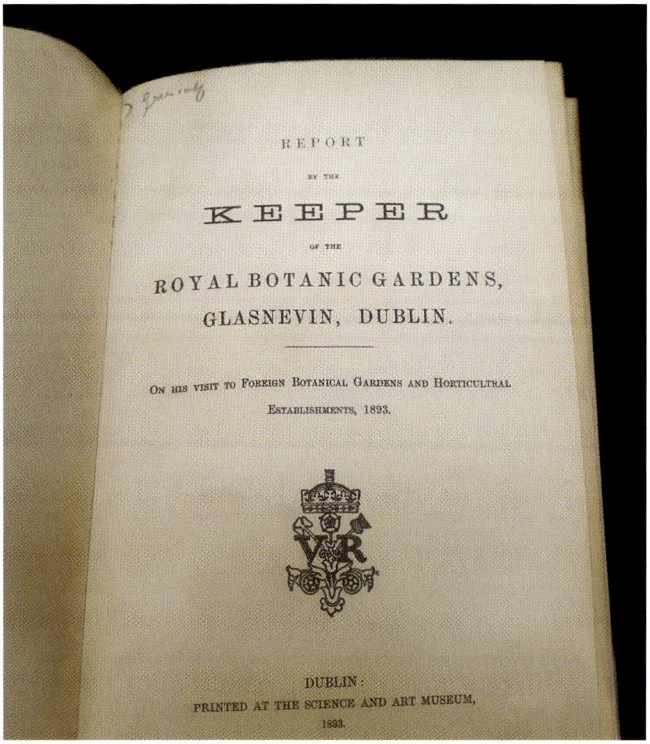


fig. 6 | David Moore and W.R. McNab, *Guide to the Royal Botanic Gardens, Glasnevin,* (HMSO, 1885), National Library of Ireland

fig. 7 | Frederick William Moore, *Report by the Keeper of the Royal Botanic Gardens, Glasnevin, Dublin, on his visit to Foreign Botanical Gardens and Horticultural Establishments* (Science and Art Museum, Dublin, 1893), National Library of Ireland

Moore, with revisions by Professor William Ramsay McNab and an introduction by the Director of the Science and Art Museum (now the National Museum of Ireland), Valentine Ball [fig. 6].[27] While the politics of the garden's management were in some upheaval at this time, and the control moving from the Royal Dublin Society to the Department of Science and Art, the last chapter on the Botanical Museum is pertinent to the current theme. In it, Moore described donations to the museum which included fruit of the oil palm, cocoa nut from the Seychelles Islands and even chocolate from J.S. Fry & Sons of Bristol. He goes on to list that one Surgeon Thornton presented Chinese paper, and Judge O'Reilly some nutmegs, and that a 'fine ball of Opium' was presented along with other valuable donations by the East India Company. This list shows not only the imperial nature of the donations, but also the enthusiasm for natural history collections by the Irish professional classes of the nineteenth century.

In 1893, the keeper of the Botanic Gardens, Sir Frederick William Moore (1857–1949) – son of David Moore – drafted a report on his visits to foreign gardens and horticultural establishments [fig. 7]. In it, Moore details his visits to thirteen different gardens, from Dijon to the Borromean Islands and Geneva, concluding that 'in none of them are the collections anything like so good as at Glasnevin'.[28] It is evident how, over the course of the nineteenth century, the focus of the Gardens had changed from an advisory role on agricultural matters to imperial plant-collecting and the pursuit of scientific botanical knowledge. The donations books in the archive of the RDS show that many people engaged in imperial employment – as well as Irish people travelling overseas – sent seeds and plants directly to Dublin rather than London, and were encouraged to do so, as Moore senior had entreated the RDS members in 1844:

> 'I may here be permitted to mention the great facilities now afforded for the transmission of Seeds, in small parcels, through the Post Office, and to beg of you, to request the members of the Royal Dublin Society, who have friends residing abroad, to recommend this mode of sending either small tubers of valuable Plants, or select Seeds.'[29]

This transmission of knowledge and material culture displays the imperial mindset, which is also evident in Glasnevin's built heritage. Only by taking care to clearly explain the engagement in the Dublin botanic gardens with these influences can we imagine different responses to the contents of the collections today.

## Imperial built heritage

THE INSTALLATION OF GLASSHOUSES FEATURED IN THE ORIGINAL PLANS FOR THE BOTANIC Gardens dating as far back as 1793. The earliest structures were wooden-framed, and throughout the nineteenth century maintenance and repair were constant preoccupations. The Curvilinear Range in Glasnevin is a long, low range of glasshouses, with a distinctive curved roofline.[30] This style and method of construction was characteristic of its designer, the celebrated Dublin iron-master Richard Turner. The east wing was constructed in 1843 by William Clancy, and the remaining sections were built by Turner and his son William. The two outer wings originally had brick walls at the back

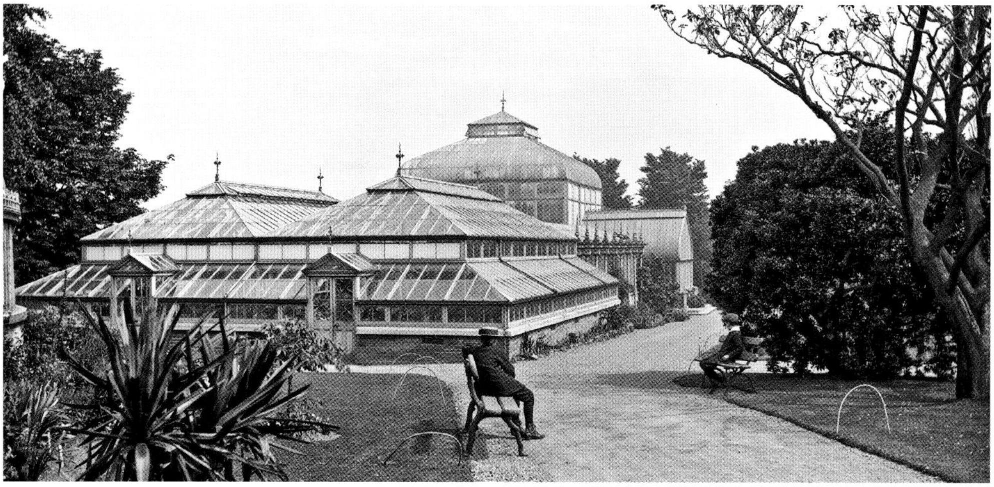

(i.e. down the middle of the existing houses), but in 1869 their size was doubled by adding a matching half to the wings. This is the most commanding building in the National Botanic Gardens. Turner also constructed the Palm House at Kew Gardens in 1844. By the later nineteenth century, the construction of buildings in the Botanic Gardens was benefiting from the industrial revolution, with timber cheaper to import and the mass production of British cast and wrought iron as well as glass.[31] The Great Palm House in Dublin was built in 1883 when the preceding glasshouse was damaged, with the new ironwork being fabricated in Glasgow and transported to Glasnevin [fig. 1].[32]

This architectural overview demonstrates how the flow of information and skills between Ireland and Britain moved through networks of specialists with knowledge of how to create spaces where tropical plants would survive and flourish. These specialists included botanists, garden designers, engineers and architects. While the glasshouses were scientific laboratories of empire to test growing conditions, they were also important cultural spaces where residents of cities at the centre of the imperial world could experience a romanticised version of tropical abundance [fig. 8].[33]

## Alternative narratives

THE NUANCED HISTORY OF THE GARDENS AND HERBARIUM AT GLASNEVIN MEANS THAT IN relation to decolonisation, there is undoubtedly a case to be made for a cross-disciplinary research project which would engage with the social history and culture of Irish science. E. Charles Nelson and Eileen McCracken's work outlines the intricacies of the overlapping family relationships and actors on the Irish botanical stage of the nineteenth century.[34] Highlighting the colonial and imperial links presents

fig. 8 | The Cactus House, the Victoria House and the Fern House, National Botanic Gardens, Glasnevin, photographed by Robert French (1841–1917), in the early twentieth century, National Library of Ireland, Lawrence Photograph Collection, L_ROY_01782
(courtesy of the National Library of Ireland)

challenges, as the research questions are of a social and cultural nature, being asked of a scientific institution. The cultural and historical significance of plant and herbaria collections must first be established; then it is necessary to consider how the collections can be made accessible. Botanic gardens are often understood as places that hold documented collections of living plants for the purposes of scientific research, conservation, display and education. However, this definition means the cultural complexity of botanic gardens remains unrecognised.

These collections are as much about the groups of people who collected them and who relinquished them as they are about the actual objects. The selection of specimens inevitably reflects a western-centric value system which may differ from that exercised by origin communities. Information recorded at the point of collection will be equally selective and biased, and much will be lost by the removal of an object from its natural habitat. When material is transferred from a living organic system to an archival system, the responsibility to it changes. Facilitating a two-way knowledge exchange with those communities today is an established best practice for institutions engaging with decolonisation, and will surely provide enriching contextual information.

## Conclusion

The National Botanic Gardens in Glasnevin states that its primary role is to function as a national scientific collection. It is actively involved in biodiversity conservation projects, thereby expanding that role to include community engagement and the preservation of local and international plant knowledges. The institution has the potential to further decolonise western knowledge practices, as articulated here. In this way, the ordered world of the Gardens could raise critical questions about how we might navigate nature, culture and education in contemporary botanic gardens in a more inclusive way, promoting knowledge decolonisation by engaging a variety of epistemological histories and futures.[35] By reinterpreting the site and collection at Glasnevin in a considered, inclusive and transdisciplinary way, the Gardens will articulate their contemporary cultural relevance, while engaging with a wider audience in the process.

---

**Audrey Walshe** is a Government of Ireland Postgraduate Scholar, funded by Taighde Éireann – Research Ireland, at the Centre for Irish Studies, University of Galway. Her current research focuses on Irish botanical illustration in the long nineteenth century. She holds an MA from IADT Dún Laoghaire (ARC) and a BA in Irish Studies from Trinity College Dublin.

**Author's acknowledgements**

With thanks to Dr Colin Kelleher, Keeper of the Herbarium, and Rachel Hynes, Botanic Gardens Assistant Librarian, for their input.

**Endnotes**

1 National Botanic Gardens, Glasnevin <www.botanicgardens.ie> [acc. May 2024].

2 E. Charles Nelson and Eileen M. McCracken, *The Brightest Jewel: a history of the National Botanic Gardens, Glasnevin, Dublin* (Kilkenny: Boethius Press, 1987).

3 Heritage Ireland / OPW site, homepage for Garden of Remembrance, Dublin <https://heritageireland.ie/places-to-visit/garden-of-remembrance/> [acc. 9 Oct 2024].

4 *Ireland's Historic Gardens in the care of the Office of Public Works* (Heritage Ireland / OPW,

2023), e-book version https://heritage ireland.ie/assets/uploads/2023/06/OPW-Heritage-Ireland-Historic-Gardens-of-Ireland-2023.pdf; 'OPW launches new visitor guide to 32 Historic Gardens', OPW press release, 2 June 2023 <https://www.gov.ie/en/press-release/587d2-opw-launches-new-visitor-guide-to-32-historic-gardens/> [acc. 9 Oct 2024].

[5] Dr Dónal Hassett, 'Decolonizing Irish Public Heritage', research spotlight article, UCC, College of Arts, Celtic Studies & Social Sciences, 18 May 2020 <https:// www.ucc.ie/en/cacsss/research/spotlight/decolonizingirishpublicheritage/> [acc. 28 May 2024].

[6] Barry Crosbie, *Irish Imperial Networks: migration, social communication and exchange in nineteenth-century India* (Cambridge: Cambridge University Press, 2012), pp.26–27.

[7] Hassett, 'Decolonizing Irish Public Heritage' webpage.

[8] C.A. Bayly, *The Birth of the Modern World, 1780–1914: global connections and comparisons* (Malden, MA: Blackwell Publishing, 2004), pp.87–93.

[9] Nuala C. Johnson, *Nature Displaced, Nature Displayed: order and beauty in botanical gardens* (London: I.B. Tauris & Co., 2011), p.36.

[10] Áine Ryan, 'Stolen skulls finally come home to Inishbofin after 133 years for poignant burial ceremony', *The Irish Times*, 16 July 2023 <https://www.irishtimes.com/ireland/2023/07/16/stolen-skulls-finally-come-home-to-inishbofin-after-133–years-for-poignant-burial-ceremony/>.

[11] Martha Ann Fleming, 'Field/work in the archive: herbaria as sites of cultural exchange', London Group of Historical Geographers seminar, Institute of Historical Research, School of Advanced Study, University of London, 6 Feb 2024 (online lecture).

[12] Ibid.

[13] Alexandre Antonelli, 'It's time to re-examine the history of botanical collections', *Royal Botanic Gardens Kew*, 25 June 2020 <www.kew.org/read-and-watch/time-to-re-examine-the-history-of-botanical-collections>. Kew Science is the research and commercial part of Kew Botanic Gardens.

[14] Ibid.

[15] A.P.W. Malcolmson, 'John Foster (1740–1828)', *Dictionary of Irish Biography* <https://doi.org/10.3318/dib.003339.v1>.

[16] Nelson and McCracken, pp.47–49.

[17] *Prospectus of the arrangements in the Dublin Society's Botanical and Agricultural Garden, at Glasnevin* (Dublin: Dublin Society, 1818).

[18] 'Carl Linnaeus – His career and legacy', *The Linnean Society of London* <https://www.linnean.org/learning/who-was-linnaeus/career-and-legacy> [acc. 9 Oct 2024].

[19] Isabelle Charmantier, 'Linnaeus and Race', *The Linnean Society of London*, 3 Sept 2020 <https://www.linnean.org/learning/who-was-linnaeus/linnaeus-and-race> [acc. 10 Oct 2024]. Linnaeus initially believed that these variations arose from different climatic conditions. In the twelfth edition of his *Systema Naturae* (1766), he proposed more hierarchical views based on differences in moral and intellectual capacities, thereby further contributing to the birth of scientific racism.

[20] Nelson and McCracken, p.143.

[21] Barry Crosbie, 'Ireland, Colonial Science, and the Geographical Construction of British Rule in India, c.1820–1870', *The Historical Journal*, vol.52, no.4 (Dec 2009), pp.963–87.

[22] Ibid.

[23] Ninian Niven, *The Visitor's Companion to the Botanic Garden, Glasnevin* (Dublin: William Curry, Jun. & Co., 1838).

[24] Ibid., p.22.

[25] Ibid., p.25.

[26] Ibid., p.179.

[27] David Moore and W.R. McNab, *Guide to the Royal Botanic Gardens, Glasnevin* (Dublin: Alex. Thom & Co., 1885).

[28] Frederick William Moore, *Report by the Keeper of the Royal Botanic Gardens, Glasnevin, Dublin, on his Visit to Foreign Botanical Gardens and Horticultural Establishments* (Dublin: Science and Art Museum, 1893), p.9.

[29] RDS Archival Collection, Misc 1845, 'Annual report on the state of the Royal Dublin Society's Botanic Garden, in November 1844. D. Moore, Curator'.

[30] Restored by OPW in the 1990s.

[31] Pat Hudson, *The Industrial Revolution* (London: Edward Arnold, 1992), p.182.

[32] A major conservation project was completed by the OPW in 2004.

[33] Johnson, p.127.

[34] Nelson and MacCracken.

[35] Dawn L. Sanders, Amy E. Ryken and Katherine Stewart, 'Navigating nature, culture and education in contemporary botanic gardens', *Environmental Education Research*, vol.24, no.8 (2018), pp.1077–84.